PART I

The Study of Primitive Law

The Law of Primitive Man

The Law of Primitive Man

A STUDY IN COMPARATIVE LEGAL DYNAMICS

E. ADAMSON HOEBEL

Originally published by Harvard University Press

New York ATHENEUM 1974

Published by Atheneum
Reprinted by arrangement with Harvard University Press
Copyright © 1954 by the President and Fellows of Harvard College
All rights reserved
Library of Congress catalog card number 54-9331
ISBN 0-689-70096-2
Manufactured in the United States of America by
The Murray Printing Company, Forge Village, Massachusetts
Published in Canada by McClelland & Stewart Ltd.
First Atheneum Printing January 1968
Second Printing November 1970
Third Printing March 1972
Fourth Printing December 1973
Fifth Printing November 1974

TO
K. N. L.
AND
M. R.

PREFACE

The study of law has challenged the Western mind for more than two thousand years. How is it then possible for more to be said on the subject? The fact is that we know all too little of the nature and functioning of law, for an understanding of the law is elusive of achievement. It has so many aspects, the tendrils of its roots and branches penetrate so finely into the interstices of society, that it is difficult to study law in its entirety. It has, in consequence, more often than not been torn from its context as an isolated phenomenon devoid of reference to the social matrix from which it naturally derives. This error must be corrected before we can achieve full understanding of the nature of law, of the ways in which it works, of the ways in which it works most effectively, of what man may hope from it, of what he has to fear of it.

Modern anthropology has its special contribution to make to the understanding of law for two reasons. The first is that the anthropologist, who has traditionally concentrated his studies on small societies with simple cultures, has been in a position to comprehend such societies each in its entirety and so to deal with cultures as integrated, working wholes. This has made possible the development of comprehensive theories of cultural dynamics embracing legal phenomena as but one aspect of culture. The second arises from the fact that anthropology is first and foremost a comparative science. It draws its data from all orders of society—primitive and civilized, prehistoric and contemporary—and from all portions of the globe. It provides the wherewithal to check hypotheses as to the nature of man and human behavior by finding ready-to-order variables somewhere in the anthropological inventory of observed societies. It thus provides a substitute (up to a point) for the experimental arrangement of variables that distinguishes laboratory control of scientific observation in the sister physical sciences. It makes it possible to move much closer to the realization of a genuine and empirical science of law. Such an approach to law through anthropology is one of functional realism by means of comparative legal dynamics.

In this book on law and anthropology the procedure will be first to develop a setting of ideas and methods for the study of law in primitive society. In the second part, seven primitive cultures will be analyzed with reference to their underlying jural postulates and to the ways in which these are translated into legal forms and action. These analyses exemplify the operation of law in total cultural settings that range on the primitive level from the most simple to the most complex. They make no pretense of typifying all forms of primitive law systems, for this book does not presume to offer an encyclopedic treatment of primitive law. Its emphasis is on function rather than on detailed diversity of form.

Professor Karl N. Llewellyn, Chicago University School of Law, who, with Max Radin, has been my preceptor in legal learning, read the manuscript of this book and lent his penetrating criticism to its improvement. Professor Charles M. Haar, Harvard University Law School, graciously performed the same service. This does not, however, in any respect imply that either of them is in full agreement with all that is written here. I am most grateful to them, to Professor Douglas Oliver, Harvard University, and to my wife, Frances Gore Hoebel, for their invaluable help.

Salt Lake City   E. A. H.
January 15, 1954

CONTENTS

I

The Cultural Background of Law

There are moments in anthropological field work that brighten the ofttimes unrelieved drudgery of patient dredging for facts—for orderly minutiae. Field work among the American Indians, especially, has long since ceased to be a larking adventure in prospecting. Civilization has washed over the Indians too much for that. The gold-panning techniques of the past century have given way to a systematic dredging, which sifts out the pay dust but only rarely excites the operator by turning up a pure nugget.

Yet moments that thrill and excite do occur. And one type of nugget which flashes to light, giving a sustaining lift to the hours of routine work, is the utterance of a pithy epigram from the mouth of an informant or interpreter—an utterance that is refined of the juices and materials which your interrogations have set to work. Your Indian co-worker has seen beyond the queries that at first were to him quite pointless; he has seen beyond the material fact and into the meaning of things; he has caught the purpose of your groping, and because he is not a professor or a social scientist, he has conceived his insight simply, and he forms his inspiration in a quietly uttered reflection that sums up in a single phrase what you must elaborate in a book.

One such bit of epigrammatic insight was dropped by High Forehead, an old-time Cheyenne. It serves well as a motif for any discussion of primitive law.

High Forehead had been both intrigued and perplexed by the line of questioning I had been following in the investigation of Cheyenne law-ways.[1] "Mr. Grinnell never used to ask questions like

[1] Field studies of Northern Cheyenne Indian law-ways were carried out in Montana during the summers of 1935 and 1936.

those," he commented again and again when we were alone in our rest periods and he was relieved of the burden of interpreting. The questions bothered him because they were, for the most part, inquiries into the ways of conduct in conflict and dispute—rules of conduct embedded in the behavior and attitudes of the Cheyenne people in action in the days before white dominance. High Forehead was bothered because the line of questioning seemed to him to put emphasis on the troublesome side of Cheyenne behavior. He was bothered, too, because he had his own traditional conception of anthropological interests based on his long experience with George Bird Grinnell. Anthropologists ought to be concerned with the more tangible and showy aspects of culture such as ceremony and ritual, hunting and war parties, food getting, bead working, and stories; but not stories about the troubles and squabbles of real people, who must be named; rather, legends and myths about culture heroes and men at war. This is what bothered High Forehead. But gradually he began to perceive that what was done about trouble was more important to our interests than mere misbehavior itself. The realization slowly obtruded upon his consciousness that the Cheyennes, his people, had on their own responsibility in their time dealt with and met many problems of social order. And one noon as we lay beneath a cottonwood tree under a blue Montana sky, beside the waters of Lame Deer creek, almost on the spot where Lame Deer, the Sioux chieftain, was killed in the spring of '77, he quietly said, "The Indian on the prairie, before there was the White Man to put him in the guardhouse, had to have something to keep him from doing wrong."

Yes, the Indian on the prairie had a social order to maintain, as has every society of man. Each people has its system of social control. And all but a few of the poorest of them have as a part of their control system a complex of behavior patterns and institutional mechanisms that we may properly treat as law. For, "anthropologically considered, law is merely one aspect of our culture—the aspect which employs the force of organized society to regulate individual and group conduct and to prevent, redress or punish deviations from prescribed social norms."[2] When this area of behavior we

[2] S. P. Simpson and Ruth Field, "Law and the Social Sciences," *Virginia Law Review,* 32:858 (1946).

speak of as law is found in the culture of a preliterate people, we call it primitive law. When it is found within the cultures of ancient societies that had in their time only recently entered the threshold of civilization, we call it archaic law.[3] And when we find it in the structure of developed civilizations, we call it modern.

But all systems of law, whatever their content and unique dynamics, must have some essential elements in common. Our first need, therefore, is to delineate the common elements. To do this we must have a look at society and culture at large in order to find the place of law within the total structure. We must have some idea of how society works before we can have a full conception of what law is and how it works. As forcefully put by Ehrlich, who did so much to free continental jurisprudence from unrealistic abstractions and the cold grip of the overt technical codes and legal method, "A juristic act is never an individual, an isolated thing, it is part of the prevailing social order."[4] Law must have its proper frame of reference.

An anthropological approach to law is flatly behavioristic and empirical in that we understand all human law to reside in human behavior and to be discernible through objective and accurate observation of what men do in relation to each other and the natural forces that impinge upon them.

We divorce ourselves, on the one hand, from the presumption of the supernatural intuitionalism characteristic of the traditional Natural Law approach. If there perchance be supernatural forces shaping, limiting, or even determining human law, these, we hold, are not subject to objective determination and are not within the scope of this book. This is not to ignore the fact that every society analyzed in this book fervently believes that the gods and other supernatural forces are active and, often, determinative forces in their law systems. Methodologically, we shall accept such beliefs as cultural facts or realities without committing ourselves to an answer as to whether they are or are not empirical realities. In other words, the approach is confined within the limits of scientific methodology—a method that may be called "functional realism."

[3] William Seagle, *The Quest for Law* (New York, 1941), chap. iii.
[4] Eugen Ehrlich, *Fundamental Principles of the Sociology of Law* (Cambridge, 1936), p. 397.

We also divorce ourselves, on the other hand, from the logical abstractionism of the Austinian approach of which Stone has recently written, "It 'belongs' neither to any actual society, nor to any actual law, but to the critique of legal propositions by reference to their logical consistency." [5] By the same token we find ourselves unable to link interest with the kind of legal positivism advanced in the so-called "pure science of law" so ably espoused by Hans Kelsen. For we see such a method not as science but logic for the sake of logical exercise, and our search is not for models of ideal perfection in law but rather the social realities of the law men have produced. Although the "pure science of law" is, as Lowie wrote of Durkheim's study of primitive religion,[6] "a noteworthy mental exercise and would rank as a landmark if dialectic ingenuity sufficed to achieve greatness in the empirical sciences," [7] the net result in the cold judgment of Sidney Post Simpson and Ruth Field, "is law without social content or significance . . . law without flesh, blood or bowels. It is not even zombie-law." [8] Functional realism seeks for the anatomy of empirically observed social systems and the physiology of the dynamics of the legal mechanisms that are inseparable parts of the functioning whole.

We do not, as shall be shown later, deny and cast out as insignificant the role of logic in law, but we take as a basic tenet Holmes' now classic dictum, "The life of law has not been logic; it has been experience." [9] Experience means men living in society.

When answering the question: "What is society?" it should be first observed that society exists only among sentient creatures. Moreover, it always involves a multitude of creatures interacting. It is, in the first instance, an animal aggregation. But it is more than *just* an animal aggregation. Some of us may hesitate to speak of the society of amoebae or fruit flies. Many of us do, however, talk glibly of ant society or see society in the organization of a flock of pigeons or a herd of wild horses. We recognize a patterned organization in the interrelations of the members of the animal group. We recognize further that the group exists with a degree of separate-

---

[5] Julius Stone, *The Province and Function of Law* (Cambridge, 1950), p. 61.
[6] Emile Durkheim, *Les formes élémentaires de la vie réligieuse* (Paris, 1912).
[7] R. H. Lowie, *Primitive Religion* (New York, 1912), p. 157.
[8] Simpson and Field, p. 862.
[9] O. W. Holmes, Jr., *The Common Law* (Boston, 1881), p. 1.

ness from all other groups—even those of the same species or variety. These traits are tacitly acknowledged as attributes of society—a measure of differentiated but organized behavior within the group and with sufficient centralized cohesion resulting from this organization to maintain the group as a discrete entity. Every society exists over and against other societies. Implied in the concept of aggregation is a spatial location of each society the members of which have in the main a closer local contiguity with one another than they do to outsiders. Almost all societies are territorially rooted to an area of more or less clearly defined limits.

It would avail us little to try to establish that human society is in kind unlike animal society. But it is important for us to understand that in degree human society is different indeed from animal society. That difference resides in the fact that the behavior characterizing animal societies is largely instinctual and only in small degree learned,[10] whereas in human societies the behavior of men is only in limited degree instinctual and in large measure learned.

This learned behavior in its aggregate is culture, and we say that culture is the integrated sum total of learned behavior patterns which are manifested and shared by the members of a society. Although chimpanzees and other primates are capable of discovering and inventing new patterns of behavior as Kohler has long since demonstrated,[11] and although these new patterns may be transmitted to a whole colony of chimpanzees through direct imitation and precept,[12] yet because of their inability to convey learned behavior through speech, and because their limited memory spans prevent them from retaining activities for long, they are capable of no more than limited protoculture. Man alone possesses significant culture-producing and culture-maintaining capacities.[13] Culture is, therefore, a distinguishing feature of human society when compared to that of lower animals.

[10] On social organization without learning among ants, see A. L. Kroeber, *Anthropology*, rev. ed. (New York, 1948), "The Social Insects," pp. 34–38.

[11] Wolfgang Kohler, *The Mentality of Apes* (New York, 1925).

[12] R. M. and A. W. Yerkes, *The Great Apes* (New Haven, 1929); and E. A. Hooton, *Man's Poor Relations* (Garden City, 1942), for the great apes and other primates.

[13] G. P. Murdock, "The Science of Culture," *American Anthropologist*, 34:200–215 (1932).

We need not dispute the cynicism of Anatole France in his dictum that that which distinguishes man from the animals is lying and literature. Nor need we feel impelled to contradict the epicure, Jean-Louys, who eloquently declaimed (if we are to believe Hendrik van Loon), "After all, in what consists the difference between man and beast except in the possibilities of the former to learn the art of dining, while the latter is forever doomed to feed?" [14] Literature, lying, and dining are nothing but cultural accomplishments. Taken together and with all else that makes up culture, they help distinguish man from the animals. A human society, therefore, is a population acting in accordance with its culture.

The phenomenon of culture presents a thorny paradox. The behavior of which a culture is built consists only of behavior made manifest by individuals. It can be seen and recorded only after the fact. Yet the cultural *patterns for behavior* exist prior to the entry of the individual into his society. And when he has departed the patterns continue for those still living and those yet to come. Culture is a continuum. Sociologists speak of it as the social heritage. So it is that although culture has its existence only in individual behavior, it is something over and above the individual.

Culture, as Kroeber recognized three decades ago, and Spencer long before that, is superorganic.[15] It exists as the highest level of natural phenomena.

The lowest level is the *inorganic,* consisting of lifeless matter— the earth stuff and cosmic materials of which our planet, the solar system, and stars are made.

Eventually, in the evolutionary reorganization of matter, life was born, and in the birth of life something new was added that had not been in existence before. So critically significant is this new aspect of matter that we identify it as a new level—the *vital organic,* consisting of protozoa, metazoa, plants, and animals that have not developed nervous systems. The new rests upon the old; living things consist of inorganic matter ordered in a peculiar relationship

[14] H. W. Van Loon, *R. v. R., The Life and Times of Rembrandt van Rijn* (New York, 1930), p. 108.

[15] A. L. Kroeber, "The Superorganic," *American Anthropologist,* 19:163–213 (1917).

that results in vitality. This new quality is so significantly different that we classify it as a difference in kind.

When the lowly organic forms ultimately evolved nervous systems and became sentient animals, this new aspect of matter acquired qualities now recognized as being so critically significant as to justify the identification of a new level of phenomena—the *psychic organic*.

Finally, as man emerged from apehood at the close of the Pliocene period, some million years ago, he developed his central nervous system to the critical point at which he was gradually able to break through the limiting bonds of instinct into an area of behavior not preset in the structure of his germ cells. He developed the capacity to produce culture, which, although rooted in the organic and finding its expression through organisms, nevertheless is superorganic. The superorganic consists of natural phenomena in the form of behavior patterns which, while they are manifest in the activity of organisms (man), are not predetermined in specific content by the inherent forms of that organism.

Law, which exists in human beings acting, also exists above and beyond the individual as one aspect of culture. It falls in the realm of the superorganic.

The concept of the superorganic is not supernatural, nor is it mystical. It embraces *natural* phenomena, for culture is as much a part of nature as is the formation of water from hydrogen and oxygen. Cultural anthropology is therefore truly a natural science, as indeed are all the so-called social sciences. Jurisprudence, too, may be treated as a natural science and will be here approached as such. Sixty years ago Holmes saw it thus and in these words, "It is perfectly proper to regard and study the law simply as a great anthropological document. It is proper to resort to it to discover what ideals of society have been strong enough to reach that final form of expression, or what have been the changes in dominant ideals from century to century. It is proper to study it as an exercise in the morphology and transformation of human ideas. The study pursued for such ends becomes science in the strictest sense." [16]

[16] O. W. Holmes, Jr., "Law in Science and Science in Law," *Harvard Law Review*, 12:99 (1899).

The next problem is a determination of the nature of social order in relation to culture.

Perhaps the greatest lesson driven home by modern anthropology is the truly remarkable adaptability of the human being as revealed through the wide range of behavior exhibited by men the world over. "Anthropology," in the words of Professor Clyde Kluckhohn, "holds up a great mirror to man and lets him look at himself in his infinite variety." [17] Man is truly capable of many things—perhaps not in infinite variety, for his finite body and the physical universe do impose real limitations—but the range is impressively wide.[18]

However, although the range of available items appears to be almost infinite, the capacity of each individual culture is inherently finite and can never be an omnibus for all possibilities. In the words of Ruth Benedict, "The culture pattern of any civilization makes use of a certain segment of the great arc of potential human purposes and motivations . . . the great arc along which all the possible human behaviours are distributed is far too immense and too full of contradictions for any one culture to utilize even any considerable portion of it. Selection is the first requirement." [19] The imperative of selection is of prime importance for an understanding of the place and role of law in human affairs.

The imperative of selection is imposed by a number of factors. The first of these is an *inherent incompatibility* among certain forms of behavior so that contradictory forms may not be performed simultaneously by the same person or persons. A people cannot cook the same piece of meat and eat it raw. They cannot practice celibacy and at the same instance enjoy free sexual license. They cannot burn off their prairies and at the same moment leave the grass standing. They cannot practice absolute celibacy and restock their population from among their own members. They cannot practice infanticide and raise all babies to maturity.

The simultaneous factor is emphasized in some of the examples just cited because, of course, with respect to some of these practices it is possible to temporize. It is possible with certain behaviors to hold to one line now and hew to its opposite on another occasion.

---

[17] Clyde Kluckhohn, *Mirror for Man* (New York, 1949), p. 11.

[18] Cf. J. P. Gillin, "Custom and the Range of Human Response," *Character an Personality*, 13:101–134 (1944).

[19] R. F. Benedict, *Patterns of Culture* (New York, 1934), p. 237.

The psychological theory of drive reduction suggests a second imperative for cultural selection. The individual is seen as fundamentally motivated by basic drives to action built up as a result of inner physiological tensions. Hunger and thirst are the most elementary and powerful, then sex. The organism seeks to reduce drives through activity that leads to a goal that in turn satisfies the basic need that has given rise to the drive. Some potential lines of behavior lead to satisfactory goals; others do not. Those that lead to culs-de-sac and not to satisfaction of needs produce no reduction in drive and must be ruled out. If they are not—if the organism persists in repetition of the behavior—it will eliminate itself. Experimental psychology indicates that in animal and self-directed human learning the line of behavior in trial-and-error activity which leads to the drive-reducing goal, since it is the last line of behavior followed before success is attained, tends to be repeated on the next attempt. Repetition reinforces the behavior and, if the stimulus situation is repeated, it tends to become a habit. The pattern of behavior set up in the habit may not be the only one that would lead to gratification of the need; it may not even be the most effective one. But if it is the one first hit upon, it may remain the only one followed. It also tends to be generalized in that it tends to be extended in the form of response patterns evoked by stimuli essentially similar but not identical to the original stimulus. It serves to reduce the drive, relieve the tension, and return the organism to an adequate (if not a complete) state of balance—and that is enough. The other potential lines of behavior are eliminated, at least for the time being.[20]

Deviation from the established pattern is upsetting to the nervous system when the goal sought is related to a basic drive, and also in the case of strongly-set derived drives. The blocking of basic drives by enforced deviation leads to neurosis and psychosis when the pressure is excessive. The adaptive mechanisms of the organism therefore tend to hold it to the habitual lines of behavior not only as a means of tension reduction but also in avoidance of tension production.[21] Self-limitation of choices among the potential varieties of behavior is thus imposed.

[20] Cf. C. L. Hull, *Principles of Behavior* (New York, 1943).
[21] Cf. J. H. Masserman, *Principles of Dynamic Psychiatry* (Philadelphia, 1946), pp. 126–129.

Third, human infants are subjected to adult control and molding in accordance with basic patterns previously established. Their powers of perception are already slanted by the time they are ready to experience much of what life will set before them. What happens between birth and maturation inevitably inhibits the capacity to react in all possible ways.[22]

A fourth factor rests in the nature of group life and is, in a sense, a corollary of the second discussed above. People living together must be able to predict what the others will do when confronted with certain situations (stimuli). Every normal man is a practicing empirical social scientist every moment of his waking day. On the basis of past experience he is ordering his own conduct in relation to the expected conduct of others. Men in society are men interacting. If each were actually liable to pop off along any one of all the different lines of behavior human beings are potentially capable of, the result would be chaotic indeed. Any organization of complex activities and social life would be quite impossible. Further, continued frustration of individual expectancies would soon reduce all men to neurotics and psychotics. The world would then, indeed, be a madhouse. Society is possible only on a basis of order.

On these grounds we recognize and accept the proposition that every society must of necessity choose a limited number of behavior possibilities for incorporation in its culture, and it must peremptorily and arbitrarily reject the admissibility for its own members of those lines of behavior which are incompatible with its selected lines as well as many others which are merely different. This does not, however, mean that absolute rigidity is imposed by the nature of things. A measure of permissible leeway exists in most cases, for some deviation is inevitable; and it is in leeway that new modifications find their soil for taking root.

Selection is therefore physiologically and sociologically imperative. This is important for any theory of law, for the basic problem confronting the creators of all law systems is one of selection: what lines of behavior is the law to support, and what lines are to be

---

[22] Cf. A. I. Hallowell, "Psychological Leads for Ethnological Field Workers" (mimeographed, National Research Council, 1937; reprinted in D. G. Haring, ed., *Personal Character and Cultural Milieu*, rev. ed., Syracuse, 1949), pp. 292–348, especially pp. 300–307.

suppressed? The theory of imperative selection here outlined as a working tool is sound in terms of present known facts and it overcomes the major shortcoming found in the *Interessenjurisprudenz* of Jhering and in the social ultilitarianism of Pound's sociology of law; namely, "the lack of any general conception of the structure and processes of society as a whole." [23]

Our next premise is that selection is by no means ever wholly fortuitous. Once a culture gets under way (and all the cultures with which social science has to deal *are* under way) there are always some criteria of choice that govern or influence selection. These criteria are the broadly generalized propositions held by the members of a society as to the nature of things and as to what is qualitatively desirable and undesirable. We prefer to call these basic propositions "postulates." Philosophers and sociologists commonly call them "values." Professor Morris Opler proposes that we call them "cultural themes." [24] Inasmuch as the members of a society ordinarily accept their basic propositions as self-evident truths and work upon them as if they were truths, and because they do reason from them, if not with perfect logic, they may best be called postulates. The particular formulations of specific customs and patterns for behavior that go into a given culture are more or less explicitly shaped by the precepts given in the basic postulates of that specific culture. New patterns are accepted, rejected, or modified with reference to the basic postulates. New patterns may be ideologically rejected as incompatible with the preëxisting postulates, but once present they may persist though "officially" banned, and in time may influence a change in the postulates themselves so that ultimately their general acceptance becomes possible. Or they may be found acceptable in terms of some of their aspects and without awareness of the potential implications of other aspects that are incompatible with existing postulates. Then when such implications are finally realized, the behavior may be so well established as to cause a modification or even overthrow of the original postulate. Cultures are never static and in the course of time change may produce results which

[23] Otis Lee, "Social Values and the Philosophy of Law," *Virginia Law Review,* 32:808 (1946).

[24] M. E. Opler, "Themes as Dynamic Forces in Culture," *American Journal of Sociology,* 51:198–206 (1945); "An Application of the Theory of Themes in Culture," *Journal of the Washington Academy of Sciences,* 36:137–166 (1946).

if compressed into a short span would be unacceptable to the members of a given society.

Nor are the basic postulates in a culture necessarily perfectly consistent among themselves. However, the measure of consistency between basic postulates, and between the postulates and the specific selected behavior patterns, will be the measure of integration of the culture. Integration, it is assumed, must be held a minimal level if any society is to continue to function effectively. Integration is achieved by selection in accordance with a body of basic postulates that are not overly inconsistent with each other. Every society maintains a social system.

As a result, the behavior of the individual members of any society (or of subgroups within a society) reveal considerable similarity in response to specific stimuli. These frequently recurring patterns we call *norms* or *ways*. Norm, in its statistical sense, is a strictly neutral term. It merely expresses what *is,* on the basis of a numerical count. It says nothing of what ought to be or what people think ought to be. It is a quantitative concept.

Whenever an anthropologist reports a culture and its ways, he presumes to present statistical modes of behavior. I say "presumes," because he rarely takes actual statistical counts of all behavior over a fixed span of time in order to determine an arithmetically exact distribution of frequency occurrences. In general, it is neither practical nor possible to do so. Therefore, the field anthropologist, observing that one line of behavior seems to crop up quite consistently, says, "This is the custom," meaning, "This is the norm (way)."

A social norm, it should be kept in mind, is a construct. It does not represent the reality of all behavior of a certain class. Consequently, an anthropological description of a culture, which consists of a series of reported norms, is no more than a *cultural construct,* not the real culture.[25] A description of the real culture would entail a running description of *all* of the behavior of *all* the members of a society over a specified period of time. No man or group of men can ever perceive all this.

Thus far the norm has been spoken of as what the greatest number do in a given situation—a mere statistical expression of behavior.

But this is not enough. As was forcibly demonstrated by William Graham Sumner some time ago, in society what *is* takes on the compulsive element of *ought*. "The folkways are the 'right' ways." [26] The *norm* takes on the quality of the *normative*. What the most do, others should do.

Most norms appear to carry their own ultimate rewards in goal achievement. However, the goal achievement is by no means necessarily immediate. What is more, nonnormal behavior may sometimes bring quick rewards to individuals or subgroups in contravention to the values of the society as a whole. "The rewards of successful iniquity," lamented Salmond, "are upon occasion very great." [27] Hence, more immediate rewards and deterrents are added in the forms of sanctions that reward or punish conformity or deviation. The positive sanctions step up all the way from the lollipop, the smile, the pat on the back, applause, to honorific positions, bonuses, medals and citations, to posthumous enshrinement. The negative sanctions range from the curled lip, the raised eyebrow, the word of scorn and ridicule, the rap on the knuckle, and refusal to invite back to dinner, through economic deprivation, physical hurt, prolonged social ostracism, through imprisonment or exile to the ultimate in social ostracism—execution.[28]

Substantively, law consists of a specially demarked set of social norms that are maintained through the application of "legal" sanctions. The entire operating system of sanctioning norms is what constitutes a system of social control. Law as a process is an aspect of the total system of social control maintained by a society.

Legal norms, like other social norms, are products of selection. They, too, are subject to the test of consistency with the guiding principles set in the basic postulates of their respective societies. Not all the basic postulates of any social system bear on legal problems, for rarely does any law system even pretend to govern all phases of

[26] W. G. Sumner, *Folkways* (Boston, 1906), p. 28.
[27] J. W. Salmond, *Jurisprudence*, 7th ed. (New York, 1924), p. 132.
[28] Cf. A. R. Radcliffe-Brown, "Sanction, Social," *Encyclopaedia of the Social Sciences*, XIII (1934), 531–534; J. R. Provinse, "The Underlying Sanctions of Plains Indian Culture," in Fred Eggan, ed., *The Social Anthropology of North American Tribes* (Chicago, 1937); R. I. MacIver, *Society, Its Structure and Changes* (New York, 1931), pp. 38–39, 249–250; E. A. Ross, *Social Control* (New York, 1901), pp. 89 ff.

life; the postulates (major and minor) that are used for operation in determination of legal principles may be isolated for separate study through comparative jurisprudence. These are the jural postulates.

"The jural postulates," as Julius Stone has described them, ". . . are generalized statements of the tendencies actually operating, of the presuppositions on which a particular civilization is based . . . They are ideals presupposed by the whole social complex, which can thus be used to bring the law into harmony with it, so that the law 'promotes rather than hampers and oppresses it.' They are, as it were, directives issuing from the particular civilized society to those who are wielding social control through law within it." [29] This is not a wholly new idea. Joseph Kohler declared some time ago that "every civilization has its definite postulates for law . . ." [30] As for Stone's formulation of the matter, he need not have limited the existence of jural postulates to civilized society, for every society, primitive or civilized, that has a law system has its jural postulates.

This is recognized in F. S. C. Northrop's recent observation that, "A study of the key basic concepts of any culture, without which the living law underlying the codified law of that culture is not understood, reveals that those key concepts not merely provide the ideas in terms of which the people of that culture conceive the facts of their existence but also define their values." [31]

A functional realistic approach to law has as one of its main problems the isolation of the basic social postulates on which the law system rests. A chief function of law is seen to be one of selecting norms for legal support that accord with the basic postulates of the culture in which the law system is set. A primary problem of comparative jurisprudence is, therefore, to seek out the jural postulates of different law systems and to determine how they find expression in the juridical institutions of the societies under consideration. Functional realism insists on this because, "before a basic norm is postulated for any legal system, this theory is purely formal and empty and inapplicable to any actual legal problems. Yet a basic

[29] Stone, p. 337.
[30] Joseph Kohler, *The Philosophy of Law* (New York, 1921), p. 5.
[31] F. S. C. Northrop, "Jurisprudence in the Law School Curriculum," *Journal of Legal Education*, 1:489 (1949).

norm cannot be postulated except after an examination of the extra legal facts of the particular society . . ."[32]

The postulates of a society may or may not be explicitly expressed by its members. There may or may not be total agreement as to what they are. The judicial duel as well as the political struggle is often a contest to determine which of several postulates shall prevail or how the specific interpretation of a postulate shall be formed in its application to the legislation being fought over or in the case at hand. In the study of a social system and its law by the specialist it is his job to abstract the postulates from the behavior he sees and from what he hears. In the analysis and formulation of his report of the postulates the statement is therefore ex post facto.

In summary: the essence of the postulation theory of law may be put in three propositions as formulated by Otis Lee.

1. Every culture, society, and in fact every group, no matter how restricted, represents a limited selection from the total of human potentialities, individual and collective.

2. The selection tends to be made in accordance with certain dominant values (postulates) basic to the group.

3. It follows that every stable group exemplifies a more or less complete and coherent pattern, structure, or system of relationships.

"The quality of a society will vary with the quality of its basic values . . . with their suitability to its needs and circumstances; and with the consistency and thoroughness with which they are worked out."[33]

[32] Stone, p. 96.

[33] Lee, pp. 811–812. Note: the theoretical approach presented in this chapter was formulated prior to the publication of Lee's frame of reference. The parallelism that has resulted follows from common inferences drawn from the trends and facts of modern social science behaviorism.

2

What is Law?

"At the very outset," wrote Hohfeld, "it seems necessary to emphasize the importance of differentiating purely legal relations from the physical and mental facts that call such relations into being. Obvious as this initial suggestion may seem to be, the arguments that one may hear in court almost any day, and likewise a considerable number of judicial opinions, afford ample evidence of the inveterate and unfortunate tendency to confuse and blend the legal and the non-legal qualities in a given problem." [1] Nevertheless, to seek a definition of the legal is like the quest for the Holy Grail. Those who have tried it will readily lend a sympathetic ear to Max Radin, who with well-seasoned wisdom warned that: "Those of us who have learned humility have given over the attempt to define law." [2] Yet it cannot be that law is incapable of definition, for a definition is merely an expression of the acknowledged attributes of a phenomenon or concept. If law were in fact beyond definition, it would be because its attributes are unknown, or law does not exist. If the latter be true, then indeed have generations of judges, advocates, prosecutors, policemen, sheriffs, and law students been living in a wonderful fool's paradise. This we hold not to have been the case.

The difficulties in achievement of a generally acceptable definition of law—a true consensus as to its essential attributes—arise from excessive parochialism, on the one hand, and more importantly from the fact that law is but part of the social web. Its strands flow without break into the total fabric of culture and it has no clear-cut edges. Law is not sharply separable from all other forms of human action.

[1] W. N. Hohfeld, *Fundamental Legal Conceptions as Applied in Judicial Reasoning and Other Legal Essays,* ed. W. W. Cook, (New Haven, 1932), p. 27.

[2] Max Radin, "A Restatement of Hohfeld," *Harvard Law Review,* 51:1145 (1938).

One may ask, "Why be concerned with definitions? Facts are the thing and quarreling over words is sterile." The answer is that although definitions are of secondary importance, they do have their functional uses.

Facts are never without their meanings, for meaningless phenomena are nonexistent. Yet, however much an overzealous empiricist may cry, "Let the facts speak for themselves!" or the rhetorician praise the persuasiveness of "eloquent facts," most phenomena are dumb and tongueless, quite incapable of speech and eloquence. If their meaning is to be put into words, man alone can do it. And to find the meaning in complex phenomena and complexes of phenomena he must abstract them, categorize them, and find realistic ways to compare one with another.

A researcher in any field must begin with the language tools and concepts that are available in his own heritage. "Language and our thought-grooves are inextricably interwoven, are, in a sense, one and the same."[3] Thinking is done within the framework of a pre-existing language. But as the researcher widens the scope of knowledge or sharpens down a point, he finds inevitably that old words must have their meanings altered or that new words must be hammered out to encompass new phenomena that are too different to be embraced in old words or concepts. New facts and new thoughts often do call for new words. However, to the scientist who is also a teacher, it will always seem preferable to couch his discourse in familiar terms, if that is at all possible without effecting distortion of the facts and their meaning.

Therefore, it is desirable in any study of law to work with the words and concepts that jurisprudence has given us—insofar as this is possible.

It will soon be seen in the study of primitive law, however, that we cannot take all traditional meanings straight. When we push out from the universe of experience based on Continental and Anglo-American law into the legal world of primitive man, we find some things that are wholly new and some that are familiar but in different form. Thus it is perfectly true, as Julius Lips warned us, "Even a simple description of *facts* pertaining to law in a primitive tribe may, if we use our legal terminology, cause a distortion of the

---

[3] Edward Sapir, *Language* (New York, 1939), p. 232.

legal content of primitive institutions."[4] This does not at all mean, however, that we must wholly reject our traditional legal terminology when we undertake an anthropology of law. It merely means that we must neither blindly nor willfully force upon primitive data that are only relatively comparable the specific content of meaning associated with our terminology.

The lawyer, or law student, who reads this book may find himself occasionally (we hope not too frequently) bristling with annoyance as he mutters to himself, "But damn it, that is not what that word means in law!" Let him remember that he means in *our* law. There is other peoples' law too, and the term in question may have been modified to suit the broader range of data.

We recognize full well that in any approach to other peoples' law, thinking at all in traditional legal concepts tends to limit our perception of unfamiliar legal forms.[5] Historians of law and analytical jurisprudes have told us, for instance, that nothing so refined and sophisticated, so well organized and logically perfected, nothing so authoritarian, so purposeful as law, could exist on the primitive level. Most anthropologists, until recently, have responded with a solemn nod. The legal life of primitive man was looked upon as being nonexistent rather than as simply unexplored.

To rationalize their blindness and to justify their neglect, they turned to the exaltation of custom. "Custom is King," became the cry. An English work bearing the title of *Primitive Law,* published as late as 1924, offered the flat introductory assertion that, "Primitive law is in truth the totality of the customs of the tribe."[6]

This, if taken literally, would mean that the patterns of pottery making, flint flaking, tooth filing, toilet training, and all the other social habits of a people, are law. Naturally enough, Sidney Hartland, the author of this assertion, did not take his proposition seriously in his subsequent discussion of what he considered to be legal topics. Yet nowhere did he indicate the basis on which he selected from the mass of customs those which he saw fit to treat as legal. Nor can the basis of selection be discerned from his treatment of

---

[4] J. E. Lips, in *General Anthropology,* ed. Franz Boas (Boston, 1938), p. 487.

[5] O. W. Holmes, Jr.: "The past gives us our vocabulary and fixes the limits of our imagination."

[6] E. S. Hartland, *Primitive Law* (London, 1924), p. 5.

the subject matter, either. Because he was committed to the proposition that law and custom are one, Hartland found himself unable to state any explicit criteria of law. Yet he had perforce to utilize a hidden concept of law, if he was to write any kind of book at all on his chosen subject.

A more recent and somewhat more discriminating approach, but still custom-enchanted, may be seen in the study of East African law by J. Driberg, who proceeds on the proposition that "law comprises all those rules of conduct which regulate the behavior of individuals and communities." [7] This, at least, rules out pottery making but still leaves us with the etiquette of handshaking as being "legal." This not uncommon fusing of law and custom by anthropologists led Clark Wissler to bless the Lynds' famous Middletown study as the first application of the methods of social anthropology to the study of an American community, embracing "the whole round of its activities," [8] in spite of the fact, as Karl Llewellyn has observed with wry cogency, that "the legal aspects of behavior there did not seem worth canvass—or capable thereof." [9] From this truly impressive anthropology of an American community a reader could carry away the impression that, like the reputed communities of primitive man, it lives under an automatic sway of custom without benefit of law. Such are the consequences of a lawless anthropology.

With such cues as these Seagle, in his recent stimulating and provocative treatise on *The Quest for Law,* labels the first of his four chapters on primitive law, "Custom is King." [10] That statement being so, he must have it that primitive societies are lawless and live under an "automatic *sway* of custom," [11] which, because it is automatic, seems to suffice. Therefore, "there is no law until there are courts," and "really primitive peoples have no courts and no conception of the state." [12] And if a people who are ordinarily recognized as primitive have courts, then *ipso facto* they are not primitive, for

[7] J. H. Driberg, "Primitive Law in East Africa," *Africa,* 1:65 (1928).

[8] Clark Wissler, Introduction to R. S. and H. M. Lynd, *Middletown* (New York, 1929), p. v.

[9] K. N. Llewellyn, "The Theory of Legal Science," *North Carolina Law Review,* 20:7, note 7a (1941).

[10] Seagle, chap. ii.

[11] *Ibid.,* p. 33.

[12] *Ibid.,* pp. 69, 60.

"to speak of the law of some African peoples as 'primitive' although they have courts and have invented many complex forms of legal transaction which compare not unfavorably with those of the ancient Babylonians is to abuse the natural [*sic*] meaning of the term." [13]

Seagle at least is cognizant of the fact that law and custom are not one, and he truly insists that, "Only confusion can result from treating law and custom as interchangeable phenomena." [14] He avoids doing a Hartland by arbitrarily denying in effect that there is any such thing as primitive law at all.

Thus, although the approach typified by Seagle makes it possible to separate law and custom, avoiding the fusion of the two, its logic forces the conclusion attacked by Malinowski some time ago when he wrote, "By defining the forces of law in terms of central authority, codes, courts, and constables, we must come to the conclusion that law needs no enforcement in a primitive community and is followed spontaneously." [15] Such a conclusion, as Malinowski effectively demonstrated, is unreal and arbitrary.

A new approach and a more realistic conception as to the nature of law is clearly necessary. To make this fresh start we may properly address the question: What is law?

It is not the fiat of a sovereign—either real or imagined. Nor is it exclusively legislative enactment. Our taking-off point will be certain modern conceptions of contemporary jurisprudence. Cardozo has given us our best lead in his now classic declaration that a law is "a principle or rule of conduct so established as to justify a prediction with reasonable certainty that it will be enforced by the courts if its authority is challenged." [16] This formula expands a little more elaborately and somewhat less bluntly the famous Holmesian dictum of 1897, "The prophecies of what the courts will do in fact, and nothing more pretentious, are what I mean by the law." [17] From Holmes' classic statement springs the stream of legal realism of today.

[13] *Ibid.*, p. 34.
[14] *Ibid.*, p. 35.
[15] Bronislaw Malinowski, *Crime and Custom in Savage Society* (New York, 1926), p. 14.
[16] B. N. Cardozo, *The Growth of the Law* (New Haven, 1924), p. 52.
[17] O. W. Holmes, Jr., "The Path of the Law," *Harvard Law Review*, 10:457 (1897).

In the Cardozian formulation we find four essential components: 1) the normative element; 2) regularity; 3) courts; 4) enforcement. In England a somewhat similar idea of law also took root and was given expression by Salmond, who wrote in his *Jurisprudence* that law consists of "the rules in accordance with which justice is administered by the judicial tribunals of the state," and, more explicitly, "the principles enforced by the state through judicial authorities by physical force in the pursuit of justice whether attained or not." [18]

Salmond with forthright vigor took his stand on the critical significance of the courts, as has many another legal thinker of more recent decades: "But all law, however made, is recognized and administered by the Courts, and no rules are recognized and administered by the Courts which are not rules of law. It is therefore to the Courts and not the legislature that we must go to ascertain the true nature of law." [19] And more succinctly: "English law is nothing but the body of rules recognized and applied by English Courts in the administration of justice." [20] In this he did not espouse the extreme position that *all* law is judge-made. He would have it that what the judges find and accept for execution or enforcement is law; what they reject is not—be it even a legislative statute. What the courts will do . . .

From the anthropological point of view such legal behaviorism makes sense and provides a handle wherewith to grasp the law. But when we consider legal matters in many primitive societies, if we must rely on courts and their predicted actions as the test of law, we are still left at sea. This is what bothered Max Radin (who well understood the anthropologist's problem) and, perhaps, led him to assert: "But there is an infallible test for recognizing whether an imagined course of conduct is lawful or unlawful. This infallible test, in our system, is to submit the question to the judgment of a court. In other systems exactly the same test will be used, but it is often difficult to recognize the court. None the less, although difficult, it can be done in almost every system at any time." [21] Max Radin was right. But what sorts of courts did he have in mind? Some

[18] Salmond, pp. 60, 62.
[19] *Ibid.*, p. 49.
[20] *Ibid.*, p. 113.
[21] Max Radin, "Restatement of Hohfeld," p. 1145, note 11.

courts are difficult to identify. Among primitives they may be regularly constituted tribal courts such as the tribal council of an American Indian pueblo sitting in judicial capacity, or a court of the West African Ashanti, constituted of the chief, his council of elders, and henchmen. And even as Seagle notes, "The court of the bush is none the less a court because it does not sit every day, because it may not always employ compulsory process, because it is not housed in a permanent structure upon whose lintel is inscribed *Fiat justitia ruat caelum.*" [22] That type of primitive court is not too hard to recognize. Any member of the American Bar Association should readily see it for what it is. But a more obscure type of "court" may be found in the Cheyenne Indian military society.

Consider the case of Wolf Lies Down, whose horse was "borrowed" by a friend in the absence of the owner. When the friend did not return from the warpath with the horse, Wolf Lies Down put the matter before his society—the Elk Soldiers. "Now I want to know what to do," he said. "I want you to tell me the right thing." The society chiefs sent a messenger to bring the friend in from the camp of a remote band. The friend gave an adequate and acceptable explanation of his conduct and offered handsome restitution to the complainant in addition to making him his blood brother. Then said the chiefs: "Now we have settled this thing." But they went on, half as a legislature: "Now we shall make a new rule. There shall be no more borrowing of horses without asking. If any man takes another's goods without asking, we will go over and get them back for him. More than that, if the taker tries to keep them, we will give him a whipping." [23] Can anyone deny that the Elk Soldiers were in effect sitting as a court for the entire tribe? The test is first, one of responsibility. That they knew. It is, second, one of authority. That they achieved. It is, third, one of method. Unhampered by a system of formal precedent which "required" them to judge according to the past, they recognized that the rule according to which they were settling this case was new, and they so announced it.

Among the Yurok Indians of California, as typical of a less specifically organized people, the "court" was less definite, but it was

22 Seagle, p. 34.
23 K. N. Llewellyn and E. A. Hoebel, *The Cheyenne Way* (Norman, 1941), p. 127, quoted here and elsewhere by permission of the University of Oklahoma Press.

nevertheless there. An aggrieved Yurok who felt he had a legitimate claim engaged the legal services of two nonrelatives from a community other than his own. The defendant then did likewise. These men were called "crossers"; they crossed back and forth between the litigants. The principals to the dispute did not ordinarily face each other during the course of the action. After hearing all that each side had to offer in evidence and pleading as to the relevant substantive law, the crossers rendered a decision for damages according to a well-established scale that was known to all. For their footwork and efforts each received a piece of shell currency called a "moccasin." [24] Here again we have a court.

On an even more primitive level, if an aggrieved party or his kinsmen must institute and carry through the prosecution without the intervention of a third party, there will still be a "court" if the proceedings follow the lines of recognized and established order— there will be then at least the compulsion of recognized "legal" procedure, though the ultimate court may be no more than the "bar of public opinion." When vigorous public opinion recognizes and accepts the procedure of the plaintiff as correct and the settlement or punishment meted out as sound, and the wrongdoer in consequence accedes to the settlement because he feels he must yield, then the plaintiff and his supporting public opinion constitute a rudimentary sort of "court," and the procedure is inescapably "legal."

Consider the Eskimo way of handling recidivist homicide. Killing on a single occasion merely leads to feud. (A feud, of course, marks an absence of law inasmuch as the counterkilling is not recognized as privileged by the opposite kin group. The so-called law of blood revenge is a sociological law but not a legal one.) But, among the Eskimos, to kill someone on a second occasion makes the culprit a dangerous public enemy.

Now arises the opportunity for some public-spirited man of initiative to perform a community service. He may undertake to interview, one after the other, all the adult males of the community to see if they agree that the killer had best be executed. If unanimous consent is given, he personally dispatches the murderer at the first

[24] A. L. Kroeber, "Yurok Law" (*22nd International Congress of Americanists,* 1924), pp. 511 ff.; Kroeber's statement of the pattern seems to be more formalized than the actual cases reveal, however.

opportunity, and no revenge may be taken on him by the murderer's relatives. Cases show that no revenge *is* taken.[25]

A community "court" has spoken and its judgment executed. Such are the kinds of courts Max Radin had in mind. And such are the courts that Seagle has in mind with his comment, "Doubtless there will be borderline cases of the existence of machinery for intervention closely approximating a court." [26]

Although courts in this sense exist in primitive societies, it is not necessary to submit the concept of courts to such a strain in order to give primitive law the recognition that is its due.

The really fundamental *sine qua non* of law in any society—primitive or civilized—is the legitimate use of physical coercion by a socially authorized agent. The law has teeth, teeth that can bite if need be, although they need not necessarily be bared. Truly, as Jhering emphasized, "Law without force is an empty name," and more poetically, "A legal rule without coercion is a fire that does not burn, a light that does not shine." [27] No matter that often the force need not be unleashed; for as Salmond notes, "Against subjects its [the law of an organized state] force is so overwhelming that its decision is usually enough to secure compliance, but force is still present though latent." [28]

The importance of force as an aspect of law has been clearly recognized by a few of the modern anthropologists who have come to grips with the problem of primitive law. A. R. Radcliffe-Brown, whose treatment of social sanctions [29] has been a helpful contribution toward clear thinking, sees law as "the maintenance or establishment of social order, within a territorial framework, by the exercise of coercive authority through the use, or the possibility of use, of physical force." [30] So, also, Thurnwald in his volume on the nature and growth of law emphasizes and reëmphasizes the importance of force in law in such terms as the following: "The instance

[25] See Chapter 5, below.

[26] Seagle, p. 34.

[27] R. von Jhering, *Law as Means to an End* (New York, 1924), p. 190.

[28] Salmond, p. 165.

[29] Radcliffe-Brown, "Sanctions, Social," pp. 532–534. For a critical application and analysis of Brown's categorical system of sanctions, see Provinse, "The Underlying Sanctions of Plains Indian Culture."

[30] A. R. Radcliffe-Brown, Preface, in *African Political Systems,* ed. M. Fortes and E. E. Evans-Pritchard (Oxford, 1949), p. xiv.

of organized force raises the legal order over and against usage and custom . . . recognized force raises it (custom) to law." [31]

However, force in law has a special meaning. Force, unqualified, means coercion—the condition that exists whenever men act, or refrain from acting, in a manner different from that which they themselves would have chosen in a given situation, because others deliberately limit the range of their choice either directly, through present control over it, or indirectly, through the threat of consequences.[32] There are, of course, as many forms of coercion as there are forms of power. Of these, only certain methods and forms are legal. Coercion by gangsters is not legal. Even physical coercion by a parent is not legal if it is too extreme. The essentials of legal coercion are general social acceptance of the application of physical power, in threat or in fact, by a privileged party, for a legitimate cause, in a legitimate way, and at a legitimate time. This distinguishes the sanction of law from that of other social rules.

The privilege of applying force constitutes the "official" element in law. He who is generally or specifically recognized as rightly exerting the element of physical coercion is a splinter of social authority. It is not necessary that he be an official with legal office or a constable's badge. In any primitive society the so-called "private prosecutor" of a private injury is implicitly a public official pro tempore, *pro eo solo delicto*. He is not and cannot be acting solely on his own, his family's, or his clan's behalf and yet enjoy the approval or tacit support of the "disinterested" remainder of his society. If the rest of the tribal population supports him in opinion, even though not in overt action, it can only mean that the society feels that the behavior of the defendant was wrong in its broadest implications, that is, against the standards of the society as a whole. Thus it is in itself an injury to the society, although the group feeling may not be strong enough to generate overt and specific action by the group as a group and on its own initiative. Yet the private prosecutor remains the representative of the general social interest as well as that which is specifically his own. This fundamental fact

[31] "Das Moment eines *organizierten* Zwanges hebt die Rechtsordnung heraus gegenüber Brauch und Sitte . . . der anerkannte Zwang erhebt sie [die Gewohnheit] zum Recht." Richard Thurnwald, *Die menschliche Gesellschaft*, V: *Werden, Wandel, und Gestaltung des Rechts* (Berlin, 1931–34), pp. 2, 4.

[32] MacIver, *Society*, p. 35.

is ordinarily ignored in discussions of primitive law, and it is in this sense that we may say that the difference between criminal law and private law is a difference in degree rather than in kind, although there can be no doubt that some matters touch the general interest much more vigorously than others in primitive law, as for example, sorcery, homicidal tendencies, and, frequently, treason.

These observations are not intended to deny the usefulness of our modern concept of "public" as against "private" law. Those concepts are of the greatest value in reaching an understanding of a difference in emphasis that tends to pervade the law of primitive societies as compared to the more highly organized legal systems of civilizations. Private law predominates on the primitive scene.

A third explicit feature of law is regularity. Regularity is what law in the legal sense has in common with law in the scientific sense. Regularity, it must be warned, does not mean absolute certainty. There can be no true certainty where human beings enter. Yet there is much regularity, for all society is based on it and regularity is a quality law shares with all other cultural norms. In law, the doctrine of precedent is not the unique possession of the Anglo-American common-law jurist. As we shall see, primitive law also builds on precedents, for there, too, new decisions rest on old rules of law or norms of custom, and new decisions which are sound tend to supply the foundations of future action.

Hence we may say that privileged force, official authority, and regularity are the elements that modern jurisprudence teaches us we must seek when we wish to identify law.

On this basis, for working purposes law may be defined in these terms: *A social norm is legal if its neglect or infraction is regularly met, in threat or in fact, by the application of physical force by an individual or group possessing the socially recognized privilege of so acting.*

3

Methods and Techniques

The law has many facets. It is no two-dimensioned thing to be comprehended from one position solely. Therefore, any method for the study of law—primitive or civilized—must be eclectic and the approach multiphasal.

Three main lines of investigation have already been worked out in anthropological studies of law. The first is "ideological and goes to 'rules' which are felt as proper for channeling and controlling behavior . . . The second road is descriptive; it deals with practice. It explores patterns according to which behavior actually occurs. The third road is a search for instances of hitch, dispute, grievance, trouble; and inquiry into what the trouble was and what was done about it. Beyond this, too, for the third approach, there lies—if it can be discovered—the problem of motivation and result of what was done." [1]

The ideological contents itself, for the most part, with an almost passive acceptance of ideal norms as truly representing the law. It undertakes to put into writing a kind of code, as it were, such as a native systematizer of the law might write, if there were native systematizers who could write. It does not concern itself to any great degree, if at all, with variations from the stated norm; nor does it test the presumed norms with cases to see whether they actually hold when challenged in real life situations. The ideological approach leads to abstractions; it is rarely clothed in flesh and blood. It portrays the ghost of the law. It looks away from the fact that ideal norms are too often pretend rules, rules mouthed but ofttimes honored only in the breach. For as Judge Jerome Frank notes, "All groups have their pseudo-standards, their 'pretend rules'; *it is part*

[1] Llewellyn and Hoebel, pp. 20–21.

of the rules of any group to break some of its own rules. Greeks and Trobrianders, New Yorkers and Hottentots, not only preserve but currently produce . . . rules which they circumvent or openly violate but which they refuse to abandon . . . The seeming lawlessness of any group is the result of the gap between the legal standards apparently set by the political community and the more exigent ethical standards and psychological drives operative within that particular group." [2]

Any investigation of a law system will record and make note of the ideal norms—the legal *rules*—for at no point can it be maintained that the ideal norms are without significance. They are guides for action, and more often than not the real norms of behavior coincide with them. Nevertheless, experience shows that there are always some real behavior norms that depart widely from the stated ideal patterns.

The older German researchers in ethnological jurisprudence, working in the tradition of Post and Kohler,[3] best represented the ideological school. As continental code-trained civil lawyers it was but natural that they should seek out the "rules" of primitive law. As men who had scarcely ever visited primitives in the field, it is hardly surprising that they failed to sense the vibrant reality of the dynamic law-life of primitive peoples. Committed as they were to the demonstration of evolutionary schemes involving specific and rather detailed stages of social and legal development, it was but

---

[2] Jerome Frank, "Lawlessness," *Encyclopaedia of the Social Sciences*, IX (1933), 277–278. (Italics mine.)

[3] A. H. Post (1839–95), *Einleitung in eine Naturwissenschaft des Rechts* (Oldenburg, 1872); *Bausteine für eine allgemeine Rechtswissenschaft auf vergleichend-ethnologischer Basis*, 2 vols. (Oldenburg, 1880–81); *Einleitung in das Studien der ethnologischen Jurisprudenz* (Oldenburg, 1887); *Grundriss der ethnologischen Jurisprudenz*, 2 vols. (1894–95). "The order of his compositions is systematic, not chronological or even ethnographical in the sense of grouping kindred races together. He takes up the different subdivisions of law and traces them through all the various tribes which present any data in regard to them. What he sought was not common origin or a common stock of ideas, but recourse to similar expedients in similar situations." P. Vinogradoff and H. Goitein, "Jurisprudence, Comparative," *Encyclopaedia Britannica*, 14th ed. (1949). Joseph Kohler (1849–1919), for many years editor of the *Zeitschrift für Vergleichende Rechtswissenschaft;* "During his lifetime Kohler was regarded by some as the greatest of living jurists while others consider him hardly more than an assiduous compiler of an almost endless series of monographs." W. Seagle, "Kohler, Joseph," *Encyclopaedia of the Social Sciences,* VIII (1932), 588.

natural that they were impelled to look at the simplified, patterned form rather than to seek the dynamics of interaction.

Post, although he tried hard to be empirical, was limited to library resources that in his day yielded little of reliable, controlled material. Feeling the need for source material more directly addressed to the subject of law, he set in motion the great *Fragebogen* effort that was later developed and pushed by Kohler, Felix Meyer, and others. The questionnaires consisted of compilations of formal queries on legal customs which were sent to colonial officers and missionaries throughout the German colonies and in such other empire holdings as would offer coöperation. In 1893, 1897, 1906, and 1907 the questionnaires were formulated, reworked, and distributed in German and other languages.[4]

The way in which the facts of law were ideologically conceived may quickly be exemplified by a few random samples drawn from Kohler's *Fragebogen:* [5]

I. Family and Personal Law

Question 1. Does mother- or father-right prevail? i.e., does the child follow the family of the mother or father? [6] Or are the children shared between both families?

Question 3. What rights does the father of the family have toward the wife and children?

Question 14. At what age is marriage consummated?

Question 24. Who has the right of divorce?

II. Property Law

Question 41. What are the laws of land and soil?

Question 42. Can property be protected by magic?

Question 43. Does ownership belong to the family or the individual alone?

[4] See Erich Schultz-Ewarth and Leonard Adam, *Das Eingeborenenrecht,* 2 vols. (Stuttgart, 1929); vol. I: *Ostafrika,* Foreword, pp. v-ix, for a brief history of the questionnaire movement. This work collates the usable data derived from the answers garnered in the surveys.

[5] Joseph Kohler, "*Fragebogen zur Erforschung der Rechstverhältnisse der sogenannten Naturvölker, namentlich in den deutschen Kolonialländer,*" *Zeitschrift für vergleichende Rechstwissenschaft,* 12:427–440 (1897).

[6] One literal-minded missionary responded to this with the following note: "When young, they follow the mother—in later years, the father." J. E. Lips, *Naskapi Law (Transactions of the American Philosophical Society,* vol. 37, 1937), p. 382.

III. Penal Law

> Question 57. Does blood revenge prevail in event of murder?
> Accidental homicide? Adultery? Other cases?
> Question 59. Who works blood revenge?
> Question 60. Is there composition?
> Question 61. What happens when not paid?
> Question 63. Is there a public [*staatliches*] penal law?
> Particularly, a penal law of the chieftain? What are the penalties? Substitution of a slave? Fines?

IV. Procedural Law

> Question 67. Can a creditor seize his debtor?
> Question 69. Is there a judicial proceeding and decision?
> Question 75. Does the principle "Where there is no complainant, then no judge" prevail in penal matters? [7]

From this sample it may readily be seen, as Lips has observed, "They . . . stressed the general culture and especially the economic background of the tribes in question . . . The main emphasis was laid on the finding of the general 'norms' and 'rules' of the primitive law in question." [8] For example, we note that only questions 59, 61, and 67 in the sample given above imply answers descriptive of going situations involving persons as principals and not principles as generalized rules. The inevitable result is seen in the following comment of Lips, who worked in the field in Kamerun in a later extension of the project and who had direct access to the questionnaire data. "From the judicial point of view it was significant that none of the answering officials—even when they were Englishmen —attempted to answer any of the questions by a collection of cases. The desire to find out the general rules was prevalent throughout." [9]

Although cases were known to the reporting officials and missionaries (they did not live with the natives with their eyes shut) and were used as background to some degree,[10] the effect of ideological emphasis is formalization and neglect of real life situations.

---

[7] Translated from the German by the author.
[8] Lips, *Naskapi Law*, p. 382.
[9] *Ibid.*
[10] *Ibid.*

To a lesser degree, but still in the main, the Dutch school of ethnological jurisprudence founded by the great van Vollenhoven also followed the ideological approach in its vast coverage of Indonesian *adat* (customary) law.[11] The Dutch monographs, however, come closer to real law-life. Field studies were made by trained legal and ethnological specialists with little use of questionnaires in the hands of missionaries and administrators. More than this, the Dutch did not commit themselves to any synthetic theory of social evolution or historical diffusion of culture. Thus, although the Dutch in their works aimed at idealized norms, their reports reveal a quality of accuracy and the feel of a greater reality than most of the German products. Nevertheless, the systematic Dutch *adat*-law studies, based as they are on the ideological approach, pay little attention to the testing of principles by cases, to the nature of the sanctions used, or to deviation and the range of permissible leeway. In another context, however, the Dutch have given a good deal of attention to case materials. As long ago as 1910, they founded a "Reporter" of court records and digests, the *Adatrechtbundels*. In addition, a series of three dissertations at the University of Leiden has collated and summarized a vast body of case law materials drawn from Dutch and Native courts.[12] Unfortunately, however, the Dutch case reports on Indonesian law are norm-oriented to such an extent that they record no more of the material fact than is necessary to demonstrate that the claim relates to some declared principle of law. Or they concentrate upon testimony as to the substantive nature of legal norms in native usage. Of details there are few, of the imponderabilia of the law-ways none.

So it is that ter Haar's comprehensive handbook on Indonesian *adat,* distilling out the essence of all Indonesian law, yields not a single case for exemplification or substantiation of the many norms it summarizes. When we were preparing the English translation of ter Haar's compendium, Arthur Schiller and I hoped to remedy

[11] See B. ter Haar, *Adat Law in Indonesia* (New York, 1948), chap. XV, for a bibliography with commentaries on the more important items of this literature.

[12] K. L. J. Enthoven, *Het adatrecht de inlanders in de jurisprudentie, 1849–1912* (Leiden, 1912); J. C. van der Meulen, *Het adatrecht de inlanders in de jurisprudentie, 1912–1923* (Leiden, 1924); E. A. Boerenbeker, *Het adatrecht de inlanders in de jurisprudentie, 1923–1933* (Bandung, 1935).

this with the inclusion of an appendix of pertinent cases from the *Adatrechtbundels*. But the *Bundels* yielded too few cases that revealed enough of substance and process to satisfy the need, and the idea was of necessity dropped.

In sum, the ideational road into law is to be appreciated since it is at least a road with law as its goal. To use it produces results of worth, but to travel it as the main highway causes one to move all too smoothly and readily to a formulation of the law that leaves out too much, misses too much, and causes a too ready acceptance of the façades and false fronts along the highway as representing the real structures.

The descriptive road is well exemplified by R. S. Rattray's study of Ashanti law, by R. F. Barton's earlier work on the Ifugao, and by the behavioristic and theoretical work of Malinowski on the Trobrianders. Such studies are behavioristic in that they eschew formulating rules of what people think or say they should do in hypothetical situations in favor of accounts of actual human behavior. Of Malinowski Sir James Frazer wrote, "It is characteristic of Dr. Malinowski's method that he takes full account of the complexity of human nature. He sees man, so to say, in the round and not in the flat. He remembers that man is a creature of emotion at least as much as reason, and he is constantly at pains to discover the emotional as well as the rational basis of human action." [13] To Malinowski man was always a being in action and for him the problem was "not to study how human life submits to rules—it simply does not; the real problem is how the rules become adapted to life." [14] With this as his fundamental premise Malinowski could not help but shun rules in favor of descriptive accounts of behavior and motivation. Deviation was held by him to be more revealing than normation. It is not that he ignored the norms, but rather that they did not hold him spellbound. Nevertheless, because he took the descriptive road and not that of the case study approach, his accounts tend to be generalized. In *Crime and Custom in Savage Society* no more than six actual cases can be found. Even these are presented in a quasi-narrative form rather than in the manner of cases as such.

[13] J. G. Frazer, Preface, in Bronislaw Malinowski, *Argonauts of the Western Pacific* (London, 1922), p. ix.

[14] Malinowski, *Crime and Custom in Savage Society*, p. 127.

In consequence, they leave much unsaid and they lack the detail necessary to the answering of many pertinent questions that may well be asked.

Much more detailed as to fact are Barton's *Ifugao Law* and Rattray's *Ashanti Law and Constitution*. Both are examples of the descriptive approach at its best. Neither author was distracted from his main task by problems of general comparative jurisprudence, for their studies are strictly monographic. Each was a field worker with long personal contact and intimate rapport with his people. No questionnaires for them. The result is that their studies consist of long, running accounts from an observer's scientific notebook. The norms are there, but they are firmly embedded in a rich lode of fact. Cases, however, although used, are few and far between, and the emphasis falls quite naturally on the substantive aspects of law to the neglect of the procedural. Barton's *Ifugao Law,* in consequence, offers seventy-three close-packed pages of substantive law (under the headings of The Family Law, The Property Law and Penal Law), while devoting but seventeen pages to procedure. In Rattray's case the disparity is even heavier.

If law, as the students of Anglo-American jurisprudence have long held, is secreted in the interstices of procedure, much is obviously missed in the substantive overemphasis characteristic of the descriptive approach.[15]

The method of emphasizing trouble cases as a road into the study of law is not a panacea in itself; it is to be used in conjunction with a full treatment of ideological problems and norms, for Cardozo's dictum is not to be forgotten: "We must not sacrifice the general to

[15] Of Barton, let it be remembered, these comments apply only to his earliest work, *Ifugao Law* (University of California Publications in American Archaeology and Ethnology, vol. 15, 1919). The deficiences of his descriptive account were more than corrected by his semipopular book, *The Half Way Sun* (New York, 1930), in which a long chapter (pp. 60–119) offers one intriguing case after another in exemplification of Ifugao law in action, while yet another chapter (pp. 232–289) highlights problems of the conflict of laws which ensnared Ifugaos in the American courts. Three cases are presented and discussed at length. Then, in a later writing covering the autobiographies of three Ifugaos, published by Barton under the title, *Philippine Pagans* (London, 1935), a number of actual cases crop up. Among the litigious Ifugaos, few men, if any, it appears, escaped involvement in legal action. Finally, in his posthumous work, *The Kalingas* (Chicago, 1949), Barton makes full and uninhibited use of the case method: every point of Kalinga law in every aspect of the system is illuminated and substantiated with cases.

the particular." [16] Cases are also to be embedded in description of the whole cultural setting. But the orientation of the case-method approach is inductive. Its user arrives at the norms of primitive law, as does the student of the common law, from the analysis of cases and more cases. His is the scientific approach—the movement from particulars to generalization and the further testing of generalizations through a return to the particular. The case-method researcher never forgets Cardozo's admonition that "We do not pick our rules of law full-blossomed from the trees." [17] And he knows that mere collection of cases as curiosa is not enough. Cases must be analyzed for what is in them, and compared for what they will yield in generalization. Dissecting tools are needed, and hypotheses related to a frame of reference are indispensable. "Cases do not unfold their principles for the asking. They yield up their kernel slowly and painfully." [18]

The eclectic approach, with its trouble case emphasis, differs from the ideological mainly in this: whereas the ideological takes the ideal norm as its starting point (and usually gets no farther than this), the case method treats the statement of norms as the end product, not the beginning. A by-product, but nevertheless very important result, is that while the results of the exclusively ideological approach tend to be tinctured with a quality of abstract unreality, the results of the case-oriented approach (when the cases are not overdistilled in the reporting) are perforce tied to the reality of life, and if there is an adequate number of cases, the range and facts of deviation from the norm cannot be missed. The case method leads to realistic jurisprudence.

Beyond the basic proposition that a scientific method in law must move out from cases there is a secondary proposition concerning the importance of cases derived from our assumptions as to the nature of law. Law focuses around conflicts of interests. [19] "A law embodies beliefs that have triumphed in the battle of ideas and then translated themselves into action." Law breeds and grows on trouble or prospect of troubles. It exists in order to channel behavior so that con-

[16] B. N. Cardozo, *The Nature of the Judicial Process* (New Haven, 1921), p. 103.
[17] *Ibid.,* p. 103.
[18] *Ibid.,* p. 29.
[19] Roscoe Pound, "The law is an attempt to reconcile, to harmonize, to compromise . . . overlapping or conflicting interests." ("A Theory of Social Interests," *Publications of the American Sociological Society,* vol. 15, 1920; p. 44.)

flicts of interests do not come to overt clash. It moves into action to clear up the social muddle when interests do clash. Indeed, as a canon of realistic law it may be said that unless a dispute arises to test the principles of law in the crucible of litigation, there can be no certainty as to whether the presumptive principle will actually prevail. One knows not whether it is merely pretend rule or genuine law. A "law" that is never broken may be nothing more than omnipotent custom. One will never know more than this until it is sustained in legal action by application of a legal sanction.

Thus it is not only a dictate of scientific method that we should deal with cases, but the nature of law-stuff (any and all of the social practices that enter into or impinge upon legal usages and institutions) is such that trouble cases lead us most directly to legal phenomena. It is obviously true that not all trouble cases in any society are legal cases, but all legal cases are trouble cases.

The recording of cases from primitive peoples involves certain techniques, and an inevitable question asked of the anthropologist is: "How do you get your data and your cases?"

It is difficult to offer an adequate answer without formulating what would amount to a handbook on field methods.[20] Such is decidedly not in order here, but it does seem likely that a précis of the elementary facts may be of use.

In the first place, the basic approach depends upon the nature of the culture under investigation, the attitudes of the subjects towards aliens in general and the anthropologist in particular, the degree to which the subjects are prone to think of their culture in formalized terms, and whether the investigators are dealing with a live and going culture or one which in its legal aspects has been overthrown and suppressed, and which hence lives only in memory and tradition. The mode of operation must always be kept flexible; the investigator must always remain alert to the need for adjustment of procedures and concepts to the demands of the situation. Further factors exist in the amount and quality of data already published on

20 Such a handbook, and a most useful one, exists; although it is designed primarily as a guide for the alert and intelligent amateur, it is a handy vade mecum for any field worker, and the last two editions have a good section on law: *Notes and Queries on Anthropology*, 6th ed. (Oxford, 1950). The *Outline of Cultural Materials* (New Haven, 1949), prepared by Human Relations Area Files, Inc., also can be used as a convenient checklist in field studies.

the culture, technical equipment of the field worker (specifically, ability to speak the language or to record it phonetically), and the amount of time available to him in the field.

The first rule of procedure is, of course, to live right in the community of the people, if at all possible. The place and role of the field ethnologist is that of the participant observer. The second requirement is a careful choice of a native sponsor or sponsors who will be the researcher's voucher in the new community. Whatever the sponsor's official position in the tribe or community, he must be a *de facto* leader of acknowledged influence or prestige among his own people. In the early days of field work it usually takes some days of oblique inquiry and observation to determine the proper person for selection and then to establish contact with him in such a way as to win his personal interest and support. The impulse to accept the more readily accessible individual who shows an eager desire to be a buddy must be held in check. Too often such men are social misfits in their own group who are anxious to find a prop in the visiting scientist for their own weak or rebellious egos. They may be talkative informants but rarely good smoothers of the way in gaining entree to the society at large. Only men of influence can open the way and grant invitations to council and ceremonial, and, negatively, they may if they so desire make work among their people difficult, if not impossible. The misfit may, for reasons of his own, be ready to spill secrets that conservative pillars of society hold back, but he should be tapped in the later, not the early, stages of field study.

Where factions exist, then indeed is the selection of a sponsor a ticklish matter of judgment, for identification with a sponsor means (in most primitive societies) identification with him in all his social ties. However, participant observation implies that one is in the social group and yet aloof. This aloofness means that unless circumstances are most unusual, one can in time get to the other factions, who may then be more than willing to see to it that their side of things is reported too.

It is a matter of routine training for all modern, professional anthropologists to acquire skill in the techniques of phonetic recording of textual transcriptions of any and all languages. A first step in any field job, whether a full analysis of the language is intended or not, is (once proper contacts have been established) to spend some time in recording ordinary passages of daily communication and longer chunks of texts—usually of folklore and myths—in the vernacular. This serves three purposes; it gives the worker a quick feel of the language (even though he cannot speak it); it greatly impresses the informants and their friends to see that the anthropologist can write down their speech and read it back to them—something none of them or their ancestors have been able to do if theirs is a primitive culture—thereby contributing to the establishment of rapport; and furthermore, "stories" are a good, innocuous starting point. They usually come easily and readily. They serve as an innocent springboard into the more esoteric and abstract phases of culture.

Beyond such use of linguistic recording for procedural convenience, it is highly desirable, time permitting, to attain at least a conversational mastery of the language itself as a surer means of sensing the covert imponderabilia of attitudes and nuances of meaning.[21] However, this ideal achievement is by no means essential to solid field work—providing a selfless and objective interpreter can be found or trained to produce unabridged and unedited two-way translations. It *is* essential, on the other hand, to subject all key words, or potential key words, to linguistic analysis. In matters of law and property, as in religion, this is especially needful. Some words, it will be found, are not exactly translatable or do not mean precisely what their apparent English synonyms convey. Words of this order must be spotted and isolated so that they may be given their full connotive value in an expanded context.

It is hardly necessary to reiterate that law divorced from its cultural matrix is meaningless. Wherefore the anthropologist who is the first of his calling to undertake the study of a particular primitive society must work out the general ethnology of the tribe in the field before he can even begin any special inquiry into its law-ways. On the other hand, many excellent general ethnological accounts, lacking adequate materials on law, are already in print. When law studies are to be done on a people so accounted for, it is obviously easy to move quickly into the legal phases of social life. Inquiry into other-than-legal aspects of the culture need be pushed only where elaboration, rechecking, or special integration are seen as necessary and desirable.

[21] See Margaret Mead, "Native Languages as Field Work Tools," *American Anthropologist*, 41:189–205 (1939).

Whether the culture is living, or whether the investigation is reaching back into the past, the initial steps of law inquiry will be the same—inquiry with competent informants. In a going culture the investigator will be able to observe some cases in action. But cases may be few and far between, for critical, law-making cases may turn up only once in a decade. It is a rare ethnologist who can stay around long enough to sit in on a bag of cases full enough to round out the law picture. Observed cases are always to be preferred over cases derived from secondary sources, but it is doubtful if there has ever been a complete study that was able to rest its analysis on direct observation only.

Whether the line of research goes directly to cases, or moves first through a recording of ideal norms, will depend upon the nature of the culture. Some cultures produce the habit of thinking in terms of formal patterns; others do not. As Linton observed, "Different cultures show a tremendous amount of difference in the degree to which their patterns are consciously formalized. My experiences with Polynesians and Comanches illustrate this: Polynesians can give you practically an Emily Post statement of what proper behavior should be on all occasions, whereas Comanches, when asked how they do anything immediately answer, 'Well, that depends.' They genuinely think of behavior as a range of unlimited, individual, freedom of choice, although when you take a series of examples of behavior . . . you find actually quite a high degree of uniformity. But you have to check Comanche behavior to arrive at this." [22]

In Polynesia and among the more elaborately organized African tribes, therefore, it might be more fruitful to get the ideal framework and then to undertake to check it against the cases in fact. Among such peoples as the Comanches, Shoshones, and most North American Indian tribes there is little gain in spending more than the briefest of time in search for verbalized ideal norms.

So far as a researcher's informants are concerned, it is quite possible, and sometimes indeed desirable, to pursue the inquiry entirely without any overt mention of law—especially if they have had

[22] Ralph Linton, comment on the paper by L. Hanks, Jr., "The Locus of Individual Differences in Certain Primitive Cultures," in *Culture and Personality,* ed. S. S. Sargent and M. W. Smith (New York, 1949), p. 123. See also Ralph Linton, *The Study of Man* (New York, 1936).

some experience with imposed European law. The inquiry may start with a simple discussion of the fact that any nation or tribe has to deal with troubles among its people. People quarrel, get angry, feel someone else has done wrong, steal, injure, insult each other, perhaps kill. "Do you know any examples of these sorts of things?" "Well, tell me just what happened." Accounts when once started are permitted to run their course uninterrupted. Statements are never (well, hardly ever) overtly challenged. The usual ethnologist's practice of showing no emotion either of approval or disapproval is adhered to as strictly as possible. Notes are made as the discourse proceeds—unless, as among the Keresan Pueblos, this is out of the question.

At the completion of the recital of the case a series of questions is put first to elicit elaboration of important details, the fixing of dates and names, and the informant's relation to the facts (whether first- or second-hand). The questioning then goes on to exploration of the informant's attitudes with respect to the actions of the principles, their kin, and the public at large—and also as to "what the people had to say, or thought, about it." Next, inquiry probes into reputed or imputed motivations: "Why did he do that?" And finally, in seeking after "felt norms," hypothetical variations on the case may be posed to see what the informant thinks would have happened if certain conditions had been different or specific acts had occurred in a different way.[23] The responses to these latter questions do not necessarily go into the ethnologist's report of the case itself, but they are most useful in the process of analysis of cases and in rounding out the covert aspects of law. Usually one case leads to another, but always more cases of the same sort must be asked for—repeatedly. Quite obviously, it will never do to be satisfied with only one informant's version of a case, wherefore cross-checking by means of inquiry with other informants is done as a matter of course, so that in the end as many accounts as it is possible to obtain are recorded.

Analysis of the cases then reveals the recurrent lines of action that may be stated as "real" norms and whether there is a single norm or alternative norms for given situations. The degree and direction of variation and leeway may then be drawn.

[23] Cf. M. J. Herskovits, "The Hypothetical Situation: A Technique of Field Research," *Southwestern Journal of Anthropology*, 6:1–20 (1950).

Determination of the validity of the recorded cases poses problems that are not always amenable to easy solution. Even though cross-checking evokes consistent responses from a number of informants, there is the possibility that the informants may all unwittingly be recasting events in the mold of ideal norms. The actors "ought" to have behaved this way. Hence, expectancy may evoke a kind of socialized projection of the expected behavior with a resultant displacement of the real behavior. Testimonials or accounts of what took place must all go through the mediating effects of language; they must pass through the mind, where filtering out and injection both may occur.

This problem, of course, obtrudes itself in every courtroom, and the potential unreliability of even the most sincerely offered evidence is axiomatic in legal psychology. In ethnological field work the difficulties are decreased in situations in which the ethnologist is an on-the-spot observer. They are increased along with the danger of distortion when the ethnologist is working with reconstructions of events long past. In either event, they are never absent.

Unfortunately, we have not yet arrived at the state wherein we can make explicit the ways in which we think we recognize projective recasting of the evidence in evaluating cases. In the gross, we take cognizance of the degree to which a culture sets up patterns of verbalization of norms. Where this tendency is strong, we are more ready to increase the discount rate. We attempt to get a measurement of the degree of development of myth fantasy in the culture. The more there is of this, the greater the caution needed in acceptance of case records. Conversely, the more prosaic and matter-of-fact the thought-patterns of a people, the safer we can feel with their law cases.

So also, the relative degrees of status-determined differentials in social roles will be recognized as factors in projective recasting. The Yuroks of California believed with ironclad dogmatism that a bastard (in this culture, a person born of a mother for whom no bride-price had been paid) was incapable of normal decency—that he was by nature an incorrigible delinquent. The likelihood of objectivity in any Yurok's account of such a person's alleged delicts would then be rather slight. Or again, we run into such asseverations as Barton's: "It is a general principle that true *kadangyang* [men of the Ifugao upper class] do not steal." [24] Or Mishkin's to the opposite effect that the Kiowa *dapom* (the lowest of four distinct social classes), "would steal from their own kin. They were shiftless and lazy." [25] We would not challenge the validity of these generalizations as to the deportment of the Ifugao men-of-distinction as against the behavior of Kiowa bums, but it is certainly likely that the fact of a theft by a *kadangyang* runs a good chance of being overlooked or minimized in any native account, while anything that borders on theft on the part of a *dapom* is quite apt to be colored in the telling so that it is presented as theft.

The relative explicitness of the informants as to name, place, and time is also a valuable key to validity. For example, one of my Comanche incest cases was wholly ambiguous on these counts. [26] On return from the field, while engaged in working up the materials, suspicion of the validity of this case grew until I wrote to two Comanche informants asking for more particulars and whether they knew for certain that this case had actually taken place. Their replies brought no further enlightenment on particulars, but two positive statements were forthcoming that this case had really happened. However, reading in American Indian mythology brought forth several almost identical stories among other Plains tribes where they were clearly recognized by informants as myths and not as cases. The ambiguity of the Comanche accounts was symptomatic. Where ambiguous "cases" have a wide distribution among a number of contiguous tribes, and where the cases all reveal internal similarity of exotic incidents, it is safe to throw them out as myth or legend.

Another problem of validity turns on whether the trouble case involves men who are tribal figures or just ordinary men. The tribal figure may tend to build into heroic legend or near-legend. Not so the little man. The case of the ordinary man is less subject to glorification than that of the hero. The most obvious check, of course, is to measure the details of the heroic case against the prosaic. If they are commensurate, it is unlikely that the cases involving heroes are distorted. If they are not commensurate it does not directly

[24] Barton, *Ifugao Law*, p. 85.
[25] Bernard Mishkin, *Rank and Warfare Among the Plains Indians* (American Ethnological Society, Monograph 4, 1940), p. 36.
[26] E. A. Hoebel, *The Political Organization and Law-ways of the Comanche Indians* (American Anthropological Association, Memoir 54, 1940), p. 110.

follow that the hero's actions are fictionally blown up. Outstanding men are outstanding because their actions are not those of the common run. But such cases call for careful scrutiny. It is here that inquiry into motivation is apt to be most useful. Informants are by this means induced to measure the purported performance against everyday expectancy—and incongruities are thrown into focus.

Yet another caution must be stated with respect to the case of the Big Men. By the very reason of their special characters and social status the litigious behavior of such personages does not give a full picture of law at large. Justice may wear a blindfold and every man be equal before the law, but in every society—primitive and civilized—personality and social status color and influence every legal situation. The field investigator must, therefore, consciously drive for a full body of cases involving the obscure and little-remembered as well as those centering on chieftains and men of affairs.

Finally, in the matter of assaying the worth of the individual report (aside from the general process of cross-checking a case by means of several independent reports of that particular case) there is the need to understand the personality of the individual informant.

The known liar can readily be disposed of. The sycophant who wants to please the investigator for ego rewards or hard cash may be useful, but his "facts" must be charily handled. It is the weighing of the testimony of normal, well-integrated informants that raises subtler problems of discrimination. Perhaps the significance of this aspect of validation may be best shown by reprinting a fragment of what was written in *The Cheyenne Way* on the characters of two contrasting individual informants.

Stump Horn was eighty-six when he was consulted. A careful, somewhat conventional gentleman, an observer of all decencies—among them, truth. His accounts began always with the location of the camp and where it moved during the story. Twice he caught himself on a point of doubt and went out to check with "another old man," and found himself correct. A number of times such consultation came before he spoke or before he stated inability to get the matter straight. Pauses for pondering on a detail, to bring either the answer or a failure of it, made accurate notes easy on the writing hand: "He says he is sending his heart back over the years." "He wants to let his mind go away to think on that." For three days Stump Horn would not address us with these accounts from the old days, but held his eagle-feather fan between his face and us, and spoke to High Forehead. If noise or movement outside attracted his attention, he would lean forward to peer out the door, under the fan. There was a flat, disruptive silence, once, when a matter touching religion had been mentioned. But later, having mentioned an oath himself, he let his "heart" go away to think, dropped the fan, and felt he might better talk out the rest of the matter, "so you could get it right." If man can be accurate in the circumstances, Stump Horn was accurate.

Calf Woman, though a most valuable informant, has her value in other characteristics. Eighty-five, the wife of a chief, an enthusiastic, gossipy *raconteuse,* a shrewd and strong-willed trader on those decencies which were to her only what they threatened in action or what they could be made to yield, Calf Woman's memory was sharp for any weakness or any discomfiture of another which a long life of eager attention to such matters had yielded her. Her placing of cases was not in terms of the camp, but by what the women—naming them—had said about it. Calf Woman had the skilled teller's nose for context and for the characteristic. Detail she may have added, and may have spiced; where that has occurred, detail was spiced and added not only for realistic effect, but by one who had sure knowledge of what effect was Cheyenne-realistic. When it was possible to check the story against another informant's version, all relevant legal points of Calf Woman's stories were corroborated, save this: that whatever in a Calf Woman story turns to the glory of Calf Woman is to be regarded with more than suspicion.[27]

With such checks as have been briefly stated above, cases may be distilled to an approximation of their true essence. Despite all care, however, it must be recognized that some residuum of non-fact will probably remain in most instances. It cannot be pretended that the cases are assuredly absolutely true. It can only be maintained that they come closer to the facts of life than do idealized norms and that they are more sharply discriminating and detailed than are broad descriptive passages penned in conventional ethnologies. The case method is not the perfect method; it is, however, the most productive and the most reliable method for getting sound raw materials. It is not an end in itself; the materials it harvests are but the grist for the analytical mill of jurisprudence. "Cases are of course themselves no substitute for sound theory; but they are the writer's and the reader's only means for checking on the theorizing." [28]

[27] Llewellyn and Hoebel, pp. 30–31.
[28] *Ibid.,* p. 40.

4

Fundamental Legal Concepts as Applied in the Study of Primitive Law

If there is law in primitive societies in the same sense as in ours, then the basic tools of the student of western jurisprudence, though originally designed to fit the needs of the student of a system of civilized law, should also, to some degree, serve the needs of the student of primitive law. The anthropologist may then find some of his tools for the study of primitive law ready-made and well designed in the *fundamental legal concepts* of modern jurisprudence. It will then behoove the anthropologist to attain the mastery of these fundamental tools to produce an ethnological jurisprudence that is sound and adequate in quantity and quality; and, what is more, the materials may then be communicated in a form that will be meaningful to the student of law.

It is, of course, true that neither courts, nor lawyers, nor jurisprudents have all of them bothered to reduce their technical concepts to clear and basic fundamentals. For, as Karl Llewellyn so cogently put it, "legal usage of technical words has sinned, and does still, in two respects; it is involved in ambiguity of two kinds: multiple senses of the same term, and terms too broad to be precise in application to the details of single disputes . . . No logician worth his salt would stand for it; no scientist would stand for it." [1]

Yet it is a happy fact that the essential and fundamental legal concepts have been reduced to simplicity, precision, and universality in the system advanced by Wesley Newcombe Hohfeld.[2] Hohfeld,

---

[1] K. N. Llewellyn, *The Bramble Bush* (New York, 1930), p. 83.

[2] W. N. Hohfeld, "Some Fundamental Legal Conceptions as Applied in Judicial Reasoning," *Yale Law Journal*, 3:16 ff. (1913); "Fundamental Legal Conceptions as Applied in Judicial Reasoning," *Yale Law Journal*, 26:710 ff. (1917). See also Hohfeld, *Fundamental Legal Conceptions as Applied in Judicial Reasoning and Other Legal Essays*.

modified, provides at hand a set of accepted instruments which deserve rigorous use in primitive jurisprudence.[3]

Max Radin has observed that "a restated Hohfeldian analysis may safely discard a great many of the detailed terms that Hohfeld—rather tentatively—used, and even some which he apparently regarded as of high importance. We may even—in fact we must—reject some of the logical relationships he found in these terms."[4] Corbin, Goebel, and others have independently reworked Hohfeld. A restatement of the Hohfeldian system formulated largely along the lines suggested by Radin is presented here for use in the analysis of primitive law.

The fundamental premise of Hohfeld was that all legal relations are between *persons,* or as put by Corbin, "There can be no such thing as a legal relation between a person and a thing."[5] A legal issue may be one that concerns the relations between two persons with respect to a thing; but the issue lies only in the relations between the persons involved: "in each case one plaintiff, one de-

---

[3] Professor Kocourek, one of Hohfeld's sharpest critics, wrote: "After Hohfeld's death various attempts were made to subject the Hohfeld formulation to critical consideration, and in one or two instances the critical findings were unfavorable. On the whole, however, the weight of opinion in America, and perhaps, also, in England, accepts the Hohfeld formulation as logically correct and as practically useful." "The Century of Analytic Jurisprudence Since John Austin," in *Law: A Century of Progress,* II, 195, 207.

"With some variation in terms Hohfeld's analysis has found acceptance . . . [it] has been taken over in the pending restatement of the law by the American Law Institute." K. N. Llewellyn, "Hohfeld, Wesley Newcombe," *Encyclopaedia of the Social Sciences,* VII, 400–401.

"It professes . . . and, I think, successfully—to be able to reduce any legal transaction, however complicated, to its actual constituent elements or atoms." Radin, "Restatement of Hohfeld," p. 1164.

"One of the greatest messages which [Hohfeld] . . . gave to the legal profession was this, that an adequate analytical jurisprudence is an absolutely indispensable tool in the equipment of the properly trained judge or lawyer—indispensable, that is, for the highest efficiency in the discharge of the daily duties of his profession." W. W. Cook, "Hohfeld's Contributions to the Science of Law," *Yale Law Journal,* 28:721 (1919). "He demonstrated its utility by many examples from the law of contracts, torts, agency, property, etc., showing how the courts are constantly confronted by the necessity of distinguishing between the eight concepts and are all too often confused by the lack of clear concepts and precise terminology." *Ibid.,* p. 729.

[4] Radin, "Restatement of Hohfeld," p. 1163. For an excellent and the most recent analysis of the Hohfeldian concepts see Stone, chap. v.

[5] A. L. Corbin, "Legal Analysis and Terminology," *Yale Law Journal,* 29:165 (1919).

fendant, one issue; one privilege or one right is all that needs examination: the one relation between these two people." [6]

Thus every legal relation is bilateral, and there are two sides to the coin in each of the four fundamental relations recognized in the Hohfeldian system. The basic concepts are therefore eight and they pair off in four fundamental reciprocal relations as follows:

Person A		Person B
I. Demand-right	←————————→	Duty
II. Privilege-right	←————————→	No-demand-right
III. Power	←————————→	Liability
IV. Immunity	←————————→	No-power

I. *Demand-right* means that A has a legal expectation that B shall behave in a certain way with respect to A. A can ask, "What must B do (or refrain from doing) for me?" A may evoke legal compulsion against B, if B fails to act in accordance with A's demand-right. Thus, in debt, B must pay A $100: this is A's demand-right.

Duty means that B must behave in a specific way with respect to A. B can ask, "What must *I* do (or refrain from doing) with respect to A?" Thus, in debt, B must pay A $100: this is B's duty. Or, A has a legal expectation that B refrain from assaulting A: this is A's demand-right; B must refrain from assaulting A: this is B's duty.

II. *Privilege-right* means that A is free to behave in a certain manner with respect to B. A may ask, "What may I do without being subject to a legal penalty invoked by B?" Thus A is free, as against B, to sell his auto (to which he has clear title) to X, Y, or Z: this is A's privilege-right.

No-demand-right means that B has no legal redress if A behaves in a certain manner with respect to B. No duty is imposed on A to behave in a particular way toward B; hence B's relation is one of no-demand-right as against A that A shall behave in that manner. Thus A is free, as against B to sell his auto (to which he has clear title) to X, Y, or Z; against this B has no-demand-right.

III. *Power* means that A may voluntarily create a new legal relation affecting B. A can ask, "If I take this step, will it impose new duties on B and establish new demand-rights for me?" Thus, B

[6] Llewellyn, *Bramble Bush*, p. 86.

may make an offer of sale or contract to A. A, by acceptance, can close the contract. He has the power to establish the new legal relation. B's offer is merely B's privilege-right. He is free to make it, but there is no power in the offer per se. A can ignore it. B's act does not create a new legal relation. But A's acceptance does.

Liability means that B is subject to a new legal relation created by a voluntary act of A. Thus, if B makes an offer, A can effect the new legal relation by closing the contract: this is B's liability.

IV. *Immunity* means that A is not subject to B's attempt voluntarily to create a new legal relation affecting A. Thus, if B makes an offer, A is free to reject or ignore it as he wishes: this is A's immunity to the act of B.

No-power means that B cannot by his own act create a new legal relation affecting A. If A rejects B's offer, B can do nothing more: this is B's no-power.

Two of the relations, it should be noted at the outset, are positive (and active) and the other two are legally negative (and passive). The demand-right ←——→ duty and the power ←——→ liability relations are positive and active, and are enforced by means of legal sanctions, for they are imperative relations subject to the coercive authority of the courts or other legal authority.

The privilege-right ←——→ no-demand-right and the immunity ←——→ no-power relations are, on the other hand, negative and passive. They are not in themselves directly subject to enforcement by legal means. Rather, they set the limits of the law's activities, for they define the types of behavior that are outside the scope of law's sphere of control and are not subject to the coercive authority of the courts or other legal authority.

When the passive relations are called legal relations, it is only in the sense that legal systems make declaratory decisions as to which acts fall into the passive privilege-right ←——→ no-demand-right and the immunity ←——→ no-power relations. Because, under our prevailing system, the majority of such decisions are made by legal agencies, we are prone to call them "legal." This leads to the common phrasing, "The law is that A can sell Blackacre to X, Y, Z." A sharper phrasing would be, "The Law says that A may sell Blackacre to X, Y, or Z." Or, better still, the statement should read, "The Law declares it is none of its concern if A sells Blackacre to X, Y,

Z." When so put, it is easy to see that the passive legal relations are statements of "no-law."

In the study of primitive law it is especially important to recognize this quality, for it will help dispel the illusion that law and custom are one among primitives. In our legal system every demand-right that A has upon B is buttressed by accompanying demand-rights upon courts that they compel B to perform his duty. In primitive society it may also be that there are courts upon which A may have demand-rights in the event another person violates his legal rights, as is the case when a system of public law exists. But more commonly, there are no formal courts and no specialized law-enforcing agents. It will frequently happen that the aggrieved person himself, or his kinsmen, must enforce the individual's demand-rights. If they do this in a socially recognized and generally accepted manner, they have the privilege-right to apply the regular legal sanctions. The outstanding difference, then, is this: in our system, a failure to meet a demand-right by one party engenders a series of further demand-rights by the aggrieved on the courts and law-enforcing agents that they compel performance, exact damages or impose penalties; in primitive systems of private law; a failure to meet a demand-right by one party engenders a privilege-right in the aggrieved party and his kinsmen to compel performance, exact damages, or impose penalties, in a regularized manner.

For primitive law, especially, but also of valid importance for general jurisprudence, there is an additional point which ought to be added to the Hohfeldian doctrine. In any society one may expect to find a series of subgroups which taken together constitute the social whole. Every one of these subgroups will have its own code of standards and norms for its own members. Some of these standards may have a genuinely imperative quality for the membership of the subgroup. They will, then, on the level of that subgroup have a quality which is significantly similar to the "legal." Many social problems arise from the fact that the individual is at one and the same time a member of a number of subgroups and of the social whole, and his legal relations on the separate levels of the several orders may be in sharp conflict. To unravel any social (and legal) situation, the analyst must be consistently aware of the possibilities of inconsistency between the legal relations on the law level and social codes on the subgroup levels. A religious conscientious objector whose cult is not recognized by the Selective Service Administration may well illustrate the conflict of duties (in the Hohfeldian sense) imposed by the legal as against the religious imperatives. Analogue after analogue will confront the investigator of primitive peoples. Even within a supposedly well-ordered and consistent civilized legal scheme the same pluralism is at work. When Hohfeld, as Seagle said, annihilated the classic theory that there was no conflict between law and equity, he brilliantly demonstrated the strong disharmony that characterized two levels of law within the larger socio-legal system.[7]

The most effective test of the usefulness of the Hohfeldian fundamental legal concepts would be to apply the system to the analysis of the most vexatious problems of primitive law. A good problem would be that of drawing the real shape of institutions said to be "communistic" as against "private," or "corporeal" as against "incorporeal." These simple, all-embracing concepts are not fundamentals in themselves and they easily become unsatisfactory substitutes for clear analysis of the ofttimes complex niceties of primitive legal institutions. Much acrimonious argumentation can be made unnecessary by accurate and precise analysis, leaving the catchall labels, which have no place in the social science of comparative jurisprudence, to the political protagonist.

To this end, materials from the Yurok Indians of northern California may be scrutinized with profit. The Yuroks are well known ethnologically by virtue of the published works of Professor Kroeber, whose writings also include some brief formal statements of Yurok law.[8]

The Yuroks live along the lower reaches of the Klamath River and the adjacent shores of the Pacific Coast where they once subsisted as a primitive fishing and food-gathering people. Their world was a precise little affair, a nicely knit cocoon which hemmed the Yuroks within the confines of their river valley and a short stretch

---

[7] Seagle, *Quest for Law*, p. 400, n. 22.

[8] A. L. Kroeber, *Handbook of the Indians of California* (Bureau of American Ethnology, Bulletin 78, 1925), pp. 20 ff. "Yurok Law," pp. 511–516. See also W. Goldschmidt, "Ethics and the Structure of Society: An Ethnological Contribution to the Sociology of Knowledge," *American Anthropologist*, 53:506–524 (1951), for a penetrating comparison of Western European and Yurok social ethics.

of the sea coast. They held a dogma that the mountain ranges forming the boundaries of the Yurok country delimit the existent world; and within their known country they defined all identifiable geographical places with names and attributes according to a traditional pattern. This is but one phase of a marked conservative-mindedness and interest in status definition of all things and persons. It may be expected, in view of their marked concern with personal status, that although the Yuroks had no formal government, they nevertheless exhibited a welter of legal relationships in the realm of personal law.

Wealth, its accumulation and display, was an interest of the greatest vitality for these people; tokens of wealth were strings of dentalium shell, woodpecker scalps, and large ceremonial obsidian blades. Symbolic wealth was found in consumable goods as well, but prestige came from goods of large nonutilitarian worth. Property was therefore of extreme importance as an instrument for the maintenance of personal status and prestige.

In this setting every person, except bastards and slaves, had a full quiver of demand-rights, privilege-rights, powers, and immunities which he could fit to his litigious bow on the slightest provocation. Although there was no specialized law-enforcing personnel among the Yuroks, there was nevertheless a regularized procedural technique for enforcing conformance to the accepted legal standards through the imposition and collection of damages, or by the infliction of bodily injury—even death—to the offender. As Kroeber has rightly observed, "In the last analysis, violence to the body is the legal force." [9] It was up to the aggrieved and his kinsmen to institute the proceedings, as is usual in the private law of primitives, but they did not themselves, in the case of the Yuroks, arraign the offender or determine the extent of the damages to be assessed. This was done by the informal court of go-betweens, or "crossers," who were chosen from among nonrelatives living in different communities than those occupied by parties to the litigation. The plaintiff named two to four such persons, and the defendant did likewise. Whatever these men decided was to be the judgment in the case. The crossers ob-

---

[9] In a discussion of Yurok culture and personality before the joint seminar (psychology and anthropology) on "Psychological Approaches to Culture" held at the University of California, Berkeley, in the spring of 1941.

tained evidence from the disputants and any other available sources; they conferred among themselves and with the litigants as to what rules of substantive law might apply to the case in hand. They then arrived at a verdict and, if they found the defendant guilty, declared an explicit judgment against him. When the crossers thus found against the defendant, they sustained the plaintiff's claim as a valid demand-right, for the defendant had been found derelict in his duty; the judgment assessed the customary damages against him, which he had to pay over to the plaintiff. In default, the defendant normally became the plaintiff's debtor-slave; otherwise, his execution by the plaintiff and his kin was warranted, although there was risk of engendering feud in this kind of action even though public opinion supported the plaintiff. Each litigant paid his crossers with a dentalium shell, symbolically known as "his moccasin" in literal compensation for the footwork involved in adjudicating the case.

In fixing damages, the crossers were guided by well-established principles of value. Except for the bastards and slaves, who had no legal rights, every person possessed a fixed and immutable wergild, every material object its fixed worth, determined by what had been paid for it in previous economic transactions, and every intangible property-right its customarily recognized valuation. Bride-purchase, which alone made a marriage valid, determined wergild, for the *laga* of a person was equivalent to the price one's father had paid for one's mother. Bastards had no wergild for the simple reason that no bride-price had ever been paid for their mothers. In consequence, they had no legal status. This fact was true in theory and in practice, for such persons had no father's kin to support them, while their mother's kin were ashamed to come forward on their behalf. In addition to being legally without *laga,* they were social pariahs, living affronts to all Yurok sensibilities, and they were therefore in the unenviable position of scapegoats.

Injury to the person was scaled in accordance with the seriousness of the trespass and the wergild evaluation of the aggrieved. Legal relations of many interesting sorts entered into the Yurok law of persons. A few examples put into Hohfeldian terms will be to the point.[10]

---

[10] All the Yurok case materials to follow were presented by Professor Kroeber in his discussion of Yurok culture-before the seminar mentioned in note 9.

The first case arises out of the broad conception of responsibility held by the Yuroks and is related to the fact that locations which are most favorable as fishing sites along the banks of the Klamath river were subject to private ownership. The holder of the hereditary title to a fishing spot enjoyed, as against any other person, the demand-right to exclusive use of the location. He possessed the power, however, to extend a temporary privilege-right to any second party to fish in his private locus. Extension of such a privilege-right to a stranger carried with it a duty on the part of the owner to see that no injury befell his guest. Failure to do so was held by the Yuroks to be a fault of the owner; should the guest have the misfortune to slip on a rock while fishing from his host's territory, suffering injury thereby, he had a legitimate demand-right for damages against his host arising out of his original demand-right that the owner protect him from injury.

In a similar vein, Kroeber recorded a case in which a visitor to three brothers went sea-lion hunting while he was yet their guest. The venture ended disastrously; he drowned. The dead man's kin demanded damages equivalent to full wergild. The three brothers denied any substantive validity in the claim, refusing thereby to acknowledge a duty. The kinsmen then initiated action, and crossers were selected to take testimony, state the law, and give judgment. Testimony adduced evidence that the brothers had invited the deceased to stay overnight with them. In Yurok law this imposed a duty to safeguard the well-being of their guest. It was further established that the drowning occurred offshore from the very beach that was privately owned by the three brothers. This was held to impose a parallel duty to safeguard the guest. The brothers were judged responsible and derelict in their duties on these two counts, and the crossers awarded full wergild to the kin of the deceased.

Land ownership involved not only powers and privilege-rights for the title holder, but unique and interesting duties as well. Another case, recorded by Kroeber as having occurred some ninety years ago, reveals further aspects of Yurok legal relations with respect to property. In this instance, the family of which M—— was headman did not own the beach as such but possessed a long-established demand-right that the flippers of all sea lions caught along the Pacific coast for a distance of about four miles in either

direction from its settlement be yielded to it. A hunter, named
L——, disregarded his duty in this respect on several occasions.
M——, instead of taking legal steps, brooded, and finally assaulted
the father of L——, wounding him with an arrow. The family of
L—— took action for assault-damages. Crossers handled the case in
the regular manner. Their verdict was that the damages sustained
by virtue of the wounding were slightly less than the damages arising from the violation of the M—— family's demand-right for the
sea-lion flippers. Ergo, the L—— family's claim was nullified. The
affair was thus presumed to be equitably settled; but, though the
claims were adjudicated, the sense of grievance was not washed out.
So, L—— nursed his sense of grievance, and, two days after the legal
settlement, he cursed M——. To lay a curse without legal justification is a violation of duty in Yurok law. On this foundation M——
entered a claim for damages against L—— for violation of his duty
to refrain from cursing. Crossers were at work on the case when
hotheaded relatives of M—— killed L——. They were terribly in the
wrong here, for they simultaneously disregarded due process and
applied a penalty that was overstrong, going beyond privilege-right.
When the sister of L——retaliated by cursing the killers, it was *her*
privilege-right to do so. But with greater effect L——'s mother entered a claim to have the hereditary demand-right for the sea-lion
flippers transferred to her as equivalent to her son's wergild. She
won the award.[11]

The examples thus far presented show two things. First, that the
presentation of primitive material by way of the Hohfeldian concepts is feasible. Second, and better, that such presentation sharpens
perception of the cases, the issues, and their more precise bearings
and limits in law.

The demonstration of a third point may now be attempted: that
unnecessary controversy and confusion engendered by the use of
labels which are overbroad and inapplicable may be avoided by substitution of Hohfeldian analysis.

One of the fields of skirmish between the collectivist and the in-
dividualistically-minded anthropologist has been the identification of

[11] Less formalized accounts of this case are given in R. Spott and A. L. Kroeber,
Yurok Narratives (University of California Publications in American Archaeology and
Ethnology, vol. 35, 1943), pp. 182–199.

certain primitive property forms as either "private" or "communal."
Legal writers have also entered the fray, as in the instance of William Seagle, who castigated Bronislaw Malinowski with the assertion that Malinowski was guilty of attacking primitive communism "with evidence from a communistic people," [12] because Malinowski undertook to demonstrate that canoe ownership in Melanesia is not the subject of common ownership, as had been maintained by the English anthropologist, W. H. R. Rivers.[13] Malinowski had gone to great lengths to show that Trobriand canoe ownership, as an exemplification of Melanesian practices, is not communism but an intricate complex of individual "duties, privileges and benefits." [14] Malinowski was wholly right in his conclusions that "ownership . . . can be defined neither by such words as 'communism,' nor 'individualism,' nor by reference to 'joint-stock company' system or 'personal enterprise,' but by the concrete facts and conditions of use. It is the sum of duties, privileges and mutualities which bind the joint owners to the object and to each other." [15] In this he is very close to the Hohfeldian type of thinking and terminology. It seems likely that if his case had been put explicitly in Hohfeldian terms, his comprehensive grasp of the nature of property forms in primitive Melanesian society could not have been grossly misconstrued, especially not by a student of law. For if a complex legal and social institution is reduced in clarity to its fundamental components, the vagary of gross catchall concepts is banished. Confusion and useless argumentation go out with the catchalls, for it is in the periphery of their fuzzy boundaries that all the fighting occurs.

Thus, if further consideration is given to the Yurok materials, the question of canoe ownership among these people is also best handled without reference to communism or private property. A Yurok boat-owner nominally "owned" his boat, but "ownership," as always, was a compound especially of demand-right ←——→ duty and privilege-right ←——→ no-demand-right relations. The "owner" had a series of demand-rights against any other person that such other person must not molest or damage his boat. He had the

---

[12] Seagle, *Quest for Law*, p. 53.
[13] W. H. R. Rivers, *Social Organization* (New York, 1924), pp. 106–107.
[14] Malinowski, *Crime and Custom in Savage Society*, pp. 17–21.
[15] *Ibid.*, pp. 20–21.

privilege-right against any other person to use it upon the public waters, and a general immunity from obligation by way of mere offers to buy. In addition, he had the power to sell or bestow it as a gift. These are all marks of private ownership. (Such an immunity, however, is not enjoyed in every primitive culture, especially where exchange operates chiefly by "gift" and "return-gift.") [16] Yet he was also subject to a series of well-recognized duties which certainly limited his exclusive prerogative over the object. For one thing, he was under a duty to respond to the demand-right of any cross-country traveler upon a canoe-owner to ferry him across a river when called upon. Failure to do so gave rise to a demand-right for damages on the part of the traveler equal to one dentalium shell. However, in balance with this duty of the canoe-owner he enjoyed a demand-right against the traveler for any injury he (the canoe owner) suffered in consequence of service rendered. A boat-owner whose house caught fire and burned while he was engaged in ferrying a passenger enjoyed a demand-right for full damages by his passenger on the presumption that he could have brought the fire under control if he had not been engaged on the river.

Analysis of these examples from primitive societies leads to concurrence with Cook's formulation of the nature of ownership as based on Roman and Anglo-American law which seems aptly tailored to suit the data just analyzed:

> The assertion that a person owns an object is a summary way of stating that he has an exceedingly complex aggregate of legal rights which relate to the object, and indirectly that all the facts necessary to give him these rights exist. This may be expressed by saying that the word ownership denotes such an aggregate of rights and connotes the existence of the facts which give rise to the rights. When the aggregate of rights denoted by ownership is analyzed, it is found to consist not only of an indefinite number of rights in the strict sense or claims available against an indefinite number of persons, each of whom is under a corresponding duty, but also of a large and indefinite number of privileges, powers and immunities, in the senses in which these terms are employed in the system of Hohfeld. The number of such claims, privileges, powers and immunities changes constantly as persons are born, become old enough

---

[16] See H. N. Wardle, "Gifts, Primitive," *Encyclopaedia of the Social Sciences,* VI (1931), p. 657.

to owe legal duties and die; they may vary also with the occurrence of other events.[17]

The anthropologist must perforce agree with the Hohfeldian view that the object is of less significance in "property" than is the network of legal relations which determine and prescribe permissible behavior with respect to that object. Property in its full sense is a web of social relations with respect to the utilization of some object (material or nonmaterial) in which a person or group is tacitly or explicitly recognized as holding quasi-exclusive and limiting demand-rights, privilege-rights, powers, and immunities in relation to that object.

Thus there are two essential aspects of property: (1) the object, (2) the web of social relations, which establishes a limiting and defined relationship between persons and the object.

This limiting relationship is traditionally referred to by orthodox lawyers and economists as an exclusive right of use,[18] but modern economists and most legal thinkers today recognize that plenary control over any object of property is relative, and that the so-called exclusive right of control is at best a quasi-exclusive right, always limited by implicit, customary claims and restraints imposed upon the property owner by others. Even when there appear to be no explicit legal limitations upon the use and disposition of a person's object of property this is true.

Even though the individual may create or acquire the object of property through his own efforts, it is society and not the individual which creates the circumstances that make property out of it. For although an individual may be the possessor of some valued object, some *res nullius* that he has picked up, occupied, or created, that object does not become property until the members of the society at large agree, tacitly or explicitly, to bestow the property attribute upon the object by regulating their behavior with respect to it in a self-limiting manner. They recognize a special status [19] in the owner with respect to the object in question.

[17] W. W. Cook, "Ownership and Possession," *Encyclopaedia of the Social Sciences,* XI (1933), p. 521.

[18] E.g., T. E. Holland, *The Elements of Jurisprudence,* 8th ed. (New York, 1896), p. 180, "It is usually defined as a plenary control over an object."

[19] Linton, *Cultural Background of Personality,* p. 76: "The place in a particular system which a certain individual occupies at a particular time."

Put in the terminology of social psychology the object of property stimulates a special complex of behavior on the part of nonowners and owner. The roles [20] of the property holder and nonholder of the same object of property are culturally determined.

Thus, where Cairns puts it that "the property relation is triadic: *A* owns *B* against *C*, where *C* represents all other individuals," a social anthropologist would phrase it: "The status and roles of A with respect to B are distinct and special, as against the status and roles of C with respect to B, where B represents the object of property and C represents all other individuals." [21]

This conception of property will help clarify inheritance—which is then to be seen not as a transference of possession, or of title after death, but as a transference of status from a deceased person to his successor. A. R. Radcliffe-Brown, in his survey of patrilineal and matrilineal succession in primitive society, came close to the realization of this fact when he concluded that inheritance tends to run down the paternal line in societies that organize the kinsmen into paternal lineages or clans, while in those societies that organize kinsmen into maternal lineages or clans property tends to run down the maternal line. Specifically, "in general, though there are a few exceptions, transmission of property follows the same line as does transmission of status." [22] What Radcliffe-Brown failed to see, although he came so close to it, is that transmission of property *is* transmission of status. It follows that if most statuses are transmitted through one kind of unilateral kin group, property status will also devolve in the same way. It also follows that a close correlation between social organization and transmission of property status is to be expected.

Thus a social anthropological approach to property as a social institution leads us to the position where we look upon inheritance not as "the entry of living persons into the possession of dead persons' property," [23] or even as "succession to all the rights of the de-

[20] *Ibid.*, p. 77: "The sum total of culture patterns associated with a particular status."

[21] H. Cairns, *Law and the Social Sciences* (New York, 1935), p. 59.

[22] A. R. Radcliffe-Brown, "Patrilineal and Matrilineal Succession," *Iowa Law Review*, 20:297 (1935).

[23] G. D. H. Cole, "Inheritance," *Encyclopaedia of the Social Sciences*, VIII (1932), p. 35.

ceased," [24] but rather as the transference of statuses from the dead to the living with respect to specific property objects that involve not only "an indefinite number of rights in the strict sense of claims available against an indefinite number of persons, each of whom is under a corresponding duty, but also a large and indefinite number of privileges, powers and immunities."

With such conceptions in mind it is not difficult to deal with the question of the existence of incorporeal property in primitive society, as well as tangible chattels. This subject first received anthropological attention in the writings of R. H. Lowie, who contends that the widely-held notion of legal historians that ideas of incorporeal property are limited to modern law systems because primitive people lack the mental sophistication necessary for so abstract a conception is false.[25]

Professor Lowie's interpretation of certain primitive data as evidence of the existence of incorporeal property rights among primitives has been sharply challenged by Seagle, who denies that the incorporeal rights of primitives are property in any sense. "The concept of 'possession' rather than ownership is far more suitable in describing the primitive institution." Incorporeal rights are not property, he holds, because they are no more than extensions of the person; they are a part of the person and hence cannot be properties in the legal sense. On these grounds, Seagle contends, "It remains true to say that early law is hostile to incorporeal rights." [26]

The Hohfeldian analysis may be effectively applied as a precipitant for these muddy waters. Taking the concept of ownership made explicit in the words of Cook, may we not usefully say that we have property when any object, tangible or intangible, is the subject of ownership? Now pick up the examples of incorporeal property advanced by Lowie and see if they may be properly treated as objects of ownership.

An Andaman Islander composes a song for the occasion of a tribal gathering—a song that is received with applause. Irrespective of its popularity, we are told that no one dares sing it except the composer

[24] *Bouvier's Law Dictionary,* ed. W. E. Baldwin (Cleveland, 1934), p. 549.

[25] R. H. Lowie, "Incorporeal Property in Primitive Society," *Yale Law Journal,* 37:551–563 (1928), and in his *Primitive Society* (New York, 1920), pp. 235–243.

[26] Seagle, *Quest for Law,* pp. 50–54.

himself.[27] Unfortunately, we are not told what happens if someone does presume to sing the song of another, and, in consequence, it is impossible to know on just what level of social control the incorporeal right to songs among the Andamanese exists.

Among the further examples set forth by Professor Lowie is the private ownership of incantations, prayers, and magical formulas. Verbal patterns of supernatural importance are often subject to sale and gift among primitives. The owner in some of the instances cited may completely alienate his property, or he may sell or give no more than a limited interest in it, retaining the right to use the song or formula while extending a similar right to the recipient.

So long, of course, as any other aspects there may be are not artificially eliminated from notice, there is no evidence at hand of any legal procedures for setting a legal claim against usurpers of incorporeal property rights of the order just described. There is no evidence that damages are claimed or that punitive penalties may be imposed by the aggrieved or that they are ever the subject of litigation in primitive courts of law. On this point, however, the negative evidence is hardly impressive, unless such evidence has first been expressly sought, because the little extant data concerning the actual subjects of litigation in primitive disputes have to date for the most part been culled without special inquiry. What we do learn and know is that trespass on these incorporeal rights of a supernatural nature brings supernatural punishments in its train. The sanctions protecting these forms of rights are apparently magico-religious rather than strictly legal. Yet the beauty of Hohfeldian analysis is that the Hohfeldian relationships can be used to make other-than-legal social relationships clear.

Thus, consider the case of a Plains Indian visionary who had fasted and sought supernatural power. A bear appeared to him in a dream; it spoke to him and taught him four new songs. It also instructed him in the preparation of a rawhide shield to be painted with a bear symbol and other devices. The bear in the vision also instructed his tutelary that the shield would provide immunity in battle if the four songs were sung before an engagement began. The visionary made a shield as instructed; he sang the songs; his comrades heard the words; and he deliberately exposed himself to the

---

[27] Lowie, *Primitive Society,* p. 236.

missiles of the enemy, coming through unscathed. The value of the shield and the songs was publicly and pragmatically demonstrated. The shield, as Professor Lowie has made clear, was a material object which was clearly personal property. But the shield as such, in the culture of the Plains Indians, was of little value. What was of value in conjunction with the shield were the songs and the mystic power which the two engendered together. The incorporeal property was the thing of worth.

The complex of shield, song, and power could be transferred as a gift to son, nephew, brother, or friend. Or this same complex could be sold in a commercial transaction which had the qualities of contractual sale. In either case, the recipient could use the complex, if he had properly acquired the rights through regularized transfer, but not otherwise. The consequence of unauthorized use of the shield and songs was that the usurper would most certainly be killed by enemy missiles, due to the punitive action of the supernatural power. But there is no reason to believe that the true owner could not recover the shield, if it had been stolen, and with it his enjoyment of the songs.

In Hohfeldian terms, all this meant simply that the owner of a vision complex could sing its songs and possess its distinctive paraphernalia, and others could not: this was his demand-right as against any other person. From the standpoint of other warriors in the tribe it meant that A alone could sing its songs and possess its distinctive paraphernalia, and B (or any other person) could not: this was the duty of every B. But B's duty is not shown to give grounds for a legal claim on A's part in the event of violation; rather, B's duty existed with respect to the supernatural order and perhaps not with respect to the legal order.

This form of statement assumes the supernatural powers to be no part of the legal order. But the fact in many primitive cultures is that they can more properly be viewed as sanctioning officials, operating, so to speak, in "equity" when the "common law" of the secular gives no remedy, or even is supposed not to. If we go further, it may be said that A could give away the entire complex: this was A's privilege-right. Suppose A was free, as against his family, to give it to a nonrelative; his son X, could not prevent him from so doing: this was X's no-power. Suppose B offered to give three horses for the complex. A could close the deal: this was A's power. Again, suppose B offered to give three horses for the complex. A could reject the offer: this was A's immunity. Or, again with respect to this offer and A's rejection of it: this was B's no-power. But in some cultures (e.g., the Cheyenne) A could not well be said to be free to reject the offer. In such a culture A holds the complex with power in various other persons to force him to alienation by such an offer. His "ownership" is accompanied by liabilities to involuntary alienation.

Do we not have here a sufficiently large aggregate of rights denoted by ownership "[which consists] not only of an indefinite number of rights in the strict sense or claims available against an indefinite number of persons, each of whom is under a corresponding duty, but also a large and indefinite number of privileges, powers and immunities . . .," so that one may properly speak of incorporeal property in these matters?

An Hohfeldian analysis makes this unambiguously clear. Because Hohfeld's fundamental concepts fit not only the fundamental legal relations, but also the fundamentals of any complex of normative or imperative social reciprocity. Thus, even were we to grant that a social relation must be recognized by courts and enforced by political agents to be legal, even though we were to accept the idea that social relations enforced by supernatural sanctions are not primarily legal, the Hohfeldian system may still effect a useful analysis of such an other-than-legal complex as incorporeal property among primitives. Above all, "thinking thus, in nicer terms, with nicer tools of thought, you pull the issue into clarity . . . unambiguously, because your terms are not ambiguous." [28]

[28] Llewellyn, *Bramble Bush*, p. 88.

PART II

Primitive Law-ways

5

The Eskimo: Rudimentary Law in a Primitive Anarchy

Although we speak and write of "the Eskimos," there is no Eskimo tribe. The 20,000 or so Eskimos are thinly spread in Arctic isolation along the northern maritime fringe of North America, western and eastern Greenland—a distance of some six thousand miles from the handful of Siberian Eskimos to the settlements of East Greenland. Population density varies of necessity from estimated ratios of from sixty-five to two hundred square miles of territory per person. Settlements are far apart. Thus, although the Eskimo is highly mobile and ordinarily travels many miles in his annual cycle of hunting and visiting, contacts between local groups are fleeting and temporary. No superstructure of social organization embracing several local groups has ever come into being.

The size of the local group, or village community, is so small that rarely does the explorer or whaler find more than a hundred persons in a single community. The primitive Eskimo local group is, therefore, a peculiarly small and intimate face-to-face aggregation. Only when an Eskimo travels across the snow and tundra, or by sea, to visit another community, does he enter into secondary group relationships.

An ordinary Eskimo local group is made up of more or less than a dozen somewhat interrelated families. Kinship, except within very close degrees, is not emphasized, and as a result there is but little institutionalization of the extended family, and that along bilateral lines. So far as social organization is concerned, this makes the Eskimos one of the most genuinely primitive groups known to anthropologists. Winter houses are usually multiple-family dwellings,

it is true, but within each household each conjugal family is autonomous. The various families may be closely related to each other,
but often they are not—for friends may hole up together on the
basis of mere personal preference. The lineage and the clan are
conspicuous only in their absence. Thus, although kinship is not
ignored, it is *not* the basic principle in the organization and integration of the local group, for the group is also defined by locality, and
this is recognized by the Eskimos themselves, who designate each
local group by a place name followed by the suffix, -*miut,* meaning,
"people of," as in the case of the Kuskokwigmiut on the lower
reaches of the Kuskokwim River.

The technological and hunting proficiency of the Eskimos have
long excited the admiration of those who have visited them. Equally
remarkable in the eyes of the anthropologist is the high degree of
uniformity of their culture and language. Rasmussen, who spoke
the Greenland Eskimo dialect, was able to communicate with all the
Eskimos he met in his memorable trek across the rim of Canada
to Siberia.[1]

Regional variations do exist in the Eskimo ways of life and beliefs, however. In southwest Alaska, for instance, social forms have
been noticeably influenced by the impress of the highly elaborate
Indian cultures of the Northwest Coast of British Columbia and
probably also directly from northeast Asia.[2] Consequently, rather
than the law of any particular Eskimo local group, a generalized
analysis is forced upon us by the scarcity of adequate materials from
any single Eskimo group or even region. Where significant regional
variations are known to occur, they will be noted, however; and
specific examples will be ascribed to the local groups from which
they are drawn.

So simple is the social life of the Eskimo, and so rudimentary his
legal institutions, that the basic premises of his culture translatable
into jural postulates are few. Naturally, none of these postulates
have been explicitly formulated by the Eskimos themselves—for that
is not their way of thought. On the contrary, as the Iglulik Eskimo,
Orulo, irritably remonstrated to Knud Rasmussen's persistent ques-

[1] Knud Rasmussen, *Across Arctic America* (New York, 1927).
[2] Cf. Margaret Lantis, *Alaskan Ceremonial Organization* (American Ethnological
Society, Monograph 10, 1947).

tioning, "Too much thought only leads to trouble . . . We Eskimos do not concern ourselves with solving all riddles. We repeat the old stories in the way they were told to us and with the words we ourselves remember . . . You always want these supernatural things to make sense, but we do not bother about that. We are content not to understand."[3] Nevertheless, although the Eskimo does not subject himself to self-analysis, nor consciously try to formulate a logically consistent system of social behavior, his system does make sense in terms of its own premises—premises that may be extracted from what has been reported of his beliefs and practices by numerous observers and formulated as they are here.

The underlying postulates of jural significance in Eskimo culture are the following:

Postulate I. Spirit beings, and all animals by virtue of possessing souls, have emotional intelligence similar to that of man.

Corollary 1. Certain acts are pleasing to them; others arouse their ire.

Postulate II. Man in important aspects of life is subordinate to the wills of animal souls and spirit beings.

Corollary 1. When displeased or angered by human acts they withhold desired things or set loose evil forces.

Postulate III. Life is hard and the margin of safety small.

Corollary 1. Unproductive members of society cannot be supported.

Postulate IV. All natural resources are free or common goods.

Postulate V. It is necessary to keep all instruments of production (hunting equipment, etc.) in effective use as much of the time as is possible.

Corollary 1. Private property is subject to use claims by others than its owners.

Corollary 2. No man may own more capital goods than he can himself utilize.

Postulate VI. The self must find its realization through action.

Corollary 1. The individual must be left free to act with a minimum of formal direction from others.

Corollary 2. The measure of the self for males is success as a food-getter and in competition for women.

[3] Knud Rasmussen, *Intellectual Culture of the Iglulik Eskimos* (Reports of the Fifth Thule Expedition, 1921–1924, vol. 7, 1929), p. 69.

Corollary 3. Those who are no longer capable of action are not worthy of living.

Corollary 4. Creation or personal use of a material object results in a special status with respect to "ownership" of the object.

Postulate VII. Women are socially inferior to men but essential in economic production and childbearing.

Postulate VIII. The bilateral small family is the basic social and economic unit *and* is autonomous in the direction of its activities.

Postulate IX. For the safety of the person and the local group, individual behavior must be predictable.

Corollary 1. Aggressive behavior must be kept within defined channels and limited within certain bounds.

How are these postulates translated into legal or quasi-legal principles and norms?

"Apprehension of unpredictable misfortune," Rasmussen wrote, "drives the Eskimo to cling to his belief that they are caused by spirits, and to hope that by discovering the desires of the spirits he may forestall their designs."

"What do we believe? We don't believe; we only fear," said Aua, the Iglulik wiseman.

Now this is true, but not wholly true. It is true in the large, but it is by no means true in the detail of Eskimo action. To accept Aua's statement for illumination of the whole of the Eskimo system would throw light on its outlines but leave the finer essence hidden in unrelieved shadow.

From the fearful state of mind emerge the thousand and one tabus that hedge every moment of the Eskimos' waking day. A people more tabu-ridden would be difficult to find. The multitude of tabus are mostly directed to spirits of animals or their controlling deities in order to guard against conduct offensive or disrespectful to them. So comprehensive is the tabu system that the paucity of legal rules in Eskimo culture is in large part caused by the encompassing supernatural sanctions which dominate Eskimo social and economic life. Magic and religion rather than law direct most of their actions. Violation is sin. And the Eskimos in their own terms are most sinful.

The immediate personal consequence of sin is illness. Each sin contributes to the formation of a dark, noxious vapor that envelops the vital soul of the offender.

Among the Central Eskimos of Canada and those of West Greenland confession in a public gathering purges the soul.[4] With dramatic intensity the shaman (or *angakok,* in Eskimo) draws forth confessed tabu violation after tabu violation from the patient. Co-villagers from a background chorus to his chanting—washing the polluted soul clean with their cries for forgiveness. The Eskimo public, although the sins of one may endanger all, is gently tolerant and compassionate of the sinner in most cases. They are one of the rare peoples who do not rally in righteous indignation to stone the exposed miscreant who has been caught in acts of which they, too, may themselves be guilty in secret.

The psychotherapy of release from guilt anxiety can easily be read in the following descriptive excerpt from Rasmussen's writings. The simple technique of the *angakok* in fishing for clues is also patently revealed. That a confessional cure is theatrics and fun for the local group who makes up the audience—a welcome diversion in an Arctic world—can scarce be doubted.

The shaman who is dancing over the patient is the interrogator. He sings:

"It is you, you are Aksharquarnilik, I ask you, my helping spirit, whence comes the sickness from which this person is suffering? Is it due to something I have eaten in defiance of taboo, lately or long since? Or is it due to the one who is wont to lie beside me, to my wife? Or is it brought about by the sick woman herself? Is she herself the cause of the disease?"

The patient answers: "The sickness is due to my own fault. I have but ill fulfilled my duties. My thoughts have been bad and my actions evil."

The shaman interrupts her, and continues: "It looks like peat, and yet is not really peat. It is that which is behind the ear, something that looks like the cartilage of the ear? There is something that gleams white. It is the edge of a pipe, or what can it be?"

The listeners cry all at once: "She has smoked a pipe that she ought

---

[4] The public confessional is absent in East Greenland.

not to have smoked. But never mind. We will not take any notice of that. Let her be forgiven. tauva!"

The shaman: "That is not all. There are yet further offenses, which have brought about this disease. Is it due to me, or to the sick person herself?"

The patient answers: "It is due to myself alone. There was something the matter with my abdomen, with my inside."

The shaman: "I espy something dark beside the house. Is it perhaps a piece of a marrow-bone, or just a bit of boiled meat, standing upright, or is it something that has been split with a chisel? That is the cause. She has split a meat bone which she ought not to have touched."

The audience: "Let her be released from her offense! tauva!"

The shaman: "She is not released from her evil. It is dangerous. It is matter for anxiety. Helping spirit, say what it is that plagues her. Is it due to me or to herself?"

Angutingmarik listens, in breathless silence, and then speaking as if he had with difficulty elicited the information from his helping spirit, he says: "She has eaten a piece of raw, frozen caribou steak at a time when that was taboo for her."

Listeners: "It is such a slight offense, and means so little, when her life is at stake. Let her be released from this burden, from this cause, from this source of illness. tauva!"

The shaman: "She is not yet released. I see a woman over in your direction, towards my audience, a woman who seems to be asking for something. A light shines out in front of her. It is as if she was asking for something with her eyes, and in front of her is something that looks like a hollow. What is it? What is it? Is it that, I wonder, which causes her to fall over on her face, stumble right into sickness, into peril of death? Can it indeed be something which will not be taken from her? Will she not be released from it? I still see before me a woman with entreating eyes, with sorrowful eyes, and she has with her a walrus tusk in which grooves have been cut."

Listeners: "Oh, is that all? It is a harpoon head that she has worked at, cutting grooves in it at a time when she ought not to touch anything made from parts of an animal. If that is all, let her be released. Let it be, tauva!"

Shaman: "Now this evil is removed, but in its place there appears something else; hair combings and sinew thread."

The patient: "Oh, I did comb my hair once when after giving birth to a child I ought not to have combed my hair; and I hid away the combings that none might see."

Listeners: "Let her be released from that. Oh, such a trifling thing; let her be released. tauva!"

And so, on and on and on.[5]

The powers of the shaman as revealed in his direction of the public confessional are not to be taken as immediately legal. The action on the part of the sinner is "voluntary" and no compulsive legal sanctions are indicated when complete and abject confession is forthcoming. Out of this context, however, the shaman *does* draw legal power, and he can initiate legal action. A forceful shaman of established reputation may denounce a member of his group as guilty of an act repulsive to animals or spirits, and on his own authority he may command penance. The lightest penance is abstention from foods designated by the shaman. An apparently common atonement is for the shaman to direct an allegedly erring woman to have intercourse with him (his supernatural power counteracts the effects of her sinning). Or, he may direct her to cohabit with some particular man. More drastically, he may declare the union of a man and wife to be obnoxious to certain spirits. On this basis, the couple may be ordered to separate with sometimes a specification added as to whom they must remarry.[6] There is a hint that some *angakoks* are not above making a racket out of this power; men who court a married woman and yet shrink from conflict with her husband may "bribe" an *angakok* to find a marriage obnoxious to the spirits. Or, viewed in a less cynical way, it may be suggested that the specialist (the *angakok*) can sell out his right for a "fee." In interior western Alaska, "he literally ordered people around, and collected considerable wealth from them."[7]

The person who fails to accede to the orders of the shaman may be driven from the community, as was the Labrador girl who was banished in the dead of winter because she persisted in eating caribou meat and seal together. Because of the imputed separatistic sentiments of the denizens of land and sea, this is a basic Eskimo tabu. Her act endangered the whole community, since the angered animals would shun the local territory: frustration of the efforts of

---

[5] Rasmussen, *Intellectual Culture*, pp. 131–140.

[6] E. W. Hawkes, *The Labrador Eskimo* (Memoir 91 of the Geological Survey of Canada, Anthropological Series No. 14, 1916), p. 21.

[7] Lantis, p. 86.

hunters and starvation for the community threatened. Like disaster impends when the *angakok*, having declared certain behavior or associations to be obnoxious to spirits, orders penance or atonement, and his instructions are ignored.

Out of Postulates I and II with their attendant corollaries one can feel emerging a legal principle that willful and persistent violation of tabus shall be sanctioned by extrusion from the community; and, if the evidence on sex matters is sound, the principle as administered by an *angakok* carries its force over into humanly very dubious cases. The violation of a tabu is a sin supernaturally sanctioned; willful and repeated sinning becomes a crime legally punished. Penalty: exile—in the Arctic.

The third basic postulate (*Life is hard*) and its corollary (*The unsupportability of unproductive members of society*) are expressed not in the form of legal injunctions but, on the contrary, in privilege-rights. Infanticide, invalidicide, senilicide, and suicide are privileged acts: socially approved homicide.

Infanticide may be considered first. Infants are only potentially productive. If conditions permit, the Eskimos will always endeavor to raise their babies to adulthood. Too often, however, harsh circumstance does not permit. It is then up to each family to decide for itself: are its present resources (both human and material) sufficient to maintain the baby through its nonproductive years? There will be no social blame or legal sanction if a negative decision is reached and acted upon.

The first limiting factor is the nursing capacity of the mothers. Eskimos, like many another primitive people, prolong the nursing period many months, and even years, beyond that to which we are accustomed. Eskimo children subsist at their mothers' breasts for two to four years at least. And a youth, even a fifteen-year-old, if not yet married, may take occasional nourishment from his mother.[8]

The need for mobility and the physical drain of unceasing work make it difficult, if not impossible, for the mother to nurse two or more children simultaneously. Furthermore, she can carry but one child at a time within her parka, as she travels and goes about her outdoor work. Newborn children, if the next oldest is not yet ready for weaning, are therefore subject to disposal. This is almost always

[8] Peter Freuchen, *Arctic Adventure* (New York, 1935), p. 9.

effected by first offering the child for adoption. Foster parenthood is taken for granted by most Eskimos, and there is little concern over biological identity of the father or mother. Childless couples are generally eager to adopt, either to be able to pass on a family name (which carries with it the name-soul and imputed personality of a recently deceased family member), or to have a backlog against old age that will provide a minimum assurance of meagre social security.

In the event of birth of twins, one infant is almost inevitably disposed of, not because of any aversion to twins such as exists in a number of primitive societies,[9] but for the reasons just cited. If one twin is a girl and the other a boy, the girl is disposed of. Most Eskimos expect compensation from the foster parents, if they accept a child for adoption. Rasmussen tells of a Netsilingmiut Eskimo who gave a dog and a frying pan for one of a pair of twins and who felt she got the short end of the deal, since the parents had kept the fatter one for themselves.[10]

If there are no takers for the surplus children, they are killed. This may be done by smothering, but it is more customary to put the infants out in the cold to freeze. Anyone who finds an abandoned child may forthwith adopt it with no duty of compensation to its parents, for exposure of a child is a quitclaim on the part of the parents.

Baby girls are the most frequent victims of infanticide because of the effects of three discriminatory factors. First, the male is the basic food producer and, hence, potentially more valuable to the group. Second, the general tendency towards virilocal residence [11] means that grown-up daughters will, at marriage, more often leave their parents than will sons. Hence, the baby girl is a poorer risk than a boy as an investment in old-age security. Third, occupational casualties and homicide drastically drain off the number of adult men in the community.

One Netsilingmiut woman known to Rasmussen had in the course of sixty years borne twenty children—fifteen girls and five

---

[9] W. I. Thomas, *Primitive Behavior* (New York, 1937), pp. 9–16.

[10] Rasmussen, *Intellectual Culture*, p. 23.

[11] The practice whereby a married couple settles in, or close by, the domicile of the husband's family.

boys. Ten of the girls she had killed at birth; four had died of illnesses; one survived. Of her five sons one had drowned at sea; four survived.[12] This is clearly an extreme case, but one which showed no group-disapproval-in-action.

Census data brought together by Weyer reveal interesting results. In fourteen groups of Eskimos for whom sex ratios on children under ten years of age could be computed the ratios ran from a minimum of 42 girls per hundred boys to a maximum of 92 girls per hundred boys. Eight of the ten groups had ratios of 71 or less. Roughly one-third of the girls had been eliminated.[13]

On the other hand, consider what is revealed when sex ratios are assembled for adults above fifteen years of age. In twenty groups only three had *fewer* women than men, and half of these groups had adult sex ratios of *more* than 110 women to 100 men, with ratios running as high as 131 women to 100 men at Chesterfield Inlet and on the northwest coast of Hudson Bay. Such are the consequences of hunting accidents and killings among the men. Were it not for female infanticide (unless starvation reduced the entire population or forced reorganization of the scheme of living) there would be approximately one-and-a-half times as many females in the average Eskimo local group as there are food-producing males.

Eskimo polyandry is obviously not due to any shortage of females caused by the practice of female infanticide, as has been suggested by some authors.[14] Its *raison d'être* rests in other sociological factors.

Senilicide, invalidicide, and suicide are expressions of the same postulate that underlies infanticide—life is hard and the margin of safety small. Those who cannot carry their full share of the productive load forfeit the right to live.

Although others may decide that the days of an aged one are done, the request for death usually comes from the old person. The actual killing should be performed by a relative to preclude the possibility of vengeance. Infanticide is casually accepted, but not so senilicide and invalidicide. Emotional bonds are not easily severed that have been built up through the years and not infrequently the aged one

---

[12] Rasmussen, *Across Arctic America*, p. 226.

[13] E. M. Weyer, *The Eskimos* (New Haven, 1924), p. 134.

[14] E.g., C. K. Garber, "Eskimo Infanticide," *Scientific Monthly*, 64:98–102 (1947).

has to insist upon his demand-right to be killed; the kinsman is forced into performance of his duty.

Weyer records a poignant example:

A hunter living on the Diomede Islands related to the writer how he killed his own father, at the latter's request. The old Eskimo was failing, he could no longer contribute what he thought should be his share as a member of the group; so he asked his son, then a lad about twelve years old, to sharpen the big hunting knife. Then he indicated the vulnerable spot over his heart where his son should stab him. The boy plunged the knife deep, but the stroke failed to take effect. The old father suggested with dignity and resignation, "Try it a little higher, my son." The second stab was effective, and the patriarch passed into the realm of the ancestral shades.[15]

Stabbing is but one form of Eskimo senilicide. Hanging, strangulation, blocking up in a snow house to freeze to death, and abandonment in the open wastes by a traveling group are all used by various Eskimos. The mental conflict entailed in these practices is revealed in Eskimo mythology, however. There may be no overt social onus toward those who destroy their aged, but the myths of the Iglulik in which the infirm or aged are abandoned, "generally provide some miraculous form of rescue . . . with a cruel and ignominious death for those who abandoned them." [16]

Between suicide and senilicide and invalidicide stands suicide-with-assistance. At Chesterfield Inlet a son-in-law helped his wife's mother, who was sick with tuberculosis, to hang herself. "She felt that she was old, and having begun to spit up blood, she wished to die quickly, and I agreed. I only made the line fast to the roof, the rest she did herself." [17]

In East Greenland, a woman who led a blind neighbor to the local suicide cliff so that she could jump off to her end, virtuously told Holm how she had refused pay for her services. She was not a relative, but after all, she was a friend.[18]

A really nice sophism in the reconciliation of two conflicting systems of values was that of the wife of Qalaseq, an old man of Ches-

[15] Weyer, p. 138.

[16] Rasmussen, *Intellectual Culture*, p. 160.

[17] *Ibid.*, p. 96.

[18] G. Holm, *Ethnological Sketch of the Angmassalik Eskimos* (Meddelelser om Grønland, vol. 39, 1914), p. 74.

terfield Inlet. After a year's illness he hanged himself with the assistance of his wife. It was not, however, she pointedly explained to
Rasmussen, a real hanging. Both she and her husband were mission-
converted Catholics and they had taken to heart the teaching that
taking a human life was for God alone. Therefore, at her husband's
request she stood by with a crucifix while he strung himself up, and
just before he expired — this can be paralleled from Inquisition practice — she released him and held up the cross. Hence, as she saw it,
he died a natural death. They had "only hurried death up a little,
as it is apt to be so very slow at times." [19]

Outright suicide seems to be practiced on rare occasions because
of "mental anguish." In the two such cases reported by Rasmussen
a pattern of freezing to death, naked, is indicated for self-destruction
motivated by such reasons. An Iglulik old woman accidentally froze
to death, whereupon her son deliberately went out naked and did
likewise.[20]

An irritable foster-father declared to his adopted son, "I wish you
were dead! You are not worth the food you eat." The youth then
declared he would never eat again. That night he went out naked
into the snow, to lie down and freeze to death.[21]

Hunters in extreme danger or about to drown may slit their own
throats. Among the Iglulik the Moon Spirit calls gently, "Come,
come to me! It is not painful to die. It is only a brief moment of
dizziness. It does not hurt to kill yourself." [22]

Yet another privilege-right resting upon the third postulate is that
of cannibalism under famine conditions.

Although epicurean cannibalism exists among some peoples, notably in Africa, and although many different primitive tribes have
practiced ritual cannibalism for the acquisition of the supernatural
power of the ingested victim, Eskimos resort to cannibalism only
with great distaste and in the extremities of hunger.

"Many people have eaten human flesh," admitted a native of King
William Island to Rasmussen, "but never from any desire for it,
only to save their lives, and that after so much suffering that in

[19] Rasmussen, *Intellectual Culture*, p. 97.
[20] *Ibid.*, p. 95.
[21] Rasmussen, *Across Arctic America*, p. 96.
[22] Rasmussen, *Intellectual Culture*, p. 74.

many cases they were not sensible of what they did . . . But we who have endured such things ourselves, we do not judge others who have acted in this way, though we may find it hard, when fed and contented ourselves, to understand how they could do such things. But then again how can one who is in good health and well fed expect to understand the madness of starvation? We only know that every one of us has the same desire to live." [23]

Postulate IV—*All natural resources are free or common goods.* Land, to begin with, is not property in any form: communal, joint, nor private. It is not even to be thought of as public domain, for it is and ever remains no-man's-land in an absolute and unconditional sense. Although each local group is traditionally associated with a particular district, it makes not the least pretension to territorial sovereignty. Anyone, whatever his local group, may hunt where he pleases, for the idea of restricting the pursuit of food is repugnant to all Eskimos, except to some extent in Western Alaska, where the individualistic or familistic notions of the Northwest Coast Indians are said to have influenced Eskimo practices. And even for Western Alaska, Margaret Lantis reports from personal observation that when mainland Eskimos cross over to hunt on Nunivak Island it apparently never occurs to the Nunivakers to object or even to resent the intrusion, although the supply of game is limited.[24] Hawkes reported of the natives of Labrador that although a given family may have habitually used a particular fishing station on a river for years, it would move to another spot rather than start a quarrel with any new arrivals who had moved in ahead of them.[25] Eskimo interest is in game per se; land is ignored and therefore not conceptualized as property.

Game and most articles of personal use, on the other hand, are objects of property notions. Deep-rooted Eskimo individualism, expressed in the postulate that the self finds its realization through action, breeds law-ways in support of private property by way of the corollary idea that the creation of an object makes it the private property of the creator, as it also does, up to a point, in hunting.

[23] Rasmussen, *Across Arctic America,* pp. 223–224. See also F. Boas, *The Eskimo of Baffinland and Hudson Bay* (Bulletin 15, American Museum of Natural History, 1907), p. 470.

[24] Oral communication, 1941.

[25] Hawkes, p. 25.

Game that can be taken by individual effort belongs to the person who makes possible the kill. Consequently, among the Ammassalik of East Greenland the hunter who chops a seal hole "has a potential right to seal caught in it." [26] More definitely, a seal which escapes with a harpoon head in it belongs to the hunter who actually succeeds in capturing and killing the creature, although the harpoon, identifiable with ownership marks, should be returned to its owner. But—any seal harpooned with a bladder float attached to its line goes to the owner of the float no matter who captures it, since it is reasoned that the capture is made possible by the drag and visibility of the float.

When the hunting is such that by its very nature more than one man is usually needed, then each man by virtue of his activity establishes demand-rights for specific portions of the kill. The Baffin Islanders furnish a typical example: "Who first strikes a walrus receives the tusk and one of the forequarters. The person who first comes to his assistance receives the other forequarter; the next man the neck and head; and each of the next two, one of the hindquarters." [27] Individual effort welded into coöperative team play gives each individual who voluntarily plunges into the team activity his carefully scaled demand-rights as against the others for a share in the products of victory over the denizens of the deep—or land, in the case of bears. By joining the fray, a hunter exercises his power to open a new legal relation with respect to the other hunters of the moment. They accept a no-power to stop him and so they become bearers of a duty correlative to his claim.

Against this postulated extension of individualism, however, the postulate that no man can have more than he can effectively use comes into play. It is the giving away of food and goods, not the possession of them, that wins honor and leadership among the simple Eskimos. In Western Alaska about the waters of Bering Strait, where the Eskimos have been influenced by the intensely developed property notions of the Indians of the Northwest Coast, a man may temporarily accumulate quantities of food and nonproductive capital. But under the legal application of Postulate X all men,

[26] W. Thalbitzer, *The Ammassalik Eskimo* (Meddelelser om Grønland, vol. 34, 1914), p. 524.

[27] Boas, *Eskimo of Baffinland and Hudson Bay*, p. 116.

even in Western Alaska, are reduced to a common level of wealth. A Western Alaskan is permitted to accumulate wealth only so long as he is felt to be a public benefactor.

It is common for the shrewdest man in each village to accumulate property and become a recognized leader among his fellows . . . In every trading expedition these men are usually the owners of the *umiaks*,[28] and control the others, even to the extent of doing their trading for them, but the authority of such a leader lasts only so long as he is looked upon as a public benefactor. Such men make a point of gathering an abundant supply of food every summer in order that they may feed the needy and give numerous festivals during the winter. . . . The Eskimo are very jealous of anyone who accumulates much property, and in consequence these rich men, in order to retain the public good will, are forced to be very open-handed with the community . . . They make little festivals at which are distributed food and other presents, so that the people appreciate the fact that it is to their interest to encourage the man in his efforts toward leadership, in order that they may be benefitted thereby.[29]

Nelson reported (albeit without cases) that the entrepreneur who accumulated too much property, i.e., kept it for himself, was looked upon as not working for the common end, so that he became hated and envied among the people. Ultimately he would be forced to give a feast upon pain of death, distributing all his goods with unrestrained largess. Nor might he ever again undertake to accumulate goods. Should he postpone the distribution too long, he was lynched, and his goods distributed among the people by his executioners. In either event his family was cut off from all the goods.[30] Prolonged possession of more capital goods than a man could himself utilize was a capital crime in Western Alaska, and the goods were subject to communal confiscation. Throughout the rest of the Arctic it never became necessary to translate the basic postulate into law; the ethics of generosity and hospitality were enough to see to it that he who had gave.

The Eskimo is what some would call an anarchist. He has no government in the formal sense, either over a territory or at all.

[28] *Umiak*: a large, skin-covered boat.
[29] E. W. Nelson, *The Eskimo About Bering Strait* (Bureau of American Ethnology, Annual Report 17, 1899), p. 305.
[30] *Ibid.*

There is no preëminent center of authority. In this, Eskimo society is notably democratic. Yet, as is the case with every human group, skills are unequal. Some people are prone to initiate action more frequently and forcefully than others. They become the nucleus for the organization of the community. The Eskimos recognize this, and they accept the proven skills of the superior hunter or *angakok* as qualification for pointing the way for the group as a whole.

The directing powers of the shaman have already been discussed. What of the secular leader, the headman? The headman, of which there is one in each local group, is he who is "tacitly, half-unconsciously recognized as first among equals." He is almost invariably the best hunter, "always up first in the morning" and "the first man out on the ice, the one who makes all the plans for hunting trips— and the lesser men respect his wisdom and intuition." [31]

Among the Caribou Eskimos he is called *ihumitak*, "he who thinks" (implying "for the others"); among the Baffin Islanders, *pimain*, "he who knows everything best"; or, as among the Unalit, *anaiyuhok*, "the one to whom all listen." Such men are usually "wealthy" by Unalit standards in that they are well equipped and maintain good households and well-stocked larders; but mere wealth does not give leadership of itself, and the "rich" who are lacking in the persuasive qualities of leadership are merely called *tu-gu*, "rich man."

Among the Unalit, as elsewhere in the Arctic, the headman possesses no fixed authority; neither does he enter into formal office. He is not elected, nor is he chosen by any formal process. When other men accept his judgment and opinions, he is a headman. When they ignore them, he is not. Headmen are those who can hunt and "who by their extended acquaintance with the traditions, customs, and rites connected with the festivals, as well as being possessed of an unusual degree of common sense, are deferred to and act as chief advisors of the community." [32] Such are the germs of political authority among the rude societies of mankind.

Although direct personal power of man over man finds no place in the Eskimo scheme of things, competitiveness and rivalries are strong. Much has been made of the peacefulness of the Eskimos among whom community does not war on community. Much has

---

[31] Freuchen, p. 138.   [32] Nelson, p. 304.

also been written on the reputed Eskimo lack of sexual jealousy: they lend and exchange their wives with a good will. True, the Eskimos do not war with each other, and they do practice wife exchange, but these facts do not prove a lack of aggressiveness or emotions of sexual jealousy. In spite of the wide latitude permitted for varied sexual experience, both pre- and postmarital, the Eskimos enter into continuous competition and often violent conflict for the possession of women in a struggle that takes the form of flagrant adultery and willful appropriation of other men's wives.

If a husband lends his wife to a friend, that is one thing and it is not adultery. If man and wife join in the game of putting out the lamp—various couples mill around in a darkened iglu seeking a partner of the opposite sex; when the lamp is lighted a man goes home for the night with whatever partner the grab-bag has produced—that also is not adultery under Eskimo usage. It is considered adultery only to have intercourse with a married woman without the previous express or implied consent of her husband. Since the consent of the husband can ordinarily be had, if a man is on good terms with him, intercourse with his wife taken without his consent can only be viewed as a challenge to his position as a man. The husband must react by assaulting the interloper or by challenging him to a song contest—or else let himself rest demeaned in the eyes of the people.

Outright appropriation of another man's wife is an even more gratuitous challenge to his status, and one of the recurrent consequences is homicide. Knud Rasmussen, when he visited the Musk Ox Eskimos in Canada, found that all adult males in the fifteen families that made up the community in the early 1920's had been involved in a homicide, either as principals or accessories, and for each of them "the motive was invariably some quarrel about a woman." [33]

In part, the Eskimo difficulties are enhanced by the lack of marriage and divorce rituals which might demarcate the beginning and the end of a marital relationship. Marriage is entered into merely by bedding down with the intention of living together; divorce is effected simply by not living together any more. A woman is as free to terminate a marriage as is a man. Shifts in marital status are so

[33] Rasmussen, *Across Arctic America*, p. 250.

easy that an open invitation to home-breaking exists as a continuous temptation. Or put otherwise, there are no cultural devices signalizing marriage in such a way as to serve to keep out trespassers. This may in part be no more than an aspect of the general lack of structure in Eskimo society. But it also reflects a lack of interest on the part of the Eskimo in stabilizing the family. It contributes to conflict by inviting intrusion. Things and wives are both easily borrowed and lent among the Eskimos, and in the case of wives there is a lack of clear demarcation of where borrowing ends and appropriation begins. A woman who has left her husband of her own volition may consider herself free for a new liaison—and so may the man who takes up with her. Her recent husband, on the other hand, who may have been off on a long trip in the meantime, may not have accepted the separation as a genuine divorce. His wife's new domestic tie-up may not seem to him to be a remarriage but rather, adultery. Trouble then brews.

The connubial ebb and flow of Eskimo life is well illustrated by a situation reported from East Greenland by Thalbitzer:

S——, a man of thirty, was an angakok and a smart hunter. Last spring he had two wives. For one of them, P——, he had given her father a knife. He had been married to her for several years and had had two sons with her. A——, the other wife, was taken from him soon after marriage by U——, in revenge for S—— having been the one to urge I—— to take U——'s former wife . . . When U—— found his wife had gone he was approached by A——'s mother who urged him to take her daughter away from S—— who, she said, could not support two wives. A—— was willing to leave S—— because he habitually scolded and abused her . . . So A—— left him for U——.

S—— unexpectedly brought back a new wife, Ut——. He was her seventh husband. She had left her sixth husband because she had, by her violent impatience, killed the child she was about to deliver and had, for this, been made to feel like a second wife. S—— had won her at the game of "Putting out the Lamps," and had carried her off, apparently by force.

When P—— saw the new wife she was very angry and began to scold her husband. He flew into a rage, beat her and even stabbed her in the knee . . .

A few days later Ut—— seized the chance to leave S—— and travel with some visitors to another settlement. There she immediately married a young man (M——). This eighth marriage of hers lasted but three weeks, when she left to go back to her sixth husband . . .

A few days after Ut—— had left S——, his housemate P—— caught him trying to get hold of his wife. P—— is now S——'s enemy and watches him covertly.[34]

In such a competitive situation the possession of the woman by the successful male is an affront to the husband's capacity to hold a wife—a challenge to his dominance prestige. Its effect is suspicion, friction, ill will, homicide, or resort to the drum dance. The arena of sex is the primary Eskimo breeding ground for trouble and law.

Cases from the Iglulik, Caribou and Copper Eskimos indicate to what homicidal extremes the prestige drive in woman-seeking can lead.

An Iglulik case: When the wife of Qijuk, a strong man, died, he gathered some friends to go to the neighboring village where lived Kinger, another man known for his physical prowess, there to abduct Kinger's wife. The vicissitudes of the road overcame all of the party save Qijuk and his two brothers. The others turned back. (Could it be that they did not have enough stomach for the venture?)

Kinger was out hunting when Qijuk arrived at his household, so Qijuk boldly established himself in the menage as the husband of Kinger's wife. Upon Kinger's return he was taunted by the insulting usurper. Kinger made no immediate issue, but retired to a nearby hut to sing magical songs, with which he put Qijuk to sleep. Thereupon, he entered his house to stab Qijuk. The butchering done, he pulled his wife from the house. Qijuk leaped up in pursuit, and spouting blood, fell dead. Kinger's villagers then attacked Qijuk's two brothers, who were still around. One brother died there; the other escaped to his home village.

Although often urged to take vengeance, this one brother never felt strong enough to try it.[35]

A Caribou Eskimo case: Igjugarjuk, a headman of Padlermiut, was rebuffed by the parents of a girl he sought as his wife. To have his way and to show his pride he lay in ambush by the door of her family's hut, shooting down the father, mother, brothers and sisters,

[34] Thalbitzer, pp. 71–73.
[35] Rasmussen, *Intellectual Culture*, pp. 297–298.

seven or eight in all, until only the girl survived, whereupon he took her to wife.

Rasmussen, who knew this man, considered him "clever, independent, intelligent, and a man of great authority among his fellows." [36]

A Copper Eskimo case: In 1905 a Netsilingmiut couple moved over to settle among the Asiagmiut, with their three grown sons. Of these sons, the eldest had an Asiagmiut wife. A local native declared he would have regular sexual intercourse with the woman. The husband did not want to acquiesce, but was not strong enough to prevent the aggressor, and in consequence, he speared his own wife so that the other could not have access to her.

Immediately, the husband was seized and killed by his father-in-law and some henchmen. In defending his brother, a younger son of the Netsilingmiut family stabbed the avenging father-in-law in the back, killing him. The boy was then seriously wounded himself.

The Asiagmiut, considering the situation, decided that wisdom counseled the complete eradication of the killer's family in order to forestall blood revenge. The remaining son, sensing the danger, escaped, though the father was brought to his doom.[37]

Freuchen recounts several Polar Eskimo murders in each of which woman trouble is a factor. The murder of Sekrusuna by Quanguaq is illustrative.

Sekrusuna had been a great one to tease poor Quanguaq (who was a young widower). He would taunt him by suggesting, when they were hunting together, that they go home to their 'wife' now . . . Sekrusuna also tantalized the poor man by promising him he might sleep with his wife when they returned, but whenever Quanguaq attempted to take advantage of this favor, he found the woman's lawful husband at her side. The husband thought this a great joke . . . Besides all this, Sekrusuna beat his wife in order to demonstrate to Quanguaq the many advantages of being happily married. He beat her only when the widower was present.

---

[36] Rasmussen, *Across Arctic America,* pp. 60–61.

[37] Diamond Jenness, *Life of The Copper Eskimo* (Report of the Canadian Arctic Expedition, 1913–18, vol. 12, 1922), p. 95. Dr. Lantis notes that among the Nunivak Islanders, where family life is more stable, murder for sexual reasons is much less frequent than among the eastern Eskimos. (Oral communication to the author.)

One day in the spring . . . Quanguaq drove his harpoon . . . straight through the body of his friend Sekrusuna . . . Quanguaq came home with both sledges and teams. He drove straight to the dead man's wife and told her that he was going to stay with her . . . The widow meekly accepted her altered status.[38]

Murder springs from other motives as well. Jenness reports trivial insults as the cause of several Copper Eskimo murders, as one woman stabbing another in the stomach because of a taunt of sterility (this is the sole reported instance of murder done by a female among the twenty-seven specific Eskimo cases found in the literature), or a man disemboweling another to demonstrate the falsehood in the victim's assertion that the slayer did not know how to make a sharp knife.[39]

Murder is followed quite regularly by the murderer taking over the widow and children of the victim. In many instances the desire to acquire the woman is the cause of the murder, but where this is not the motive, a social principle requiring provision for the bereaved family places the responsibility directly upon the murderer.

Blood revenge executed by kinsmen of a murdered party is expected among all Eskimos (so far as the data go), save the Copper, Iglulik, and East Greenlanders. Among these latter it is optional according to the "strength" of the surviving kinsmen. This, coupled with the protectorate principle means, as Birket-Smith notes,[40] that a man will raise as his own stepson the son of his victim, a boy who, when he grows to manhood, may be the one to exact long-delayed blood vengeance upon his foster father, as in ancient Iceland, too.

The execution of blood revenge may be immediate or long postponed. In the latter case, a Central Eskimo murderer may live on amicable terms with the people who must take vengeance on him, until one day, perhaps after years, he is suddenly stabbed or shot in the back. Nelson records the murder of a Bering Strait Eskimo who was survived by his infant son. When the boy had reached the age of fourteen, the murderer, who was in the boy's camp, was one day harnessing his dog. The youth's uncle, telling the boy it was

[38] Freuchen, pp. 297–299.
[39] Jenness, pp. 94–95.
[40] K. Birket-Smith, *The Eskimos* (New York, 1936), p. 152.

time to take revenge, handed him a loaded rifle. With the weapon in hand the boy went out, took deliberate aim and so destroyed his father's killer.[41] If the revenge-takers wish to be more sporting, the murderer is reputedly challenged to a wrestling match, to suffer death if he loses, and, again reputedly, to have the privilege of killing another of the victim's family if he wins.[42] (Without the evidence of substantiating cases this does not seem to fit comfortably into the Eskimo context, however.)

Revenge killing does not evoke a display of bravery, for it is generally exacted by stealth while the murderer is busily engaged at some task and not aware of what is about to happen. Only in West Greenland does the avenger give preliminary warning by announcing the offense for which the victim is about to die. In this connection, H. König calls attention to the fact that old Scandinavian law demanded the verbal pronouncement of the death warrant before the slaying of an outlaw and suggests that the practice was transmitted from the Scandinavians to the Greenland Eskimos.[43]

A killer who murders several persons at once may enhance, not injure, his prestige in the community. Not so, the homicidal recidivist. He becomes a social menace liable at any time to strike down another victim. As a general menace, he becomes a public enemy. As a public enemy, he becomes the object of public action. The action is legal execution: a privilege-right of the executioner. The single murder is a private wrong redressed by the kinsmen of the victim. Repeated murder becomes a public crime punishable by death at the hands of an agent of the community.

The classic case has been given by Boas, who wrote:

The fact that the custom is found among tribes so widely separated will justify a description of those events which came under my own observation. There was a native of Padli by the name of Padlu. He had induced the wife of a native of Cumberland Sound to desert her husband and follow him. The deserted husband, meditating revenge . . . visited his friends in Padli, but before he could accomplish his intention of

---

[41] Nelson, p. 293.

[42] Franz Boas, *The Central Eskimos* (Bureau of American Ethnology, Annual Report, 6, 1888), p. 582.

[43] H. König, "Der Rechtsbruch und sein Ausgleich bei den Eskimo," *Anthropos,* 18-19:306 (1923).

killing Padlu, the latter shot him . . . A brother of the murdered man went to Padli to avenge the death of his brother; but he also was killed by Padlu. A third native of Cumberland Sound, who wished to avenge the death of his relatives was also murdered by him.

On account of all these outrages the natives wanted to get rid of Padlu, but yet they did not dare to attack him. When the *pimain* (headman) of the Akudmirmiut learned of these events he started southward and *asked every man in Padli whether Padlu should be killed. All agreed;* so he went with the latter deer hunting . . . and . . . shot Padlu in the back.[44]

Similar practices exist among all the Eskimos on whom we have reports, save the East Greenlanders. The important element is that the executioner, who undertakes the slaying, seeks and obtains, in advance, community approval for his act of riddance. When such approval is obtained no blood revenge may be taken on the executioner, for his act is not murder. It is the execution of a public sentence in the name of the people, and the responsibility is theirs. Furthermore, revenge is precluded for the simple reason that unanimous consent involves also the consent of the murderer's relatives, if any be in the community.

As a double safeguard against blood revenge on the executioner, close kinsmen may be themselves called upon to carry out the community will. In 1921, for instance, the headman of the Arviligjuarmiut was deputed by his fifty-four co-villagers to execute his own brother, who occasionally went berserk, having killed one man and wounded others in his fits. The headman went reluctantly to his brother and explaining his position, asked how he chose to die— by steel, thong, or shot? The brother chose the latter, and was killed on the spot.[45]

At Point Barrow, on the north Alaskan coast, a brother and an uncle shot and killed their kinsman who had murdered ten to twelve victims whom he had ambushed on his march from Herschel Island to the Point. The man had been publicly whipped by the whaling captains at Herschel on injunction of the local missionary, because he had exposed a baby to die. All the Eskimos had reacted

---

[44] Boas, *Central Eskimos*, p. 668.
[45] Rasmussen, *Across Arctic America*, p. 175.

with disgust to such unheard-of punishment, for, to their mind, "to whip a man does not cure him." But even so, the man had become a homicidal maniac to be removed.[46]

It is generally reported for the Eskimos that *de facto* murder is not essential in establishing one as a public enemy. Threats and abuse of others may lead to the same end. The obnoxious person is first ostracized, then liquidated if he continues his bothersome behavior.

Sorcery and chronic lying are also placed in the same category as homicidal recidivism. Because the sorcerer is a killer, and because the perfidious man is thought to be a public danger, both are liable to execution at the public command. Outside of West Greenland, when a shaman names a sorcerer as guilty, the sorcerer may be killed by the relatives of a victim of sorcery.

In West Greenland the natives treat all sorcery as an offense against the group punishable by death.[47] Widows without protectors and grown men without sons are said to be the ones usually singled out as sorcerers by the shaman. They are easy marks who have no survivors to protect them, and so in consequence, the community task is easy enough.

Boas reported the destruction of a sorcerer among the Baffinland Eskimos "who was attempting to kill a lot of people by magic." The community talked it over and decided he should die; he was stabbed in the back by an old man, who was thanked for the job.[48] Rasmussen noted a similar case among the Polar Eskimos.[49]

The execution of liars is reported from Greenland to Alaska. Although the reason for such drastic action is not given, it would appear that it rests on Postulate IX, and that such persons raise themselves to the status of the not-to-be-borne-any-longer. They fall in the same category as recidivist killers who must be removed from the community for the good of all. Chronic lying is outrageous, and like the outrageous conduct of the willful son of Kullabak on the northwest coast of Greenland, recounted by Freuchen, it is not to be countenanced.

---

[46] Vilhjálmur Stefánsson, oral communication to the author, February, 1938.

[47] K. Birket-Smith, *The Country of Eggedesminde and Its Inhabitants* (Meddelelser om Grønland, vol. 66, 1924).

[48] Boas, *Eskimo of Baffinland and Hudson Bay*, pp. 117–118.

[49] Knud Rasmussen, *The People of the Polar North* (New York, 1908), p. 156.

The boy's debut in terrorism had taken place at Cape York where he collected a load of rotten birds' eggs and hid them high up on a hillside. Then one day he became loudly hysterical and shouted: "A ship! A ship! A big ship is coming!" Magic words, of course, to natives who were seldom visited by outsiders.

They all hurried up on the hillside to get a look at the boat. Meanwhile the boy crouched behind a rock, and when his friends were close enough he jumped out and pelted them with his peculiarly offensive cache. This naturally reflected upon Kullabak's house, and she had tried to apologize, but being a lone woman, without a husband, there was not much she could say to reëstablish herself.

So she asked Mayark to help her get rid of the boy, and Mayark took him up onto the glacier and pushed him down in a crevasse. That, by all rights, should have been the end of him. Kullabak went into traditional mourning, but her mourning was pretty effectively interrupted when the boy came walking into the house. By some miracle he had escaped death in the fall, and had followed the crevasse to its portal near the sea.

After that no one dared touch him, and the boy played all manner of tricks to revenge himself. He was a big, strapping youngster, but he had no hunting gear of his own and had to borrow what he wanted from the hunters while they slept. One day, while Mayark was away on a hunting trip, he went to Mayark's house and told his wife that he had followed Mayark some distance and that when they had parted, Mayark had told him that he might stay in his house and take all a husband's privileges. Mayark's wife was an obedient, loving wife, and not until her husband returned home did she realize that she had been tricked. All the villagers had the laugh on Mayark.

The boy also helped himself from various caches and never took the trouble to close them. His mother was at her wit's end, and finally decided that if she wanted to save the honor of her house she must do something desperate. One night while he was asleep with his head protruding beyond the end of the ledge, she made a sealskin-line noose, slipped it over his head and pulled it tight.

Thus ended the criminal pranks of one young man, and his mother was highly honored for her good deed. Now she was remarried, and her great, booming voice was always an asset at parties.[50]

In the small Eskimo community the question of evidence in disputes does not raise a great problem; sufficient direct information

---

[50] Freuchen, pp. 123-124. (With the permission of Rhinehart & Co.)

seems usually to be at hand. When fact is not known, however, resort may be had to divination, but apparently only when an element of sin enters into the offense, or as among the Copper Eskimos at least, when a death through sorcery has occurred.[51] Divination is by weighing. A thong is looped around the head of a reclining person, or a bundled coat, or even the diviner's own foot. When the proper spirit has entered the object, the question may be put. As the object is hard or easy to lift, the answer is "yes" or "no." In Nunivak, according to Dr. Lantis, divination is done by peering into still water which has been poured into the abdominal cavity of a dressed animal. The image of the guilty person may then be seen.

Homicidal dispute, though prevalent, is made less frequent in many Eskimo groups by recourse to regulated combat—wrestling, buffeting, and butting. Buffeting is found among the central tribes along the Arctic Circle from Hudson Bay to Bering Straits. Wrestling occurs in Siberia, Alaska, Baffinland, and Northwest Greenland.[52] Head-butting as a feature of the song duel occurs in West and East Greenland. All three forms are a type of wager by battle without the element of divine judgment.

In buffeting, the opponents face each other, alternately delivering straight-armed blows on the side of the head, until one is felled and thereby vanquished. Butting accompanies the singing in the song duel in Greenland. The singer, if so inclined, butts his opponent with his forehead while delivering his excoriation. The opponent moves his head forward to meet the blow. He who is upset is derided by the onlookers and comes out badly in the singing. As juridical forms, boxing and butting are more regulated than feudistic homicide, since the contests are announced and occur on festive occasions when they are looked upon as a sort of sporting performance before the assembled community. Stealth, cunning, and ambush are not part of such contests; the strongest wins by pitted strength. The object of the boxing and butting contests is not annihilation, but subjection. Nor is there any more or less concern with basic justice than there was in the medieval wager of battle. Whatever the facts underlying the dispute, they are irrelevant to the outcome. The man who wins, wins social esteem. He who loses, suffers loss of social rank.

[51] Jenness, pp. 212–217.   [52] König, p. 295.

Boxing and butting are apparently available as means of settling all disputes except homicide.

Wrestling serves much the same function, though it may have a more deadly outcome in Baffinland and Labrador, where the loser may be slain by the victor. The wrestling duel is occasionally used as the means through which blood revenge may be carried out.

Deserving of fame are the *nith* songs of the eastern and western Eskimos. Elevating the duel to a higher plane, the weapons used are words — "little, sharp words, like the wooden splinters which I hack off with my ax." [53]

Song duels are used to work off grudges and disputes of all orders, save murder. An East Greenlander, however, may seek his satisfaction for the murder of a relative through a song contest if he is physically too weak to gain his end, or if he is so skilled in singing as to feel certain of victory.[54] Inasmuch as East Greenlanders get so engrossed in the mere artistry of the singing as to forget the cause of the grudge, this is understandable. Singing skill among these Eskimos equals or outranks gross physical prowess.

The singing style is highly conventionalized. The successful singer uses the traditional patterns of composition which he attempts to deliver with such finesse as to delight the audience to enthusiastic applause. He who is most heartily applauded is "winner." To win a song contest brings no restitution in its train. The sole advantage is in prestige.

Among the East Greenlanders song duels may be carried on for years, just for the fun of it. But elsewhere, grudge contests are usually finished in a single season. Traditional songs are used, but special compositions are created for each occasion to ridicule the opponent and capitalize his vulnerable foibles and frailties.

Some situations and their songs will illustrate the institution as it functions.

Ipa—— took Igsia——'s third wife away from him. Igsia—— challenged Ipa—— to a song contest. Because he was not really competent, Ipa—— had his former stepson, M——, sing for him. M—— accused Igsia—— of attempted murder. When Igsia——'s turn came

---

[53] From the song of Kilini; Knud Rasmussen, *Grønlandsagen* (Berlin, 1922), p. 236.

[54] Holm, p. 87.

to sing he replied with proper ridicule and satirical antics as follows:

"I cannot help my opponent not being able to sing or bring forth his voice." (He put a block of wood in his opponent's mouth and pretended to sew the mouth shut.)

"What shall we do with my opponent? He can neither sing anything, nor bring forth his voice. Since one cannot hear him, I had better stretch out his mouth and try to make it larger." (He stretched his opponent's mouth to the sides with his fingers, crammed it full of blubber, then gagged it with a stick.)

"My opponent has much to say against me. He says I wanted to do A—— a hurt and would have slain him. When we came hither from the south, it was thou didst first challenge A—— to a drum match." (He put a thong in his opponent's mouth and tied it up under the rafters.)

Etc., etc., etc. The song lasted one hour. Whenever Igsia—— made mockery of his opponent with such tricks, M—— showed his indifference by encouraging the audience to shout and laugh at him.[55]

Other songs rely less on buffoonery, placing greater reliance on innuendo and deprecation. When K—— and E—— confronted each other they sang with dancing and mimicry in the following manner (E—— had married the divorced wife of old man K——. Now that she was gone K—— wanted her back. E—— would not give her up, and a song duel occurred):

K——:

> Now shall I split off words—little,
>   sharp words
> Like the wooden splinters which I
>   hack off with my ax.
> A song from ancient times—a breath
>   of the ancestors
> A song of longing—for my wife.
> An impudent, black skinned oaf has
>   stolen her,
> Has tried to belittle her.
> A miserable wretch who loves
>   human flesh—
> A cannibal from famine days.

[55] *Ibid.*

E——, in his defense, replied:

> Insolence that takes the breath away
> Such laughable arrogance and ef-
>   frontery.
> What a satirical song! Supposed to
>   place blame on me.
> You would drive fear into my heart!
> I who care not about death.
> Hi! You sing about my woman who
>   was your wench.
> You weren't so loving then—she was
>   much alone.
> You forgot to prize her in song, in
>   stout, contest songs.
> Now she is mine.
> And never shall she visit singing,
>   false lovers.
> Betrayer of women in strange house-
>   holds.

K—— and E—— taunt each other in like manner as they sing out their dispute:

K——:

> Let me too follow the Umiak as kayak man!
> To follow the boat with the singers
> As if I could be afraid!
> As if I were possessed of weak-kneed ways!
> When I pursue the kayak paddler.
> It is not to be wondered at
> That he is pleased,
> He who has nearly killed his cousin
> He who has nearly harpooned his cousin
> No wonder that he was so self-satisfied
> That he felt such joy.

E—— hurls back in rebuttal:

> But I merely laugh at it
> But I but make merry over it
> That you K——, *are* a murderer
> That you are jealous from the ground up.

Given to envy
Because you do not have more than three wives
And you think them too few
So are you jealous.
You should marry them to some other men.
Then you could have what their husbands bring in.
K——, because you do not concern yourself
    with these things
Because your women eat you out of house and
    home
So you have taken to murdering your fellow men.[56]

In West Greenland, the singer has the vocal backing of his household. In preparing for the contest he sings his songs until all his household knows them perfectly. When the actual contest is in full swing, his householders reinforce his words in chorus. In spite of the nastiness of the insults hurled, it is good form for neither party to show anger or passion. And it is expected that the participants will remain the best of friends thereafter. The West Greenlanders, in contrast to the men of the East Coast, use self-deprecation, "the self-irony which is so significant in the Eskimo character," though at the same time the opponent is lashed with weighty accusations and sneering references. Here, for example, is the song which a husband hurled at the man who had induced the singer's wife to so gash the covering of his kayak that it would open and drown him. Then she and the plotter could marry. The plot failed; the wife received a physical mauling, and the co-conspirator received a verbal mauling:

Ah, how doubtful I feel about it!
How I feel about having to sing.
In my soul, which is not strong!
However could it occur to me to make a song
    of charge against him.
How stupid that now I really have to
    trouble on his account.
When we were up North there,
When we were up at Kialineq
It happened as usual that she made me
    angry,

[56] Rasmussen, *Grønlandsagen*, pp. 235–236.

That as usual I gave my wife a trouncing.
I was not angry without cause.
I was as usual displeased with her work,
Because my kayak cover was torn.
It had got an opening;
When I, a moment, went outside, they say,
You appear to have made a remark about me:
That I am always accustomed to behave so
    devilishly considerately:
That I on every occasion act so extraordinarily
    leniently.
How stupid I was then not to give him the
    same treatment,
That I did not also give him a stab with
    the knife.
What a pity that I acted so leniently
    towards you.
What a pity that I showed myself so
    considerate towards you,
You scoundrel, who so thoughtlessly
    received my anger.[57]

Among the Polar Eskimos the song duel is also used, but without
the head-butting and buffeting. A dramatic presentation of a Polar
song duel is portrayed in the motion picture, "The Wedding of
Paloa," made by Rasmussen and released in 1937.

Among the Iglulik Eskimos, north of Hudson Bay, contest singing is also an important art. Among these people, anyone who would
be considered an effective singer must have a "song cousin." This
is an institution built upon the basis of "formal friendship," a com-
radeship bond which was widespread among the aborigines of the
Western Hemisphere. Song cousins try to outdo each other in all
things, exchanging costly gifts and their wives whenever they meet.
Each delights to compete with the other in the beauty of his songs
as such, or in the skillful composition and delivery of metrical
abuse. When song cousins castigate each other, it is for fun, and is
done in a lighthearted, humorous manner. When a man takes up a
grudge song duel, however, the tenor of the songs is different.
Though the cast of the songs is humorous for effect, insolence, de-

[57] After König, p. 313.

rision, and the pictured ludicrousness of the opponents are the stuff
they are made of. As in Greenland, the one who can win the audience, or silence his opponent, is victor, but in any event, winner and
loser are expected to be reconciled, and they exchange presents as a
token of settlement.[58]

Further inland, among the Caribou Eskimos, who are located at
the very center of the whole Eskimo territory, the song duel is also
found. From Rasmussen we have the composition of a man who
is chastizing the deserted husband of a woman, who, mistreated by
her spouse, ran away to join the singer. Its quality will by now be
familiar to the reader.

> Something was whispered
> Of a man and wife
> Who could not agree
> And what was it all about?
> A wife who in rightful anger
> Tore her husband's furs across
> Took their canoe
> And rowed away with her son.
> Ay-ay, all who listen,
> What do you think of him?
> Is he to be envied,
> Who is great in his anger
> But faint in strength
> Blubbering helplessly
> Properly chastized?
> Though it was he who foolishly proud
> Started the quarrel with stupid words.

The occurrence of the song-duel complex all down the west coast
of Alaska and even out into the Aleutian Islands (reported by the
Russian missionary Weniamenow),[59] shows how basic (and possibly, ancient) a form it is among the Eskimos.

The song duels are juridical instruments insofar as they do serve
to settle disputes and restore normal relations between estranged
members of the community. One of the contestants receives a "judg-

[58] Rasmussen, *Intellectual Culture*, pp. 231–232.
[59] Cf. Weyer, pp. 227–228.

ment" in his favor. There is, however, no attempt to mete justice according to rights and privileges defined by substantive law. It is sufficient that the litigants (contestants) feel relieved—the complaint laid to rest—a psychological satisfaction attained and balance restored. This is justice sufficient unto the needs of Eskimo society as the Eskimos conceive it. It is, so far as here achieved, an element in which "higher" cultures often fail.

Unlike wager of battle, however, there is no ordeal element in the song duel. Supernatural forces do not operate to enhance the prowess of the singer who has "right" on his side. Let it be remembered that "right" is immaterial to the singing or its outcome (though the singer who can pile up scurrilous accusations of more or less truth against his opponent has an advantage in fact). As the courtroom joust may become a sporting game between sparring attorneys-at-law, so the juridical song contest is above all things a contest in which pleasurable delight is richly served, so richly that the dispute-settlement function is nearly forgotten. And in the forgetting the original end is the better served.

In these ways, Eskimo society, without government, courts, constables, or written law, maintains its social equilibrium, channeling human behavior, buttressing the control dikes along the channels with primitive legal mechanisms, or their equivalents. In these ways a social system is shaped in accordance with the social principles and values laid down in the basic postulates held by the members of Eskimo society. Here we have come the nearest we can, in observation, to the bare-bones of the legal. But the weaknesses of the Eskimo system are evident. In a society in which manpower is desperately needed, in which occupational hazards destroy more men than the society can well afford, there is additional tragic waste in the killings which the inchoate system permits—indeed, encourages.

6

The Ifugao: Private Law in Northern Luzon

The great significance of the Ifugao for the study of the nature and function of primitive legal and political institutions rests in the fact that they reveal how far it is possible to elaborate a system of interfamilial law on the foundation of a quite elementary social structure. They reveal how wrong are the political theorists who hold that law and government are wholly indivisible.[1] They reveal, also, the limitations inherent in the operation of a law system without benefit of formal government. For the data on Ifugao law we are indebted to the late R. F. Barton for his penetrating powers of observation and his accurate and vivid reporting.

Deep in the interior recesses of the rugged mountain country of Luzon the Ifugao have practiced wet-rice husbandry for untold centuries. Theirs is not a level terrain easily graded into rice paddies. On the contrary, rugged and sharply eroded mountains are gashed and cut into thousands of segments by deep valleys which offer precious little flat space in their constricted bottoms. Generations of labor have gone into the building of narrow terraces climbing the shoulders of the mountains, mile on long mile along the valley walls. Those who have seen it say there is nothing like it in all the world. To obtain twenty feet of flat surface whereon to grow his rice the Ifugao will sometimes build a terrace wall fifty feet high.[2] And all

---

[1] E.g., R. M. MacIver: "Property rights are legal rights, in other words they are dependent upon government. They exist *only because* government recognizes and protects them," in "Government and Property," *Journal of Legal and Political Sociology*, 4:5 (1946). (Italics mine.)

[2] Barton, *Ifugao Law*, p. 9.

this has been done by hand labor with no more effective tools than wooden spades and crowbars. Irrigation ditches carry water from mountain streams and springs to flood the fields behind the retaining dikes along the edges of the terraces.

The Ifugao, then, are gardeners whose economy centers about intensive irrigation hoe culture. An irrigation culture inevitably breeds law, for the control of water rights and the maintenance of the elaborate real-estate system that it entails demand effective mechanisms of adjudication and protection. This has happened in the case of the Ifugao so far as the elaboration of details of substantive law are concerned. Indeed, the substantive side of Ifugao law is comparable to that of the early civilizations in its complexity. But in ways of procedure the legal mechanisms of the Ifugao are most primitive and only slightly developed. Their social structure admits of little centralization or delegation of authority: there has been little explicit basis for the exercise of compulsive sanctions on behalf of the community.

The Ifugao as a people number some 70,000.[3] Although ethnologically they may be said to constitute a tribe, politically they do not. Governmentally no man is recognized as chieftain. Nor is there a tribal, district, or village council. Only the family possesses a full-fledged leader, and he is not in the Ifugao view a headman but rather the "center." Although he leads the family in legal and economic enterprise, its members think of him more as an integrating core than as a head who in any way dominates.

Villages in Ifugaoland are of little functional significance. Houses generally are scattered up and down the valley troughs. In some places a dozen or so houses may form a cluster that constitutes a village. But a village is only in the broadest sense a political or defensive unit. Headhunters bent on killing the members of one family are not usually attacked by unrelated members of the victim's village unless they come from the feud zone. Revenge expeditions are organized on a kinship basis and never on a village footing. Although, as we shall see later on, village sentiment works to ameliorate the harshness of sanctions in disputes between co-villagers, the village still does not enter into legal actions as a village.

The kinship group of the Ifugao is all-important and yet it is

[3] Barton, *The Kalingas*, p. 15.

very simple in its structure. From the point of view of the individual it includes relatives of both the father and mother to the third degree on either side in ascent and descent. More remote relationships are acknowledged on an individual basis determined by personal reputation, influence and reciprocal services. Lineages and clans are nonexistent. The simplicity and compactness of the kinship system is reflected in the terminology of relationship which distinguishes neither cousins, aunts, uncles, nor nephews and nieces. All kinsmen of a person's own generation (brother, sisters, cousins) are collectively lumped as *tulang* (sibling). All kin of the parents' generation are called "male parent" (*ana*) or "female parent" (*ina*). All kin of the offspring generation (son, daughter, nephew, niece) are lumped in one term, *anak*. All kin on both the grandparental and grandchild levels are grouped as *apo*. Kinsmen are kinsmen: a solid unit to be differentiated only on the basis of generations, except that on the parental level difference in sex is also recognized in the changing of one vowel.[4]

When a man or woman marries, he also takes on a degree of identity to his spouse's family, from whom he receives support and to whom he lends his aid—providing always that his identity to his own genetic group takes precedence in any legal squabble.

Far more striking than the simple familial system of the Ifugao, albeit of secondary importance in their point of view, is the class system of the society. Prestige-seeking drives the normal Ifugao in his everyday striving for wealth. The goal is to achieve the status of *kadangyang:* the top rung of the stratified social ladder. To be a *kadangyang* a man must have *kadangyang* ancestry; "but who so poor as to be unable to rake up a kadangyang ancestor in a land where family trees are known clear back to Ancestor Gold and his sister who survived the Great Flood?"[5] The real essential is wealth. Wealth means the possession of enough rice fields to produce more of the life-sustaining kernels than a man's family need eat in a year. With surplus wealth a man may enter the loan business, and what with the usurious rates that are customary in the land, he may with

---

[4] This type of kinship system is called *Hawaiian* by anthropologists after the usage introduced by Lewis H. Morgan. It represents the "classificatory principle" carried to its farthest point.

[5] Barton, *Half Way Sun*, p. 68.

good luck and skill amass an estate. Then he can undertake to build a *hagahi,* the ostentatious lounging bench that only a *kadangyang* is privileged to install before his house. But he is not privileged to use the bench until he has given the *uyuawae* feasts—a series of pretentious banquets to which he invites the whole district. His surplus substance is joyously consumed by the enthusiastic populace, and what does not go down their gullets is religiously sacrificed to the deities. By their presence and gustatory participation his compatriots acknowledge his elevation to the exalted rank of *kadangyang.* The *kadangyang* on his part is fairly stripped of his liquid capital, but he still has his fields and, barring too much illness in his family (which calls for expensive sacrifices) or injudicious conduct such as will cause him to get bilked in a legal fracas, he may remain a wealthy man throughout his days. As for his sons, they can become *kadangyangs* only by repeating the process.

The middle class in Ifugao, called *tumok,* comprises those persons who own fields enough to yield a full year's supply of rice in normal times. They may have a bit more or a bit less than what they ordinarily eat, but they do not have sufficient surplus to become genuine market operators.

The *nawatwat* are the poverty-stricken substratum who have to hack out from the forested or grass-covered mountain slopes above the irrigation levels temporary fields on which to grow camotes (a form of sweet potato) with which to round out their vegetable diet. A generation ago more camotes than rice were consumed by the Ifugao at large. But rice is prized and camotes despised, so it is felt to be a hard lot to be a camote-eater.

Barton does not hazard an estimate of the relative frequencies of Ifugao class membership. However, most Ifugao live close to the subsistence minimum and the gap between *kadangyang* and *nawatwat,* although great in prestige, is not so great in real goods. Of one hundred and nine families in the Kiangan district of Ifugaoland some forty years ago twenty held two acres of rice fields; forty held one to two acres; a like number had but one acre, and only nine were wholly landless.

With this general background the basic postulates of legal significance for the Ifugao as they may be abstracted from the Ifugao data are as follows:

Postulate I. The bilateral kinship group is the primary social and legal unit, consisting of the dead, the living, and the yet unborn.

Corollary 1. An individual's responsibility to his kinship group takes precedence over any self-interest.

Corollary 2. The kinship group is responsible for the acts of its individual members.

Corollary 3. The kinship group shall provide protection for its members and punish outside aggression against them.

Corollary 4. The kinship group shall control all basic capital goods.

Corollary 4'. Individual possession of rice lands and ritual heirlooms is limited to trust administration on behalf of the kin group.

Corollary 5. Marriage imposes strict and limiting reciprocal obligations on husband and wife, but the obligations of each to his own kinship group take priority.

Corollary 5'. Sex rights in marriage are exclusive between husband and wife.

Corollary 6. Because children provide the continuity essential to the perpetuation of the kinship group, the small family exists primarily for its child members.

Postulate II. Men and women are of equal social and economic worth.

Postulate III. Supernatural forces control most activities, and the actions of human beings are either compatible or incompatible with the predilections of the supernaturals.

Corollary 1. Compatibility should be determined for the most important activities by means of divination.

Corollary 2. The supernaturals may be controlled to some extent by magic and influenced to a considerable degree by extensive sacrifice and appeasement.

Corollary 3. The taking of enemy heads is religiously and magically necessary.

Corollary 3'. A record of successful head-hunting gives a man (and his kinship group) power and social prestige.

Postulate IV. Capital goods may be lent at interest.

Corollary 1. Control of wealth gives power and social prestige: property is important.

Corollary 1'. A debt never dies.

Postulate V. Rice is the one *good* food.

Corollary 1. Ownership of rice lands is the most important means for control of wealth.

Corollary 2. Since water is necessary for the growing of good rice, control of water is essential to useful ownership of rice lands.

Postulate VI. Propinquity of residence ameliorates the absoluteness of the primacy of kinship ties and, conversely, outside the kinship group responsibility to others diminishes with distance.

Corollary 1. People should avoid quarrels and quickly settle disputes with non-related neighbors.

Corollary 2. A person may ordinarily kill a distant stranger on sight.

Let us first look at the substantive law and then turn to procedure, in spite of the fact that this is somewhat artificial inasmuch as Ifugao conceptions of the different forms of property rest on procedural rather than substantive distinctions.

Property is of two kinds: that which requires and that which does not require an *ibuy* ceremony to effect alienation. The *ibuy* ceremony is a ritual feast held in the buyer's house at which final payments are made to the seller, along with the customary fees (*luklu*) to the agent (*monbaga*) and witnesses. With the consummation of the feast and its accompanying payments the alienation of the *ibuy* property is completed.

Ibuy property itself is of three orders: 1) rice fields; 2) heirlooms, consisting of gold neck ornaments, strings of glass, agate, and bloodstone beads, rice wine jars, gongs, and the jawbones of decapitated enemies; 3) forest lands.

Such property is in fact family property, for no individual possessor of any of these articles may sell them except under dire necessity and only with full approval of his kin. To ignore the kinsmen in a sale of *ibuy* property would mean their alienation along with the goods. In the Ifugao setting this is a truly effective sanction, for without kin support a man is helpless.

Property *adi-ma-ibuy* is personal and may be transferred without any ceremony. It consists of such movables as ordinary utensils, blankets, animals, fowl, houses and certain forms of immovables, to wit: coffee trees, coconut trees, areca palms, and camote fields. An agent, or go-between, may be used in arranging a sale or pledge of these articles, but no ceremonies are involved, nor are witnesses required. Neither is approval of kinsmen necessary for their alienation.

It is obvious that the *ibuy* ceremony functions to provide a public record of transfer of title for important forms of property in a land that has no writing. And important property is that which is rare and upon which family economic and psychic security rests—the rice fields and the magically potent heirlooms. "The Ifugao attitude," as Barton succinctly put it, "is that lands and articles of value that have been handed down from generation to generation cannot be the property of any individual. Present holders possess only a transient and fleeting possession, or better, occupation, insignificant in duration in comparison with the decades and perhaps centuries that have usually elapsed since the field or heirloom came into the possession of the family. Their possession is more in the nature of a trust than an absolute ownership—a holding in trust for future generations." [6]

The concept of trust and trusteeship with a fairly clear-cut distinction between trustee occupation and individual ownership is thus well developed in Ifugao legal thinking. This is one outgrowth of Postulate I.

Because the Ifugao family consists of the dead, the living, and the unborn, with concern for the well-being of the dead outranking that of those who live in the present or the future (the dead enter the realm of the supernatural and so control the present and the future: Postulate III), family fields may be sold if necessary to buy sacrificial animals to accompany the spirit of a deceased ancestor. They may also be sold to bring about the recovery of a family member from a dangerous illness. Fields which have been in a family for a long time naturally acquire for that family a greater psychological worth than more recently acquired lands. The sale price is concomitantly higher.

In the purchase of a field, service charges by the *monbaga* (agent) and witnesses, plus interest on the unpaid balance, plus gifts to the seller's kinsmen for the quit on their family interest in the field almost equal the "price" paid on the field itself. The price is paid in units of one-tenth: two units, or a down payment of 20 per cent, are required as the initial installment. On this the buyer gets pos-

[6] Barton, *Ifugao Law*, p. 39.

session and use but not title. When the last installment has been met, the payment of extras then begins. The extras are small in individual economic value but great in number and even greater in psychological and magical significance. Each carries a metaphorical name that brings forth the imagery of some step in the cultivation of the field itself or some act in the process of transference such as "the cutting of the rice," "the tying of the rice," "the flooding of the field," "the surplus of rice produced by the field." The growing of rice is fraught with magical overtones, and it seems clear that the transference of a field effects not only the alienation of the tangible real estate but also the *incorporeal property rights* in the magic that makes the particular field really productive.

This inference is made inescapable by the fact that the buyer within a year of the *ibuy* transaction, if the field has been washed out or the terrace walls have collapsed, may nullify the sale and recover his total costs on the ground that the seller "did not relinquish his hold on its welfare and fertility." [7]

Rather than sell a field, a trustee who needs goods to set up a funeral feast, or make sacrifices, or to pay a fine or damages consequent to a law suit will, if it is at all possible, obtain a loan on a piece of his land, pledging it to his creditor as security on the debt. The Ifugao call this *balal*. The creditor is well protected inasmuch as it is never customary to loan a sum greater than half the current value of the land pledged, and, further, the field is his to have and to hold until such time as the debt is repaid in full even though this be a generation or more. Debts devolve on the debtor's heirs, and credits are inheritable assets on the other side of the picture. The interest on a land loan that accrues to the lender is the usufruct of the field.

Real-estate loans are arranged through the medium of a *monbaga* for a fee of from 5 to 12 per cent of the sum of the loan. The fee is paid by the lender, but ultimately it is footed by the borrower, since the charge is added to the sum of the basic debt. No *ibuy* rites are involved in consummating a land pledge, and the only necessary witness is the *monbaga*.

The law permits the creditor to repledge the land at any time that he needs liquid capital. He is subject only to the limitation that he

[7] *Ibid.*, p. 50.

may not borrow more on the piece than he himself lent. This is, of course, a wise protection on behalf of the original debtor trustee. Violation of this duty is a legal offense, but with what exact consequences we do not know, except that Barton cryptically remarks, "there would be an excellent beginning for a quarrel that might end in lance throwing." [8]

A rice field without water is useless. Therefore, any transfer of rice lands *ipso facto* includes the rights to the water that ordinarily services the field.

Water rights once established are perpetual but also transferable. Sources of water are both common and private property. Water flowing from springs on public domain to land on public domain is available to all takers on a priority basis; i.e., the first man to subjugate a field below the spring has first rights to all the water his field requires. Even though a second comer builds a field between his plot and the spring, the newcomer may divert only so much water as the first comer does not need. If a spring is on private land, all the water flowing from it belongs to the family that owns it. Its members may, however, and customarily do, sell rights in the surplus water to others, and these rights are in perpetuity.

Ditches are constructed by the men of a family working together. Perpetual interest in a ditch may be sold to others, and then the task of maintaining the ditch becomes the equal duty of all members of the "water company." No new construction may impair the previously laid waterworks of others. But the maintenance of fields requires occasional sluicing of quantities of clay or leaf mold onto them for fertilization. Then the owner of a field has the privilege-right to cut a temporary sluice through any and all fields above his, providing he also fulfills his duty to restore them to their former condition.

Borrowing and lending of minor items and livestock is carried on at a lively rate among the Ifugao. Any large ceremonial event— funerals, recovery from illness, elevation to *ḳadangyang,* marriage— launches a family into extensive borrowing. Except as kinsmen go easy on each other, the minimal interest rate (*lupe*) is ordinarily 100 per cent for even the shortest term. When repayment is deferred for more than a year the rate leaps to 300 to 400 per cent. Small

[8] *Ibid.,* p. 45.

wonder the Ifugao says a debtor's goods go away in great heaps! Small wonder that so much of Ifugao litigation turns on questions of debt! For there is no statute of limitations and "a debt never sleeps."

Before considering Ifugao laws of inheritance it is necessary first to discuss the essentials of marriage. This, too, is a piece of business. Under Postulate I, 5 it is stated to be a secular, civil contract between two families. The man and woman who enter into marriage are, under Postulate II, equals. This is so, because each ideally brings into the marriage exactly equivalent amounts of property—for women inherit and hold on the same basis as men, and men and women both work the fields.

The years before marriage are carefree and fancy-free. Parents are most indulgent, and at adolescence both boys and girls leave their homes to avoid the incestuous implications of brother and sister sleeping under the same roof.[9] The girls resort to an *angamang:* a deserted house or the home of a widow that serves as a dormitory for maidens. The boys roam at large, seeking shelter and a night's bedmate in any *angamang* that does not house a "sister." Love is free and transient—until a boy and girl begin sleeping together regularly, ultimately to decide (or be convinced by their families) that it is time to begin getting married. Four ceremonial feasts, involving animal sacrifices and gift exchanges, must be consummated, each accompanied by favorable divinations, before the marriage transaction is completed and the fields finally settled on the conjugal pair. This may, in the case of a poor man, take many years. The couple, however, after the *mommon,* or first marriage feast, live together as man and wife, each with a limited claim on the other, and low damages may then be assessed for sexual infidelity as fourth degree adultery.[10]

The important fact is that parents assign some land and other fam-

---

[9] "Are your people like the lowlanders—do they sleep in the same house with their sisters?" (An Ifugao is quizzing Barton.)

"Our houses are very big; they often have as many rooms as all of the houses of one of your villages."

"*Nakayang!* . . . If they are as big as a large village and if brothers and sisters sleep at opposite ends of them, it is perhaps not so bad. But the way the *Piscao* ('fish-eaters,' i.e., lowlanders) do is a custom that stinks." Barton, *Half Way Sun,* p. 58.

[10] See p. 117, below.

ily property to each child at or before marriage, if there is enough to go around. Otherwise, the first-born gets it all, and his brothers and sisters are dependent upon him. He becomes the "center" of the family. It is better, the Ifugao feel, to have one strong "center" than a handful of weak fractions. Possession is given to the child when the marriage is completed and he sets up his own household. By the time the last child is married the parents have wholly stripped themselves of the management of family property; it is up to the children to provide for them from then on. The father contents himself thereafter by serving as a family priest.

For the children of *kadangyangs* and would-be *kadangyangs,* there is no freedom of the *angamang*. Free experimentation in the girls' dormitories might lead to misalliance: a rich boy with a poor girl, or vice versa. This would never do, for it means putting personal predilection before family interests; there would be no property equivalence in the marriage. To avoid such contretemps wealthy parents arrange marriages for their offspring while the children are yet in infancy.[11] Indeed, far-seeing fathers who want to make a good alliance even arrange potential marriages for children as yet unborn— with the ever-useful *monbaga* doing all the negotiating. Specific assignments of family property are agreed upon in advance, and once the first marriage feast has been performed, the youngsters are provisionally married. They take turns living in each other's homes [12] and grow to maturity together. When at last the final feast is held, they receive their full inheritances. Sexual infidelity by either party prior to completion of the marriage is penalized as fourth- to second-degree adultery.

All marriages, whether ended by death or in divorce, must be terminated by a formal abrogation of the marriage contract through a payment called *gibu,* which literally means "finish." Remarriage without payment of *gibu* to the kin of the other spouse is severely sanctioned, as in the case of Liuliwa.

Liuliwa had deserted his wife and refused to pay the *gibu* demanded by her kinsmen. He was stiff-necked and arrogant (appar-

---

[11] Barton calls such marriages "contract marriage" as against "trial marriage" for the other kind (*Ifugao Law,* p. 19). The distinction is spurious, however, since both marriages are contracts; both are equally binding, and the only essential difference is in the preliminary procedures leading up to the contract.

[12] The *binawit* relation.

ently nursing a grudge). To the *monkalun* (procedural go-between) who came to press the demands on him he sneered, "Her kin will be bald-headed, and even then they won't have received any *gibu.*" Four *monkalun* were sent, one ofter the other, without budging him.

At last his wife's "brothers" made the magic customary for a head-hunting expedition. Three of them ambushed Liuliwa and speared him in the back. He was wrong, and his own kin made no attempt to avenge his death.[13] To overlook even so much as one relative among a spouse's kin can have dire consequences, if that one person is strong to demand and the other is too strong in resisting demands.

Nangligan of Mampoyla lost his wife, who was from Luhadan, through death. He paid the customary *gibu* to terminate the marriage. But Ohunda, a "brother-in-law" was absent at the time of the distribution. On his return he sent a go-between to collect *tokdang,* an addenda payment.

Nangligan was stiff-necked: "I have given them their kettle-skillets and their bolos. They've had all they are going to get out of me. Don't keep coming back to me with this demand."

The go-between withdrew from the case.

Ohunda, working in his field one day, saw Nangligan coming down the path well-armed. He hid his own spear until after Nangligan had passed by. Then he speared him in the back. No revenge was taken for the execution.[14]

A release from the marriage contract must be absolute and unconditional.

Death terminates marriage; so does divorce. It is rather surprising in view of the elaborated emphasis on getting married that divorce is as frequent as it seems to be. It seems, however, that the very specificity and elaborateness of mutual marital obligations contributes to the brittleness of many marriages. Certainly an examination of the numerous specific grounds for divorce indicates just this. As listed by Barton they are:

1. A bad omen of the bile sac of the sacrificial animal at any one of the four feasts of the marriage ritual.
2. A bad omen of the bile sac at any of the three principal rice

---

[13] R. F. Barton, *Philippine Pagans* (London, 1935), p. 250.
[14] *Ibid.,* pp. 49–50.

feasts of either family during the first year after the completion of the marriage rituals.

3. Barrenness.
4. Continuous dying of offspring.
5. Permanent sexual disability.
6. Unwillingness to perform the sexual act.
7. Neglect in time of sickness, "failure to cherish."
8. Insulting language by an in-law.
9. Reduction of the area of fields agreed on in the marriage contract.
10. Selling of a rice field for insufficient reason and without consent of the other spouse.
11. Continued refusal of a father-in-law to deliver the fields called for in the marriage contract when the couple reaches a reasonable age.
12. Incurring of unreasonable debts.
13. Chronic laziness or shiftless conduct.
14. Failure to perform certain special duties involved in getting married.
15. Any legal offense by a kinsman of one spouse against a kinsman of the other.
16. Insanity.
17. Extreme jealousy.
18. Incompatibility.
19. Dereliction of affection.
20. Desertion.
21. Adultery.[15]

Barton also notes, "It cannot be too strongly emphasized that husband and wife *are never united into one family. They are merely allies.* The ties that bind each to his own family are much stronger than the ties that bind them together. An Ifugao explained this to me by putting his hands parallel, forefingers together. The forefingers represent the two spouses; the hands the two families. Should the two families separate, should they withdraw from amity and agreement, the two spouses, the forefingers, of necessity withdraw, because they are attached to different hands." [16]

---

[15] Barton, *Ifugao Law*, pp. 30–31.   [16] *Ibid.*, p. 25.

The separation is not wholly cold-blooded so far as legal form is concerned. In addition to *gibu,* the party that gave cause has to pay a small amount in token damages, called *hudhud,* to assuage the mental anguish caused the aggrieved partner, literally, *"hakit di nemnem,* hurt of the mind."[17] The causing of mental anguish is not a ground for divorce among the Ifugao, however. It is much too broad and indefinite a category for that. The grounds are detailed and specific; assuagement of mental anguish is merely a minor by-product.

Property settlements in cases of divorce are simply and rationally achieved. When there are children their interests come first.[18] All the property of both parents (except personal property) must be assigned to the children at the time of the divorce. Except in unusual cases of mature children whose father has fields and whose mother does not, the children go with the mother, who administers their fields for them until they marry and take over on their own.

In cases involving no children, all family property brought into the marriage by each of the spouses reverts with the spouse to the family from which it came. All property of any sort acquired through the joint efforts of the couple during the time of their married life is equally divided between them according to the decision of two referees. These *monhangdad,* who are chosen by the separating spouses, one by each, get a small part of the property for their efforts.

So much for the substance of basic property law, family law, and the laws of irrigation, sale, and indebtedness, all of which are in the nature of contract.

By virtue of the nature of Ifugao social organization there can be no criminal acts.[19] All other legally recognized offenses are of the type known in Anglo-American law as torts: private (or civil) wrongs or injuries independent of contract. Among the Ifugao the responsibility for initiating any prosecution rests with the aggrieved;

[17] *Ibid.,* p. 32.

[18] *Postulate I,* Corollary 6. The conjugal family exists primarily for its child members.

[19] Barton treats all aggressive acts which carry customary penalties as crimes under the heading, *Penal Law.* However, violations of contracts are also penalized, and mere penalty does not distinguish one form from the other. *Ifugao Law,* pp. 61–90.

any damages, penal assessments, or physical punishment inflicted upon the defendant are imposed by the plaintiff and his kinsmen. The lines of procedure are anything but raw self-help, however. Custom requires that proper procedural protocol be carefully exhausted before resort to direct seizure or the lance is taken.

Legal coercion occurs only when its applicator enjoys a socially recognized privilege-right to proceed in a legitimate way at a legitimate time for a legitimate cause. Legitimate cause is defined by the substantive law. The legitimate way and legitimate times are defined by the adjective law.

Procedure among the Ifugao, except in homicide cases calling for direct blood revenge, requires the use of a go-between as in all interfamilial negotiations. In arranging contracts, we have already recognized this functionary in the person of the *monbaga*. The go-between in litigational procedure may be the very same individual, but in such a situation he is known as a *monkalun*. A *monbaga* is, literally, an "asker," "requester." A *monkalun*, on the other hand, is, literally, an "advisor," or functionally, a "mediator." [20] He is always the key figure in the adjustment of any trouble case.

The existence of the *monkalun* represents a first step in the development of juridical institutions. He explicitly expresses the general societal interest in the clearing up of tensions, the punishment of wrongs and the reëstablishment of social equilibrium when the normal balance has been disturbed by an alleged illegitimate act. He is to be recognized as a quasi-public official: the "disinterested" third party who represents the public interest in seeing that justice is done. He is not an outright public official, because his office is not explicit; he is a *monkalun* only when acting as a *monkalun*, and he is not chosen by the public to serve in that post. He is not a judge; for he makes no judgments. He is not an arbiter; for he hands down no decrees. He is merely a forceful go-between—an admonishing mediator of limited authority but of usually persuasive effectiveness.

The *monkalun* is always a member of the *kadangyang* class and ordinarily a man of reputation as a head hunter. This means that he enjoys general influence emanating from his personal prestige; but more than this he is in a position to marshal effective support from his own kinsmen in the pinch.

[20] *Ibid.*, pp. 95–125.

The *monkalun* in any legal action is chosen by the plaintiff. Any *kadangyang* not related to either party may be asked to take the case, although a man who has already built up a name as a successful settler of cases is preferred. In cases arising out of breach of contract and debt the aggrieved ordinarily makes repeated efforts to collect his due for himself before resorting to the intervention of a *monkalun*. In tort actions he immediately consults his kin and with their consent seeks out a *monkalun* with little delay.

Barton is of the opinion that the *monkalun* exercises no authority, but this is hardly born out by the evidence Barton himself adduces. The *monkalun* exercises no authority insofar as it is true that he cannot himself declare a judgment or personally enforce the settlement that is ultimately agreed upon. He definitely has the authority to force the defendant to join the issue, however; for when a *monkalun* approaches an alleged transgressor, if the "accused be not disposed to listen to reason and runs away or 'shows fight' when approached, the *monkalun* waits till the former ascends into his house, follows him, and, *war-knife in hand,* sits in front of him and compels him to listen." [21] In the hands of a wealthy and powerful man with a head-hunting record, acting in the public interest, the war knife is an instrument of authority!

The *monkalun* is not an advocate of the plaintiff. He is equally interested in seeing that the defendant's rights are met. Or better, he strives to bring about a settlement of the issue in accordance with generally recognized cultural standards. He is a pipeline between the two antagonists, who, once the issue is joined, may not confront each other or speak one to the other until the issue is settled one way or the other. So—the *monkalun* shuttles back and forth between the embroiled parties (which means not only the two principals but also their family centers) first stating the demands of the plaintiff and then carrying back the counterproposals of the defendant. Whatever his ultimate intent, it is unlikely that the defendant will come to terms easily, for, "self-interest and self-respect demand that the accused shall not accept punishment too tamely or with undue haste, and that he shall not pay an exorbitant fine. If he can manage to beat the demands of the complainant down below those usually met in like cases, he even gains in prestige. But the *monkalun* never lets

[21] *Ibid.*, p. 94 (Italics Barton's.)

him forget that the lance has been scoured and sharpened for him and that he walks and lives in daily danger of it."

"It is the part of the accused to dally with danger for a time, however, and at last to accede to the best terms he can get, if they be within reason." [22]

This the *monkalun* knows full well, so he scolds, wheedles, lashes with sarcasm, insinuates the ill-temper of the other side, exaggerates the ferocity of its warriors, blows up the number of kinsmen who have gathered at the call of the plaintiff, scoffs at the weakness of the defendant's supporters and at the thinness of his argument. Resentment of his remarks would render him no longer a go-between but an ally of the other family. He is also perfectly free to give the plaintiff the same treatment when he returns with the defendant's response. Since he knows the propensity of plaintiffs to overstate their grievances and expected damages, he works to whittle down the original demands to a point where in time an agreeable settlement is reached.

Thus, although the *monkalun* has to deal with a good deal of intransigence, and "the lance is back of every demand of importance," [23] the plaintiff is not overanxious to kill the defendant, nor is the defendant for his part overly eager to be killed. "The kin of each party are anxious for a peaceable settlement, if such can be honorably brought about. They have feuds a-plenty on their hands already. Neighbors and co-villagers do not want to see their neighborhood torn by internal dissension and thus weakened as to the conduct of warfare against enemies. All these forces make for a peaceful settlement." [24]

As for the *monkalun,* aside from the matter of his own social interest in serving his people, aside from the ego gratification of personal prestige enhanced by a successful record, each success brings new cases to him, and each case brings fat fees in pigs or other goods of value—fees which are added in costs to the defendants.

In the determination of damages five factors are critical: 1) the nature of the offense; 2) the relative class positions of the litigants; 3) the solidarity and behavior of the two kinship groups involved in the dispute; 4) the personal tempers and reputations of the two principals; 5) the geographical position of the two kin groups.

[22] *Ibid.,* p. 95.   [23] *Ibid.,* p. 94.   [24] *Ibid.,* p. 95.

1. Customary scales of payments and damages are rather definitely fixed for all types of transactions and torts.

2. There are at least three grades of penalties: one each for the *kadangyang, tokum,* and *nawatwat* classes. When both litigants are of the same class the customary penalty is easily arrived at. It is when they are of different classes that the lines are not so clear. In any event, the defendant will most likely have to pay over the sum that is characteristically linked to his class status, but it may be somewhat more or less, depending on the other factors entering the total situation. Thus if the plaintiff is a *kadangyang* and the defendant *tokum* or *nawatwat,* the defendant will perforce pay the most that is expected of a *tokum* or *nawatwat.* If the classes of plaintiff and defendant are reversed, the *kadangyang* defendant will pay the least that is expected of a rich man. Or, it may be that the settlement arrived at rests about halfway between the scales set for the two classes. Such is the legal consequence of Postulate IV, 1.

As an indication of the relative scales the accompanying table shows the customary damages paid over in cases of unaggravated adultery committed after the first marriage feast.[25]

Damages paid by *kadangyang*		Damages paid by *tokum*	
Pu-u	1 death blanket	Pu-u	1 expensive kettle
Haynub	1 expensive kettle	Natauwinan	1 kettle
Natauwinan	4 iron implements	Natauwinan	1 kettle
Natauwinan	4 iron implements	Nataku	1 cheap kettle
Nataku	3 iron implements	Nataku	1 cheap kettle
Nataku	3 iron implements	Na-oha	1 cheap kettle
Liwa		Liwa	1 kettle
(*monkalun's* fee)	1 ceremonial clout		

Damages paid by *nawatwat*	
Pu-u	1 middle-price kettle
Natauwinan	1 kettle
Nataku	1 cheap kettle
Nataku	1 cheap kettle
Nunbadi	2 iron implements
Na-oha	2 iron implements
Liwa	1 cheap kettle

[25] *Ibid.*, p. 62.

If the four feasts and property transfers have been completed, the penalties are increased from "sixes" to "tens" and multiplied in value about six times. "Sixes" and "tens" refer to the named portions of the payment. In this chart there are six parts. "Tens" are for more serious offenses.

Ifugao offenses of a tortious nature are sorcery, murder, accessory to homicide, adultery, putting an innocent person in the position of being considered an accessory to an offense, manslaughter, malicious killing of animals, arson, incest, insult, slander and false accusation, unjustified seizure.

Sorcery is by means of the evil eye, cursing, and soul capture. Among the Ifugao, as elsewhere in the primitive world, magic and sorcery are not confused. The one is used in a multitude of ways to grow the rice, protect the fields, and miraculously to increase the rice once it is lodged in the storehouse. It is used to aid in cures and to help in war. It is socially encouraged and a legal privilege-right. But sorcery is another matter; it is homicide within the community itself.

The evil eye is a personal affliction not a result of evil volition; its effects are not ordinarily deadly, and where there is no intent, except for minor restitution on occasion, no damages are sought. It is only necessary that the evil eyed make ritual sacrifices and be cured.

A curse by an ordinary person calls for only moderately heavy damages of "tens" for the upper two classes and "sixes" for the lower. But repeated sorcerery is not to be borne. Ultimately the death penalty will be imposed.

Soul capture involves such an elaborate technique of invocation of the victim's ancestral spirits and sundry other spirits, culminating in the capture and bottling up of the victim's soul in the form of a bee or fly, that there is no question of premeditated malice. It is prima facie. Such sorcerers are sure to be speared, and perhaps even by their own kin.

Adultery, as we have already seen, is graded in accordance with the number of stages of the marriage rituals that have been completed. Intent also influences the degree of seriousness of the act. Simple adultery, called *luktap,* is discreet and limited. Aggravated adultery, *howkit,* is open and flagrant—a genuine insult to the injured spouse. Women in particular are apt to overlook their husband's derelictions if only they do not come to general public attention. Then the pressures of "public opinion" are on them to sue. Again reflecting the group contract nature of Ifugao marriage, only the first part of the "sixes" or "tens" paid as damages goes to the offended spouse. The rest is divided among his or her kinsmen.

One interesting aspect of the Ifugao conception of adultery is that a married corespondent in a divorce suit has to pay damages two ways: to the in-laws of his partner in adultery and also to his own wife's kinsmen as a penalty for the breach of his own marital contract. The same holds for a married adulteress as well. Adultery is, as noted, a ground for divorce, but it need not be so used. However, if the marriage is to be continued, the offender must then put up a "general welfare" feast at which he regales both his wife's and his own kinsmen. Eating together restores and renews the equable relations of the two groups.

It is wholly possible for an offended spouse to forgive the erring partner and still to sue the interloper, although legally he may stand on his (or her) demand-right for damages from each of them.

When it comes to a husband surprising his wife *in flagrante delicto,* law and custom are apt to be in conflict. Or, perhaps it would be more accurate to state that the lines of the law are not clearly drawn. Barton mentions having heard several stories of lovers impaled by a single thrust of an outraged husband's spear. The kin of the slaughtered victims are reported not to have accepted the killing as justified and to have taken revenge. Whether the wife's or the paramour's kinsmen did the job is not made explicit. They hold that the husband should at least try to collect *howkit* damages before resorting to the spear. General opinion, on the contrary, holds that a man whose rage is so slight as not to kill under such circumstances must love "money" more than his self-respect. So a self-respecting man should use his lance in hot blood and get one in the back in cold revenge. The alternative would seem to be to look the other way and sue later.

Incest, which is very rare among the Ifugao, is not a legally punishable offense. It is solely an intrafamily affair, and an Ifugao family does not proceed against itself—except in the case of members who indulge in soul capture.

Rape crops up as a common legal issue because of the contradictory nature of Ifugao sex patterns. Among the unmarried love is free, but it should not come too easily. It is the pattern for a girl to be coy and resistant on the first approach of a boy. He, poor chap, has a tough time knowing whether the girl is putting on an act or is really fending him off. He finds out when the *monkalun* comes with charges. The traditional scales of damages are not high, but they are big enough to make it worthwhile for some girls to lure unwary youths into the snare.

Married women are in a different class from maidens. Rape of a married woman by a married man offends both her own and her husband's kin groups. Each collects damages equivalent to those paid in a case of aggravated adultery. And then, if the rapist is married, he pays not only the woman's, her husband's, but also his wife's kin the damages that go with aggravated adultery. This is really enough to break his back financially.

Although the customary damages arising from actions for slander and insult are not so great, the actions are many. The Ifugao has a powerful sense of "face" and his character is easily defamed and derogated. False accusation as a tortious act springs from the same sentiments; the damages are not heavy for this offense either, but among a litigious people it should work as a socially useful check on the impulse to sue too readily. An innocent man suffers no expense in defending himself, since the defeated plaintiff must pay the *monkalun* fee in addition to damages for attempted injury to the defendant's reputation.

Theft calls for restitution plus punitive damages, if the thief be a *kadangyang* or *tokum*. For a *kadangyang* the punitive damages are quadruple the value of the stolen article; for a *tokum* merely equivalent. A lowly *nawatwat* merely makes restitution. All must pay the *monkalun's* fee; but this, of course, is graded according to the rank of the culprit.

Animals are attributed with legal personalities. Maliciously to kill an animal is akin to killing a person; an animal is a sort of household member, and to the Ifugao mind the assault is an assault of a personal nature. The damages are called *labod,* exactly as the damages assessed in the homicide cases that may be composed—and they are heavy indeed. A dog, on biting a person, may be killed in self-defense and with immunity. So also a pig that eats rice from a drying-stack.

Such killings are not malicious. If, however, the victim of the depredations does not kill the beast, but merely drives it off, its owner is subject to a claim for damages.

The Ifugao, it is now clear, are a property-minded people. Violations of contracts and the commission of torts are almost always sanctioned by property assessments. But always there is the lance in the background. The defendant who will not come to terms will be speared. Nevertheless, so long as the case is in the hands of a *monkalun* the spear cannot be raised. To do so would line up the *monkalun* and his family against the killer along with the kin of the victim.

A *monkalun,* when utterly stymied by the stubbornness of his two litigants, can always withdraw from the case. On doing so, he makes a formal announcement to this effect and imposes a truce of from two weeks to a month on the two parties. If either raises an aggressive hand against the other during the period of the truce, he automatically lines up the *monkalun* as an ally of the other side.

When the truce has run out, the plaintiff has two courses. He may get a new *monkalun* to try to bring the defendant to terms. Or, if his kinsmen are with him, they perform war rituals preparatory to ambushing the defendant. This is the last resort.

"If a family conduct its case faultlessly, even though the issue be only a debt, and especially if a monkalun be sent, they may, at the termination of the truce, slay the culprit. Public opinion will uphold, and the kin of the slain are not very likely to retaliate." [26] "Are not very likely to retaliate"—but not infrequently they do, and it is here that Ifugao law breaks down. Feud frequently results, and the festering wound may be a social drain for generations until a marriage heals the breach and halts the killing and counterkilling.

Within the "home district" (i.e., a given valley system) resort to killing is rare, however. Neighbors not involved in the dispute exert pressure on the litigants to come to terms. The *monkalun* extends his efforts to the utmost. And the litigants also feel an obligation not to endanger home security. When a killing does occur in the home district it is not aggravated by taking the victim's head, and although counterkillings are almost sure to occur, the feud will be brought to a close before too long.

The home district shades off into a "neutral area." Numerous kins-

[26] Barton, *Half Way Sun*, p. 115.

men live in this peripheral zone, but there are nonkinsmen with whom one need not be too patient in a law suit. A *monkalun* ought to be sent in a dispute with a party living in the neutral zone. Heads are not taken in executions of tortfeasors, but are sometimes in feuds.

As distance increases, a man enters the "feudist zone." Except for a small number of relatives, everybody here is "bad." Permanent feuding relations with certain families in this area are the thing. Fresh feuds are not ordinarily sought, but legal procedures are apt to be perfunctory and to lead quickly to killings. Heads are usually taken. Travel is dangerous in the feudist zone.

The "war zone" is country out of bounds. Anybody in this area is killed on sight. Head-taking expeditions make their stealthy raids in such areas whenever heads are wanted for purely prestige or religious reasons. The relation is one of permanent enmity unmitigated by any limitations of law except for a few powerful men who have entered into *biyao* pacts.

Propinquity, as Lowie has pointed out,[27] is an ameliorating factor in the operation of Ifugao law, and although the system rests primarily on the kinship principle, the territorial principle goes by no means wholly unrecognized. It is also clear that Ifugao social morality is strong in inverse proportion to distance. But distances are not very great.

As Barton puts it, "The tie of propinquity, a weak one, is of two kinds: *positive,* which allies a man with his fellows in proportion to their nearness; and *negative,* which intensifies the accursedness of his own or his neighbor's enemies in proportion to their remoteness."[28]

In passing, let us note that the Ifugao do not practice war as an instrument of politics. Indeed, they do not know war as a social institution; for they merely head-hunt, a form of aggression but not of war.

The tie of propinquity has one specific institutional expression in Ifugao usage. If a "neutral zoner" or a person from the "feudist zone" enters the "home district" to kidnap a woman or child, or perhaps to make a forcible seizure of some object in enforcement of a debt payment—and a co-villager who is not a kinsman of the vic-

[27] Lowie, *Origin of the State,* pp. 58–59.
[28] Barton, *Half Way Sun,* p. 106.

tim is present at the time of the depredation—he must if he is a *kadangyang,* and probably will, if he is a *tokum,* demand and collect a payment from the aggressor known as *tokom.* Barton originally treated this as an assessment of damages for putting the bystander under suspicion of being an accomplice of the marauder. His demanding of the *tokom* is an overt disclaimer of responsibility. The marauder's payment of the *tokom* is a public confirmation of the bystander's innocence. The bystander who does not collect *tokom* at the least loses prestige, at the most his life, by the hands of the victim's kin, as a participant in the deed. There is, of course, the alternative possibility that he could actively intervene to protect his neighbor, but without a kin bond it is unlikely that he would do so.[29]

In his posthumously published work on the Kalingas Barton expressed the feeling that the I-am-not-an-accomplice meaning of *tokom* is an ideological, reinforcing rationalization of the practice. The essence, he felt in his later work, lies in a kind of blackmailing of the raider, an "aha, I-caught-you-in-the-act, fork-over-or-else" extortion which is to be looked upon as much as the price of nonintervention as evidence of noncomplicity. The nonrelative of a co-villager has to be bought off by an outside kidnaper or seizer.[30]

Whatever the mixed motives may be, it is clear that the collection of *tokom* rests on a territorial conscience, however weak.

Against the deadly particularistic tendencies of feud and breakdown of peaceful procedure that disrupt Ifugao life there are in addition to the restraints of the territorial tie two other working forces. Travel in the feud and war zones is always extremely dangerous—except in the cases of courting swains and the *kadangyang,* or his agents, who has entered into a *biyao* pact with other *kadangyangs* residing in the alien districts. The *biyao* is a contract for mutual protection ostensibly arranged to make trading expeditions possible. Both the courting swain and the *biyao* pact holder are granted a special immunity from attack.

The sociological importance of the lover's immunity escaped Barton and he failed to explore further or report any details on it. Nothing is said as to how lovers distinguish themselves from mere intruders so as to avoid being speared. There was no inquiry as to how

[29] Barton, *Ifugao Law,* pp. 83–85; also, *The Kalingas,* p. 140.
[30] Barton, *The Kalingas,* pp. 141–142.

the Ifugao would explain this remarkable break in the wall of hostility.

A hypothesis can and should be offered, however, and it is not the romantic one that all the world loves a lover. There are economic and social advantages in peace. Too much hostility is destructive of many of the goals of man. For the Ifugao, as for any other people, one way of effecting constructive, peaceful relations is by intermarriage. Indeed, in Ifugaoland, one certain way of ending a feud is by intermarriage.[31] The one way of uniting two kinship groups into a larger structure of social coöperation is through intermarriage. And one workable way of achieving these benefits and neutralizing the social destructiveness of chronic hostility is to let the boys seek out the girls in safety. Sir Edward Tylor argued that, "Again and again in the world's history, savage tribes must have had plainly before their minds the simple practical alternative between marrying-out and being killed out."[32] For the Ifuago it was hardly such a clear-cut either/or set of alternatives, but they clearly chose a means of cutting down the number of killings—and, what is more important, of stepping up the possibilities of economic and social coöperation.

The same end is achieved by the *biyao* pact. Under its terms each partner guarantees the personal safety of the other and any companions or agents of the other while in his home district. An assault upon the visitor by anyone in the district means that the protecting partner is under the duty to collect customary damages on behalf of his injured *biyao* partner. If he is murdered, he must obtain vengeance.

While such a pact is in effect, it operates to extend the rule of law to both districts, especially if both partners be strong characters of sufficient prestige. However, among the Ifugao such pacts are reported to be short-lived because of the heavy burdens they impose upon the *ḳadangyang* and his kinship group. Then the two districts may be without one and they lapse to the lower levels of hostile

[31] Barton, *Ifugao Law*, p. 108.

[32] E. B. Tylor, "On a Method of Investigating the Development of Institutions; Applied to Laws of Marriage and Descent," *Journal of the Royal Anthropological Institute*, 18:267 (1888). A similar argument was advanced a century earlier by Lord Bolingbroke. See A. O. Aldridge, "The Meaning of Incest from Hutcheson to Gibbon," *Ethics*, 61:309–313 (1951).

relations until two other *ḳadangyangs* take it upon themselves to set up and enforce a new *biyao*. It is thus a fitfully working institution, but it is the foundation for a loftier and permanent structure.

In summing up and weighing Ifugao legal institutions we find their most significant aspect lies not in their remarkably complex substantive law but rather in their use of the *monḳalun*. He represents the judicial process in one of its prenascent forms. Here, in the intervention of an official (or quasi-official) representative of the society at large in the squabbles and troubles of its subgroups, we see the community interest striving toward expression. So-called self-help is limited and guided to a "correct" solution by social intervention.

If we look for the moment upon the two disputing kin groups as analogous to two contemporary national states, we may note a similarity between the process of the *monḳalun* as juridical go-between and the process of mediation in international affairs. If international mediation "is the action of one or more states in suggesting to two or more disputing states a possible form of settlement of their dispute," and if "the absence of any obligation to accept the suggestion made is an essential element in the situation," [33] then this is exactly what we find among the Ifugao.

In all four of the additional essential characteristics of mediation cited by Potter the Ifugao conform exactly. What is the justification for mediatory intervention where the subject of dispute does not concern the mediator? "The interest of the third state in seeing averted any grave impairment of friendly relations and peace among its fellow members of the international community has been held . . . , where the facts justify such apprehension, to constitute the interest necessary to justify representation, including a suggestion of settlement." [34] This is the justification and motivation of the *monḳalun,* reinforced by the fees that accrue to him. "The action of mediation may be initiated upon the request of one or more parties to a dispute." This follows in Ifugao, with the limitation of initiation to the plaintiff. "The action of the mediator is ordinarily prolonged until it amounts to repetition and revision of the suggestion for a settlement." And finally, "when the suggested formula has been ac-

[33] P. B. Potter, "Mediation," *Encyclopaedia of the Social Sciences,* X (1933), 272.
[34] *Ibid.*

cepted by the parties to the dispute it becomes binding upon them." [35] The Ifugao go two steps beyond modern international law in stiffening the mediation process. Ifugao mediation, if requested by the aggrieved party, is compulsory. Further, the peace may not be broken while the mediation is in process, nor for the period of the enforced truce that follows its unsuccessful termination upon the withdrawal of the *monkalun*.

The Ifugao in their legal processes have therefore risen beyond the level of mediation attained in international affairs, and yet they have stopped far short of the level represented in arbitration—the *monkalum* makes no decision. Of true juridical process they have not a glimmer.

[35] *Ibid.*

7

Comanche, Kiowa and Cheyenne: Plains Indian Law in Development

Men have occupied the Great Plains of the West for a good ten thousand years or more. They came in, apparently, when the last ice sheet was in its northward retreat, and their archaeological culture seems to have been fairly stable over long periods of time. But the horse-riding, buffalo-hunting, tipi-dwelling culture of the eighteenth-century Plains Indian was something quite new in its development.

Before the coming of Columbus the Indians of the Plains were largely riverbound and not overly inclined to venture afar into the vast, poorly watered stretches of open grasslands. They had to go afoot.

The coming of the European altered the situation with drastic effect. The Spaniard to the south introduced the horse and thereby provided the means for extensive penetration of the Plains by native populations, for which the thick herds of buffalo and fleet antelope were an enticing lure. On the eastern frontier the French and British were working to cause a far-reaching displacement of the Woodland tribes. White settlements forced some tribes to move westward at an early date. And out beyond the frontier, other displacements were accelerated ahead of the line of settlement by the imperialistic rivalry of the fur trade.

The fur trading tribes sought ever to enlarge their trapping and hunting domains at the expense of some of their neighbors. The British companies encouraged their tribes to drive off the French-allied tribes, and they gave them guns wherewith to do it. The French responded in kind, and the tribes of either party used their new weapons to drive the unarmed tribes on the western frontier before them. Thus with pressure behind them and an attractive lure before them, a number of the tribes of the Mississippi Valley sought sanctuary and prosperity in the relatively unpopulated lands of the West. The Cheyennes were among them.

Prior to 1600 the Cheyennes were a simple food-gathering people who lived in the lake country near the headwaters of the Mississippi. Shortly after the opening of the century they began moving westward until they came to the Missouri River in the Dakotas. Here they settled into earth-lodge villages and took to tilling corn in the manner they learned from the Arikara tribe. Toward the end of the eighteenth century they were moving on again, this time out into the Plains to become a nomadic horse tribe.[1]

The Comanches, on the other hand, appear in the sixteenth century to have occupied the country that lay around the headwaters of the Yellowstone and Missouri Rivers. They were an eastern branch of the far-flung Shoshonean group of tribes and at that time it is unlikely that they would have been distinguishable from other eastern Shoshoneans. But in the eighteenth century the Comanches moved down into the southern Plains, while the Shoshones were driven back over the Rocky Mountains by invaders from the east. The Comanches became a discrete entity and one of the first, if not the first, of the Plains tribes to acquire horses.[2]

The Kiowas came into the Plains from the north at a fairly late date. Thus each of the three tribes came originally from areas peripheral to the Plains. Each carried a different language and cultural tradition into the new homeland. Yet the ferment of life on the Plains was such, and the interaction of the tribes so great, that in the details of subsistence and in the general features of clothing, housing, war, and religion they, like all the nomadic Plains tribes, developed broadly similar ways of life.

The Comanche cultural background was the most meager of the three. It was that of the so-called "Digger Indians" of the Great Basin. In the tradition of these tribes there was no great social or-

[1] G. B. Grinnell, *The Cheyenne Indians*, 2 vols. (New Haven, 1923), I, 1–45; Joseph Jablow, *The Cheyennes in Plains Indian Trade Relations, 1795–1840* (American Ethnological Society, Monograph 19, 1951), pp. 1–10.

[2] Wallace and Hoebel, pp. 3–16.

ganization. People moved and lived in small isolated family bands. Each was autonomous and economically self-sufficient on a low subsistence level. Religion was vaguely defined and almost wholly devoid of ceremonial structure. Arts were thin, and life offered little of richer satisfactions. War was a thing to be avoided, for the Basin Shoshoneans had no military organization and were wholly lacking in fighting prowess.[3]

In the Plains the Comanches never wholly shed this heritage, but in the new setting they wrought some mighty changes in their way of life. With adequate food resources and the horse they were able to prosper in numbers and so to enlarge the size of their bands. Yet they never forsook band autonomy for tribal government. Religion remained to the very end almost wholly an individual enterprise with few group rituals and no tribal ceremonials.

It was in warring and raiding that the great transformation took place. Out of apparent weakness emerged the wildest marauding brigandage. The Comanches whipped and drove the Apaches from the southern Plains. They stalemated the Spanish. They decimated the pueblo of Pecos. They ranged far below the Rio Grande on slave- and booty-taking raids into Old Mexico. They blocked the westward expansion of the Texas frontier for several decades. They became "The Spartans of the Prairies." They were rough, tough, aggressive and militant individualists. They gave trouble to all their enemies and to themselves. And in their way, out of the nothingness of Shoshone legal backgrounds they shaped a crude but effective system of law to cope with the clashes of individual with individual within their ranks.

The Cheyennes were also militaristic. They, too, fought for booty and pleasure; the war cult was wholly theirs. They also acquired the horse and prospered on the buffalo. But somewhere in their background, deep in their Algonkian heritage, was a tradition that give them a sense of form, a feel for structured order, a maturity of emotion and action. They lived without the Comanche's frenetic stridency and assertiveness.

The Cheyennes possessed a ritualized tribal government. They had a well-developed system of military societies. In the Sun Dance,

[3] J. H. Steward, *Basin–Plateau Aboriginal Socio-political Groups* (Bureau of American Ethnology, Bulletin 120, 1938).

Animal Dance, and Sacred Arrow Renewal ceremonies they possessed tribal rituals that served to express their consciousness of being as one people. In the performance of these great ceremonies they
also enjoyed a common emotional experience that built a bond of
common tribal loyalty. The Cheyennes were socialized in a way that
the Comanches never approached. The Cheyenne law system was
sedate and effective, calm and mature, when measured against the
adolescence of Comanche behavior. Above all, in legal action the
Cheyennes revealed a feeling for the social purposes of law.

The social position of the Cheyenne warrior was achieved by individual striving, as it was among the Comanches—and all other
Plains Indians. Yet, where the Comanche could never rest on his
laurels or hold his high social position with the glory of past deeds
(he had constantly to add to them lest some other man pass him),
a Cheyenne who had achieved a high position in the eyes of his
fellow men could rest secure for the rest of his days. He did not
have to be contentious to prove and re-prove his greatness. The two
law systems reflected the differences.

The Kiowas were intermediate, geographically and socially. They
were aggressive in the Comanche way. Army men who had to deal
with them called them insolent. Young warriors on the make were
blatantly contentious and aggressive troublemakers who generated
a need for legal mechanisms. But they could be held in check by
the legal use of certain tribal religious fetishes. Like the Cheyenne
men who had reached the top social rank, the Kiowa elite were so
secure that they could ignore the striving that led to clash and litigation in the case of younger men. Their system of control was not
as well developed as that of the Cheyennes, however, nor was it as
effective, but it must be ranked above the Comanches'.

These three contiguous tribes therefore offer a good comparative
case study. Their geographical environments and economic systems
were virtually identical. In familial structure they were quite alike
(all three were clanless). Their fundamental religious ideas were
essentially similar in the use of the vision quest to obtain supernatural power from guardian spirits.[4] Their war patterns were one.
They differed only in language, in minor details of their general

[4] See Ruth Benedict, *The Guardian Spirit Complex in North America* (American
Anthropological Association, Memoir 29, 1923).

cultures, and in the degree of integration of tribal government, control of the individual, and in the elaboration of their religious systems. Hence, with these three tribes we can look at the comparative effects upon the law of differing social emphases within a single cultural area.

Because the Comanche system is the most rudimentary, it will be discussed first.

The basic postulates of the Comanche way of life are simple and few. They express a strong individualism and man-to-man aggressiveness in the following terms:

Postulate I. The individual is supreme in all things.

Postulate II. The self of the male is realized in striving for accumulated war honors, horses, and women.

Postulate III. Women are sexually and economically desirable but are inferior and subordinate to men.

Corollary 1. The sex rights of a husband to his wife are limited to himself and his brothers.

Postulate IV. The strongest social tie is that of brother to brother.

Postulate V. Sexual relations between kin (incest) constitutes subhuman behavior.

Postulate VI. War is essential to the prosperity of the tribe and the individual self-expression of the male.

Postulate VII. The great spirits (Sun and Earth) have powers of "legal" judgment.

Postulate VIII. Each Comanche ought to coöperate with others and help them in their life's activities.

Corollary 1. Altruism and sharing of goods is socially desirable.

Corollary 2. The killing of a fellow tribesman is not permissible.

Postulate IX. Horses, especially favorite horses, have quasi-human personalities.

The simple needs of Comanche society did not impose any great social pressure for governmental controls, and the high value placed upon individual freedom of action also worked to hold government at a minimum. If a Comanche had been invited to subscribe to a political slogan, he would have given his assent to the proposition that "that government is best which governs least." So fully was this precept expressed in a lack of political action that That's It, one of the most acute of our Comanche informants, in commenting on the band headmen, or peace chiefs, remarked, "I hardly know how to tell about them; they never had much to do except to hold the band together." The headman was a magnet at the core of the band, but his influence was so subtle that it almost defies explicit description. He worked through precept, advice, and good humor, expressing his wisdom through well-chosen words and persuasive common sense. He was not elected to office or even chosen. "He just got that way." His role and status were only slightly more institutionalized than were those of the Eskimo headman. In the making of any important decisions of group policy all men were free to have their say. Yet among them all, the wiser old head, whose time-tested judgment the people respected, was the leader. In matters of daily routine, such as camp moving, he merely made the decisions himself, announcing them through a camp crier. Anyone who did not like his decision simply ignored it. If in time a good many people ignored his announcements and preferred to stay behind with some other man of influence, or perhaps to move in another direction with that man, the chief had then lost his following. He was no longer chief, and another had quietly superseded him.

War chiefs were outstanding fighters whose accumulated records of honored deeds were tangible evidence of their prestige status. Any Comanche was free to initiate a raid or organize a war party—if he could muster a band of followers. The Comanches were chronically at war with the Ute, Pawnee, Apache, Osage, Tonkaway, and sundry other tribes. In later days, the whites of Texas and the Mexicans on both sides of the Rio Grande were fair game. War, for the Comanches, was certainly a national pastime, if not the conscious practice of a national political policy. We suspect it was both. But so far as it was a national policy, it was not explicitly directed by a governing military or political body. It was a matter of individual motivation, prepared by training since infancy and spurred by a social system that gave rich psychological rewards to the men who were bravest in the face of the enemy or most successful in running off the horses of hostile tribes or the horses and cattle of Texas ranchers.

On the raid the leader of the war party—the man who had organized it—had temporary dictatorial powers such as a peace chief never enjoyed. He determined the objectives of the raid; he appointed scouts, cooks and water carriers; he set the camping places and the route of march; he divided the booty, if booty there was. In all his directives he was implicitly obeyed. If anyone seriously objected, he was free to leave the party and go his own way. Success on the raid demanded tough leadership, and the followers of a war chief submitted to it. Yet so strong was the Comanche sense of individual freedom that at any point a man could pick up his arrows and go home.

In view of their basic values of individual supremacy and the related ambiguity of powers of the chieftains, it is not surprising that in this tribe there were no public officials endowed with law-speaking or law-enforcing authority. The law of the Comanche was neither legislative nor judge-made. It was, as we have written elsewhere, "hammered out on the hard anvil of individual cases by claimant and defendant pressing the issues in terms of Comanche notions of individual rights and tribal standards of right conduct." [5] Thus it was almost exclusively a system of private law: a system of individual responsibility and individual action; a law that was case made.

The Comanches surely had no love of legalistic formalism, but they were a most litigious people. Their way of life engendered considerable internal friction. It might almost be said that the Comanches savored trouble-making. Their own accounts of their war parties as often as not begin with a laconic "once there was a bunch of Comanches out looking for trouble."

So, also, a man was often moved to take steps that made trouble. He stole another man's wife, or he secretly consorted with her. When this was done, the husband had no choice but to initiate legal action. Magnanimity on his part would bring no praise, for there was no doctrine of turning the other cheek. A man's status turned on his bravery, and for an offended husband not to act reflected merely on his courage; it was seen not as an act of forgiveness but as an expression of lily-livered cowardice. Wife-stealing and adultery were not the result of any sexual deprivation on the part of the offender; they were in effect deliberate challenges to the prestige of the husband. As such, he was forced in the eyes of the people to respond to them.

The way was open to him in legal action. Custom impelled men

[5] Wallace and Hoebel, p. 224.

to violate the marital rights of other men. The culture also provided a legal remedy for the wronged man. Except in a few rare and extreme cases, the wrongdoer fully expected to pay the legal price—and did so without forcing the injured husband to a violent bodily attack. He knew well that he would have to pay a price, but he also knew that if he was steadfast and could outface the other man, the price would be light. In that case he would come out of the affair with greater public respect than the husband and he might get the woman to boot. So he took the risk.

In the memory of a dozen old Comanche informants still living in 1933 forty-five cases of old-time legal actions involving wife-stealing and adultery were still vivid enough for detailed recording.[6] Twenty-two were wife-absconding cases and twenty-three involved adultery.

As it takes two to make a contract it also takes two to commit adultery or a wife-absconding (Comanche women were not forcibly stolen). The woman's role in these affairs was very frequently an expression of individual revolt against the workings of Postulate III. Theoretically in all instances, and actually in many, a girl had no formal voice in the choice of her husband. Her brothers gave her away in exchange for a consideration. The takers were usually older and established warriors and hunters who had the goods. In the Comanche ideal such arrangements made for the best marriages. But they were marriages in which the woman was at the mercy of her husband. Working against the stability of such marriages was a strong current of romantic idealism among the young. The ambition of the adolescent girl was to be a *naiβi*,[7] i.e., a beautiful maiden with lustrous, black hair hanging in long braids, and dressed in a fine fringed buckskin dress. The young bucks for their part strove to attract the attention of the girls by playing the role of *tuiɡ:ɪsʋ* "a handsome young man who looks good on a horse." Wife-absconding was really an escape in which a frustrated wife sought a more romantic match with a daring warrior.

Comanche elopements were invariably linked to a war party. The man in the case would be going on a raid with his friends, and he would make an assignation with the woman to go along. It

[6] Cf. Hoebel, *Political Organization and Law-ways*, pp. 49–59.

[7] Phonetic symbols are used as in the International Phonetics System.

was a way provided by custom to violate the marriage rights of the rightful husband as defined by custom and sustained by law! A nice example of internal inconsistency in the ways of a culture.

When a woman and her lover took off with a war party, two courses were open to the jilted husband. He could mount in hot pursuit in the hope that he could overtake them before they reached enemy territory. Or he could bide his time until they returned from the raid. In enemy country he could not press his suit; here all Comanches had to stand shoulder to shoulder. Aside from this, he could institute his action wherever he might be able to confront his tortfeasor. He might take along some compatriots—brothers, real or putative—to strengthen his courage and his arm, if need be. A real man, however, went alone. It was not necessary for him to gather witnesses, for a Comanche legal action was in no sense a trial. Questions of evidence rarely, if ever, entered. The wife-stealer, or even the adulterer, had no desire to conceal his deed; his aim was to flaunt his prestige in the face of the challenged husband.

If he followed the dictates of decorum, he politely addressed the defendant as "brother." The defendant replied in kind. Did not Comanche brothers share their wives? Syllogistically the reasoning runs:

Men who share a wife are brothers.
This man has assumed a share in my wife.
Therefore, he is my brother.
(But he is going to pay for the privilege!)

The immediate goal of the prosecuting husband was to get *nanɛwɔkə,* restitutive damages. As an opening gambit he placed his demands high, customarily asking for four different kinds of articles (four was the mystic number in which most Indians conceived things). Horses were always demanded, numbering from one to ten. The size of the demand varied directly with the wealth of the defendant and the fortitude of the husband and inversely with the war record of the defendant. The husband hoped to squeeze out as much as the traffic would bear and the wrongdoer was willing to yield.

The defendant on his side would pay in the end, but it would be unseemly to yield readily or to first demands. The procedure was one of higgling and haggling—with always the risk of a violent breakdown in the offing. For the husband, if mean-tempered or short of patience, might well cut the palavering short with a quick attack upon the defendant. Theoretically, then, the injured husband had recourse to use of physical force, if the offender failed to recognize his duty to pay up with a settlement that was reasonable in the eyes of the injured party. In fact, however, this was not a genuine legal privilege-right, since in event of homicide retaliation prevailed. The husband who pressed his suit to the killing point was bound to be slain in turn by the defendant's kinsmen. Here was the fatal weakness of the primitive system of the Comanches. Yet in forty-one of the forty-five recorded adultery and absconding cases the offender paid up and the matter became *res judicata* with an award in favor of the plaintiff. It is evident that the Comanches had a strong sense of the fitness of the law and that, willful as they were, wrongdoers submitted to its dictates.

This condition was implemented by two facts: 1) action was not initiated unless the facts were predetermined—guilt, as we have said, was rarely an issue except in sorcery cases; 2) the elopement pattern worked to tone down the first burst of anger; 3) usage saw to it that the husband could in the final resort always muster a greater amount of force than could the defendant.

In the nature of things, the adulterer or wife-absconder was (or thought he was) a more dangerous man than the husband he was wronging. If he had been left wholly to his own resources, the aggrieved husband would more often than not have been in a poor way to exact restitution. In the achievement of justice Comanche practice saw to it that if the husband were man-to-man on the short end of the power stick, he could marshal his brothers or friends to go a-lawing with, or for, him. When confronted with this deputation, the defendant rarely had recourse to marshaling *his* friends or brothers. It was not good form. And more than that—he had made his bid for prestige, and he would surely look bad if he failed to carry it through alone.

The plaintiff who called to his brothers for help naturally lost prestige to some degree, and in addition he had to turn over all that he received in damages. His "lawyers" got the a' of it.

Comanche society in the nineteenth century was constantly recouping its losses by incorporating captives into the tribe. Such captives were taken as children and mildly exploited as houseworkers, if they were girls, or put to work as herders, if boys. The girls were ultimately married by their captors and so acquired full citizenship. The boys were allowed to join war parties and they, too, were incorporated after a time into the kinship system through adoption as "brothers" or "sons" by their captors or some other Comanche friend. Some captives, however, although they achieved free status in manhood, were not absorbed into a family by adoption. Conversely, attrition so decimated a number of Comanche families that only one or two males were left as survivors. These men and unadopted captives had no brothers upon whom to call when hard put to prosecute a wrong. In such a plight there could be no justice for them if left to their own resources. Aggressors would have a free hand.

At this point the Comanches met the social need for a check on aggression and the provision of redress by means of a simple utilization of the materials at hand. They held no constitutional convention to devise new instruments of government. Personal power was the recognized basis of social relations between men. Power out of control was the threat. Controlled power was the countercheck naturally hit upon. The weak-kneed victim of aggression who had no kin to back him turned to some great warrior to press his cause for him "A brave, well-known warrior," runs the stock phrase.

The brave, well-known warrior simply took over the case on behalf of the injured party and prosecuted it as his own. It gave him a neat chance to face down an upstart warrior, to serve his own ends of self-glorification while acting in the interest of the general social welfare—not against it. He could add to the luster of his status while upholding the law of marriage, instead of flouting it. Vanity and social altruism were wedded in one act and both were exploited for the social good. Their gratification was the sole reward, for the warrior champion received no compensation nor any share of the damages collected.

The intervening warrior was acting as a legal champion. He made no pretense of judging the case or of mediating. He entered with the aim of *forcing* the defendant to pay damages exactly as the injured party would have forced him, if he could. And if damages could not be squeezed out, he personally assaulted the defendant with all the violence he could muster. The ultimate sanction was his to use, if need be.

Comanche procedure in the wife absconding cases never involved questions of fact, for fact and evidence were cleared in preliminary investigation by the husband. He had no problem; the presence of the wife with her lover was enough. Adultery, however, was usually surreptitious. And this posed problems. To meet them the suspecting husband had recourse to several violent privilege-rights. A married woman could be wholly at the mercy of her husband's whim. He was free to extort from her a confession, as well as the name of her lover, by use of the cruelest third-degree methods. He either choked her until she gasped out the required information, or he took her out to a spot some distance from the camp where he built a fire over which he slowly lowered his terrorized wife until she gave him the information he wanted.

More refined men put the matter in the hands of the Sun and Earth. They took their wives to a lonely spot for *taß βekʌt,* "sun killing." The suspecting husband filled his ceremonial pipe and smoked to the great powers, addressing first the Sun. "You, Father, know the truth of this matter. As you look down upon them don't let them live until fall." Then to the Earth he said, "You, Mother Earth, as you know what is true, don't let them live a happy life on you."

Thereupon the wife smoked the pipe and avowed her innocence with an appeal to the Sun and Earth to kill her if she lied. Comanche dogma has it, and supporting cases are offered, that when women made this ritual conditioned curse, the Sun knew if they were guilty, and it killed them. Its penalty for perjury was death.[8]

Women, for their part, had no demand-rights against their husbands that they be faithful in marriage; they could exact no penalties from them. Hence, they had no opportunities to put their husbands to the test. But in recent decades some did turn the tables by demanding of the Sun and Earth, when they took the oath, that the powers kill the husband if the wife were innocent of the act.

Finally, it should be noted that when the issue was put to the

---

[8] Hoebel, *Political Organization and Law-ways,* pp. 90–91.

Sun and Earth, no legal action against the corespondent followed. The death of the wife ended the matter.

On the other hand, the collecting of damages from the offending male did not necessarily absolve the wife. If her absconder was strong enough, she had a good chance of escaping her husband's ire. But she ran terrible risks. In seven of forty-five Comanche adultery and wife-absconding cases the women were slain by their husbands—one in seven! Three of these were adulteresses; four were absconders. Of the twenty other adulteresses five were mutilated by their husbands; four had their noses cut off, and one had the soles of her feet slashed so she could not walk.

One may wonder that any Comanche woman played the game against such odds. We see it as additional evidence that mere severity of the law is not enough by itself to make people behave.

The Comanche law of murder was most simple. For a Comanche husband to kill his wife—with or without good cause—was not murder. It was an absolute privilege-right, which not even her family would move to challenge.

On the other hand, for one Comanche male to kill another was never a privilege-right, even when applying force to an over-stubborn defendant. Any willful killing required a revenge killing of the slayer. Here was the fatal weakness of Comanche law, as indeed of so much primitive law. The culture provided right ways of procedure and defined the substance of tortious acts. But the primacy of the kin group came to the fore whenever a prosecutor felt he had pushed negotiation as far as it would carry and then had taken recourse to arms. The kin of the defendant whom he had killed did not accept the killing, although general public opinion may have held that the victim had it coming to him. The Comanche kinsmen took revenge on the prosecutor regardless of the rightness of his original grievance. In enforcing the law he lost his life, a victim of *lex talionis*.

However much Comanche law fell short in this respect, custom remedied the defect in another. Blood-revenge killing was only of the first killer and retaliation did not lead to feud. The kinship principle, while extant, was nevertheless weak among the Comanches, and general fighting within the tribe was not to be countenanced when there were always outside enemies to be confronted. The killer, and the killer alone, had to die. There it stopped. No religious sanction, no tribal authority, was necessary to suppress the feuding tendency. Custom was sufficient restraint, and in this the Comanches were fortunate, for thereby they escaped the self-renewing curse that plagues so many primitive law systems.

Willful killing of a man's favorite horse was an act akin to murder, especially if the horse had been bequeathed to him by a best friend. Retaliation was taken not in killing the favorite horse of the transgressor but in slaying the transgressor himself. A favorite horse had a legal personality and was equated with a human being. Consequently, no further blood revenge followed, for things were already equal: a man for a horse.

Every Comanche male at one time or another went on a vision quest in search of power. He did not abase himself before the supernatural spirits or masochistically mutilate and torture himself to arouse their compassion. Nor did he weep before them to arouse their pity. Unlike the tribesmen of the Plains to the north, he assumed that the spirits were generally benign toward him; they needed no coaxing to share the benefits of their power with him. If he fasted and waited in a lonely place, they would help him. Nor did they interfere in his daily living except as they put conditions on the use of the power they gave him. A Comanche had to observe no supernatural tabus save those that went with his own personal medicine. Under Postulate VIII most Comanche medicine men used their powers to help the people. They cured and used their medicine to bring success in war and the hunt. They even, for a contractual consideration, helped others to get a share in their power. Although they were paid for their healing efforts, they did not attempt to milk the public or use their supernatural potency for exploitative purposes. Comanche magic was mostly white.

Occasional older medicine men, however, became "mean medicine men." Unable any longer to maintain their prestige by war prowess, they struck out at enterprising youngsters. They shot their medicine into them. The detection of sorcery was the job of a curing medicine man. In the first instance, after diagnosing the nature of the illness and who caused it, he always tried to effect a cure with a counter medicine. If he was successful, nothing more was done. If he failed, legal action was in order. The brothers of the sorcerized victim would call upon the sorcerer to remove the curse. If he refused, which he usually did by denying that he had anything to do with the affair, they could move to an attack with weapons or the threat of such an attack. But whether they did or not depended upon their strength of character. In sorcery cases where the aggrieved party was a weakling (and apparently not backed by brothers) there was no prosecution; and one Comanche, Salt Worn Out, even shifted to another band, to get out of the sorcerer's sphere of influence.[9] In one instance where the aggrieved brothers started an apparently forceful prosecution, they backed down when the sorcerer put up an even more forceful defense—a threat of *more* sorcery.[10] In the event both parties took equally strong positions, one accused sorcerer took a voluntary conditional curse on the sun—and was killed by lightning the following spring. Thus he paid the price of his guilt.[11]

In another instance the alleged sorcerer was forthwith stabbed and killed by his own sister's son, the brother of his victim. The slayer's elder brother was appalled by the act. But Chew Up, the knife wielder, retorted, "Is it as nothing that I should sit and watch my brother being murdered? Should I have done nothing?" And here there was no blood revenge in counteraction, "Because," in the very words of a Comanche, "the quarrel was in the family, no one else could take it up or do anything about it." [12] Homicide was not legally a tribal or public affair.

The cases in general indicate that the Comanches preferred not to tangle with sorcerers. A cure by a good doctor was much to be preferred. This failing, a kinsman did not have to prosecute as did a cuckolded husband, but he legitimately could, if he had the guts. Otherwise the individual act of sorcery went unpunished. Brave warriors as champions at law did not enter these cases. A warrior outfacing another warrior was one thing, but to have to threaten a sorcerer was not an inviting prospect for even the bravest.

Repeated sorcery was another matter. As among the Eskimos it became a threat to all the people—a threat not to be borne. The fact that the sorcerer was believed to have killed a number of people was evidence that he was "getting away with murder," evidence that

[9] Hoebel, *Political Organization and Law-ways*, case 25, p. 92.
[10] *Ibid.*, case 24, p. 91.
[11] *Ibid.*, case 23, pp. 89–90.
[12] *Ibid.*, case 27, pp. 94–95.

no one dared to face up to him. In the need to remove the threat to their common security the members of the band drew together in the sole communal action that the Comanches took against any sort of offender. They lynched him. Or together they tricked him into breaking his tabus so that he died of the effects of his own powers. In each of these instances his fate was discussed and ordained in a meeting of all the men of the band. Excessive sorcery thus became the sole crime in the Comanche legal system.

Let us now have a look at the Cheyennes, who were so similar to, and yet so different from, the Comanches. Most importantly, they were not as politically naïve as the Comanches. They had a nicely institutionalized system of government and a working legal order and "worked out their nice cases with an intuitive juristic precision which among us marks a judge as good." [13] For them it was clearly a tool to be used in adjusting the balance between freedom of action for the individual and the need for constraint among the members of the society. The Cheyennes, to a surprising degree, looked upon and treated their culture and the law within it as a medium to be manipulated and not as an absolute verity before which they had to prostrate themselves. They were a genuinely socially mature people—except in a few glaring weak spots.

To achieve this the Cheyennes held fast to a few well-chosen basic values which, through skillful use of social techniques, they were able to transform into effective patterns of legal action. They combined sound ideology with manipulative aptitude.

As in most primitive belief systems their first postulate was religious.

Postulate I. Man is subordinate to supernatural forces and spirit beings, *which are benevolent in nature.*

Corollary 1. Individual success and tribal well-being are abetted by the beneficent assistance of the supernaturals.

Postulate II. The killing of a Cheyenne by a fellow Cheyenne pollutes the tribal fetishes and also the murderer.

Corollary 1. Bad luck will dog the tribe until the fetishes are purified.

---

[13] Llewellyn and Hoebel, p. 313.

Corollary 2. The murderer must be temporarily separated from the social body.

Corollary 3. Violent behavior that may lead to homicide within the tribe must be avoided.

Corollary 4. Killing an enemy while in the presence of a tribal fetish is inimical to the supernaturals.

Postulate III. The authority of the tribal council is derived from the supernaturals and is supreme over all other elements in the society.

Postulate IV. The individual is important and shall be permitted and encouraged to express his potentialities with the greatest possible freedom compatible with group existence, but at the same time the individual is subordinate to the group, and all first obligations are to the maintenance of the well-being of the *tribe.*

Corollary 1. Rehabilitation of the recalcitrant individual after punishment is extremely important.

Postulate V. War is necessary to defend the interests of the tribe and to permit individual self-expression of the male.

Postulate VI. All land is public property.

Postulate VII. Except for land and the tribal fetishes all material goods are private property, but they should be generously shared with others.

Postulate VIII. Women are subject to the direction of men, but they have personal value in their own right.

Corollary 1. The sex rights of a husband to his wife are exclusive (except in certain ceremonial situations).

Postulate IX. Sexual activity should be held to a minimum.

In Postulate IV the Cheyennes possessed the basic values of a true democracy. The simultaneous high valuation of the individual and the maintenance of group supremacy are not self-contradictory. The social problem is merely one of achievement of adequate balance between complementary forces. How did the Cheyennes manage it?

The informal base of Cheyenne society was the conjugal family which was woven into the fabric of the extended bilateral family.

But this was a unit with little formal structure; "relatives tended to camp together."

The really important unit of organization was the band. During the winter months, when the Cheyennes scattered over the country-side so as not to overstrain the meager winter food resources, they broke up into widely separated village camps. Each of these camps had one or more natural leaders as a headman—a headman in exactly the same sense as the Comanche peace chief. The headmen among the Cheyennes, however, were more than band headmen. They were also tribal chiefs. For in the summer months the Cheyennes were drawn together into one great tribal family governed by a tribal council.

One or another of their great religious rituals was used as the catalyzer for the event—the Sun Dance, The Medicine Arrows Renewal, or the Animal Dance (Massaum Ceremony). Which ceremony was given in any one year depended upon circumstance, but at least one of them was given every spring or summer. And every decade a great chief-renewal was held.

In the winter of each tenth year, word was passed among the bands that there would be a chief-renewal the coming spring. The chiefs themselves had declared the rendezvous. As the snows melted and game again was plentiful, all the Cheyennes from the far-flung territories began their annual drifting together. Within a few weeks, band after band converged; there was the great in-gathering. Each group came marching or riding into the camp, whooping, shouting, and singing as they circled the lodges, while those already there cheered and applauded. The groups arranged their lodges in a large circle by bands, each in a traditional position.[14]

The camp circle had a wide opening at the east, just as the individual lodge always was placed with the door facing the first rays of the morning sun. Thus, the Cheyenne camp circle symbolized a giant family lodge, the dwelling of the whole tribe. In the center of the circle, like the hearth in the lodge, was raised the ceremonial structure for whatever ritual was to be the event of the tribal gathering. If it was to be a decennial chief-renewal, it was the double-size chiefs' lodge.

The council of chiefs numbered forty-four. These were not men

[14] *Ibid.,* p. 74.

"who just got that way." They were honored office holders, who were explicitly appointed to chieftainship with a definite tenure.

The Cheyennes have a semimythical legend telling how the council of forty-four first came into being, not as a social contract but as an act of creation of a supernaturally aided woman. It was she who told them to renew their numbers every ten years, and so it was done down to 1892.

At the renewal each chief appointed his own successor, who was usually a man from within his own band but who should not be his own son. The Cheyennes wanted no hereditary dynasties. A chief could not succeed himself, but he could be "held in the lodge": i.e., be reappointed to succeed another man. Vacancies caused by death during the preceding decade were filled by common choice of the surviving chiefs. Among the forty-four were five priest-chiefs, ceremonial officers, who stood above the rest. Among them was the supreme priest-chief, the Sweet Medicine Man, who represented Sweet Medicine, the Cheyenne culture hero and innovator.

The character of a Cheyenne tribal chief was expected to be exemplary.

"In the Cheyenne view," wrote Grinnell, "the first duty of a chief . . . was that he should care for the widows and the orphans; and the second that he should be a peace maker—should act as mediator between any in the camp who quarreled. The dignity of a chief did not permit him to take part in any quarrel; he might not take personal vengeance for an offense committed against himself; to do so would result in loss of influence."

Since so much depended on his example and precept, a chief must be brave in war, generous in disposition, liberal in temper, deliberate in making up his mind, and of good judgment. A good chief gave his whole heart and his whole mind to the work of helping his people, and strove for their welfare with an earnestness and a devotion rarely equalled by other rulers of men. Such thought for his fellows was not without its influence on the man himself; after a time the spirit of good will which animated him became reflected in his countenance, so that as he grew old such a chief often came to have a most benevolent and kindly expression. Yet, though simple, honest, generous, tender-hearted, and often merry and jolly, when occasion demanded he could be stern, severe, and inflexible of purpose. Such men, once known, commanded general respect and admiration. They were like the conventional notion of Indians in nothing save in the color of the skin. True friends, delightful companions, wise counselors, they were men whose attitude toward their fellows we might all emulate.[15]

Some men felt they could not sustain this high level of conduct, as did Sun Road, who explained his rejection of the Sweet Medicine (the foremost) chieftainship in 1892 in these words: "When a dog is running after a bitch in heat—if my wife is chased by another man, I might weaken and open my mouth. Then it would be well if another had the medicine and not I." [16]

The council as a council functioned only during the summer months, but the chiefs exercised their leadership at all times in whatever situations they found themselves. The activity of High Backed Wolf in the affair of Pawnee is a good case in point.

Pawnee was a Southern Cheyenne when he was a very young man, but in his later years he lived up here with us. He was all the time looking out after the people's morals and counseling the boys on good behavior. I have heard him tell his story many times when I was a youth, because he was always telling it to us as a lesson. He had been an awful rascal down there in Oklahoma when he was young, stealing meat from people's racks, taking their horses for joy-rides without asking them for them, and then when he got to where he was going he would just turn the horse loose and let it wander back to its owner—if it did. He was disrespectful to people and sassed them back. Everyone thought he was a mean boy, and whatever happened in camp he got blamed for it. This story I am going to tell happened just after that trouble Wolf Lies Down had over the borrowed horse when the soldiers made the rule that no one in camp could take another person's horse without permission. This is what Pawnee used to tell us:

"Down there (in Oklahoma) were two spotted horses well liked in their family. One day I took them and headed west. Three days passed and I found myself still safe. Now I was out of trouble's way, so I began to feel pretty good. On the fourth day, as I looked back, I saw some people coming up. 'It is nothing,' I thought, 'just some people traveling.' When they overtook me, I saw they were Bowstring Soldiers out after me.

" 'You have stolen those horses,' they cried as they pulled me from

15 Grinnell, *Cheyenne Indians*, I, 336–337.
16 Llewellyn and Hoebel, p. 79.

my horse. 'Now we have trailed you down.' They threw me on the ground and beat me until I could not stand; they broke up my weapons and ruined my saddle; they cut my blankets, moccasins, and kit to shreds. When they had finished they took all my food and went off with the horses, leaving me alone on the prairie, sore and destitute, too weak and hurt to move.

"The next day I started back, traveling as best I could all day long. I knew there was a small camp of buffalo hunters out and for them I was looking. I traveled all day. The next day I thought I would die. I had no food, only water. Late in the afternoon I camped on a creek. My feet were bleeding and I could not walk farther. I crawled slowly on my hands and knees to the brow of a high hill to find a place to die. I waited in mourning. Far to the south of me I could see the rolling country; to the west my view was blocked. My pipe and tobacco were gone. Without smoke I sat there thinking of a great many things as I watched the blood drip from my swollen feet.

"As I gazed steadfastly into the south, a hunter came up the hill from behind me. When he saw me he stopped and watched me for a long time. After three days and two nights in my condition I must have been nearly deaf, for I did not hear him until he spoke from his horse right behind me. I was naked. I fell over in a fright when I heard his voice start out in the silence.

"This man dismounted and hugged me. He wept, he felt so bad at seeing my plight. It was High Backed Wolf,[17] a young man, but a chief. He put his blanket about me and took me home. The camp was on the creek below, hidden just around a bend where I had not seen it. His wife gave me food and nourished me.

"Then High Backed Wolf sent for the chiefs who were in the camp. Four or five came, one of whom was a soldier chief.

"High Backed Wolf spoke to the soldier chief first. 'This is the first time since I have become a big [tribal] chief that I have happened upon such a poor man; now I am going to outfit him. Until he is fixed up, I shall ask no questions. Then we shall learn how he came to be naked. I am not going to ask you to give anything unless you wish to do so. I know this man,' he said. 'He is a great smoker. But I shall give him no smoke until he has first eaten.' (In my own mind I said, 'I'd rather smoke first.')

"First they gave me a little soup; then some meat.

"High Backed Wolf then filled the pipe. As he held it to the five di-

[17] Later a famous chief killed in a skirmish with American troops at the Platte Bridge, July 25, 1865. Grinnell, *Fighting Cheyennes*, p. 218.

rections he prayed, 'This is my first good act as a chief. Help this man to tell the truth.' Then he held the pipe for me to smoke; then he gave it to the next man and to the others. Now he faced me again. 'Now you tell the truth. Have you been caught by enemies and stripped? Or was it something else? You saw me smoke this pipe; you have touched it with your own lips. That is to help you tell the truth. If you tell us straightly, Maiyun will help you.'

"I told them the whole story. I told them whose horses they were, and told them it was the Bowstrings who had punished me.

"High Backed Wolf knew I was a rascal, so he lectured to me. 'You are old enough now to know what is right,' he preached. 'You have been to war. Now leave off this foolishness. If it had been that I had not ridden out into the hills today you would have died. No one would have known the end of you. You know how we Cheyennes try to live. You know how we hunt, how we go to war. When we take horses, we take them from enemies, not from Cheyennes. You had better join a military society. You can learn good behavior from the soldiers. Yet I ask only one thing of you. Be decent from now on! Stop stealing! Stop making fun of people! Use no more bad language in the camp! Lead a good life!

" 'Now I am going to help you out. That is what I am here for, because I am a chief of the people. Here are your clothes. Outside are three horses. You may take your choice!' He gave me a six-shooter. 'Here is a mountain-lion skin. I used to wear this in the parades. Now I give it to you.' He offered me all these things and I took them.

"The others gave me beaver skins to braid in my hair, beads, and extra moccasins, and two more horses.

"Then High Backed Wolf ended it. 'Now I am not going to tell you to leave this camp. You may stay here as long as you wish. I shall not tell you which direction to go, west or south.'

"I had a sweetheart in the south, but when these people did this for me, I felt ashamed. I had all those things with which to look beautiful, but I did not dare to go back, for I knew she would have heard what the Bowstrings had done to me. I thought it wisest to go north until the thing was dead.

"When the Arrows were next renewed, the Foxes put up their lodge to get more men. I went in [joined]. Still, I never got it out of my heart that it had been those Bowstrings. Whenever my Fox troop was on duty I was out looking for those men or their families to do something wrong. I always looked for a Bowstring to slip, so I could beat him well. I stayed with the Northern Cheyennes a long, long time, until the Horse

Creek Treaty. Though I came to be a chief of the Fox Soldiers among the Northern people, I never amounted to much with the Southern bands. Those people always remembered me as a no-good.

"You boys remember that. You may run away, but your people always remember. You just obey the rules of the camp, and you'll do all right." [18]

The powers of the council were both executive and judicial. It alone had the peace-making authority, and it imposed the sentence of banishment on murderers; likewise, it commuted the sentence when in its judgment the murderer had expiated his offense. Individual chiefs served as mediators in the settlement of adultery cases. They also directed the movements of the camp.

The other branch of Cheyenne government, and a mighty legal factor, was found in the Soldiers' Societies, or military associations. Of these there were six: the Fox, Elk, Shield, Bowstring, Dog, and Northern Crazy Dogs. Together their membership embraced all the fighting men of the tribe. They were not age classes, and except for the Dog Soldiers, the members of each society were drawn from any or all of the bands. This meant that like the council of chiefs the members of the various societies met together as a unit only during the summer months of the tribal get-together. The Dog Soldiers were an exception, for they were constituted of the warriors of one band and none but members of the Dog band could join the Dog Soldiers society.

Each military association had four elected chiefs. These were the recognized war chiefs of the tribe, although any outstanding warrior could organize and lead a raiding party. In keeping with the constitutional supremacy of the peace chiefs, any warrior society chief who was appointed to the tribal council had to resign his military chieftainship, although he could and did retain his membership in the society.

The authority of the heads of the military societies over their constituents was absolute in action. Nevertheless their power, in the Hohfeldian sense of initiating new legal relations, was restricted in practice, although not in theory. New lines of social policy were constitutionally to be determined by general consensus.

Thus in two great crisis situations Dog Soldier chiefs were forbidden to have contact with American officials lest they make un-

[18] Llewellyn and Hoebel, pp. 6–9.

authorized and unwanted yet binding decisions. Bull Bear, in 1863, was restrained from meeting in treaty council with the American Commissioners. More spectacularly, the Cheyennes threatened to kill Tangle Hair, head chief of the Dog Soldiers, in 1873 when Captain Wessels offered to release him and his family from the freezing and starving confinement to which Dull Knife's band was being subjected in the Fort Robinson barracks. The Cheyennes were determined to die rather than capitulate to the United States government's demand that they return to Oklahoma from whence they had fled. They feared that Tangle Hair, given freedom, would order them to capitulate. "This man cannot go out; he owns us and can do what he likes with us," declared Little Shield. That being his constitutional power, they were going to see to it that he got into no position wherein he might exercise his power contrary to the wishes of his followers. The limitation of legal power by degree was not a shading found in Cheyenne law. But social control over the exercise of a theoretically absolute power was not lacking in case of need.

The legal role of the military societies was centered mostly around the maintenance of order on the communal hunt and at the time of the great tribal ceremonial rituals—but it was by no means limited to these occasions, as shall soon be seen.

The communal hunts were in themselves integrative forces in the cementing of tribal consciousness as they were also an expression of the strong corporate feeling that had been built up during the days of common worship just preceding the hunt. It is hardly likely that a mass hunt by hundreds of warriors followed by all their women and children was more efficient than would have been a dozen separate hunts by the various bands. An adequate meat supply could have been won just as easily and with less organization in the second way. But the national interests of the Cheyennes as a tribe would not have enjoyed the kind of nourishment that the communal enterprise cultivated. So a-hunting went the tribe.

The military society of the man who had sponsored the dance of the season was in charge. Its scouts located the herd, and the people moved up into position under its direction. When the hunters went out the next morning the military police worked them out in a long attack line. No man could charge the herd until the signal was given. Then the two ends of the line raced out to close a circle around the herd so that it could not break away but would mill wildly while the slaughter went on.

But highstrung and overeager warriors did frequently jump the gun. What then? A case recorded in 1935 in the words of an old-time Cheyenne, Stump Horn, will give the answer.

The tribe was moving in a body up the Rosebud River toward the Big Horn Mountain country in search of buffalo. The Shield Soldiers, who were in charge on that occasion, had their scouts out looking for the herds, and when the scouts came in with their report, the order was given that no one should leave the camp or attack the buffalo. . .

All the hunters went out in a line with the Shield Soldiers in front to hold them back. Just as they were coming up over a long ridge down wind from where the scouts had reported the herd they saw two men down in the valley riding in among the buffalo. A Shield Soldier chief gave the signal to his men. They paid no attention to the buffalo, but charged in a long line on the two violators of the rules. Little Old Man shouted out for everyone to whip them: "Those who fail or hesitate shall get a good beating themselves."

The first men to reach the spot shot and killed the horses from under the hunters. As each soldier reached the miscreants he slashed them with his riding whip. Then some seized the guns of the two and smashed them.

When the punishment was done, the father of these two boys rode up. It was Two Forks, a member of the Dakota tribe, who had been living with the Cheyennes for some time. He looked at his sons before talking. "Now you have done wrong. You failed to obey the law of this tribe. You went out alone and you did not give the other people a chance. This is what has happened to you."

Then the Shield Soldier chiefs took up the talk. "Now you know what we do when anyone disobeys our orders," they declared. "Now you know we mean what we say." The boys did not say anything.

After that the chiefs relented. This was not alone because of the fact that the culprits were Dakotas. They called their men to gather around. "Look how these two boys are here in our midst. Now they have no horses and no weapons. What do you men want to do about it?"

One of the soldiers spoke up, "Well, I have some extra horses. I will give one of them to them." Then another soldier did the same thing.

Bear Standing On A Ridge was the third to speak out, "Well," he announced, "we broke those guns they had. I have two guns. I will give them one."

All the others said, "*Ipewa,* good."

Meanwhile, someone had been counting up the men. There were forty-nine in the troop at that time, and now it was noticed that five or six were not at hand. When they began looking around, they saw these men way down the creek chasing bison. "Now we will give them a good whipping," shouted one of the chiefs. "Charge on them and whip them, but don't kill their horses."

They all leaped to their mounts to see who could get there first. When the slackers saw them coming, Big Footed Bull, who was among them, took off the blanket he was wearing and spread it on the ground. It was one of those fine Hudson's Bay blankets which the government used to issue to the Indians. He stood behind it with his friends, because he meant it as an offering to the troop. Last Bull, who was one of the Shield Soldier chiefs at that time, called to his men to halt. They stopped, and then they split into two columns which rode slowly around the men by the blanket and circled around to the front again. The soldiers dismounted and divided the blanket among themselves, tearing it into long narrow strips of cloth to wear as tail pieces when they were having a dance. They finished by cutting an ear off each of the horses of the culprits. That was how they punished them.[19]

Two things stand out in this account: two characteristics of Cheyenne law in action, characteristics that run through case after case. First, the rehabilitation of the miscreant boys. They were severely punished. The law was sustained. And then, when they showed no willful defiance, when it was clear that they had learned their lesson, they were immediately rehabilitated by the very law-enforcers who had destroyed their guns, killed their horses, and given them a bodily whipping. Cheyenne law was not vindictive. It could be harsh and swift, but its aim was conformance to essential rules, not social vengeance. The second point is that dereliction of duty by any of the police was also punished. It was essential that all of the troop carry their full share of the responsibility to see that things were done right. The fact that the miscreant Shields were able to fend off a beating for themselves by offering a blanket was not mere bribery. It was an act of contrition, an open confession of error, and

19 Llewellyn and Hoebel, pp. 112–113.

an expression of humility. And humiliated they were, for none of them would dare to ride his ear-cropped horse again; it would be a constant public reminder of disgrace.

So many other Cheyennes received a beating in their time for going out to hunt too soon that one gets the flavor (along with that of occasional greed or fear of being left behind) of a recognized dangerous sport for the adventurous daredevil: beating the cops when the police were peculiarly on the alert.

The police also acted as a Tribal Bureau of Investigation when surreptitious hunters were reported or suspected. Then they exercised the right of search. If, as they approached the suspect's lodge, he rushed out holding up his hands, they made a careful search for fresh meat. If they found none, they retired. If they did find any, however, they slashed his lodge to shreds.

"The soldiers were not working for themselves; they were working for the people." [20]

The role of the military societies in the legal life of Plains Indian tribes along the lines just described was first brought to attention by Professor Robert Lowie in his *Primitive Society,* which book, Holmes wrote to his friend, Sir Frederick Pollock, "seems to be an advance on all previous books in the same sense as Tourtoulon's *Principes philosophique de l'histoire du droit,* distrusting and even discrediting the too sweeping and easy generalizations of our earlier day." [21]

In his early work Lowie wrote the following:

Circumstances affecting the weal and woe of the community required more concentration of power than was commonly vouchsafed to a more or less honored figurehead. This is illustrated by the Plains Indian police organizations at the time of a communal buffalo hunt, when a single false step might have scared off the entire herd and jeopardized the food supply of the entire camp. Hence the utmost rigor temporarily supplanted the extreme individualism of normal times. Women were not allowed to chop trees, men were not permitted to go hunting by themselves lest their premature efforts imperil the success of the cooperative enterprise. The police not only confiscated an offender's game, but se-

---

[20] Calf Woman, a Cheyenne informant, in Llewellyn and Hoebel, p. 118.
[21] M. de Howe, *Holmes–Pollock Letters,* 2 vols. (Cambridge, 1942), II, 59.

verely beat him, broke up his weapons, and destroyed his tent. If he offered resistance, he was likely to be killed on the spot.[22]

The author then went on to note that the police had other "less conspicuous" functions as well, such as restraining ill-timed war parties and checking dangerous hostilities among the tribesmen.

In his later treatise on primitive polity, *The Origin of the State,* Professor Lowie greatly expanded his treatment of state germination as exemplified by the Plains Indian military societies. But he narrowed his conception of their state-making activities while stepping up his estimate of their importance. His emphasis was now on the emergency and temporary nature of the assumption of police powers. In Lowie's words, "Everywhere the basic idea is that during the hunt a group is vested with the power forcibly to prevent premature attacks on the herd and to punish offenders by corporal punishment . . . by destruction of their property generally, and in extreme cases by killing them." And further, "for the brief period of the hunt the unchallenged supremacy of the police unified the entire population and created a state 'towering immeasurably above single individuals,' but which disappeared again as rapidly as it had come into being. No other feature of Plains Indian life approached the buffalo police as an effective territorial unifier." [23]

The most important implication of Lowie's discussion is in its empirical demonstration of the multiple nature of the emergent state—the internal growth of various types of control organs to meet felt social needs. He was explicitly arguing against Oppenheimer's single-line theory of the conquest and caste origin of the state.[24] Indirectly, he was also disproving the Marxist notion of the state as being exclusively an instrument of exploitation devised by a ruling class for the domination and exploitation of a submerged class. In the noncapitalistic, non-land-owning Plains tribes there was no permanent mastery of one tribe by another. Yet coercive legal power was exercised. It was a result of democratic self-determination in response to a felt social need.

The interesting and utterly reasonable thing about it all is that the need did not result in the creation of new social agencies to wield

[22] Lowie, *Primitive Society,* p. 385.
[23] Lowie, *Origin of the State,* pp. 103–105.
[24] Franz Oppenheimer, *The State* (New York, 1922).

the stick of power but that already-existing agencies were drafted into the job. The primary interests of the military associations had been social. They were nothing more than men's clubs: fraternal orders whose members got together for camaraderie, feasting, singing, dancing, and parades to tickle their egos before the public eye. They were military in that all their members were soldiers. Only rarely did they go to war as units. They were not tactical bodies of standing armies nor even militia companies as we understand them. But they were *organized*. And when a job requiring the exercise of force by an organized unit representing not kinship interests, but the tribal whole came up, what was more natural than that the tribes should acquiesce in their taking on of *secondary* functions: the administration of policing and of summary justice where summary action was necessary? Thus an entirely nongovernmental type of organization became a legitimatized branch of the government of the tribes.

As against the tribal council it was to be expected that the military societies were constitutionally subordinate. This was the case inasmuch as the council was officially and exclusively an agent of government and apparently much older than the military associations. Yet in the dynamic flow of crisis and culture change in which the Cheyennes were caught in the nineteenth century the military societies were steadily expanding the area of their legal powers— not by encroachment on the powers of the council but by moving in where one new situation after another called for new law and where new or old law called for new types of enforcement. The council tended to be traditional in accordance with its original religious endowment. Not so the warrior associations.

The Cheyenne military societies assumed jurisdiction in a large variety of dispute and misbehavior situations, except those of adultery and homicide (which had from "time immemorial" been the chiefs' jurisdiction). And in marginal homicide cases calling for new decision, they entered even here.

In a case where an aborted fetus was found near the camp one of the societies lined up all the women, ordered them to expose their breasts for evidence of recent lactation, judged one girl guilty, and ordered her banished from the camp.[25]

[25] Llewellyn and Hoebel, case 14, pp. 118–119.

It has already been seen how summarily and roughly they punished the horse-stealing Pawnee. That, however, was but a follow-up to a carefully considered judicial decision that had made new law in a previous case. This was none other than the horse-borrowing case laid before the Elk Soldiers by Wolf Lies Down which was discussed in Chapter II.

The Cheyenne military societies even intervened judicially in intrafamily fracases on occasion. In the case of Bird Face *vs.* Sleeping Rabbit the latter shot an arrow into the arm of Bird Face because of a rebuke the Bird Face gave him for letting Elk Woman, niece of Bird Face and wife of Sleeping Rabbit, struggle afoot through deep snow when the camp was on the move. The arrowhead would not come out, and the Fox Soldiers were convened "to see what they would do about it." They decided they should beat Sleeping Rabbit "until he was as sore as Bird Face's arm." This they did. They also ordered him to amputate Bird Face's arm and to sit up with him every night until he was well again. When other soldier societies began agitating to exile him, he publicly confessed repentance and gave five horses to the Fox Soldiers. These worthies converted the "fine" into a barrel of whiskey in a deal with a trader. With this and some food the Foxes threw a big ceremonial feast for all the soldier bands. *No compensation passed from Sleeping Rabbit to Bird Face.*[26]

Such had become the law-making power of the Cheyenne military associations.

The older and more deeply rooted law of the Cheyennes lay within the jurisdiction of the tribal chiefs and centered about the problems of homicide and marital infidelity.

Homicide, as indicated under Postulate II, was truly a serious matter of tribal concern. Very little of the law of the tribes thus far considered sprang from religious notions, but the Cheyenne law of homicide was quite definitely religiously shaped.

The tribe possesses two sacred fetishes of great antiquity. One is the Medicine Arrows bundle. The other, the Holy Hat bundle. The Medicine Arrows have been with the tribe since time beyond the memory of man. In the Four Arrows are symbolized the entity and

[26] *Ibid.,* case 16, pp. 122–123.

the integrity of the tribe. When the Arrows are properly treated all goes well with the tribe. Failure to perform the proper ceremonies on behalf of the Arrows before the great tribal attack on the Pawnee Indians on the South Loup River of Nebraska in 1830 led, in Cheyenne belief, to the capture of the Arrows by the Skidi Pawnees. The Cheyennes believe that all their misfortunes began with this catastrophe, although two of the Arrows were recovered and substitutes were provided for the others.

Among the several circumstances that affected the well-being of the Arrows, and thereby of the tribe, was the killing of a Cheyenne by a Cheyenne. This was a stain on the tribal "soul," and it was revealed by the miraculous appearance of blood on the feathers of the Arrows. A curse fell on the whole nation. While the blood yet remained on the feathers "bad luck dogged the tribe." No war party could dare to hope for success; hunting parties would return empty-handed. All the people suffered for the act of one man.

As for him, he was doomed with the mark of Cain. His viscera, it was said, rotted within him. From his corrupting vitals emanated a noisome odor repugnant to the beasts of the prairie. That is why "game shunned the territory; it made the tribe lonesome." So much was the sin corruption of the man to the fore in the minds of the Cheyennes that it became the byword for murder, *hejoxow3s,* "putrid."

Murder was thus, in the first instance, a sin. The sanctions were supernatural and automatic. It is interesting, however, that the penalty was neither religiously nor mythologically explained as flowing from the anger or disapproval of any god or nature or ancestral spirits. The Cheyennes held to no image of a punishing father or brooding ancestors. True, the injunction against murder came from the "Deserted Daughter" who gave the Cheyennes their form of government. She had induced a mountain lion and bear to kill her nefarious and evil father for his deeds—and this done, had said, "Hereafter we shall make a rule that if anyone kills a fellow tribesman he shall be ordered out of camp for from one to five years. Whatever the people decide." [27] Yet it is not her spirit that punishes the Cheyenne Cain. Nor were the animals angry with the tribe

[27] *Ibid.,* pp. 71–72.

for what had been done. They were merely distressed by the smell, and so took themselves elsewhere. In other words, this evil was evil for its own sake. The consequences, though supernatural, were in the nature of things.

The consequences for the Cheyennes were in fact most salubrious, for they placed an immediate check on the impulse for a counter-killing. Revenge could not rest in the hands of the deceased victim's kinsmen. That would merely compound sin with sin.

Judgment lay with the tribe in the persons of the tribal council. Nor could the tribal council impose the death penalty. Yet extrusion was necessary to cleanse the putrid infection from the body politic. The solution was exile, and this was the sentence. Thus homicide was made a crime against the people.

Simple banishment of the offender was not enough, however. The tribe as well as the man was stained. Purification was called for, and this was done through the ritual of Renewal of the Medicine Arrows. For this undertaking every Cheyenne was under obligation to be present—excepting murderers and their families. This rule was law enforced by the military societies. If need be, they drove absentees in for the great ceremony.[28] The law also required a reign of absolute silence during the hours in which the Sacred Arrows were taken from their bundle and given fresh, unbloodied feathers. The police patrolled the camp to see that all women and small children remained quietly in the lodges, and they summarily brained any dog that chose to break the silence with a bark.

The impressiveness of the Renewal Ritual is difficult to sense. Its emotional effect must have been great. And by means of it the Cheyennes achieved a positive social result of tremendous value. As an integrator of the tribe nothing equaled it. The feeling of oneness was not to be escaped. So it was that the act which could shatter the unity of the tribe—homicide—was made the incident that formally reinforced the integrity of the people as a people. Not vengeance, not further bloodletting, not the cruel punishment of imprisonment, but purification from a sin shared by all and a reinforcement of the social bond were the results achieved by the Cheyenne action.

As for the murderer, he could continue his life among the friendly

[28] *Ibid.*, pp. 126–127.

Arapahos or Sioux. In due course, normally after five years, he could petition the tribal council for reinstatement to the tribe. In the meantime all his civil rights as a Cheyenne were nullified, except the position of chieftainship as a member of the tribal council (for such a chief could not be deposed for any act prior to the completion of his ten-year term of office). But, as always, the Cheyennes looked toward rehabilitation and reinstatement of the wayward tribesman. Hence, if there was no objection from the kin of the murderer's victim, the council usually granted a commutation of exile to the murderer who promised to walk straight. Nevertheless, not all was forgiven. Although his internal disintegration was checked, a faint odor of pollution remained, and for this he was forever barred from smoking the common pipe in manly gatherings or eating and drinking from a common bowl.

The feudistic tendency is the bane of primitive societies that rely on private law to control their members. This the Cheyennes mastered in a simple way through use of a unifying religious concept.

The concept of murder as sin also reached out to impose moderation in parental treatment of daughters. Suicide or the threat of suicide is not uncommonly used among various peoples to control the actions of persons in close relations to the suicide. Cheyenne daughters in resentment against overstrict maternal control occasionally took their own lives by hanging. Brothers who had promised a sister in marriage, only to have the girl elope with some other man, fought conspicuously in battle in order to get themselves killed. These acts of driving a close relative to suicide were looked upon as killing that person: the responsible person was banished and the Arrows were usually renewed.[29]

If the virtue of the Cheyenne law of homicide was in its humaneness and moral decency and its strength in its effectiveness in checking feuds, it must be acknowledged that it exhibited some ineffectiveness in the prevention of killings. Sixteen case records of intratribal killings between 1835 and 1879 were recorded by George Bird Grinnell and us. It is as though a pioneer territory of 8,500 population suffered a homicide a year—a rate which would seem very low in the light of our own frontier history. The Cheyennes

[29] *Ibid.*, cases 25–27, pp. 154–160.

were trained to be aggressive warriors, and the impulse to kill could not always be channeled outside the tribe.

In sharp contrast to the Comanches and Eskimos, the Cheyennes turned the prestige struggle among the men away from the arena of sex. Adultery raised its head rarely, and wife-absconding was faced as a legal issue only in an indirect way. It may be said from this that the Cheyennes had successfully channeled the prestige competition among men (which they encouraged) into other lines. With their institutionalized chieftainship in the council and warrior fraternities the status placing of successful men was assured and clear-cut. There was little need to prove one's worth by stealing another man's wife.

Marital shifts did take place with moderate frequency, but such incidents were commonly devoid of tension. In the exemplary behavior of a chieftain such a man would studiously—nay, ostentatiously—ignore his wife's defection. One chieftain when engaged in the very serious act of having a scalp shirt dedicated, was informed that someone had run off with his wife. He paused only to comment, "A dog has pissed on my tent." He gave no further notice to the affair. A scalp-shirt wearer was brave beyond all other men and not subject to any reflections cast on his status by an interloper.

This should be true of any Cheyenne chieftain, and a chief sorely beset would sometimes seize and light his pipe to remind himself of his obligation not to take offense. Other men of good manners and serene disposition tried to deport themselves like chiefs. Obviously then, when their wives deserted them for other men they did not rant like a Kiowa. In fact, they did nothing but sit it out as did our friend, Stump Horn, who was a meticulous observer of tribal decencies. In his own words:

My wife ran off with a certain man. For a while I said nothing, but simply studied the best way to do. To other people I simply carried on as though not a thing had happened.

Then one day I saw a man coming my way leading a spotted horse. It was Crazy Head, a chief. I would not say anything to a chief. Crazy Head said he was pulling for me not to cause trouble. Would I accept the horse and settle it?

I said to him, "Do not talk about such things" (i.e., the causing of trouble). But I did tell Crazy Head this, "I am very sorry you brought that horse. I would much rather have had a saddle and some blankets. However, since you brought the horse, I shall take it."

So we smoked, and I took the horse, and that other man had my wife.

This case was in the ideal pattern: the proper Cheyenne husband took wifely defection in good grace and inaction. The corespondent, if proper in his behavior, soon took a horse and other goods to a chief with the request that the chief carry his pipe to the husband and proffer him the restitutive gifts. The sending of a chief almost guaranteed a smooth and peaceful settlement, for the reverence toward the tribal leaders was such that "a man cannot refuse a request of a chief," though even that did occur. The smoking of the pipe by the husband indicated acceptance of the gifts and the closing of the issue. It was not, incidently, a "peace pipe" that was smoked. True, internal peace was assured by the act, but the real meaning of ritual smoking among the Plains Indians was that it bound the parties to an agreement to keep their word. It was the sealer of an agreement and a sacred testimonial to truth.

The ideal was by no means achieved in all cases, however. If, after a few days, no chiefly emissary was forthcoming from the wife-taker—and an occasional warrior taunted another in this way—then a proper husband sent a chief himself, stating a demand as to what it would take to satisfy him. This almost always produced results, since recalcitrance on the part of the wife-taker would then put him in a very bad light before all the people.

Yet other husbands were shorter tempered. Iron Shirt shot and killed two of She Bear's best horses when no emissary was sent to him by She Bear. This is the only reported case of this kind. She Bear acknowledged the justice of the act by making no overt reaction.

Once in a while a warrior on the make—a warrior who was concentrating on the war leader ideal and who had not yet achieved the status of a peace chief on the tribal council—tossed all restraint to the winds. He took the stealing of his wife as an act of personal insult and attempted to recoup his status through violence.

Red Eagle, who was a chief of the Fox Soldiers, gave Coyote, the stealer of his wife, a beating and then went to his lodge to find his gun. He made it clear he was going to kill him. Coyote, however, was a man of more discretion than valor. He hid. But the next day, when the camp was on the move Red Eagle spotted him. The case continues:

Red Eagle was with the Fox Soldiers, who were marching in a bunch singing. He ordered the Foxes to keep marching, while he dropped out of the ranks. Coyote saw him at that moment, so he rushed in among the soldiers. Red Eagle rode up pointing his gun. "Move!" he cried to the soldiers, "Move, so I can shoot him." At first the soldiers scattered a bit, but as soon as they recovered, they closed in on Red Eagle and seized him. They argued with him. They said, "You are one of our chiefs. We think a lot of you. Don't do this thing. You will spoil your reputation."

Red Eagle answered back, "If there is one thing I hate, it is to see a man let another get away with his wife." But the soldiers held him in check.

Red Eagle's own Foxes then sent an old chief to him with the pipe, but he refused to smoke. His threats toward Coyote continued. After he had refused several chiefs, the Foxes advised Coyote [who had been in hiding under their care] to leave the camp. This was ten years before the Custer fight. Coyote went south and did not return until a few years ago, long after the death of Red Eagle. In a joking mood he began to say to the folks, "I am looking for that wife of mine. Where is she?" She, on the other hand, announced that she hated him for the trouble he had caused her. For though Red Eagle did not mutilate her, and kept her as wife, he beat her regularly until she wounded him in the armpit with her six shooter.[30]

In one other Cheyenne case that violates Corollary 3 of Postulate II is seen the uncontrolled reaction of a man who was more Comanche- and Kiowa-like than Cheyenne in his recalcitrance.

One time one man's wife ran off with another. Before anything could be done, the husband sent word over to the absconder.

"Don't try to send me any gifts! Send no chief to tell me a story about what you are going to do to get this thing settled," was his message. "I want nothing from *you*."

Then he went on talking to his friends. "That man thinks nothing of me," he told them. "He thinks I am a coward who will do nothing. Well, some day we are going to meet the enemy together. There is where

30 Llewellyn and Hoebel, pp. 197–198.

I am going to see my friend. If he shows any cowardice then, there is where I'll come in."

The husband was a noted warrior among the people.

The camp was moved to the south, down toward Oklahoma. It was a big camp, for they were getting all the tribe together. When they got in the south country, a big war party was made up.

After the declaration of the husband, that wife-taker always went in war parties in which the husband was not a member. This time the husband hung back several days before starting out, then trailed down the group the absconder was with. When he overtook them, they were at rest in camp. They saw him coming and heard him singing a soldier song—a death song. When he got into camp, he rode right over some of the men as they were sitting there. That meant he intended to charge right into the enemy breastworks. If the campers ran into a lodge, they were safe from him, but if he came upon one, he struck him hard with his whip. That was the way he would count coup on the enemy. He could take whatever meat he wanted from any pot.

The absconder looked scared.

Three days later, he walked up to the husband. "Friend," he said, "as long as we are on this war party, it is my desire to look after you. I want to make your camp, to cook your food, to look after your horses. I know what you have declared as your intention. You are on this war path never to return."

He got no satisfaction from the other. Came the rebuff, "I haven't finished this thing yet. You acted as though you did not think so much of me when you were making off with my wife. You put on as though you were the better man then. I still think I am good. I could have accepted gifts from you. But that is not what I want. Now we are out to see who *is* the better man."

That began to worry the absconder. "If I turn back, he'll kill me. If I go on, I must die before the enemy."

In his dilemma he went to the leader of the war party and to the Holy Hat Keeper to see if they could do something. He was asking them if they would not carry the pipe to the husband.

Again he was rebuffed. "No," they told him, "the pipe is still filled.[81] But, even so, we'll go talk to him without a smoke. We'll see if he won't agree to leave some things out which he has in mind. That kind of man is hard to handle. It will take a lot of talking."

They went to see him as they had said. And they told him the old-time history [way of doing things]. "In the old times," they pointed out

[81] The meaning of this statement is made clear in the account on p. 165.

to him, "people went to war like you to get killed. That is all right. But you are up to something else. You want to scare him so he'll run off by himself where you can kill him. Can't you leave our friend alone?"

"Well," said the husband, "I'll leave him alone on this trip. But you chiefs know how it is when a man steps in and induces your wife to run off with him. He acts as though you were nothing. That is what makes me angry—for him to act as though he were not afraid of me! Now what I want to know is, is he the better man? When we find the enemy, I am going right in. If he leads me in and counts coup before I do, I am satisfied."

When they charged the enemies, the husband counted two coups, but the enemies were well armed and turned the Cheyennes to rout. When the wife-taker lighted out with the others, the husband took after him and quirted him. "Just as I thought," he yelled, "you are no man. When we get back, I take my wife from you."

But when he started to do this thing, his father-in-law intervened, saying that his daughter had made a poor wife. Now he had another who had come of age and he was giving her to his son-in-law instead.[32]

This man was a courageous warrior. But he was not yet a chief. His drive for status was great, and dominance was his personal need. The giving of restitutive gifts by the wrongdoer acknowledged no particular superiority to the wronged husband among the Cheyennes; at the most it merely acknowledged an obligation to balance the loss suffered and to maintain the peace. For this particular warrior's ego it was not enough. Although he was un-Cheyenne in his personal demands, he was truly Cheyenne in the skill with which he built up the situation to serve his ends.

If further evidence is needed of the Cheyenne concern for maintenance of intragroup tranquillity and the checking of interpersonal aggression and their "legislative" finesse in formulating social policy in critical situations, the case of Walking Rabbit, who was perhaps too "slick" a lawyer, should answer. This is the case as told by Black Wolf.

A war party was organizing. Walking Rabbit approached the leader with a question. "Is it true that you have declared we must all go afoot? If so, I would like to be able to lead a horse to pack my moccasins and possibles." The leader gave him an answer. "There is a reason for my

32 Llewellyn and Hoebel, pp. 199–201.

ruling. I want no horses, that it may be easier for us to conceal our movements. However, you may bring one horse." Then Walking Rabbit asked for instructions concerning the location of the first and second nights' camps, for he would start late and overtake the party.

Walking Rabbit's sweetheart had been married only recently to another. "My husband is not the man I thought he was," she told her former suitor. So Walking Rabbit took her to join the war party. [The Cheyennes have a phrase for the single man who marries a one-time married woman—"putting on the old moccasin."] In this way, it turned out that the "moccasin" he was packing was a big woman.

When they saw this woman there, the warriors got excited. The party turned into the hills and stopped. The leader opened his pipe. The leader's pipe was always filled before they left the camp, but it was not smoked until the enemy was seen or their tracks reported. Now the leader spoke. "When we take a woman with us it is usually known in the camp. Here is a man who has sneaked off with another's wife. Now what is going to happen?" That is what they were talking about.

The leader declared, "The only thing this man can do is return and make a settlement with the husband. Then he may follow us up."

One warrior was for aiding Walking Rabbit. "Why can't we let him stay?" was his proposal. "If we take any horses, we can give them to her husband." That was rejected.

The decision was that he had to go back. "If you had told us you wanted her so badly, we might have waited for you to settle for her. Then we could have taken her the right way. If you really want to go to war with us, you will be able to overtake us. We are afoot."

Then three or four warriors spoke up, each promising Walking Rabbit a horse to send to the husband. Everyone gave one or two arrows to be sent as well.

In the meantime Walking Rabbit's father had fixed it up with the aggrieved husband. Since he and his wife were incompatible, he was willing to release her. When Walking Rabbit came in and told his father the story of the soldiers' action, the father said, "Just let that stand. The thing is fixed. When those fighters come back they may want to give to the girl's parents. You go back after your party." But Walking Rabbit preferred to stay at home.

When Walking Rabbit did not go out, his closest relatives raised a big tipi. When they heard of the approach of the returning party, everything was in readiness.

The warriors came charging in, shooting; they had taken many horses. The first coup-counters were in the van. Walking Rabbit's father had a right to harangue; he was a crier. "Don't go to your homes! Don't go to your own lodges! Come here to the lodge of Walking Rabbit, your friend!"

When they were all in this lodge the old man entered and told them his story. "I had this thing all settled before my son returned. You have sent arrows and promised horses. Now I have kept this girl here pending your return. I shall send her back to her parents with presents. I have waited to see what you are going to do."

The leader replied for his followers. "Yes, we will help you. We promised to help your son. When you send her back, we'll send presents with her." The men who had promised horses went out to get them. Others gave captured horses.

Sending her back with these presents was giving wedding gifts. Her relatives got them all. They gathered up their goods to send back. The war party was called together once more; to them this stuff was given. It was a great thing for the people to talk about. It was the first and last time a woman was sent home on enemy horses the day they came in.[33]

In this we have a nice instance of intertribal diffusion blocked because of inconsistency with the basic postulates of the receiving tribe. Walking Rabbit may have been stimulated to his bright idea by Comanche example. He was to be the initiator of it in his own tribe. He even proceeded with great skill and subtlety, a subtlety so smooth that it borders on chicanery. What a nice lawyer's fiction— "I would like to be able to lead a horse to pack my moccasins and possibles." And with what skill he maneuvered his delayed departure so as to present his fellow warriors (who he knew would be his judges) with a *fait accompli* and thus increase the possibility of acceptance of his innovation. It worked with one of the war party.

Wiser heads saw through the scheme. They quickly measured the trouble-making potentialities of this new proposal. They realized fully the consequences of letting even this one venture stand as a precedent. They rebuffed him decisively. And then, in typical Cheyenne fashion, they capitalized on the situation dramatically to achieve a twofold effect: they handsomely got Walking Rabbit out of the pit he had dug for himself; they memorialized their ruling of law with a grand gesture that was "a great thing for the people to talk about." It was not forgotten—and never tried again.

[33] Llewellyn and Hoebel, pp. 13–15.

Can it still be said that primitive peoples do not legislate, that custom takes care of all things?

In one area of domestic relations and sex the Cheyennes were badly muddled: suppressed male aggressions sometimes burst the dams of restraint in an orgy of sadism focused on a hapless female. The Cheyennes did not look upon sex gratification as sinful, but they certainly did not value it highly. I believe I am correct in formulating Postulate IX (*Sexual activity should be held to a minimum*) as the best way of stating their basic attitude toward sex. It has already been shown that sex competition was ruled out as a vehicle for status achievement. Great precautions were taken to see that women remained chaste. Every postpubescent girl is reputed to have worn a chastity belt at all times. Every married woman was supposed to wear one whenever her husband was away on a journey or whenever she went out alone away from her lodge. Molestation of the belt (attempted rape) was severely punished by the woman's female relatives. Under "Black Letter Law" they would stone him to death, and in one case briefly reported by George Bird Grinnell the victimized girl and her mother stoned the molester until they left him for dead.[34] In the other recorded Cheyenne case of this sort the offender was a mere youngster. His parents' lodge was totally destroyed by the girl's female relatives, even as the father and mother of the boy stood watching with no show of resistance. This much of the law was clear; attempted rape was a delict of the first order.

The ideal of chastity was usually held to by the women themselves. The contrast of their behavior when compared to that of other Plains Indian women was such that Grinnell wrote that the women of the Cheyenne tribe "are famous among all western tribes for their chastity," adding, "she who had yielded was disgraced forever." [35]

The men, for their part, were not quite so universally restrained. Yet a good husband of strong character and high idealism took vows upon the birth of his first son not to have intercourse with the mother for a period of seven or fourteen years. The Cheyennes believed that this concentrated all their diffuse supernatural pow-

[34] Grinnell, *Cheyenne Indians*, I, 131.
[35] *Ibid.*, I, 156.

ers on the growing child, thus aiding him to become a great man. "The people talked about it and praised the parents' self-control." [36] Failure to live up to the vow was punished supernaturally, not legally; the dedicated child sickened and died.

We now come to the legal muddle that, as we see it, grew out of the normal Cheyenne sexual repressions. The wife who was suspected of being unfaithful by her husband (theoretically, the wife who four times erred) could be "put on the prairie" or "be made a free woman." Her husband invited his military society confreres to a "feast" on the prairie. The *pièce de résistance* of this stag party was his wife, who was made the victim of a mass raping. Thereafter, if she survived, she was to be free game for any man—in effect, an outlaw. The husband and his fraternity considered this to be their legal privilege-right.

In all four of the recorded cases of this practice, however, the husband's claim was technically dubious and seems to have lacked public acceptance. Certainly among the four histories, outside intervention blocked the undertaking completely in two cases and by ruse rescued the woman in one other. In two cases the father and brothers of the woman challenged the participating soldiers to armed combat. In all cases the women of the tribe taunted and heckled them for their deed.[37] There was no tribal consensus granting to the military societies a socially recognized privilege-right to apply this fearful sanction. The claim of the husband and his cronies to the privilege-right was derived from Postulate IX. Yet the action as a sanction clearly went beyond the limits of what was necessary, and it violated the conditioning clause of Postulate VIII (*Women have personal value in their own right*). The Cheyennes failed fully to resolve this conflict.

Problems of evidence in cases of private delict were even less a matter for procedural concern among the Cheyennes than it was for the Comanches, for the fact is that few actions in private law were initiated. Adultery, we have seen, was rare. Sorcery occurred occasionally. Yet it was not particularly bothersome, and such as occurred was cured by a medicine man. There are no cases of physical threats or even quasi-legal action against alleged sorcerers.

A fair amount of petty pilfering took place in the camps, but theft was never made a legal issue. A known thief was publicly shamed with the remark, "If I had known you wanted that thing, I would have given it to you." Gift-giving was a high virtue, and good Cheyennes were not supposed to value their material possessions too highly. Hence, they did not strive to discover the less proper persons who lifted that which was not theirs.

In public law, however, the penalties were so severe that clear-cut evidence was wanted. This was arrived at in a number of ways. A man about to testify on his own behalf could take an oath on a pipe. Perjury meant death by ill luck. A man suspected of illegal buffalo hunting on his own found his tipi subject to search by the hunt police. In the case of the aborted fetus, a military society lined up all the women to inspect their breasts for signs of recent lactation. But no use of the conditional curse was made in any situation. No third degree techniques were used at any time.

One other positive feature of Cheyenne law must be mentioned. This was the right of religious asylum. The lodge of the Holy Hat Keeper was a refuge for anyone. Even an enemy horse stealer, if he could make the Holy Hat lodge, was safe and would be given a safe conduct out of the Cheyenne territory. In a neat instance of fiction, the wife of the Hat Keeper made a symbolic lodge when the tribe was on the move by throwing her arms about a girl who —without justifiable cause—was about to be "put on the prairie." She held the stick on which the Hat was hung in her hands, and the girl was safe.[38]

With the Comanche and Cheyenne pictures in mind, let us now consider the Kiowas. No attempt will be made here to describe the Kiowa system in full detail. Our purpose will be to show how it struggled to deal with a Comanche-like individualism with control mechanisms that were more like those used by the Cheyennes and yet not handled with Cheyenne skill.

The chief problem faced by all three societies was the resolution of the dilemma that rested in the incompatible values of individual aggressiveness coupled with military glorification and the ideal of internal peace and the democratic order.

In social structure the Kiowas were much more akin to their

38 *Ibid.*, pp. 206–208.

Cheyenne neighbors on the north than they were to their close Comanche allies to the south. They possessed a series of military associations which were ranked in a prestige order but not age-graded. These military associations policed much as did the Cheyenne. They had the Sun Dance. They had a group of tribal fetishes —ten special medicine bundles known as The Grandmothers. These had their legal effect, as did the Cheyenne Medicine Arrows and Holy Hat, but in a different manner. The Kiowas had a definite system of chieftainship. Unlike the other two tribes, however, they did not distinguish war chief from peace chief. This produced special difficulties, as will soon be seen, for where the Cheyennes and Comanches separated the two conflicting ideal personality types of aggressive, narcissistic warrior and generous, gentle, kind, and even-tempered peace chief into two distinct status configurations, the Kiowas rolled them into one. Their tribal political officers then frequently proved unable to resolve the conflict of the two systems of personality orientation within themselves.

A system of horizontal rating unique for the Plains was used instead to arrange for the status identification of the different personality types. This gave rise to the Kiowa system of four social classes.

The top social rank was called *onde*. The men who were *onde* were all top-flight warriors with records of great achievement. They were also "wealthy" in the sense that they had well-kept and -appointed lodges, plenty of food with which to entertain, and a constant surplus of horses to give away. Above all, they were self-assured in personal bearing, "an *ondei* must exercise restraint at all times and never exhibit his emotions." [39] They were "pre-eminently the level of the 'brave and courteous.' " [40]

These were the Kiowa men of distinction who had proven themselves by all tests. In normal circumstances their individual status was beyond challenge; like members of the Cheyenne Council of Forty-four they were ideally immune to personal affront, and they rarely were involved in litigation.

[39] Bernard Mishkin, *Rank and Warfare Among the Plains Indians* (American Ethnological Society, Monograph 3, 1940), p. 50.

[40] Jane Richardson, *Law and Status Among the Kiowa Indians* (American Ethnological Society, Monograph 1, 1940), p. 15.

Beneath the *onde* were the *ondegupa*. They were extremely rival-rous and in their outfacing activities generated trouble case after trouble case. Kiowa law was mostly concerned with their obstrep-erous activities. In this rank were found able artisans, medicine men, hunters, and horse owners. Most of them were also warriors, but all of them were lacking in one thing: their war records were not out-standing.

Yet lower down were the *kɔɔn,* or the common men. They were honest and decent, but poor and undistinguished. They rarely raised legal difficulties inasmuch as they were not in a position to chal-lenge the status ranking of others.

Down in the ruck were the *dapom:* the dregs of Kiowa society. They were shiftless and lazy, without ambition and with little self-respect. They filched and stole within the camp. Virtually disowned by their own relatives, they made out as parasitic hangers-on to out-standing men of high rank. They were utterly *déclassé* and in effect without the law. They were so far beneath contempt and attention that their thefts went unpunished. Nor were they driven from the group; they were simply suffered and scorned—the botched jobs of Kiowa youth, sufficient in number to form a recognized "class."

The special tribal functionaries among the Kiowa were the *topa-doki* or headmen of the bands, the *toyopki* or war party leaders, the Keepers of the Ten Medicine Bundles, and the *Taime* (Sun Dance fetish) Keeper. Virtually all headmen were of *onde* rank, as were most of the Ten Medicine Bundle owners. The *Taime* Keeper was the nominal grand chief of the tribe, and although all impor-tant decisions of policy were announced as his, they were actually made by the *topadoki*.[41]

The role of the military fraternities in Kiowa government and law was essentially that of the Cheyenne soldier societies. They po-liced the Sun Dance camp and the communal hunt, meting out punishment when deemed necessary. They intervened in certain private disputes to prevent outbreaks of fighting. We do not find them, however, generating new law in the Cheyenne manner.

The unique aspect of Kiowa law upon which we shall concen-trate our attention is the use of the ceremonial pipes that went with the Ten Medicine Bundles.

[41] Richardson, p. 9.

Kiowa violence in interpersonal relations was ostensibly much more threatening than was that of the Comanches and certainly a good deal more so than was the Cheyennes'. A wronged Kiowa *ondegupa* was a terrible man to behold. He raged and gestured and made loud noises about "going to get my gun" and what he was going to do to that fellow when he laid eyes on him. Crowds gathered, the women crying, "Somebody stop him." In nine cases reported by Richardson, in the words of the informant "people held (the quarrelers)." In all cases where violence seemed to threaten, a Ten Medicine Bundle Keeper appeared on the scene to intervene with his sacred pipe. He asked the aggrieved demonstrator not to take violent vengeance on the aggressor but to promise to accept a peaceful settlement with compensation. To refuse the request of a Ten Medicine Keeper with his pipe was very bad form and supernaturally dangerous. In most cases the request was heeded. Genuinely adamant men might refuse three times, but when the fourth pipe-bearer came they gave in, for four refusals meant ultimate death from supernatural action. The act was tantamount to suicide.

The Kiowa procedure was generally similar to Cheyenne patterns in form yet utterly different in flavor. The personally aggrieved Cheyenne usually made no scene nor took any action. A chief came bearing his personal pipe, but he was not called by excited bystanders to come posthaste, lest there be a killing. He was sent in a day or two by the wrongdoer. In only one reported instance was word put out that the wronged man wanted no chief to come. The whole business was calm and quiet and effective.

Richardson in her report emphasizes that the Kiowas were extremely anxious for internal peace. "Popular sentiment for peace was probably the keystone which permitted the successful functioning of all legal institutions, and in itself was responsible ultimately for more adjustments than the formal mechanisms." To this she adds the opinion that "without this diffuse pressure and self-discipline, there might have been frequent feuds in this braggadocian society." [42]

The Kiowa apparent public concern lest a dispute lead to violence really led to what we see as bogus vociferousness rather than as a genuine intent to do violence in retaliation for a wrong. It should

---

[42] *Ibid.*, pp. 18–19.

be remembered that most Kiowa delicts occurred among the up-and-coming *ondegupa* and were almost always status challenges. The challenged victim naturally reacted emotionally and with a display of counteraggressiveness. But all the time he knew that by-standers, or the soldiers, or a Ten Medicine Keeper would intervene to stop him. He had only to make a loud noise and prolong it long enough to let someone arrive to take charge of the affair. Then he could "reluctantly" subside and accept the pipe without loss of status. Indeed, he would be thanked by the officials for not causing real trouble. In other words, the formal religious–legal mechanisms made it possible to disturb the peace without intent actually to break it.

The people, in all probability, were genuinely anxious, however, because this Kiowa pattern was inherently defective as a legal mechanism. Acting emotional can engender real emotions; warriors could and did slide over from play acting to the real thing. Men did refuse the pipe and did kill, unless the original offender so debased himself as to ruin his reputation for life. One other factor should be mentioned. Attainment of *onde* status was extraordinarily difficult. By estimate of modern Kiowas the *onde* class embraced no more than 10 per cent of the men in the tribe at any one time; yet 40 or 50 per cent were *ondegupa*. This meant that most of them could never rise to the position where they were above rivalry. The majority of them were bound to be frustrated in their hopes in a society in which success was constantly stressed and so neatly institutionalized. They could very easily lose control of themselves and thrash out wildly. If a man murdered, he might be killed in return, but the acceptance of the pipe on the other side, plus compensation offered by his kinsman could spare his life. Then in a vague reflection of the strong Cheyenne belief he became *taido,* weak and unsuccessful in all ventures, so that he sank to the level of the *ƙɔɔn,* and sooner or later suffered a premature death. But his bad luck was purely personal and did not pollute the tribal fetishes or extend to the tribe as a whole.

Yet in the final pinch it was the military societies who brought real legal powers to bear on the man who was out of control. They were the true linchpin of the Kiowa law system. One extraordinary trouble case cited *in extenso* will sum it all up.

The trouble maker was Guibɔde, himself a Ten Medicine Bundle Keeper, a good enough warrior but not an *onde*. He was a generally mean man and a bully. He had shortly before the great trouble led a war party on which his conduct as leader was offensive and over-officious. He had been publicly cut down to size by Saondeton, who although head of Guibɔde's own military fraternity (the *Tonkongya* society, the third highest ranking society), was a member of this war party in the capacity of cook, for he had joined it with the express intention of teaching Guibɔde a lesson. Guibɔde had his wife along, and with the purpose of testing him, Saondeton, after the group was several days out on the war trail, took his leader's wife away for two days. He then brought her back, courteously thanking her husband for the pleasant time he had had. The other men held their breaths, expecting a terrible explosion at this mortal insult. Nothing happened right away, and then white soldiers appeared. The Kiowas prepared for battle. Guibɔde's wife was holding his spear as he prepared for battle. Saondeton asked for it. With the leader's spear in hand he rushed fearlessly into the fray, speared several whites and returned unhurt. Then he returned the spear politely to Guibɔde.

Guibɔde said, "Saondeton, if you had not performed that deed, I would have killed you."

Saondeton in turn replied, "Guibɔde, if you had laid a finger on your wife, I would have killed you."

A little later the whole tribe came together for the Rice or Maggot Creek Sun Dance of 1873. Guibɔde belonged to the *Kiep* group, which was supposed to camp on the south side of the camp circle. He didn't like the location, so he moved over to where the *Koigu* group was.

The *Daimbega* military society was in charge of policing the camp. They told him to move back to where he belonged. He rejoined that he would camp where he pleased. The soldiers then carried his tipi and belongings back to their proper place. The chief of the *Daimbega* (probably White Bear) went up to him with his gun and told him to calm down and go back to where he belonged. If he did, there would be no trouble and nothing further said; at the same time he warned him that if he wanted trouble, he would get it.

Guibɔde then raised his bow as if to shoot. The chief acted quickly and knocked him cold with a blow on the head. When Guibɔde came to, he told him to move or he would give him some more. Guibɔde just sat there and glared defiance, whereupon the chief called on all the society members to hit him over the head with whatever they had. When they were through, Guibɔde got up without a word and went back to the *Kiep* territory.

A year later he caught his wife *in flagrante delicto* with Pɔkongiai, son of a wealthy man. The adulterer got away, but the enraged Guibɔde beat his wife unmercifully. Her father interfered, and the wife escaped out the back of the tipi.

Guibɔde went out in the camp crying threats of death against the life of Pɔkongiai. Immediately, the father of the latter appeared with four horses and accompanied by *three* Ten Medicine Bundle Keepers. Guibɔde threw the father out of his tipi and refused to listen to the Ten Medicine Keepers. When a fourth pipe-bearer came, he even refused the request of his sister's son that he smoke the pipe.

Soon afterward the Sun Dance camp was set up. The *Taime* Keeper warned the soldiers to prevent Guibɔde from carrying out his threats to kill Pɔkongiai. He heard of it and said they better not try to stop him. Then he went and killed a number of horses from the herd of the adulterer's father. After this he sat down in front of his tipi with his rifle across his knees, announcing, "Now that I have disposed of this, anyone who has business with me can come and talk with me here."

Meanwhile Pɔkongiai was hiding out and could not attend his military fraternity meetings. "Even the Ten Medicine tipis were no sanctuary for him now that the angry Guibɔde had refused four pipes."

Finally, Big Bow (head of the *Adltoyui* society) and White Bear announced, "We are tired of having our member imposed upon." They proposed to take action. All the societies were visited, and all agreed. Pɔkongiai's father gave two horses for the delegation to take to Guibɔde. Guibɔde was still sullen and recalcitrant, but after White Bear sang a *Daimbega* war song and threatened to spear him, he said he submitted but wanted to do what he would with his wife.

The soldiers left with a warning. White Bear reported to the other societies that he felt Guibɔde had not submitted completely. He said the test would come when the time was at hand for the camp to break up.

The time came and the trouble-maker announced that he was not going to move. The people moved out, leaving the soldiers behind. White Bear came forward to kill him, but just as he raised his spear, Saondeton, chief of Guibɔde's own society, interceded with the request that he be permitted to make the resister move. Guibɔde sat. Then the *Tonkongya* tore down his tipi, packed it up, saddled Guibɔde's horse, put him on it and drove him and his pack horses after the moving camp as fast as they could go. When they got to the next camping place, they told him where to camp and made him unpack.

He died a couple of years later, "because he had refused the pipe." [43]

So ran the law in this group of Plains tribes. Comanche law expressed individualism checked at critical points by social use of other individuals. Cheyenne law expressed a supreme sense of social well-being kept flexible by a continuous concern for individualism. The Kiowas never had a clear idea of which they preferred and muddled along trying to serve both ends.

When cultural goals are not clear-cut, it is not likely that social action will be either.

[43] This account is condensed and paraphrased in part from cases 55 and 2 in Richardson, pp. 91–92, 22–27.

8

The Trobriand Islanders: Primitive Law as Seen by Bronislaw Malinowski

In the science of man the dark-skinned Melanesians of the Trobriand Islands, lying off the northeast coast of New Guinea, and Bronislaw Malinowski are inseparable. He gave them to the world through his ethnological reports on their way of life. More than that, he raised them to a position of preëminence in the thought and theoretical literature of anthropology and social science at large. This was accomplished because Malinowski was no mere ethnographer, no dry-bones reporter. He was one of our most resourceful developers of method and theory. In the field he constantly asked "Why?" He, more than any other anthropologist, was responsible for formulating and establishing "the most fundamental anthropological postulate that every culture is an organized whole, in which even apparently strange or disparate elements can be made comprehensible in relation to the whole." [1] He saw and treated all phases of culture as multidimensional with all facets impinging on many others. Culture, like man, he treated in dynamic terms and both he saw always "in the round." As he followed the ramifying threads of an institution, he improvised new theory to guide his explorations. He did this for tribal economics, magic and religion, language, mythology, ritual, sex, kinship—and law. Each of these was the subject of at least one book, and each was treated in one or more of his many articles. [2]

[1] J. H. Weakland, "Method in Cultural Anthropology," *Philosophy of Science*, 18:58 (1951).
[2] For a complete bibliography of Malinowski's contributions see the obituary by G. P. Murdock, *American Anthropologist*, 45:445–451 (1943).

His concept of law as he saw it from the vantage point of the Trobriand Islands was developed in a widely spaced series of writings produced over a period of a decade and a half. His treatment of primitive law began with a lecture delivered before the Royal Institution of Great Britain in February, 1923, and published in the *Proceedings of the Royal Institution of Great Britain* [3] in 1925 under the title, "The Forces of Law and Order in a Primitive Community." It was only the legal forces of *a* primitive community—the Trobriand Islands—with which his thinking was at first ostensibly concerned. Nevertheless, it set his fertile mind to work on the wider implications of his data. The results were two supplementary articles on "Primitive Law and Order," published in *Nature* in 1925 and 1926. The three contributions were then immediately pulled together in a small book of great impact. It appeared in 1926 with the title, *Crime and Custom in Savage Society*. In this, Malinowski summarily described what he saw as the legal life of the Trobriand Islanders, and he also vigorously advanced his own unique conception of law in relation to custom. He set the foundations of a more embracing theory to be formulated later in the "Introduction" to Hogbin's *Law and Order in Polynesia* (1934) and in his ultimate, posthumously published restatement in 1942.[4]

In *Crime and Custom in Savage Society* Malinowski insisted that law exists in primitive societies as distinct from mere custom. Custom is *not* king. He vigorously asserted that primitive man is not the supine slave of custom; on the contrary he is quite as prone to misbehave as anyone else; he does not automatically or spontaneously follow the rules of his society. He has to be controlled. He is not, as Hartland would have it, "bound in the chains of immemorial tradition"—chains which "are accepted by him as a matter of course"—chains from which "he never seeks to break forth." [5] In opposition to this point of view, Malinowski asked, "Is it not contrary to human nature to accept any constraint as a matter of course, and does man, whether civilized or savage, ever carry out unpleasant, burdensome, cruel regulations and taboos without being

[3] Vol. 24, pp. 529–547.
[4] Bronislaw Malinowski, "A New Instrument for the Study of Law—Especially Primitive," *Lawyers Guild Review*, 2:1–12 (1942), republished on Malinowski's death in *The Yale Law Journal*, 51:1237–1254 (1942).
[5] Hartland, *Primitive Law*, p. 138.

compelled to? And compelled by some force or motive which he cannot resist?" [6]

In this rhetoric is implied a theory of human nature which answers, "No!" The problem then is to find out the nature of the irresistible and compelling forces. The procedure shall be to look for law and legal forces, "to discover and analyse all the rules conceived and acted upon as binding obligations, to find out the nature of the binding forces, and to classify the rules according to the manner in which they are made valid." Then, "we shall be enabled to arrive at a satisfactory classification of the norms and rules of a primitive community, at a clear distinction of primitive law from other forms of custom, and at a new, dynamic conception of the social organization of savages." [7]

The criteria of distinction of legal norms will not be in terms of "central authority, codes, courts and constables" but in terms of some more general attributes. For Malinowski wisely and vigorously reminded us that many primitives achieve compulsion without the aid of such institutions or worthies. [8]

The quest shall be for the less obvious compulsive forces. Malinowski set out in a canoe to find them, for the Trobrianders are the argonauts of the western Pacific. A lot can be learned about such doughty seafarers from the thwart of a canoe. The Trobriand lagoon is revealed as alive with canoes—an apparent anarchy of flashing movement. But the discerning eye and patient ear of the ethnologist learn in the course of time that the apparent disorder is ruled by a meticulous and methodical order. Each canoe is "owned" by one man, perhaps a village leader. But his fellow crewmen, who are all his kinsmen, have their places as demand-rights on the owner. Each and all must fulfill his duties to the others so that the canoe can be operated to full efficiency whenever the occasion demands. Each, if it is fishing they are engaged in, receives his fair share of the catch. Each is bound to the others in a system of mutual obligation. Each crew, in turn, has to come out when a communal fishing venture is under way. Each has its part to play in the total operation.

---

[6] Malinowski, *Crime and Custom in Savage Society*, p. 10.
[7] *Ibid.*, pp. 15–16.
[8] *Ibid.*, p. 14.

The whole is regulated by the "sum of duties, privileges and mutualities which bind the joint owners to the object and to each other." [9] Here, we are told, we are met by law, order, definite privileges and a well-developed system of obligations. [10]

The reader may be surprised to learn that he has met law on his placid trip on the lagoon; he may think he has not perceived it. However, he is assured that law in Malinowski's terms is there.

Next, in writing *Crime and Custom* Malinowski puts us ashore to find a bevy of inland dwellers waiting to receive a share of fish which they hurry off to their homes. Later they bring back vegetables in exchange. The exchange is economic and ritualized, "but there is also the legal side, a system of mutual obligations which forces the fisherman to repay whenever he has received a gift from his inland partner [it is not an open market barter but a man-to-man exchange partnership], and vice versa." [11] The foodstuffs are needed not only for eating but for important periodic public displays. Each individual and each community is economically and socially dependent upon others. They are all bound together in reciprocity. This makes it legal in Malinowski's view, for any undue chiselling by the one side will lead the other to withhold its services.

Malinowski identified these activities as rules of conduct which are "unquestionably rules of binding law" that stand out from mere rules of custom. [12] Law, it appears at this stage of the discussion in *Crime and Custom,* is that which a man has to do because another man will refuse to do something for him if he does not do what he is supposed to do in the first place. The key is in the vital reciprocity which runs throughout the various levels of Trobriand society. In sum, "the claims of chief over commoners, husband over wife, parent over child, and vice versa, are not exercised arbitrarily and one-sidedly, but according to definite rules, and arranged into well-balanced chains of reciprocal services." [13]

Thus, with reciprocity as the *leitmotif* Malinowski advanced "an anthropological definition of law." [14] The concept was phrased in

[9] *Ibid.*, pp. 20–21.
[10] *Ibid.*
[11] *Ibid.*, p. 22.
[12] *Ibid.*, p. 30–31.
[13] *Ibid.*, p. 46.
[14] *Ibid.*, title to chap. xi of *Crime and Custom in Savage Society.*

these terms, " 'Civil law,' the positive law governing all the phases of tribal life, consists then of a body of binding obligations, regarded as a right by one party and acknowledged as a duty by the other, kept in force by a specific mechanism of reciprocity and publicity inherent in the structure of their society." [15]

It is significant that Malinowski's anthropological definition of law was expressed only in terms of what he called "civil law," or positive law, and was without reference to use of the sanctions of legitimatized physical coercion. At this point in his book the reader is definitely given to believe that law operates without the aid of physical force, although it does bind behavior. Throughout this and all his subsequent writings on law Malinowski exhibited a definite distaste for forces of social coercion and he exerted himself to the utmost to minimize—even banish—them as significant operative elements in the regulation of human relations. Whether it was because in his own person he was irked by the institutional restraints of the civilizations in which he lived, or whether through lofty idealism his intellect was fixed on the Utopia in which men would conform without the need of gross physical punishment, we may never know. At any rate, the law he saw and reiterated was the law of reciprocity in which men bowed politely to each other in the rendering of mutual services and turned their backs on a culprit when he sneakingly reduced the level of mutuality below par.

Now this, it may be contended, is not the most meaningful, certainly not the most useful, concept of law. And when Malinowski implicitly recognized this by qualifying it merely as "civil law" he did not help to clarify the situation. As Seagle trenchantly notes, he then became guilty of "the pathetic fallacy of primitive jurisprudence. He has transferred to primitive law the legal emotions of his own culture. He has simply sought in primitive society those institutions which *in the modern world have come to be the subject matter of legal obligation.* He has selected the *customs* relating to marriage, inheritance and property, and pronounced these to be *primitive law.*" [16] Civil law is no more positive than criminal, or public, law. It merely happens that in Anglo-American and Con-

[15] *Ibid.,* p. 58.
[16] William Seagle, "Primitive Law and Professor Malinowski," *American Anthropologist,* 39:283 (1937).

tinental law systems it is preponderantly concerned with property and economic relations and less with matters of personal violence, while the reverse tends to be true of the criminal law. But the true basis of the distinction between the two categories of law is not in these terms, as we have already seen.[17]

Malinowski only obfuscated matters in an uncritical retreat to a false concept of civil law. He went further in attempting to escape from the obvious dilemma into which his concept of law led him. He knew full well that there is a large area of social activity which is generally recognized as law and which is not allowed for in the approach to law that is climaxed midway in *Crime and Custom* with his "anthropological definition." Hence, the last half of the book (Part II) is a patchwork of instances of disorders of one kind or another that ruffle the idyllic reciprocal tranquillity of the islands. These are labeled, "Primitive Crime and Its Punishment."

What constitutes a crime Malinowski never made clear, and the critical reader can only guess what he had in mind. The best one can say is that apparently, if an act produced disorder of any sort, he looked upon it as a criminal act. But concern with problems of social disorder was deprecated offhand as a manifestation of the immature development of anthropology in his time. Although he granted that progress had been achieved in 1926, "even then there remains something of the old 'shocker' interest in the over-emphasis of criminal justice, in the attention devoted to the breaches of the law and their punishment. Law in modern Anthropology is still almost exclusively studied in its singular and sensational manipulations, in cases of blood-curdling crime followed by tribal vendetta, in accounts of criminal sorcery with retaliation, of incest, adultery, breach of taboo or murder. In all this, besides the dramatic piquancy of the incidents, the anthropologist can, or thinks he can, trace certain unexpected, exotic, astonishing features of primitive law."[18]

Of whom was he writing? Of Sir Henry Maine, Hobhouse, Steinmetz, Post, Kohler, Lowie, Barton? More soberly motivated scientists would be hard to find. Malinowski wished emphatically to contrast his own handling of the subject with all that had gone

17 Page 28, above.
18 Malinowski, *Crime and Custom in Savage Society*, pp. 72–73.

before; ergo, he set an extreme (and fictitious) picture of his predecessors' and contemporaries' work to lend virtue to his own.[19]

Yet perforce he, too, was forced to take cognizance of incest, murder, and sorcery. Trobrianders are not flawless paragons of reciprocal perfection. They copulate with forbidden women, they steal crops, they spear each other, and they practice black magic; so that a description of the "criminal and dramatic issues" was advanced as being necessary—but promised grudgingly and with the condition that it should not be unduly emphasized.[20]

What then do we learn about crime in *Crime and Custom?*

We are introduced to a true dramatic shocker at the outset—the now famous case of Kima'i, the incestuous youth who committed suicide in the grand manner.

Kima'i had been consorting with his mother's sister's daughter—in the matrilineal society of the Trobriands, his own clan sister. Under the rules of strict clan exogamy such behavior is forbidden incest. The fact was both known and gossiped about, but no explicit action had been taken in the community until a jilted lover with a case of sour grapes, nursing a jealous grievance against the illegitimately successful Kima'i, threatened him with sorcery. Kima'i scoffed at it and did not become ill as he ought.

Then one evening, in the hearing of the whole community, his antagonist accused Kima'i of incest and insulted him with "certain expressions intolerable to a native." [21]

The next morning Kima'i dressed up in his best, climbed a tall coconut palm and delivered his swan song. He explained to all why he was about to kill himself. He placed the onus for his plight not on himself but on the one who had exposed him. He then ended his oration with the customary wailing, and leaped sixty feet to his death.

His kinsmen thereupon set upon the defender of public decency, seriously wounding him in a general brawl that was repeated at the funeral the next day.[22]

---

19 This was not an uncommon dialectic device in Malinowski's works.
20 Malinowski, *Crime and Custom in Savage Society,* p. 74.
21 Their nature is unfortunately not further indicated.
22 Malinowski, *Crime and Custom in Savage Society,* pp. 77–78.

What did Malinowski do with this case? At first, he confessed, his interest was so concentrated on recording the ceremonies of mourning and burial that he neglected to investigate the factors behind the event. Only "much later" did he piece them together.[23] Then he found himself "in the presence of a pronounced crime: the breach of totemic clan exogamy."

The fact that the public had overtly ignored the incestuous activities of Kima'i until he was jealously denounced opened up a series of highly significant revelations about social morality.

It is a basic postulate among the Trobriand Islanders, as it is among every other known society of men, that sex relations among members of a sociologically defined kinship group (incest) is evil. It is a universally forbidden activity, except for a few persons (usually divine royalty) in a limited number of societies. In support of the basic values defined by the anti-incest postulates, the Trobrianders show horror at the very idea of violating the tabu, and they unctuously recite the loathsome sores and diseases that follow in its train. Even death, they say, may be the consequence of incest. The ancestral spirits of the clan are angered.

But neither the living clan members nor the public at large ordinarily move a finger to punish the transgressors. This responsibility is left to the supernaturals. In what sense then is clan incest a *pronounced crime?* Is it not, rather, a sin?

Realistically, the incest prohibition, at least in its application to clan brothers and sisters, is actually no more than a pretend rule. Here Malinowski brilliantly exposed the gap that often exists between the ideal norms of social morality and the facts of going behavior. More than that, he showed that indulging in incest is one of the chief sports of the Trobriand Islanders. "From the point of view of the native libertine, *suvasova* (the breach of exogamy) is indeed a specially interesting and spicy form of erotic experience. Most of my informants would not only admit but actually did boast about having committed this offense or that of adultery (*kaylasi*); and I have many concrete, well-attested cases on record." [24]

---

[23] Actually, three years later, on his last field trip to the Trobriahds. B. Malinowski, *The Sexual Life of Savages in North-Western Melanesia* (London, 1929), p. 567.

[24] Malinowski, *Crime and Custom in Savage Society*, p. 84. Unfortunately, few of these cases were published.

Even more revealing is the fact that Trobriand rakes do not merely disregard the dogma of the supernatural consequences of sexual sin. Their behavior is in fact no denial of the dogma at all. On the contrary, they use magical prophylactics for the prevention of disease in the form of incantations and spells provided in the culture and thus protect themselves against the supernatural consequences of their misbehavior. Only a stupid Trobriander or an absolute heretic would dally in incest without first indulging in preventive magic.

Here, then, is a beautiful example of a customary way of circumventing custom: an instance of conflicting behavior, inconsistency, and lack of integration.

If we theorize, we can explain the basic tabu as existing to protect the solidarity and security of the kinship group from the disrupting influences of sexual jealousy.[25] This in turn enhances the solidarity of the society at large, which rests primarily on the foundation of the kin group. The interest to be protected is a *group* interest. The sex desire, on the other hand, springs from powerful *individual* drives and interests. The individual Trobriander when speaking in a public situation responds in terms of the public interest: incest is horrible. In intimate confidence he may reveal the secret derelictions born of his own philandering urges.

Even when incest becomes known, the Trobrianders retain the atomistic point of view. They gossip and tongue-wag, but barring public denouncement, no more. "Public opinion is lenient, though decidedly hypocritical." [26] On the contrary, there is no public opinion at this stage. The matter is studiously kept from becoming a public affair even though it may be known to many persons. In Malinowski's own terms, it is kept *sub rosa*. The conflict between tribal "law" and inconsistent individual behavior is customarily prevented from coming to overt attention.

When the issue *is* publicly forced into the open, the social handling of it becomes quite a different matter. The rule of law—if there be one in fact—will in most instances prevail. Indeed, we put it as a proposition that in the event of any conflict between the legal

[25] See Bronislaw Malinowski, "Culture," *Encyclopaedia of the Social Sciences,* IV (1931), p. 630.
[26] Malinowski, *Crime and Custom in Savage Society,* p. 80.

and any other well-established norm, you will know the legal by the fact that if appealed to, it is recognized as proper to prevail, and usually does in fact prevail.

This is exactly what happened in the case of Kima'i. Trobriand incest is in dogma a sin supernaturally punished. But the Trobrianders, who are ingenious magicians, learn how to nullify the supernatural sanctions, which then become impotent in their effect. Enough Trobrianders seem to enjoy plucking the forbidden fruits so that they all tacitly agree to overlook individual derelictions. But when a personally motivated citizen becomes a public denouncer, the law prevails and the death sentence is self-imposed. No other alternative exists, if we are to believe Malinowski's report. (He gives only one case, and Kima'i played it to get revenge: his suicide involved at least a double motive.) The reaction was swift and automatic. In this sense, incest publicly exposed becomes a capital crime sanctioned by self-imposed death. Everyman his own executioner.

Yet the role of the pillar of society is not a happy one. He receives no universal acclaim for his moral rectitude. His social reward is a severe beating and wounding. If he had kept his mouth shut, it would not have been necessary for the criminal to execute himself. The kinsmen of the dead Kima'i clearly felt that his accuser had gone too far in tripping the delicately poised balance to force the legal prescriptions of the Trobriand code into action. Hence, their venting of anger against him.

It is a hard and disillusioning lesson for an idealist to learn, who believes that a people mean what they say when they explicitly expound their virtues. Well may he be confounded to find them turning on him in anger or away from him in disgust when he exposes the breaker of those rules. Consider the reception of the pupil who tells Teacher that half the class has been cheating.

Malinowski was at this point one of the early Legal Realists in his awareness that law has a fullness wider in range than that given in its formal statement.

We next find Malinowski considering "Sorcery and Suicide as Legal Influences." Magic pervades most aspects of Trobriand life in a positive way. It is an integral and, from the native point of view, a necessary adjunct to all the techniques of gardening, manufacture, seafaring, and trade. It is highly socialized and serves constructive ends. Certain magicians such as the *towosi,* or village garden magician, who holds a hereditary office of the utmost importance, are outright public officials working for the general benefit of all. Nonetheless, like any instrument of power its use may be turned to destructive and antisocial ends.

There are men who are downright sorcerers. These men use their dark powers to work injury on others. "They exercise their power on their own behalf, and also professionally for a fee." [27] They are said to be generally men of outstanding personality and intelligence, men who are held in great awe because "every" serious illness and death is loosely said to be the result of their craftsmanship. They use their powers to achieve wealth and influence. But there are limits to their self-enriching activities, for flagrant use of the power makes a sorcerer a marked man who will be put away by another sorcerer at the behest of a chief. Excessive use of sorcery is a public crime. This much we learn from the study of *Crime and Custom,* but no more in detail, for Malinowski is much more concerned with showing how sorcery works to support the social system than with analyzing its disruptive nature.

Sorcerers are at the beck and call of chiefs and men of rank and wealth who have a number of special privileges denied to lesser persons. Obeisance is done them; they have larger and more elaborate houses; they possess a number of wives; they have more yams. Any man who overreaches his lower rank by failure to do proper obeisance, by overdecorating his house, by philandering with chiefs' wives, by getting too rich, may be bewitched at the chief's bidding, albeit for a royal fee. The sorcerer is a kind of royal executioner for *lèse majesté* and for status-breaking, which has politically dangerous implications. "In such cases also the victim, on learning that a sorcerer is at work against him, may quail and make amends or come to an equitable arrangement. Thus ordinarily, black magic acts as a genuine legal force, for it is used in carrying out the rules of tribal law, it prevents the use of violence and restores equilibrium." [28] The last part of this statement is hardly true: sorcery is indirect violence; it causes death. Furthermore, although no one would discern it in this book, it leads to a good deal

---

[27] Malinowski, *Crime and Custom in Savage Society,* p. 85.   [28] *Ibid.,* p. 86.

of physical violence as well. For Malinowski's other works make it clear that few Trobrianders are willing to be made victims of sorcery without striking back at the sorcerer.

Malinowski is so bent on scolding the government official, planter, and missionary for the "pernicious interference" with which they pursue the sorcerer that he overenthusiastically plays up the supposed culture-preserving aspect of black magic. As a force which maintains the *status quo* in favor of the vested interests of the powerful, wealthy and influential, he boldly asserts that in the long run it remains a support of law and order. In a sense this is, of course, true. But since he indicates that many a man is put on the spot for overreaching, and darkly states that he could mention a number of concrete instances of cases of actual oppression and crass injustice,[29] it appears that there are strong drives in Trobriand social life toward nonacceptance of the sacrosanct privileges of the chief. In the Trobriand Islands we have a hint of an unholy alliance between shaman and chief to nurture the seeds of tyranny. Sorcery serves to provide "really the main source of the wholesome fear of punishment and retribution indispensable in any orderly society."[30] Something more than reciprocity is necessary to the maintenance of social order!

What other "crimes" can a Trobriander commit? He may, in cahoots with his father, flout "the legal system of Mother-right." Under the formal organization of Trobriand society with its matrilineal clan system a boy and his father belong to separate clans. By sociological fiction they are not related. According to the Trobriand dogma of spiritual reincarnation of deceased clan ancestors (*baloma*) in the wombs of living mothers and its concomitant shibboleth of ignorance of the physiology of paternity, the father contributes nothing to the conception of his sons and daughters. He is merely a good companion in the household: genuine affection marks the usual father–son relation, which is devoid of customary authoritarianism.

Inheritance of position, privileges, magic, and responsibility devolves from the mother's brother—the maternal uncle. In prepara-

---

[29] *Ibid.*, pp. 92–93. He does not, however, describe, to say nothing of analyze them.

[30] *Ibid.*

tion for reception of this avuncular devolution a boy should leave his father's house sometime before marriage to sojourn with his uncle for the rest of his days. This is the normal and legitimate course of events. Between the young man and his uncle, however, exists a certain tension born of rivalry in succession, while between the boy and his father there are reputedly few tensions. The father "naturally" prefers his son, but "legally" must endow and foster his nephew.[31]

"Thus the powerful legal system of Mother-right is associated with a rather weak sentiment, while Father-love, much less important in law, is backed by a strong personal feeling." [32]

The result is that some fathers, especially if they are men of high rank who dare to flout the "law," keep their sons at home and bestow favors on them that by rights belong to their sisters' sons. Between sons and their maternal cousins bad feeling frequently exists.

In one of the rare cases presented in some detail by Malinowski, Namwana Guya'u, son of the paramount chief of Omarakana, was permitted by his father to stay at home and enjoy a position of influence in the village even though he was a grown man. Mitakata, the chief's nephew and legitimate heir, had a smoldering hatred for him, born of resentment of usurpation by Namwana Guya'u of rights that should have devolved only on him. At length Namwana Guya'u went beyond all bounds. He lodged charges with the Resident Magistrate alleging that Mitakata was guilty of adultery with his, Namwana Guya'u's, wife.[33] In the course of the hearing they brawled; Mitakata was wounded and on top of it received a month's sentence in jail. When the news reached Omarakana, the outraged kinsmen of Mitakata read their chief's errant nephew out of the village in a formal expulsion called *yoba*.

"These words, very rarely uttered in dead earnest, have a binding force and almost ritual power, when pronounced by the citizens of a place against a resident outsider. A man who would try to brave the dreadful insult involved in them and remain in spite of

[31] "Naturally" and "legally" are Malinowski's terms in this context.
[32] *Ibid.*, p. 101.
[33] The cause of the complaint does not appear in *Crime and Custom* but is given in *Sexual Life of Savages*, p. 12, where the account of the entire case is more detailed than that presented in *Crime and Custom*.

them, would be dishonoured forever. In fact, anything but immediate compliance with a ritual request is unthinkable for a Trobriand Islander." [34]

If this be all there is to it, and apparently there is nothing more, then the matrilineal principle of inheritance and avunculocal residence is no system of law at all, but a strong rule of custom, albeit an important one.

So much has Malinowski dwelt on reciprocity and the conflict of the matrilineal principle with the paternal tendency that he has neither the interest nor space to give more than the briefest of nods to what he acknowledges as the remainder of Trobriand law. Feud, of tremendous potential importance in any socio-legal system, is disposed of in two short paragraphs. We learn it is obligatory in the killing of a man of high rank and is called *lugawa*. Feuds are ended with the payment of *lula,* composition for every one killed or wounded. Feuds may be also avoided by paying *lula* immediately when there has been a killing. This is all we learn.

One cryptic line notes the application of the death penalty for adultery exposed *in flagrante delicto* and for insults to persons of high rank. Nothing more. Malinowski high-mindedly dissociated himself from the "shocker" school of scholars who are concerned with "cases of blood-curdling crime, followed by vendetta," with "accounts of criminal sorcery with retaliation, of incest, breach of taboo, or murder." The picture of the law system of the Trobriand Islands that we have thus had set before us is queerly confused and distorted.

Yet Malinowski, who constantly extolled the virtues of "The Functionalist Method," claimed for that method a real virtue of which we can take advantage for a new look at Trobriand law, namely, "that the reader is enabled to disagree with the author's conclusions, and to disagree on the basis of the detailed information presented by the author himself." Facts are presented with "such lucidity, precision and detachment from his generalizations that a complete theoretical reinterpretation of his material is perfectly

[34] Malinowski, *Crime and Custom in Savage Society,* p. 104; also *Sexual Life of Savages,* p. 14.

possible." [35] While this is not true of Malinowski's *Crime and Custom in Savage Society*, it is true of his *Argonauts of the Western Pacific*, of *Coral Gardens and Their Magic*, and of *The Sexual Life of Savages in North-Western Melanesia*. None of these books is about law, but each is rich in detail, and scattered in their many pages is enough law-stuff to make possible a restatement of the law of the Trobriand Islanders.

The social system of the Trobriand Islands rests on a basic postulate of matrilineality.

Postulate I. Reproduction results from entry into the body of a woman by the spirit (*baloma*) of a dead ancestor.

Corollary 1. The father is not genetically related to the child.

Corollary 2. A person belongs to the lineage of his mother only.

Postulate II. There must be an adult male in every household.

Corollary 1. Every family must have a father.

Corollary 1′. A woman must marry before she may have children.

Postulate III. A father feels great affection for his sons.

Postulate IV. Sex rights in marriage are mutually exclusive.

Postulate V. Incest is evil and offensive to the ancestral spirits.

Postulate VI. Men and women are of equal social value.

Postulate VII. Political, economic and religious capabilities are largely limited to men, although they operate and are transmitted through the female line.

Corollary 1. A man must provide for his sister's family.

Corollary 2. Property and rank are inherited from the mother's brother.

Postulate VIII. "Humanity" is divided into four clans.

Postulate IX. Priority in claims to land and rank is determined by the order of emergence from holes in the ground by the subclan ancestors.

Postulate X. High rank entails privileges not to be enjoyed by commoners.

Postulate XI. Magic is necessary to the success of all major activities.

Corollary 1. Garden magic is necessary to the production of crops.

[35] B. Malinowski, Introduction to R. F. Fortune's *Sorcerers of Dobu* (New York, 1932), pp. xxvi–xxvii.

Postulate XII. All serious diseases are the work of sorcerers or a punishment for certain sins.

Postulate XIII. Work and effort are good for their own sakes, but they are also means to ends.

Corollary 1. Personal prestige is derived from the number of gardens a man can work well.

Corollary 2. Plenty of food and wealth, combined with a careless generosity, are praiseworthy.

Before embarking on a reëxamination of the law of the Trobrianders, a brief summary of the social organization of this interesting people is in order.

The Trobriand Islanders live in permanent villages arranged in a circular pattern. The village belongs to a matrilineal subclan. Surrounding the village are the lands belonging to the subclan. The incest prohibition requires a man to marry outside his village and subclan. Therefore, because the men of the matrilineal group exercise the main economic and political functions, each man brings his wife to live in his own village. The children born in a village do not "belong" there; they are members of the subclans and clans of their mothers; the villages in which they have proprietary interests are the villages of their mothers. Because, on growing up, women cannot marry into their own subclans, they are always separated from "their" villages. Boys and young men, however, are expected to move over to the villages of their maternal uncles as they approach adulthood, and certainly on getting married. They have their economic and political functions to perform on their mother's land. Here they have their inheritance.

Although the mother never lives in the midst of her ancestral lands, her right to the product of these lands for the support of herself and her children is inviolable. It is her *urigubi,* the harvest offering of all the largest and best yams (distinguished as *taytu*) raised by her brothers. These yams are displayed in conical heaps in the gardens when harvested, and they are left on display for a short period devoted to their admiration. Then they are ceremonially transported to the villages where the growers' sisters live and there they are again carefully piled up for display in front of the yam houses in which they will ultimately be stored.

Fully half a man's garden crops—and the very best half at that—goes to feed not his own household but his sisters'. Yet he is not really giving away the product of his garden. Rather, he is turning over to his sister her share-claim to the product of the kin-owned lands. Only the seed yams and the inferior tubers plus a limited number of *taytu* may be held back as his share. The rest of his yam supply is received from his brother-in-law through his own wife.

Every now and then each husband "pays" his brother-in-law for that part of the *urigubi* that he eats from his wife's storehouse by giving his brother-in-law a present of a "valuable" (some material object).

Leadership rests on the combined principles of rank and wealth. Every village, which belongs to a subclan, has its headman who is nominally the senior member of the senior lineage within the subclan. If an ordinary headman, a lesser chief called *gumguya'u,* his powers extend only to the boundaries of his own village. If he is a full chief (*guya'u*), his influence will spread over several villages and their subchiefs. If he is a paramount chief among the full chiefs, it will extend over an entire district. There is no chief for the Trobriands as a whole.

The relative ranks of the chiefs are, in the first instance, dependent on the ranks of their clans and subclans. These in turn are fixed by the mythological order of their emergence.

The highest ranking chieftains have larger houses with elaborate decorations set conspicuously and alone in the middle area of the village circle. Full chiefs wear decorative shells in numbers; lesser chiefs wear fewer, and people of lowest rank may wear none at all.

Obeisance must always be done a person of high rank. When a person is about to pass a chieftain who is squatting on the ground, he cries out, *"tokagi"* (arise!); the chief stands, and the commoner, bent low, goes slowly by. No man's head may ever be on a higher plane than that of a chief.

The greatest power of the chief is in control of the village garden magic. He may perform the rites himself or delegate them to a brother, son (which is not strictly proper), or nephew. But the magic is his. As *towasi* (garden magician) he directly organizes the common efforts of his related co-villagers. He assigns the individual garden plots for the coming season, and from then on every step in preparing the fields, planting, and harvesting requires his ritual efforts on behalf of the community, for through his magic and his alone are the forces of fertility controlled.

He also exposes laggards to public censure and so exerts control on their behavior.

"Time after time," wrote Malinowski, ". . . I would hear the voice of Bagido'u of Omarakana or Navavile of Oburaku or Motago'i of Sinaketa rising from somewhere in front of his house. In a public harangue, he would accuse such and such a one of not having completed his share of the fence . . . Or again he would impose one of the public taboos on work, saying that as in a few days the large kamkokola would be erected, everybody must stop all other work, and bring in the long stout poles necessary for the magical structure and for the final yam supports." [36]

The ultimate power of a paramount chief is in his magical control of rain, for he can produce a prolonged and dreaded drought by use of his magic. Then starvation sets in; the people are in dire straits; and in the struggle for food wars break out between districts. The paramount chief wields this power openly "as an expression of his anger and as a means of collective punishment and enforcement of his will. The wielding of rain and drought magic is, as a matter of fact, one of the most dreaded and coveted privileges of the paramount chief of Omarakana." [37]

The Trobriand chief regulates economic activity in another way as well. Through the exercise of his right of polygynous marriage he gets the *urigubu* of a great number of wives. He marries at least one woman in each village under his suzerainty, excepting, of course, his own. Then not only her brother but also her entire subclan combine to give *urigubu* to him as "a glorified brother-in-law of the whole community." Not only do they turn over roughly five times as much as given to the wife of a commoner, but they also select finer *taytu* and give them with greater display. In the old days, when a great chief had as many as eighty wives, Malinowski estimated that he received about *four hundred times* as many yams as did a commoner.

[36] Bronislaw Malinowski, *Coral Gardens and Their Magic*, 2 vols. (London and New York, 1935) I, 67.
[37] *Ibid.*, p. 78.

A chief always has plenty to eat, but in accordance with the value placed on generosity he dispenses most of his provender in ceremonial feasts and payments for special services.

The chief, like anyone else, gardens to provide *urigubu* for his wives, and he is expected to set the pace in quality of horticulture. Indeed, "only chiefs are allowed to have first class gardens."

Like Oriental sultans, they also have their pick of the more attractive younger girls. "The chief simply indicates which of the girls pleases him best, and, irrespective of her previous attachments, she is given to him." [38]

Thus we see a hereditary nobility wielding ceremonial and political power and enjoying privileges of rank far above the ruck of ordinary men. Here is the seed that flowers noxiously in the more developed societies of early and recent civilizations; the society of the Trobriands has developed beyond that of more primitive orders.

The behavioral privileges of the Trobriand chief are maintained by direct force and *not* by any withdrawal of reciprocity. He can crush his entire territory with drought if he suspects any collective dereliction by his subjects in fulfillment of their duties to him. Individual disloyalty, discourtesy or overstepping the bounds of propriety once meant immediate death without benefit of trial. The paramount chief has demand-rights against his subjects, and the privilege-rights to enforce them, of the quality enjoyed only by despots. He has, we are told, one or two hereditary executioners, whose duty it is to kill any man who has deeply offended him. [39]

Etiquette demands, for example, that the vulgar word for defecation (*popu*) must never be used by a commoner in the presence of the chief. Nor, obviously, may a commoner climb a tree in the presence of a chief, for that would put him above the chief's head. One rash Trobriander did both of these illegal acts simultaneously, and look what happened to him!

"The following incident," wrote Malinowski, "which took place during the last war between To'uluwa, high chief of Omarakana, and his traditional foe, the headman of Kabwaku, is a good illustration of the native attitude towards this insult when directed against a chief. During a lull in the fighting, when the two forces were

[38] Malinowski, *Sexual Life of Savages*, p. 137.
[39] Malinowski, *Argonauts of the Western Pacific*, p. 65.

facing each other, a Kabwaku man, Si'ulobubu, climbed a tree and addressed To'uluwa in a loud voice: *'Kukome kam popu, To'-uluwa.'* [40] Here was insult delivered with every aggravating circumstance. It was addressed to a chief, it was said aloud and in public, and the personal name was added, the form in which the insult is deadliest. After the war, when peace was concluded and all other enmities forgotten, Si'ulobubu was openly speared in broad daylight by a few men sent by To'uluwa for that purpose. The victim's family and clansmen did not even raise a protest, still less did they ask for 'blood money,' or start a *lugwa* (vendetta). Everybody knew that the man had deserved this punishment and that his death was a just and adequate *mapula* (payment, retribution) for his crime. It is even an insult to make this remark to a chief's pig in his hearing, though it is permitted so to address his dog." [41]

More commonly, a chief now employs a sorcerer to execute the offender, as was indicated in *Crime and Custom*.[42] Two recent and specific cases, briefly presented in *Coral Gardens,* are worth quoting.

Yogaru [was] the husband of Ibo'una, the grand-niece on the distaff side of To'uluwa, the chief. Yogaru had beautiful big gardens, and since the chief and his wife's kinsmen had also to provide him with taytu as he was their [classificatory] sister's husband, he accumulated too much food. He died, and though nobody would openly say so, I was informed by several men privately that he died of sorcery by the orders of To'uluwa. Again a man who had been married to the sister of Mitakata . . . the chief of Gumilababa . . . was "killed by sorcery" because he was getting too influential through his wealth in garden produce.[43]

We can therefore recognize the following as capital offenses against the person of the paramount chief: 1) being too successful as a gardener, 2) possessing too many goods, 3) wearing personal ornaments reserved only for chiefs, or overdecorating a house, 4) boasting about one's wealth in the presence of a person of higher

[40] "Eat your own feces, To'uluwa."

[41] Malinowski, *Sexual Life of Savages,* p. 447.

[42] There is a hint that direct execution was used much more extensively in the old days when there was no Resident Magistrate to limit the powers of chiefs. Sorcery can be exercised with less likelihood of difficulty with the Government.

[43] Malinowski, *Coral Gardens and Their Magic,* I, 175–176.

rank, 5) failure to do proper obeisance, 6) use of improper language directed toward a chief. Execution for such offenses is privileged. Between commoner and chief there may be no disputes.

Between individuals of like social status and between villages disputes are regular, however. There is no inkling of this in *Crime and Custom,* but it is made very clear in the details of gardening arrangements in *Coral Gardens.* Trobriand society is crosscut with tension.

"The under-current of malice, suspicion and envy which accompanies the display of food and the show of praise and admiration, may lead to bitter personal animosity, which in the Trobriands usually ends in attempts to kill by witchcraft." [44]

The ordinary Trobriander, then, behaves exactly like his chief. He is jealous and touchy over his status. The difference is that the chief may legitimately use sorcery and he may not.

Such quarrels are most bitter as between members of different communities. But even between members of the same lineage they are common in the form of disputes over the boundaries and assignment of garden plots. A man "never" demurs in the *kayaku* (council meeting) at which the chief is assigning the plots for any given year, but when the men go forth to cut the scrub it is a different story.

Here severe quarrels may break out if two people want to cut the same plot, or if they cannot agree on the boundary line, though this is usually pretty clear. Or again, a man may regret having chosen an inferior plot at the *kayaku*. He will then pretend that his choice was different and start cutting the plot he now covets.

Whatever the cause, quarrelling frequently occurs. Even during my stay in the Trobriands I was told that there were long *yakala,* native litigations, arising out of disputes at cutting.[45]

Trouble cases there seem to have been aplenty. Yet when we turn back from *Coral Gardens* to *Crime and Custom* to find out more about *yakala,* "native litigations," all we can learn is that it is a sort of fishwife's yelling match. To wit:

44 *Ibid.,* I, 181.
45 *Ibid.,* I, 103.

The *rare* [46] quarrels which occur at times take the form of . . . public expostulation (*yakala*) in which the two parties assisted by friends and relatives meet, harangue one another, hurl and hurl back recriminations. Such litigation allows people to give vent to their feelings and shows the trend of public opinion, and thus it may be of assistance in settling disputes. Sometimes it seems, however, only to harden the litigants. In no case is there any definite sentence pronounced by a third party, and agreement is but seldom reached then and there. The *yakala* therefore is a special legal arrangement, but of small importance and not really touching the heart of legal constraint. [47]

If "litigation" and "litigant" mean "lawsuit" and "party to a lawsuit," this is surely a strange lawsuit. *Yakala* is not litigation nor even an equivalent of such. It stems from disputes, but unlike the Eskimo *nith* song contest it settles nothing.

The quarreling parties may let it go with a lot of noise, however, and this does accomplish something; the alternative is an all-out melee with spears and clubs. When this occurs people may get hurt but rarely is anyone killed, unless the melee becomes a war between villages.

More commonly a melee will be brought to a halt with a challenge to a competitive food exchange called *buritila'ulo*.

A commoner of the village of Kabwaku, by name Kalaviya Kalasia, quarrelled in the garden with Mweyoyu, a commoner of Wakayse. Both villages, which lie near to each other, belong to the district of Tilataula, which is ruled by the chief of Kabwaku, Moliasi. War could never occur between the two communities since they owe allegiance to the same chief, but quarrels are frequent, and small fights (*pulukuvalu*) are not unknown. The two men quarrelled as usual about the quantity and quality of their harvest products. The Kabwaku man in the course of the quarrel destroyed the garden arbour of Mweyoyu. A fight took place on the spot, but was stopped. Later on, however, the headman of Wakayse went to the chief of Kabwaku and remonstrated with him about the destruction of the garden. The chief of Kabwaku, Moliasi, backed up his subject, and said something to the effect that since the people of Wakayse had no decent gardens and could not give proper tribute, they should not boast about their food. In reply to this challenge

---

[46] (Italics mine.) In *Crime and Custom,* Malinowski was playing up reciprocity and slighting discord as a legal factor.
[47] Malinowski, *Crime and Custom in Savage Society,* p. 60.

the headman of Wakayse offered to present the village of Kabwaku with all the yams produced by the people of his village. This was the announcement of the *buritila'ulo,* which was accepted by Moliasi, the chief of Kabwaku, and immediately put into action.

Now the principles underlying a *buritila'ulo* are in brief the following: Community A, which is either worsted in the quarrel as Wakayse had been, or which received an injury, or which is first severely taunted, issues the challenge. This community then has to muster all the yams possible, for the *buritila'ulo* is invariably carried out in terms of *kuvi,* large yams, and never in taytu. All the yams which community A can muster will be accumulated, carried over to community B, displayed there, ceremonially given, and then community B will make a return gift. If the return is made in exactly the same quantity, all comes to a happy ending; otherwise, as said already, further trouble will arise.

. . . The initiative in the quarrel was taken by the people of Kabwaku, hence the challenge to the *buritila'ulo* came from the people of Wakayse who were insulted. The assertion of the last verse that war would arise, is so far correct that probably in old days there would have been some fighting between Kabwaku and Wakayse. But not real war, only the *pulukuvalu;* that is, an encounter between two normally friendly villages in which blood might be spilled, but usually no deaths occurred. This text gives a good idea of the type of information which a native will give spontaneously. Had I not been on the spot, observed the details of the quarrel and of the transaction, and elicited concrete facts by direct questions, it would have taken a very long time for me to get to the real inwardness of this custom.

Returning to the facts observed, let us start with the preparations. All the large yams have to be taken out of the *bwayma* (storehouses) and displayed in heaps in the village. The long yams called *kwibanena* are then sandwiched between two sticks and ornamented with pandanus streamers and dabs of white paint . . . Then as much sugar-cane and betel-nut as possible is accumulated. Only these two products may be used besides the large yams. The contributions in yams have to be made exclusively from the villagers' own produce. No one from the outside is allowed to contribute to the joint store. There is no *dodige bwala,* that is helping out by relatives-in-law, as at ordinary displays or distributions. On the other hand every man has to give all the yams he possesses. Each man carefully counts his contribution and keeps a rough tally of the size of each tuber. The long yams are measured by sticks of equivalent length, one stick for each yam. The round yams are measured by means of string, knots being made to indicate their size. Each owner keeps this private tally of yams so that he can claim back his share and neither more nor less from the common pool of the return gift.

Then the natives have to make an approximate computation of the cubic capacity necessary to contain their accumulated yams. They go to the bush and collect a few stout poles and some sticks. With these they roughly construct a crate (called *liku*) and fill it with the yams to test its capacity. Then they take it to pieces again, and the whole village (A) starts on the work of transporting the yams and the component parts of the crate to the challenged village (B). Here the yams are deposited on the *baku* while the crate is reconstructed, this time more solidly, because it will have to be carried bodily by the men of village B back to village A.

When the crate is finished, each man places his contribution into it. The long tubers, each tied between two sticks, as well as pieces of sugar-cane and bunches of betel-nut are put on top . . . Sometimes, the natives told me, a number of *pwata'i*, prism-shaped receptacles, are also erected, and filled with smaller *kuvi* and topped with betel-nut and sugar-cane. When there is a great wealth of produce, vertical frames (*lalogwa*) are set up, decorated with yams, bananas and betel-nut.

Then comes the actual transaction. First of all the exact measurements of the crate are taken. Community B will have to return the same crate, in no way changed, to community A, and fill it exactly to the same height. In order to ensure against any fraud and have a clear standard of measurement, a number of sticks are cut on which the length, width and height of the *liku* are recorded. Then the size and quality of the most important of the gifts, the long yams, is measured. Community B have by this time prepared their *kaydavi,* that is their yams tied between sticks, and for each *kaydavi* brought to them by A, they check off a corresponding *kaydavi*, which, however, they do not yet present . . . Then the number of bunches of betel-nut is ascertained and their size roughly estimated and recorded. The contents of the *liku* are now distributed; each man in community B receives his share in exchange for an exactly corresponding contribution to the return gift from his own storehouse. Next day the *liku* is transported bodily to village A where it was first built. Some twenty men were necessary to lift and transport it on the occasion when I was present. The rest of the villagers, men, women and children, were busy carrying the yams. Arrived at village A, the proceedings of the previous day are exactly repeated, only now the transfer is from community B to community A.

And now comes the dramatic moment. Community B have been

straining all their resources not only to repay the full quantity of yams but to provide a surplus. The strict return measure is called *kalamelu,* which might perhaps be translated "its equivalent", "the equivalent of the gift received." If they can offer an extra quantity, this will be put on the ground and declared to be *kalamata* "its eye." The word "eye" is here used in the figurative sense of something which is ahead of, which overtakes, goes beyond.

Now such a surplus gift would not be offered in a very friendly spirit. Community B would boast of having given it. They would also immediately clamour for a repayment of it. But since community A have strained all their resources for their original gift, they cannot repay. They would have recourse to argument, they would say that the surplus was not a real surplus but due to the fact that the *kalamelu* was not honestly and fully meted out. A quarrel will break out again and another fight arise from the *buritila'ulo.*

Since, however, community B, by supposition the richer one, would also be stronger, the people of A would obviously be beaten on every point. But two communities practising a *buritila'ulo* against each other are not essentially hostile, so the fight would probably have no very serious consequences. I was told, however, that in old days, especially when the *buritila'ulo* was not between two adjoining communities normally friendly, but between two communities who, though not on terms of recurrent warfare might yet fight if occasion arose, a serious regulated combat might follow.

But I will exemplify one or two points in this general account by what occurred between Wakayse, which corresponds here to community A, and Kabwaku, corresponding to community B. Here the Wakayse men were obviously the weaker; they had been insulted, they had been told that they had no food, and they issued the first challenge . . . Feeling ran high. In spite of the fact that Moliasi was the acknowledged chief of the whole district, there were several quarrels between him and Kulubwaga, the head-man of Wakayse and between their people . . .

Both headmen from time to time made impassioned speeches, ostensibly addressing their own subjects, but really directing their adverse comments at the other side. Moliasi, for instance, while the Wakayse men were rushing into Kabwaku with poles and yams and erecting the *liku* rather effectively and quickly, commented on the slowness with which everything was being done. Remarking on the betel-nut which was offered, he directly taunted the Wakayse people with having no betel-nut of their own and having to get it from other villages . . .

"Why do you bring betel-nut from Kaybola, from Kwaybwaga? Take back this betel-nut of other villages, of Kwaybwaga and Kaybola. I do not want it. Bring us your own betel-nut from Wakayse."

These insults were not replied to directly because the native is always subdued in another man's village, but on the following day in Wakayse I overheard a great many insulting remarks levelled at the Kabwaku men.

For when, breathless from their hard work of carrying the crate and the yams, these were moving as in a trance, excited and absorbed in their task, they were taunted with slowness, with the *prima facie* inadequacy of their return gift and the distortion of the *liku's* shape in process of carrying.

Discussing what happened that day with some Omarakana men who had been present there with me, an informant thus reproduced the boasting of the Kabwaku men.

"Some of them said: 'Let us throw away this crate. Let us take a new one. Let us exceed the people of Wakayse.' "

Such words were obviously boasting because it would be very incorrect in a *buritila'ulo* to construct a larger crate. In fact, this is never done. Any excess should be presented by laying down the *kalamata* on the ground beside the crate.

To this the Wakayse men retorted that the *liku* had been too small from the outset, and that they really wanted to build a much bigger one to accommodate their gift.

The comparison of the long yams was by no means . . . peaceful and pleasant . . . On the whole it was riotous, full of quarrelling and threatening.

However, nothing serious occurred, and the people of Kabwaku refrained from adding the insulting surplus to their return gift. The natives are now afraid of fighting and try to avoid such situations as would almost inevitably tempt them to use spears and throwing-sticks . . .

Even about the reapportionment of yams within the village there is always some dissatisfaction and quarrelling, but on the whole this arises more from personal ambition and vanity than from actual greed, and springs from a desire to prove that one has given more than one receives.[48]

Here again is found a substitute for judicial process, and it is clearly an unsatisfactory device that is as apt to stir up conflicts of feelings as it is to settle them.

[48] Malinowski, *Coral Gardens and Their Magic*, I, 182–187.

The steam generated by quarrels can also be let off through a somewhat similar competitive display at harvest time—a form of *kayasa* or coöperative enterprise set under way by a chief. The usual onset of such quarrels is brought about by insulting references to the poor gardening ability of some other village. In 1918 it was over the score of a cricket match.

These people quarrelled because of the cricket. The people of Kwaybwaga went to M'tawa and cricketed. They cricketed, they finished, they counted; they counted and they said: "Who has won?" The people of Kwaybwaga spoke and addressed the people of M'tawa: "You lie, we others have won." The M'tawa people answered: "No, you have not really won." They quarrelled: "Good, we shall beat you." They hit one another with throwing-sticks. The people of M'tawa drove off the people of Kwaybwaga, and these latter departed to their village, saying: "Good, you have driven us off; but to-morrow come you to Omarakana. We shall beat you." Later on they came to Omarakana, the people of Kwaybwaga stood up against the people of M'tawa, they took their revenge, fighting with spear and shield. The people of M'tawa and Liluta ran away. They went to their village and said: "We have quarrelled, but let us make a *kayasa* and see who is more efficient in gardening." The master of the *kayasa* is Kwoyavila of Liluta. In old days it was like that: they quarrelled, they fought, and then they arranged for a *kayasa*. The quarrelling was because of women, garden plots, or food.[49]

The *kayasa* lasted a month, each village making a great to-do and display of the giant tubers it brought in to fill the storehouses of their paramount chief in the capital village of Omarakana. During the *kayasa* itself many insults are passed between the two groups, who stand always ready to fight, and in the old days frequently did.

Intercommunity violence reaches disastrous proportions in times of drought-created famines. The vaunted reciprocity of coastal fisherman and inland yam-grower, that legal binder of social order, backfires hideously. The inlanders have no yams from their parched fields; they are desperate for fish to keep them alive. No yams, no fish.

Starving, they steal to the western shore to poach on the lagoon at night, hiding throughout the day in remote jungle patches. The men from the coastal village, unwilling to share their supposedly limited supplies of fish "scour the jungle for the encampments, attack the thin, hunted and exhausted inlanders, and kill them by the score." Malinowski knew several caves on the west coast which "are full of bones," relics of such wholesale slaughters, when inlanders were defeated, eaten, and their bones thrown into a cave.[50]

A sorcerer bent on killing a victim, when caught *in flagrante delicto* by his victim's kinsmen, is said to be speared and killed with no more ado. His offense is a tort, however; no crime.

The method of a Trobriand sorcerer is to cast a light spell over the habitual haunts of his intended victim so as to make him feel indisposed and take to his bed over a burning fire to keep warm. The sorcerer then steals close in the dark shadows of night to poke a stick bearing charmed herbs through the walls and into the fire. The fumes of the herbs make the victim deathly sick. The magician then slinks far off into the jungle to prepare a charm to be smeared on a pointed bone. With this diabolical device he again approaches the house and points his magical needle at his victim, twisting and turning it the while. This final act is fatal.

To guard against this dire fate a sick man's friends, kinsmen, and wife's brothers keep all-night vigils with spears wherewith to kill the sorcerer, when he approaches.

Whenever a woman goes into confinement a like watch is kept, for it is believed sorcerers are especially likely to come at such times. Perhaps there is such concern at the time of confinement because a sorcerer must first kill a close female relative before his power will work against other people, and this is the time when a woman is easy to bewitch.

The one outright killing that occurred during Malinowski's stay in the Trobriands was the spearing of a notorious sorcerer at night while he was approaching a village. This man was killed by an armed guard of a sick man, but no details of the case are given.[51]

Most unfortunately, nothing is reported on the aftermath of the spearing of sorcerers. The implication, however, seems to be that such killings are privileged and that no revenge is taken or composition demanded.

[50] *Ibid.*, I, 162. Since white control was established such famines and massacres have become things of the past.

[51] Malinowski, *Crime and Custom in Savage Society*, p. 118.

In the old times, fragmentary evidence indicates that quite a few people were killed in the constantly recurring brawls and fights that spice life in the Trobriand Islands. However, the little that is reported on the legal aspects of such tribal turmoil is that "in all cases when a man is killed by people of another sub-clan, there is the obligation of *talion*. This, in theory, is absolute, in practice it is regarded as obligatory only in cases of a male adult of rank or importance; and even then it is considered superfluous when the deceased had met his fate for a fault clearly his own. In other cases, when vendetta is obviously demanded by the honour of the sub-clan, it is still evaded by the substitution of blood-money (*lula*)." [52]

"It is considered superfluous when the deceased had met his fate for a fault clearly his own." Superfluous? More likely, out of order. Is it not more probable that the killing of the victim is looked upon by the Trobrianders as a privilege-right? If so, there is then an unspecified series of acts for which the legitimate penalty is death, acts which Malinowski obstinately neglects to mention, for as Seagle rightly comments, "It is perhaps the most serious defect of Malinowski's work that he refuses to admit the overshadowing importance of breach in the formation of legal institutions." [53]

We do discover in *The Sexual Life of Savages* that an adulterer caught *in flagrante delicto* may be killed, "and this will be recognized as legal retribution." [54]

Thus sorcery and adultery exposed in the act are capital private delicts. It is also reported by Malinowski that adultery with the wives of chiefs was a capital offense in the old days, as it was also in feudal times in Europe.[55] No indication is given of the collection of damages in instances in which the adulterer is not killed.

The final area of misbehavior which Malinowski thought deserving of mention is theft, and that in the Trobriands does not fall under the jurisdiction of law, for "the dangers of exposure and the shame of it are apparently a sufficiently strong protection against possible trespass." [56]

Outlying fruit trees that cannot be kept under surveillance are

[52] *Ibid.*, pp. 118–119.
[53] Seagle, "Primitive Law and Professor Malinowski," p. 284.
[54] Malinowski, *Sexual Life of Savages*, p. 459. A case is briefly given on page 118.
[55] *Ibid.*, p. 324.
[56] Malinowski, *Coral Gardens and Their Magic*, I, 374.

protected by magical charms visible to all. Theft from charmed trees is sanctioned by the onset of loathsome diseases. "The natives believe that disease invariably follows the violation of such a protective mark, and everybody pays very great respect to such 'Beware of Danger' signals." [57] The penalty is "automatic." [58] In this instance there is no prophylactic magic mentioned by Malinowski such as confounds the effectiveness of the incest tabu. Its apparent absence indicates a much lower individual valuation of fruit as compared to sexual intercourse with a clan sister.

It should now be evident that a restatement of Trobriand law offers a picture quite different from that portrayed in *Crime and Custom*. It is hardly one that would lead to the conclusion that, "The whole of Trobriand culture with its mutual obligations and exchanges rests upon economic sanctions, personal vanity, and public opinion." [59]

Trobriand law differs from the law of the tribes previously discussed in that the social organization of the Islanders has certain important institutional features not possessed by any of the other groups: clans (in this case matrilineal), plus hereditary chieftainship and generally rigid status, plus exceptionally frequent sorcery, and (for a society with highly centralized political controls) amazingly undeveloped machinery for handling the trouble case. Juristic skill is not a Trobriand attribute.

In the Trobriand instance, however, offenses are still treated as private delicts for the most part, and offenses against the chief appear to be offenses against him as a privileged person more than against him as the agent of the society as a whole. The legal system of the Trobrianders has not been well consolidated, nor does it compare with that of the Cheyennes in effectiveness.

Leaving the Trobriand Islands, there are still Malinowski's later ideas on law to consider. His introduction to Hogbin's *Law and Order in Polynesia* needs but brief comment. As an *Introduction* it is, in the opinion of Seagle, "not so much an act of piety towards a disciple as an attempt by Malinowski to reply to a growing number

---

[57] *Ibid.*, p. 375.
[58] Malinowski, *Crime and Custom in Savage Society*, p. 50.
[59] Daniel Katz and R. L. Schanck, *Social Psychology* (New York, 1938), p. 20.

of critics." [60] In reaffirming the thesis of *Crime and Custom,* it also plants two new seeds of theory that grow to great importance in his final system. The first is the hypothesis of basic biological needs as cultural determinants along with derived or instrumental needs "such as that of education, legal order, economic organization, social groupings; needs which have to be satisfied as urgently as biological requirements if man is to survive." [61] The second is the idea of *neutral custom* as opposed to *sanctioned custom.*[62] Each is only lightly touched on, but together they become the crux of his argument on the nature of law, as stated in 1942, in which he enumerated four classes of law, called Law (1), Law (2), Law (3), and Law (4).[63] What are their meanings?

Law (1) is used as in "law of science." With respect to culture it embraces the rules of imperative determinism imposed by "nature." These are natural laws acted upon by human beings but not put into words by them, if they are primitive men. These are the laws which give form to the biological base to which Malinowski insists all culture must be functionally oriented.

Law (2) is "the rule of conduct standardized in behavior or verbally formulated." It corresponds in general to what is otherwise known as custom, and also, but not explicitly, to the sociologists' folkways. This is the "neutral custom" introduced in the Introduction to Hogbin. Law (2) consists of supposedly unsanctioned rules of conduct in that Malinowski thinks the conduct they call for is taken for granted and is so socially unimportant that no one is moved to raise a fuss, or hardly an eyebrow, when a deviant departs from the lines of conduct prescribed by the rules that fall in this category.

Law (3) consists of rules of conduct "which refer to relations between individuals and groups, delimit divergent interests, and curtail disruptive physiological and sociological tendencies" (sexual and acquisitive, for instance). "It is the law of order and law maintained." Like Law (2) it prevails without any sanctions recognizable by Professor Malinowski. It differs from Law (2) only in that

[60] Seagle, "Primitive Law and Professor Malinowski," p. 280, n. 12.

[61] Malinowski, Introduction to H. I. Hogbin's *Law and Order in Polynesia,* p. xxxii.

[62] *Ibid.,* pp. xxv–xxvi, lxii.

[63] Malinowski, "A New Instrument for the Study of Law—Especially Primitive."

its rules are regulative in spheres of conduct where clashes of interests and cross-purposes are likely to occur among the members of a society. It is positively restrictive but "always" successfully so.

Law (4) is defined as the specific mechanism which is brought into play when a conflict of claims occurs or a rule of social conduct is broken. It is said to be the law of retributive and restitutive social action.

The one element that these several expressions of law have in common is regularity. A law is a statement of what has been regularly observed to have occurred under certain conditions. Law (1) consists of laws of natural science. Laws (2), (3), (4) consist of laws of the science of culture. Law (1) has meaning in generally accepted usage. Laws (2), (3), (4) have meaning only in the senses given to them by Malinowski. They are not, we hold, conducive to a clearer understanding of the nature of law and its relation to other social phenomena. Law (2) is a spurious concept because few, if any, customs are actually unsanctioned in any society. Law (3) is a concept inconsistent with the whole system because it is identified as the law of order and law maintained. "When we speak of a law-abiding community, we mean Law (3)." Yet Law (4), "the law of retributive and restitutive social action" can exist only in terms of the breach of Law (3)—which supposedly does not occur.

In part, Malinowski's Law (3) coincides with Substantive Law. His Law (4) coincides with Adjective Law. But—Law (3) contains many rules which are not breached, or which, if they are, may be sanctioned by supernatural consequences or other nonlegal devices. In other words, it embraces many rules which are not legally sanctioned and are not therefore Rules of Substantive Law. As a system of distinction and analysis Malinowski's final formulation lends little aid to the isolation and understanding of the legal aspects of human culture.

In sum: Malinowski's positive contribution to the theory of law has been in his vigorous insistence on law as an aspect of society and culture at large and on the occurrence of gaps between the ideal and the actual norm of law. He broke the crust of legal formalism in anthropology and gave a new impetus to the anthropology of law. For this service social science is in his debt. That he overshot the mark and became to some degree an obscurantist of law by fusing law overmuch with the matrix from which it emerges is a serious defect in his system. His approach has enabled him and his students to shed much light on social control at large as it operates in the cultures which they have studied in the field, while at the same time it led them into a virtual ignoring of the more strictly legal phases of the cultures.[64]

At the very end of his life, however, when confronted by problems of freedom and law in modern civilization in the face of the totalitarian threats of Fascism and Communism, Malinowski realized how deficient his "anthropological approach to law" really was. In *Freedom and Civilization* (published posthumously in 1944) we find him saying, "By law in the sense of a socially established rule we mean a command or rule of conduct sanctioned by organized constraints." [65] Here he wrote of Law (1) and Law (2) as before. But the concepts of Law (3) and (4) were dropped. Sanctions were no longer abjured. In a *volte-face*, he now gave authority and coercive sanctions a preëminent role in social control.

Let him speak for himself:

Our argument leads us to the conclusion that authority or the raw material thereof is a natural and indispensable by-product of education, of organized life, and of the normal, ordinary carrying out of all concerted and purposeful activities . . .

Now the thesis which is being here presented is that no human culture, however democratic, constructive, peaceful, and liberal, as well as libertarian, can exist without the political factor, that is, the factor of discipline established by drill and ultimately sanctioned by force.[66]

The principle of authority comes into being from the beginnings of mankind. In disciplining the individual, authority is an indispensable factor in the process of training at any level of culture. In the enforcement of criminal law it is at all stages and in all societies a *conditio sine qua non.*[67]

Political authority as we know it is indispensable even at primitive levels; we have defined it as the legally vested power to establish norms,

---

[64] E.g., Hogbin's *Law and Order in Polynesia,* and Green, *Ibo Village Affairs.* For a critical appraisal of the "legal" approach used in this book see the review by M. D. W. Jeffreys in *African Studies,* 9:99–104 (1950).

[65] Bronislaw Malinowski, *Freedom and Civilization* (New York, 1944), p. 175.

[66] *Ibid.,* pp. 187–188.

[67] *Ibid.,* p. 234.

to take decisions and to enforce them through the use of sanction by coercion.[68]

The concept of reciprocity, important though it is for the understanding of social relations (for no social relations are unilateral), was at long last recognized by Malinowski to be wholly inadequate when taken by itself in the attempt to understand the nature and function of power in social organization. When he addressed himself to the pressing matter of freedom in civilization the necessary allocation and delegation of power, as against the tendencies to usurp and corrupt power by self-centered interests, could not help but be the chief concern of his thoughts. Then, and only then, did he realize that this is the concern of law in all societies.

[68] *Ibid.*, p. 248.

9

The Ashanti: Constitutional Monarchy and the Triumph of Public Law

With the last of our selected societies we now stand on the threshold of civilization. For with the Ashanti of the Gold Coast of West Africa we are confronted with an elaborate primitive social system that is sophisticated in political structure and to a certain degree in matters of law. Theirs was a massive military state with cities and towns that had all the elements of a nascent civilization save writing, which is the anthropologists' usual criterion of civilization. In general terms their law was comparable to that of the ancient civilizations so ably analyzed by Sir Henry Maine.

The Ashanti were under British domination from the close of the Ashanti war of 1873–1874 until the opening of this decade, but Ashanti legal institutions were not seriously limited by foreign sovereignty until after the opening of the present century. The War of the Golden Stool (1900–1901), which gave the small British forces in West Africa a nasty time, ended with the annexation of Ashanti as a British possession. However, the English policy of indirect rule through native chieftains left a good part of the Ashanti political and legal structure intact. The Ashanti lost their sovereignty but not the essential integrity of their socio-political system. In 1935, limited self-determination for the Ashanti was officially regularized in the formal establishment of the Ashanti Confederacy of the Union of Ashanti States under British aegis. In 1946, the Ashanti joined with their hereditary enemies to the south to form the Ashanti–Fanti Confederacy, and five years later, in 1951, just a half century after the final defeat in The War of the Golden Stool, they were freed from colonial status through transformation of the Gold Coast

Protectorate into a free modern state known as The Gold Coast Nation. The viability of the primitive Ashanti state provided the structure that made it possible for the Ashanti (with the Fanti) to be the first native African state in modern times to emerge from colonial "tutelage" into the fellowship of free nations.[1]

Our concern in this study is with Ashanti law and its accompanying state system as it existed prior to 1875.[2] The basic sources on Ashanti law are the three books by Captain R. S. Rattray, *Ashanti, Religion and Art in Ashanti, Ashanti Law and Constitution*, plus the more recent Ashanti studies by K. A. Busia. Rattray's materials provide not only an excellent descriptive account of nineteenth-century Ashanti institutions but also a picture rich in historical depth. With these resources it is possible to follow the development of a society from a fragmented collection of clans to the consolidation of a huge tribal state embracing more than 200,000 persons under a primitive confederated monarchy.

Originally the Ashanti lived in the grasslands of the western Sudan where presumably they were sedentary gardeners. This we know only from their oral traditions. When first they became known to Europeans they had rooted themselves in the heavy equatorial forests of the Gold Coast. The forest was their place of refuge. Moslem nomads, swift-mounted on horses, had scourged the Ashanti from the open Sudan, driving them southward into the forests. There the cavalry tactics of the tormentors were neutralized, for the great trees and vines formed an impenetrable barrier except where narrow paths were laboriously hacked out by hand and the trees girdled and burned for garden patches.

How numerous were the original refugee groups we have no way of knowing, but it is clear that at first there was not much communication between the various local settlements. Social organization was simple and democratically directed by village headmen and elders who were also leaders of lineages. By the beginning of the sixteenth century the local groups within a given territory had been consolidated under the leadership of a dominant lineage whose

---

[1] Excepting, of course, the temporary yoke worn by Abyssinia.

[2] The vicissitudes and readjustments of the Ashanti system in the twentieth century are ably analyzed in the work of K. A. Busia, *The Position of the Chief in the Modern Political System of Ashanti* (Oxford, 1951). This book also provides a remarkably clear *précis* of the basic principles of the old Ashanti system.

headman became the head chieftain of the territory. Such territories then became tribal units, each with its own name and governmental structure (e.g., Bekwai, Adansi, Juabin, Kokofu, Denkyira, Nauta, Mampon, Kumasi, Wenchi). Each tribe had its own capital town where the head chief held court.

During the seventeenth century the Ashanti found themselves under military pressure from the outside and engaged in some internal strife among themselves. Kumasi, for example, was forced to pay tribute to the Denkyira, a hostile division to the south. An end to this was made by the great Osai Tutu, fourth head chief of Kumasi, military hero and statesman. His prowess at arms, wedded to the political genius of his priest and counselor, Komfo Anokye, forged the union that made the Ashanti nation a powerful native state.

Osai Tutu first defied the tribute demands of the king of Denkyira, and war resulted. He defeated Denkyira in contest of arms in 1719. As an aftermath to his victory he killed both its king and queen, destroying the Denkyira yoke completely. He pressed to the north and subdued the Moslem states of Gaman and Banna. He fought and bested other Ashanti tribes to the east and west of Kumasi. These he linked to his throne in the manner that became the traditional form of the Ashanti constitution. He symbolized the unity of the burgeoning Ashanti state by adding a miraculously delivered national Golden Stool to that which was his by ancient right as the head chief of Kumasi. The stool was produced, according to Ashanti legend, by the priest Komfo Anokye, "who by his magic powers brought the Golden Stool down from the skies, and told the Ashanti it was the symbol of their unity." [3] Because of their creative genius as builders of the Ashanti state, "No memories are more revered in Ashanti than those of Osei Tutu and Komfo Anokye." [4] The great king was slain in battle in 1731, after a rule of more than three decades, but his work was carried on, and the state expanded steadily until the defeat of the Ashanti by the British in 1874.

What was their handiwork?

The foundation of the Ashanti political structure is the maternal lineage, a social group consisting of the descendants, reckoned through the female line, of a known female ancestor who lived not

[3] Busia, p. 4.   [4] *Ibid.*, p. 96.

more than five or six generations back. True, the conjugal family is the necessary unit for procreation, but it is of slight significance in Ashanti ideology, or even in function, when compared to the unilateral maternal kinship group.

Ashanti precepts set forth two principles of biological continuity. Blood (*mogya*) is inherited by direct transfer from the mother. It is the bond that is the basis of the clan (*abusua*) and the lineage within it. The *ntoro*, or "spirit," of a person is received through the semen of the father. Blood is female; semen is male. Not only is the blood principle the foundation of a descent group, but so also is the *ntoro* principle. Both principles define exogamous groups of relatives within which marriage is banned, and which are characterized by distinctive food tabus, and are also totemic. The spirit principle has some religious manifestations beyond mere control of marriage. But the blood principle controls land rights, succession to other kinds of property, to offices and titles; it determines political status almost entirely, as well as legal responsibilities, and it is the focus of the ancestor cult. The emotional ties of blood outweigh those of spirit. Thus, although the Ashanti have organized their society in terms of double descent,[5] only the matrilineal principle figures prominently in law and politics. The blood forms the body, and so the physical links between the generations of today, yesterday, and back into the remote times of long ago are to and through the mothers.

The male line within the lineage is spatially identifiable; for males ideally stay in the place of their births, while wives go to their husbands' on marriage. Each lineage is centered in a special section of a given town and the male residents of a precinct are all theoretically members of the same lineage. Their wives are outsiders, but their widowed mothers, unmarried sisters, and daughters are with them. The unity of the lineage is further cemented by the grouping of individual family houses about the dwelling of the lineage head *in whose home all the men take their evening meals.* If the hearth and common meal be a mainspring of family unity, then in Ashanti the fostered loyalty for the men is in the home of the lineage leader rather than in the family dwelling. In modern Ashanti

---

[5] Cf. G. P. Murdock, "Double Descent," *American Anthropologist*, 42:555–561 (1940). Also, M. J. Herskovits, "The Ashanti Ntoro: a Re-examination," *Journal of the Royal Anthropological Institute*, 67:287–296 (1937).

there is a good deal of variation from the norm so far as actual residence is concerned, as has been shown by statistical analysis of household censuses by Meyer Fortes. Men no longer necessarily live in their own houses in their traditional lineage sections, but the dominant norm is still that they do so.[6] And when they do not do so, even though a man may live for years in distant towns, he looks upon the village of his lineage as home. "That was where he looked forward to being buried when he died, so that he might join his ancestors . . . the relatives of a dead man regard it as a solemn duty to bury their kinsmen in the ancestral village. Dead bodies are conveyed many miles at great expense in order that this obligation may be fulfilled."[7]

Thus the kinship and territorial principles tend to be fused, but not entirely, because while the lineage is localized, the clan of which it is a part is not.

The lineage head is an important figure who is chosen by all the adult men and senior women of the lineage. In most cases the headship is hereditary within certain families within the lineage. All the males of such families are eligible for nomination, and from among them the most suitable one is named. If the lineage is an important one, the nominee's name must be presented to the district chief for approval, for he will also sit on the chief's council. If he is approved, he is later on presented to the chief, but not until all the grown members of his lineage have met in the house of the senior woman and each kinsman in turn has sworn to serve "you whom we have chosen to occupy the stool of our ancestors, so that you in turn may serve the chief." Before the chief, he receives admonishments and is sworn in, becoming an agent of the chief and the leader of his lineage. The Ashanti conception is that he is the earthly agent of the ancestral spirits.

The most overriding of all Ashanti postulates, however, is that "the well-being of a society depends upon the maintenance of good relations with the ancestors on whom the living depend for help and protection."[8] The interest of the ancestors in the doings of their lineage descendants remains lively and continuous. They set the

---

[6] Meyer Fortes, "Time and Social Structure: An Ashanti Case Study" in Meyer Fortes, *Social Structure: Studies Presented to A. R. Radcliffe-Brown* (Oxford, 1949) pp. 54–84.

[7] Busia, p. 7.

[8] Busia, p. 26.

standards of right and wrong conduct. The business of the lineage headman is to see that his people do not transgress, to see that respect is paid the ancestors, to see that all interests of the lineage are fully regarded by its members and to represent the lineage in its relations to other groups.

The heads of the several lineages residing in a village make up the village council. Once again the kinship and territorial principles are fused. The headman of one lineage, and that usually the first lineage to have settled in the village, is also the village headman, the *odekuro*, or "owner of the village." With the council he regulates the affairs of the village.

In earlier times, when the village was the supreme autonomous unit, all legal matters were believed by Rattray to have been *efisem*, "household affairs." They consisted of private wrongs that were adjusted by arbitration without recourse to physical force.

A lineage member wronged by a kinsman could take the affair to any elderly and respected member of his group who then undertook to bring the two quarrelers into conciliation. If the problem was more serious, the plaintiff took the matter to his lineage head. Or by swearing the name of the lineage ancestor in the hearing of others, he directly brought the lineage headman in to represent the ancestors whose interests were evoked in swearing the oath. Procedure was informal; the objective is said to have been reconciliation. "We look in vain," wrote Rattray, "in the majority of these household-settled disputes for any very elaborate system of fines or sanctions." [9] The mediator had no personal machinery for enforcing his demands. But the belief system did. His judgments, his advice, were held not to be his own making. They were the will of the ancestors in whose displeasure and power to punish the sanctions lay. Rattray was thinking in terms too narrowly legal. No mediator commands, and remains a mediator. Wherever mediation is an effective institutional device it has its informal cultural machinery to make it effective. Such machinery may be diffuse, but not in the case of the Ashanti. It had its foundations in the carefully fostered loyalty of the members to their lineage, and its compulsive effect flowed from the dogma of the powers of the ancestors over their descendants. The headman, be it remembered, was the power line of communication

[9] R. S. Rattray, *Ashanti Law and Constitution* (Oxford, 1929), p. 329.

from the ancestors to the lineage members. To flaunt defiance of the headman's suggested settlements would be to thumb the nose at the ancestors. They would refuse to stand for it. The obligation to settle intralineage disputes was strong. "Repairing the house, so that it became dry," it is called. A wet house is one in which the head sits moody and brooding because of trouble.[10]

Dr. Busia, writing a generation later than Rattray, is thoroughly aware of the importance of the ancestral sanctions. He concludes, "The respect in which the elders were held secured obedience to their judgments. So although their decisions could not be legally enforced, they were generally accepted." [11] And why? "The ancestors are believed to be the custodians of the laws and customs of the tribe. They punish with sickness or misfortune those who infringe them . . . Constantly before the Ashanti, and serving to regulate his conduct, is the thought that his ancestors are watching him, and that one day, when he rejoins them in the world of spirits, they will ask him to give an account of his conduct, especially of his conduct towards his kinsmen. This thought is a very potent sanction of morality." [12]

Even in 1942 this view had not lost its effectiveness, as witness what happened in the following instance.

A slave woman bought by a former chief had two daughters. The original purchaser's successor, a chief, married the older daughter; the other was married to a commoner. The chief's wife had four children and her sister two. When the chief died both the women refused to live with his sisters, with whom they had lived all their lives. They went and lived in a village three miles away. Within a short time the chief's former wife had lost two of her children and her sister had lost both of hers. When they consulted the local god (*obosom*) to find out the cause of this misfortune, the priest told them that since they had left the chief's house the ancestral spirits were angry and no longer protected them. If they wished to avoid further deaths they should give a sheep to the chief's sister to be sacrificed to the ancestral spirits, and they should return to the house.[13]

The legal essence in Hohfeldian terms was there, although a

[10] *Ibid.*, p. 390.
[11] Busia, p. 69.
[12] *Ibid.*, p. 24–25.
[13] *Ibid.*, p. 25.

strictly legal sanction was not—unless we hold, with the Ashanti, that the ancestors are really part of the community and do their own judging and punishing.

When a settlement was achieved, the restoration of equilibrium and a closure of the issue was sealed through the offering of *mpata* ("pacification"). It consisted of a gift of a chicken or a few eggs, "to wash the soul of the aggrieved party." Perhaps, if the offense was more weighty, a bit of gold dust or a lamb would be given. The affronted soul of the plaintiff had to be cleansed of ill-feeling, his hurt assuaged. The plaintiff on his part was expected to accept it, and the matter was settled and done. Sometimes the disputants also swore on the household oath of the arbiter that they would remain friends.

When the alleged "household offense" was between the members of two different lineages, the plaintiff could take his grievance to any respected elder of the community or to his own lineage head. In any event, the headmen of the lineages of offender and plaintiff met together with such third-party elders as might be called upon to talk the matter out. In such cases not only was *mpata* given to the injured person, but also restitutive damages equal to the injury done, plus an apology tendered through the elders. The elders for their part received a token fee (*aseda*) or a small gift of palm-wine (*noa*).

"The elders of a community were frequently engaged in this way, settling differences, determining the satisfaction to be paid, and reconciling estranged persons or groups so as to ensure order and amicable relations in the community." [14]

So strong was the feeling for "rightness" that not infrequently, we are told, the man who had done wrong went of his own volition to an elder and, confessing his error, begged, "Komo, no dibem mame" ("Go and give him the right or justice of his cause"). What had become the most regular procedure in Cheyenne wife-taking was alternative high form in Ashanti.

Such was the nature of procedure for minor offenses in Ashanti law. Four or five centuries ago most, if not all, Ashanti offenses were purportedly handled in this mild and gentle manner, for Ashanti tradition has it that there was then no criminal law nor any violence that bred retaliation.

[14] *Ibid.*, p. 69.

Feud is said to have been conspicuously absent through the legal history of Ashanti. This, as Rattray notes, is remarkable, considering the strong group feeling and corporate responsibility for individual acts that was so characteristic of the Ashanti. It is all the more remarkable, we would add, in the face of the warlike proclivities of the Ashanti as a people and the prevalence of the feuding tendency among primitives with strong clan systems. Rattray lays the absence of feuding to the Ashanti practice of turning to the lineage or clan headman to act on behalf of individual members, plus a reliance on forensic rather than lethal methods of settling disputes. More than this, the old Ashanti clan would brook no unruly behavior from its members. A man who was so untoward as to kill a member of his own clan was extruded. He was then at the mercy of outsiders, and the best he could hope for was a life as a slave. A man who killed a fellow Ashanti outside of his clan, or otherwise outrageously offended one, was expelled by his own clan elders. "Corporate responsibility for his act ceased to operate, and the vendetta . . . was thus avoided." [15]

The ideal was one of internal peace and conciliation. There was no defense for the man who flagrantly ignored the ideal, and internal tensions were, if we can believe tradition, kept at a low level.

On general principles, however, we must confess to skepticism. The contrast between the later temper of criminal law and the ideal picture of early "household law" is too great to make it seem possible that early Ashanti society was quite as peaceful as the Ashanti of today make out. The tradition is too much in the pattern of Golden Age thinking.

We have thus far considered the organization of the village, the lineage, and the law that prevailed on the early level of development.

What happened when villages were cemented into tribes? And the tribes into the confederated nation?

The basic principle remained unchanged as it worked up through each succeeding level. The tie was one of kinship: the chief became the ancestral viceroy in affairs political.

A minor theme was subsequently added: loyalty to the chief is bound by oath of personal allegiance.

[15] Rattray, *Ashanti Law and Constitution*, p. 289.

Let us see how the structure of a territorial, or tribal, division, of which there were some twenty, was built up. We shall consider Wenchi. Its capital town, Wenchi, gave its name to the whole division, as is usual. The organization of the capital town was roughly the same as that of any other town as it has already been described. Wenchi embraced seven lineages. Each lineage lived in a traditional section of the town. Two lineages (the *Nkwaduasefo* and *Sofoasefo*) were senior; they were also called *Yefrefo,* "those who first emerged [from a hole in the ground]." The other lineages were made up of descendants of refugees from other Ashanti towns shattered in the wars of the seventeenth and eighteenth centuries. They were given asylum and a section of Wenchi in which to live. If numerous enough, they were given an outlying site on which to build their own satellite town, the land still belonging to the *Yefrefo,* but usufruct allowed to the newcomers. Each village had its lineage headmen, but the head of the *Sofoasefo* lineage in Wenchi, as the lineal descendant of the original female ancestress of the area, became not only the town headman of Wenchi but also the *Wenchihene,* head chief of the Wenchi tribe. Beneath him and bound to him by oaths of personal loyalty were the several headmen of the outlying villages. These were the *odekuro.*

Administratively, the *odekuro* never dealt directly with the head chief, nor he with them. Just as the village head was surrounded by his council of local elders, so the chief at Wenchi was surrounded by the council of elders from the lineages in the capital. Each of these was appointed to represent the interests of an outlying village at the seat of government. His voice was the line of communication from the *Wenchihene* to the village officials, and his ear the receiver of their desires. Thus each village was subject to an overseer who was part of the central government, while at the same time it had a friend in court to see that its interests were well represented.

These same elders at Wenchi were the commanders of the several units of the territorial army in which every able-bodied man had to serve as a member of his lineage. The battle organization of an Ashanti field force was traditional; it moved into the field in the following pattern.[16]

[16] The old Ashanti armies were supplanted by the British in the twentieth century.

Scouts
(*akwansrefo*)
Advance Guard
(*twafo*)

Left Flank	Main combat force in two sections	Right Flank
(*benkum*)	(*adonten*)	(*nifa*)
	(*konti*)	

Palace Guard
(the *Wenchihene* and his *gyase*)
Rear Guard
(*kyidom*)

Each lineage in the tribe had its traditional place in one of these units with its court representative as its field officer. Civil and military office were fused, for Ashanti had become a military state. Yet by the nature of its constitutional form, which balanced centralization and decentralization in function, it never became a military dictatorship or despotism.

Although the paramount chieftainship of Wenchi was hereditary in the *Sofoasefo* lineage, succession was not automatic. All the people had a say in the choice of the man who was to fill the office. Each of the brothers, maternal cousins, and sororate nephews (in fact, all adult males of the ex-chief's lineage) were eligible. When a chief died or was impeached, the council of elders met and chose a committee of two to approach the queen mother and ask her to nominate a successor. This woman was the senior female of the royal lineage—often a sister to the chief rather than a mother in fact.

She in turn convened all the adult males and senior females of the royal lineage in an open session. Each of the eligible males of the lineage was then discussed in turn until agreement was reached on the man to be nominated. Thus the Ashanti avoided the defects of automatic hereditary succession: the enthronement of a feeble incompetent or, more dangerous, of an egomaniac.

The name of the nominee was sent by the queen mother to the Wenchi council, which replied with thanks and the information (which, of course, she knew already) that the appointment could not be confirmed until all the people of the tribe had been heard from. To achieve this the council summoned the headmen of all the villages to be present in the capitol on a certain day for an electoral meeting. Everyone, including the young men, came to the great event.

A very important feature of the Ashanti constitutional machinery was the organization of young men, the *Nkwankwaa*. Although each young man was represented in his lineage, the formal seats of power were in the seniors and elders. The Ashanti had no highly organized age-classes among which the class of young fighters could take an important role as was done in East Africa (Masai, for instance). They fought as members of their lineage levies. But they were nevertheless important members of the society, and the voice of youth had to be heard.

Therefore each village had its association of young men, or "commoners." They chose from among themselves an able representative, brave and skilled in oratory, to represent their views. He had no official status on the council of elders, but his voice was listened to by officialdom. Unlike the headmen, the elders, and the paramount chieftains, he took no oath of personal allegiance to a higher chieftain. He, unlike them, could vociferously voice opposition to chiefly policies without risk of suspicion of treason. No council would act without hearing the Voice of the Young Men.[17]

So—at the electoral general assembly, as the council of elders took its place around their temporary presiding head, the commoners sat together behind their *Nkwankwaahene* (chief of the commoners).

Also sitting as a separate group—a short distance away or in the queen mother's house—were the members of the royal lineage.

The session opened with an address by the Talking Chief (*Okyeame*) of the tribe, who announced the name of the candidate who had been put forth by the royal lineage. The crowd let its sentiment be known through silence, grunts, hisses, derisive laughter, or applause.

There then occurred some byplay between the council and the elders, with the commoners vetoing or approving the decision of the

---

[17] The place of the *Nkwankwaahene* was recently abolished in the formal structure of the modern Ashanti Confederacy council with results that have not, in the judgment of Dr. Busia, been beneficial to smooth operation of the government. (Busia, pp. 215–216.)

elders on the acceptability of the nominee. If he was rejected, word was sent to the queen mother to turn in another nomination. If three unacceptable candidates proposed by the royal lineage were rejected, the council proceeded to name one of the line themselves—always with the approval of the commoners required. The queen mother had then only to certify that the new paramount chief-to-be was a legitimate member of her lineage. Without this approval he could not qualify.

Subsequently, the chosen chief was "enstooled." If the selective process were not enough to impress upon him that he ruled by the will of the people, the enstoolment rites put the seal upon it. In the presence of the elders and the members of the royal lineage the *Okyeame* admonished him.

"All the elders say that I should give you the Stool. Do not go after women. Do not become a drunkard. When we give you advice, listen to it. Do not gamble. We do not want you to disclose the origin of your subjects.[18] We do not want you to abuse us. We do not want you to be miserly; we do not want one who disregards advice; we do not want you to regard us as fools; we do not want autocratic ways; we do not want bullying; we do not like beating. Take the Stool. We bless the Stool and give it to you. The elders say they give the Stool to you."[19] Clearly the Ashanti knew the corrupting tendency of power.

Admonishment was not enough, however. After paying the elders their *aseda* (token payment of acknowledgment) the new chief stood before them and swore the most solemn oath of Ashantiland: the oath of the Earth Goddess, whose sacred day is Thursday.

"I ask your permission," he said, "to speak the forbidden oath of Thursday. I am the grandson of Anye Amoampon Tabraku. Today you have elected me: . . . if I do not listen to the advice of my elders; if I make war upon them; if I run away from battle; then have I violated the oath."[20] Violation of the oath means destoolment (impeachment), and destoolment was by no means rare.[21]

The Ashanti chief, surrounded by the panoply of an elaborate

[18] I.e., reproach them for being descendants of slaves.

[19] Busia, p. 12; Rattray, *Ashanti Law and Constitution*, p. 82.

[20] Busia, p. 12.

[21] In present-day Ashanti it is as plaguing as the overthrow of French governments. During the 1940's an average of three out of the twenty-one paramount chiefs were destooled every year.

court and object of high honors, holding the judgment of life and death over his subjects, looked for all the world like the popular conception of an oriental sultan. But the trappings of autocratic power were external and not real. His were not the despotic privileges of a Trobriand paramount chief. He was sacred only so long as he sat on the stool, for then he was the holy intermediary between his people and the great tribal ancestors. When destooled he was as profane as any man—and less honored. He administered the tribal lands in trust for the ancestors. And so also the stool properties. When he was destooled, any personal estate he brought to the stool remained with it—impeachment meant impoverishment.

We have thus far set the relation of the household head to lineage, the lineage head to the village, the village head to the tribe, and the paramount chief to his people. Each was selected on a kinship–territorial basis and each held power as the surrogate of household, lineage, village, and tribal ancestral spirit. The position and relationship of the *Ashantihene* (king of all Ashanti) was exactly the same. By virtue of his direct overlordship of Kumasi, the national capital, he was (and is) paramount chief of the Kumasi division or tribe. After 1719 he became successively the overlord of more and more Ashanti tribes as Osai Tutu and his followers extended their dominance and built the Ashanti Union. Although no tribe could secede—secession meant immediate war by the majority that supported Kumasi—it never lost its rights in its own lands, and all together held a constitutional check on the king.

The most obvious focal point of Ashanti social ideology was the importance of the ancestors as vital forces in everyday affairs. More deep-lying, however, was a genuine cosmic philosophy that gave rise to a native conception of Natural Law. Remote and high above all the ancestors was the supreme creator: a true High God. Beneath him were many departmental or executive deities, the *obosom,* who had their many shrines with their attendant priests who spoke the minds of the gods. Rattray understood the Earth to be a goddess,[22] but Busia with the knowledge of a born African feels that it is closer to the Ashanti feeling to say only that the Earth was conceived as a female principle. This was a society, remember, in which the female principle permeates descent and social loyalties. The

---

[22] Rattray, *Ashanti Law and Constitution,* chap. xxi.

Earth, like the Supreme Deity, had no shrines, no priests, and was not appealed to in divination. She was the giver of life itself, not of little things.[23]

The Natural Law idea of the Ashanti flowed from the belief that the Supreme Deity, the Earth, and all the gods, as well as the ancestors, had their ways, and the natural world pulsated in accord with the way of the supernaturals.

Man, for the Ashanti, was never the measure of all things. The works of man were destined to be but the working out of the universe forces.

Constitution as a structure and in function, in its Ashanti context, meant the attempt to correlate human laws with Nature's laws and the conditions to which human laws are subject. Thus, as Rattray phrased it: the lawmakers were responsible for the even and normal working of the cosmic forces. They were to make decisions and promulgate regulations that would order the workings of their evergrowing society in accord with the order of the universe. They had to see to it that the constitution of the tribe was such that it would ensure and not militate against the workings of the laws of nature.[24] This was the bedrock religious and philosophical basis of Ashanti law and government.

The people decided for themselves what was in accord with the nature of things, and the priests as mouthpieces of the gods and ancestors had their special say. The chief who acted contrariwise was soon a destooled ex-chief.

What was the substantive law thus ordained by Nature?

First, as to real estate: the land was of the Earth itself. The Earth giveth and the Earth can withhold. Her birthday is Thursday, a day when there shall be no tilling. Divisions of the Earth belonged to the ancestors collectively; no man could claim to own a part of her. Clan ancestors came to be associated with plots of land through burial in sacred groves. Earlier, and not too far back, the Ashanti were a neolithic, hunting, and mussel-eating people. As such they had only a limited interest in land, largely as hunting areas—except for the spot where the ancestors lay. As gardeners they never abandoned the idea that land and the ancestors were insepa-

---

[23] Busia, pp. 40 ff.
[24] Rattray, *Ashanti Law and Constitution,* chap. xxxviii.

rable. What *was* separable was the usufruct of the land and the crops the usufruct brought forth.[25]

"As the land belonged to the ancestors it was a link between them and their living descendants. In Ashanti the object which symbolized the unity of the ancestors and their descendants was the stool which the chief occupied. In any Ashanti village the inquirer was informed, 'The land belongs to the stool,' or 'The land belongs to the chief.' Further investigation revealed that both expressions meant the same thing: 'The land belongs to the ancestors.' " [26]

However it acquired the land in the first place (usually by the taking of unoccupied domain), the stool, i.e., the tribal chief as an officer, held it as trustee. But the individual plots that had been cleared from the forest were held *de facto* by the separate lineages from the time the lineage ancestors had first worked them. In legal theory the chief had apportioned the land to the lineage; indeed, in some instances he had actually done so. Within the lineage the plots were held by individual households; but again the theory was that the lineage headman had assigned them. An Ashanti farmer would always, on the asking, trace his descent in the matrilineal line from an ancestor known to have farmed his plot in the beginning. His right to farm there was proven by his kinship to the ancestor.

Externally viewed, this looks like a chain of enfeoffments. Indeed, Rattray, as an English-law-trained scholar, saw it as "an almost exact replica" of English laws and medieval feudalism which he described in terms of freehold, leasehold, lords, vassals, fiefs, aids, levies, and escheat.[27]

True, each successive chief in the political chain, and each elder as well, swore personal loyalty to the chief above him, and it was said, "The chief owns the land." But this was only figurative.

Lineage rights in land were inalienable. They belonged solely to the stool spirits. "The farm is mine; the soil is the king's"; and no man could be separated from his farm except for certain high criminal acts.

Conversely, no individual could alienate his right of usufruct by

[25] *Ibid.*, p. 340; R. S. Rattray, *Ashanti* (Oxford, 1923), pp. 121–122.
[26] Busia, p. 44.
[27] Rattray, *Ashanti Law and Constitution*, chap. xxxiii.

his own action, for that would deprive his ancestors' descendants of their source of living. If the right of usufruct were to be sold, it would have to be by action of the entire lineage. Such would be only a last resort.

In the larger political structure all this meant that a conquered Ashanti division kept its essential control over its land. Kumasi demanded political fealty and military aid but never sought to dispossess those who acceded to political control. Chiefs claimed a share of all mineral rights and other dues, to be sure, but they did not meddle with usufruct.

Chattels were in three categories: stool, family, and personal. Stool property made up the royal estate. It consisted of the royal stools with all their appurtenances. There were the drums, umbrellas, the palace, and the royal treasury. Each of the main items was under the custody of a palace official, a member of the royal line. The chief himself never had direct access to the royal treasury, which was handled by the *Sannahene* and his assistants.[28] The chief personally had little or no opportunity to enrich himself. On behalf of the stool he set his agents to engage in trade. He could levy special taxes, especially for war, but only with the consent of his council. His fields were worked by public corvée, and he had other sources of revenue. He needed a large income, for he had to be lavish in gift-giving and feasting. Chiefs who were not generous were destooled.

As already remarked, all personal property that the chief possessed on ascension to the stool became irrevocably stool property. Like the cagey modern business man, some chiefs before coronation turned a good part of their personal property over to their mothers or sisters against the evil day when they might be destooled.

Family property (also lineage properties) consisted of the kindred stool, household gods, fetishes, and such other heirlooms as might be borrowed by members for certain ceremonies. It was administered by the lineage or household head as trustee and custodian.

Personal property consisted of the chattels acquired by a man's individual efforts or the work of his slaves, wives and children. It could include anything, save land, even family heirlooms that had

[28] See Busia, pp. 80–84, for a summary description of the interesting accounting system that was employed.

been pledged on a family loan and then redeemed through a man's sole efforts or money. Women, too, could possess property in their own right, and children possessed their pets, which not even the king could appropriate.

Originally, all property passed to the clan or lineage on the death of its owner, but devolution of personal property to individuals within the maternal kindred became established several centuries ago at the latest. A man's personal goods then went first to his brothers and then to his sister's sons.

Any alteration of normal intestate devolution had to be done by public testament, and by this means alone could a father pass goods to his son. Before witnesses he could declare his will; if his son, or other beneficiary, gave *aseda* in palm wine or money, and the *aseda* was accepted, the testamentary disposition was valid. Such testaments are known as *samansie,* "that which is set aside by the ghost."

But the testament was not always carried out; it had no direct legal binding force. "When a ghost has made an improper distribution of his (private) property, the living will make a new one," said Rattray's Ashanti.[29] What this means is that if the maternal kin do not like the arrangement, they overrule it.

If the beneficiary decided on litigation, the issue would be an interhousehold one to be decided between his lineage and that of the deceased, and legally a will received little support as against the demands of the maternal kin of the ghost. The situation of conflict between father-love and avuncular duty in Ashanti parallels the tensions of the Trobrianders. "Ashanti," says Meyer Fortes out of his personal experience, "discuss the subject interminably, stressing especially the inevitability of conflicting loyalties."[30] This may well be, and Ashanti fathers, too, strain against the dictates of the maternal principle, but the ideology of the society and the law that supports it, now as in the past, rule in favor of the maternal heirs as against paternal testamentary disposition.

"A woman and her children constitute the insoluble core of Ashanti social organization."[31]

The difficulties of reducing legal practice to simple precept are

[29] Rattray, *Ashanti Law and Constitution,* p. 339.
[30] Fortes, "Time and Social Structure," p. 75.
[31] *Ibid.,* p. 72.

always with us. Rattray was essentially right when he said the living will set aside an improper will. The maternal descent rule is the rule with legal authority. But—ancestors (paternal?) are not wholly supine, and there *is* the conflict of ties. Note what happened in 1942!

A man when on his death-bed made a dying declaration giving one of his cocoa-farms to his son, and swore an oath enjoining his brother, who was his successor, to see that the gift was honoured. "If you do not give it to him," said the dying man, "I shall call you before the ancestors for our case to be judged." . . .

The man died and his brother succeeded to his property, but refused, with the concurrence of the other members of the family, to give the cocoa-farm to his deceased brother's son. Three months later a fire broke out in the village. The surviving brother fell from a roof while helping to put out one of the fires, and sustained an injury to his leg from which he subsequently died. Before he died, he told his family that he believed his deceased brother was summoning him to the spirit world to answer for his conduct in not honouring his brother's death-bed declaration. The general belief was that his death was due to his failure to carry out his deceased brother's instructions. The next successor to the property duly gave the cocoa-farm to the son to whom it had been left.[32]

Unfortunately we are not told whether it was the paternal or maternal ancestors who killed the man. We presume it to be the paternal representatives of the *ntoro*, since it is hardly reasonable to suppose that *abusua* spirits would rule so harshly against the interests of the *abusua* merely to uphold the abstract principle that a man's will should be upheld for its own sake.

This case also illustrates a feature of Ashanti law emphasized by Busia but slighted by Rattray, namely, if the mundane courts and legal processes which operate in the name of the ancestors fail to translate the ancestral will into proper action, the ancestors will act in accordance with their right notions of due process and "try" the case themselves. All spirits, after they have climbed the steep hill into the world of spirits are called upon by the ancestors to give an account of their actions on behalf of the kindred while on earth.[33] Is a person killed by his ancestors for wrongdoing, so that

[32] Busia, p. 43.
[33] *Ibid.*, p. 25.

his released spirit may appear before the ancestors for a hearing and trial? "If you do not give it to him, I shall call you before the ancestors for our case to be judged." Was the fall and death of the man his punishment after judgments? Or did he have a trial before the ghosts awaiting him after his death? And if so, what punishment was meted to his soul?

A stool could borrow on its lands from another stool, but the elders and subjects of a chief would ordinarily be pledged as debt slaves before the stool lands would be mortgaged. The right of usufruct to rivers could be pledged on a loan without encumbrance to the land through which the waters flowed. Interest was paid in exclusive fishing rights for the duration of the debt.

Family property could be pledged in security for a loan on decision of the family council of elders. Private property could be pledged for individual loans at any time. As in most advanced primitive tribes where capital transactions are performed an agent was used to arrange the deal, while witnesses were convened to record the transfer orally and by eye in the absence of written documents. The agent in a debt transaction assumed a greater personal responsibility than did the Ifugao *mongaba,* for he was a personal friend of the borrower and acted as surety for him. The primary surety, however, was found in the chattel given as pledge. A loan would be for only half the value of the pledge—security in the amount of 200 per cent of the loan was called for as in standard American first mortgage practice. Interest consisted of the use of the article without responsibility for ordinary wear and tear. The borrower was forced to divest himself of the *total* productive capacity of the pledged resource. The possibility of a production loan was therefore completely barred and the difficulties of redemption greatly increased. The interest might or might not be high percentagewise. Yet it was devastating in its net effect. Add to this, "service charges" to the witnesses, the agent, and the creditor, which ate up the equivalent of two shillings to the pound, and you get the Ashanti proverb: "A debtor's things go away in great heaps."

Not all loans were on pledges. Some rested only on the credit of the borrower and his surety. In this case in event of default it was up to the surety to act. He swore an oath on one of his own gods to relieve himself of the obligation and forthwith informed the head chief of the district; swearing the oath made the default, for reasons we shall later see, into a criminal act. The chief then had the debtor seized and informed his lineage of the fact. It was then up to the lineage to pay the debt or forfeit the debtor as a debt slave who could be sold to pay the principal. Responsibility for any debt was in the last analysis collective; loss of the debtor as a slave was a loss to the kindred even as paying his debt would have been. So much was this so that a less valued kinsman could and often would be offered and accepted in his stead. In like wise, debts were inheritable within the maternal group (a nephew rather than a son would have to accept the burden), and on debts there was no statute of limitations. "A debt never rots," says the Ashanti, almost paraphrasing the Ifugao adage, "A debt never sleeps."

Finally, in loans wherein there was no pledge and no surety the creditor had two sure-fire avenues of collection. He could call upon a god to kill the debtor. The debtor would then pay up through the priest of the god evoked. Or, the creditor would "flee to the chief" with a petition for intervention. The chief, for a fee and as a public service, sent his treasurer as a collector. Refusal to pay over to the royal treasurer brought from his lips the dread oath on the forbidden name of a tribal god that the debtor "hated the king." To the Ashanti this was a declaration that it was the intention of the debtor to assassinate the king. The charge was one of treason and the penalty death. To prove his innocence of the dread charge, the recalcitrant debtor paid up immediately—or lost his head.

The slightest case of indebtedness in Ashanti could thus become a capital crime. Indeed, a minor tort—any minor tort—could instantaneously be converted into a heinous criminal offense. Such was the exaggerated effect of the emergence of centralized government with its chiefs' and king's courts working on the old principle that the ancestors are the source of all morality and all law.

Crimes were sins. To this there was no exception. The basic function of Ashanti criminal law was in theory to support and maintain the religious system. In fact, the religious postulates were also used to justify a system of criminal law that ran almost wild. It was a new tool that the Ashanti had not yet learned to control and use with finesse. The corrupting corrosions of bureaucratic self-interest worked on the germ of the Ashanti juridical organism to stimulate a gross mutation.

Criminal acts were *oman akyiwadie*—"hated by the tribe." More generically, they were hated by the ancestors. They were acts deemed to affect the relations of the community of Ashanti with the ancestors of the chief, who had become in the process of state consolidation the ancestors of the entire tribe. Acts deemed offensive to the tribal ancestral spirits were held to affect the well-being of the tribe as a whole. Were they not to be punished by the chief on behalf of the tribe, the ancestors would punish the entire tribe for its negligence and disregard of the natural law set by the supernatural ghosts of the departed.[34]

The earlier "household law" in the primitive democracy of Ashanti had been a gentle thing. It aimed at the pristine function of law as a social instrument: to channel behavior and maintain a quiet equilibrium among the various members of the society. The chief aim of the central authority (household and lineage heads) was the avoidance of disputes and the conciliation of estranged parties.[35] Now it was different. A military state, pyramided through household, lineage, subdistrict, district organization, to the Ashanti kingdom with the *Kumasihene* as *Ashantihene* at the top, had been forged. A class of royal bureaucrats had arisen about the paramount chiefs and the king to administer the new political machine. The monarchy was constitutional and limited; central power was checked by decentralized rights of self-determination. There was no superimposed tyranny. But—the superstate, which existed primarily for military reasons, was a power instrument that also turned its power inward. Its supporting sanction was death—the legal penalty for all crimes. Furthermore, it arrogated unto itself an absolute monopoly of this right, for "only the king may wield the knife." It was probably not hard to achieve this monopoly, since blood-feud was not a characteristic of old Ashanti.

It is easy, however, to be misled by the Ashanti dogma that the penalty for all crimes was death. This was merely a threat—a real threat, to be sure—but not a certain result. The bureaucracy needed

---

[34] Busia, p. 67; Rattray, *Ashanti Law and Constitution*, chaps. xxv–xxvii.
[35] Rattray, *Ashanti Law and Constitution*, p. 292.

income. General assessments, except for war, were unconstitutional. There were other possibilities in the law. And these were quickly spotted and exploited. The Ashanti criminal law assumed a secondary and important function that is not primarily a law job but one that becomes inevitable once the law-ways are elaborated: revenue must be raised—the machinery must be supported. The power to fine is used to implement this function, and when limited to provision of reasonable support of the machinery, it is, as Karl Llewellyn maintains, a proper function of law. More than support is abuse of a proper function.[36]

There were, strictly speaking, few fines in the Ashanti system of public law. Various court fees such as *aseda* were collected, but these did not loom large. The dodge was to permit a dead man to "buy his own head." By payment to the stool of a heavy ransom he could keep his head on his shoulders and go his way a chastened man, leaving the stool so much the richer for his misdeed. The power to commute the death sentence belonged solely to the chiefs, who had to decide between the extreme penalty of the law and the palace advantage of getting commutation ransom. To what extent mercy as such entered into the mitigation of the harsh death sentence we do not know. We do know that the courts were avid for money. Litigation was eagerly encouraged for the benefit of the royal coffers, and justice became a royal prostitute. The chiefs' courts became more indifferent to the attainment of conciliation, as cash, not social tranquillity, became their concern.

"The central authority, once it began to feel its strength, began to welcome litigation and quarrels as a means of raising revenue for the Stool. This was an attitude of the official mind which was the direct antithesis to that found in the original courts."[37]

A chief who encouraged settlement of minor disputes in the old way was apt to be needled by his elders. "That chief has not a good head; since his succession we cannot get court cases to settle," became their lament. A new Ashanti adage was formed: "If the chief tries to conciliate parties in a street quarrel, he will soon be starving." Even the gods were brought into play, not as of old to keep peo-

---

[36] K. N. Llewellyn, personal communication.
[37] Rattray, *Ashanti Law and Constitution*, p. 388.

ple from breaking the law and custom, but to encourage them to do so. Outside the houses of the talking chiefs, the *Okyeame,* who, as will soon be seen, played an important role in court hearings, were raised litigation fetishes. Small portions of the *aseda* fees paid by acquitted litigants were regularly set aside in an earmarked fund. When enough had been accumulated from the cases, the fund was used to buy a thank offering (a kind of *aseda*) for the fetish. And when the court calendar had been too long uncrowded the *Okyeame* offered a special prayer. He stood before the litigation fetish with a palm-oil offering which he poured on the fetish, intoning, "Case-hearing rock, these days of hunger are killing us, let me get cases to settle." In other words, let men put their lives in jeopardy so that we may condemn them to death and let them off by buying their heads!

The functionaries of the Ashanti legal institutions had come to forget that the institutions had been created for the benefit of society; they had come to think that they existed to serve their own selfish interests. They had succumbed to the eternal danger that besets any institution that has become so complex that its services require full-time experts. Experts are tempted to treat the institution as existing to support them rather than perceiving that they themselves exist as servants of the institution and of the people who created and sustain it. The Ashanti elders had become shysters and fee-grabbers.

An interesting little side light is also shown by Robert Marshall in his fascinating study of an Alaskan community. "When the commissioner's office was first established in 1901," he notes, "there were forty minor criminal suits and twenty-five civil suits tried in the first two years. However, the old timers who still survive those days are unanimous in their contention that most of the trouble was stirred by the Commissioner who wanted fees, and by two shysters who were later debarred. Since 1904, when Frank E. Howard, commencing a long term as commissioner, started the precedent of avoiding trouble, the lawsuits have been few. During the past ten years there have been but three cases tried in the commissioner's court." [38]

The main categories of criminal offenses in Ashanti were not many. The "chapters" of the unwritten criminal code may be listed as follows:

[38] Robert Marshall, *Arctic Village* (New York, 1933), p. 196.

1. Homicide
2. Suicide
3. Certain forms of sexual offenses (others were private offenses)
4. Certain kinds of assault (others were private offenses)
5. Certain kinds of stealing (others were private offenses)
6. Cursing the chief
7. Treason
8. Cowardice
9. Sorcery
10. Violation of royal legislation conditioned by a royal curse
11. Violation of any established local tabu
12. Certain forms of abuse involving the use of a royal oath

Each of these may now be examined in detail.

Murder, called *"awudie,"* was looked upon with particular abhorrence. Unless a man died a natural death, which included death on the field of battle, his spirit wanted to know why he died. He had to have a trial at which the death warrant was recited in detail. Else, if the ghost knew not why it had died, it would trouble the chief and the villagers and perhaps cause bad luck. This they wanted to avoid. Secondarily, to murder was to usurp a power reserved to the king alone. Not even a district head chief, although his court had initial jurisdiction over most crimes committed within his district, could try a murder case. Such went directly to the national, or supreme, court at Kumasi.

Awudie as a concept of criminal law included sexual intercourse with a woman who was already pregnant by another man, as well as intercourse with a prepubescent girl. The concept was apparently not so much one of actual homicide as one that embraced acts of extreme repugnance to the Ashanti. *Awudie* = "the Heinous." This would satisfy Rattray's puzzlement as to why these last offenses were classified with murder. They were in the Ashanti view as repugnant as murder and hence lumped with it.

Careful attention was given to the question of intent in Ashanti murder trials. A *mens rea* had definitely to be established. Otherwise a plea of accidental homicide would hold and the slaying would be accepted as the action of an evil spirit misdirecting the activity of the killer. The court examined all the possible motives it could think of, and if none could be definitely tied to the defendant, he was to be acquitted on the criminal count. "Civil" damages were in order, however. An ordinary judgment on behalf of the deceased's maternal kin would run to £7 of gold dust, a case of rum wherewith to drown their sorrows and make funeral libations, a good piece of cloth, and a coffin. These were to be paid over to the lineage of the deceased by the killer. In other words, a heavy composition settled an accidental slaying.

A lamb had to be given to the chief to sacrifice for the absolution of the community. Furthermore, the defendant had to confess his unintentional sin to one of the lesser gods and beg that further misfortune be forestalled. These were heavy burdens but at least they were not death.

The consideration given to intent in the Ashanti law of homicide resulted not only in a clear distinction between unintentional and malicious killing but it undertook to forestall what it thought to be potential killings through identification of certain acts as declarations of intent to kill. Intention to commit a homicide was a criminal act treated as no less heinous than murder by the Ashanti, who themselves classified it as *awudie*. Exposure of intent to kill came about not as the result of any super-detective-work or skilled psychological investigation. Performance of one of three simple symbolic acts was enough. To declare in public, "I shall not eat again," was one. To cut on an object with the knife held at right angles, if done in public, was another! For a man not a priest to let his hair grow long was the third. The reasons for this last are clear. There was a time when a man contemplating war left his head unshorn. The first two may seem capricious and irrelevant, but it is enough that Ashanti men understood their meaning. And, their meaning understood, these deeds were perhaps more akin to suicide than murder, since a man committed himself to death by saying or doing them without the chance to kill. They were not penalized as suicide, however.

As to suicide itself, the Ashanti legal postulate that only the king may kill an Ashanti gave to it a bizarre twist. The penalty for suicide was decapitation, as for any other homicide. More than that, it involved "contempt of court." When a suicide occurred, the corpse was brought into court, even though the body had to be disinterred if the relatives had tried to hide the crime by burying the body. The proceedings, as usual, were in charge of the *Okyeame*. To the chief he said, "This is your slave. No one knows what he had done, and today he has hanged himself."

Then to the corpse, "No man knows a single thing that came into your head, but, because you did not bring your case here that we might take good ears to hear it, but took a club and struck the *Akyeame* [sic]—and when you kill us (thus) you regard us as brute beasts—therefore you are guilty." [39] Forthwith they chopped off his head.

Then more realistically, since in this situation the already be-corpsed criminal was in no position to buy back his head and thus enrich the stool, and also to give the sanction a more deterrent effect, one of the rare fines was added to make the proceedings more practical. All his private property was confiscated and his heirs dispossessed, an act which Llewellyn notes as practically medieval English. His standing crops went to the chief, but his right of usufruct was resumed by his heirs after the first harvest. The "attainder of blood" was not vindictively prolonged. The fruit of his trees was henceforth garnered, however, by the chief so long as the trees stood and bore. Suicide did not pay, except in one situation. War captains who lost a battle were expected to kill themselves. For this there was no punishment and they were honored rather than disgraced.

A few other interesting turns of the law of homicide deserve to be noted. In the matter of intent, drunkenness was a valid defense for all crimes but homicide and cursing the king. A plea of insanity held for all criminal offenses, and a madman would not be executed. He was not turned loose to run wild, however; he was chained to a tree and left to die, unless his relatives chose to feed him. This, incidentally, is the first mention of "imprisonment" as a legal incapacitation among the primitives reviewed in this book. Here, the important thing is that the Ashanti had a perfectly modern notion that a demented person is not responsible for his acts. And if they confined him in a brutal manner, it was not as punishment, but as a social precaution, and their brutality was hardly more calloused than that still reported for some of our backward

---

[39] The presumption was that he had committed a sin for which he would have been tried and executed. Rattray, *Ashanti Law and Constitution,* p. 300.

institutions for the mentally deficient. The Ashanti were trying to be reasonable.

In the reign of King Osai Yao this rule of law was set aside. Osai Yao was apparently very much a rationalist in some matters and, in the following instance, a bumbling empiricist. He decided to examine first premises. In a Baconian manner he set up an experiment. He ordered his flunkies to place a madman and a drunk in a house. It was then put to the torch. As the flames took hold, the madman, taking to his heels, screamed that he was being burned. The drunk, in oblivious stupor, was cremated. The conclusion was obvious to Osai Yao. A drunk does not know what is going on. Ergo, drunkenness shall remain as a mitigating plea in defense. Insanity, though it may impair, does not completely paralyze perception. Ergo, there is no validity to the old plea of insanity as a defense. The plea was abolished.

Such are the pitfalls of science and logic when the scale of observation is too gross. Osai Yao's approach to the problem was scientific and his logic correct. Lamentably, the experimental technique was faulty.

When a pregnant woman was to be decapitated for murder, another special problem arose that was handled with a nice sense of discrimination by the Ashanti. Within her womb was another Ashanti. Whether it was to be a real child or a ghost child, no one knew. A newborn Ashanti infant was not consecrated through ceremonial bestowal of name and presentation to the public until eight days after its birth. Should it die before that time, it was casually thrown on the refuse heap and not buried, because it was believed that it was no more than the husk of a ghost child whose mother in the spirit world had pawned it off on a living mother while she went off on a junket. On her return she had recalled her little spirit baby. It had never really lived. A baby was not truly a member of the society of the living until after a week had passed.

On the other hand, if an Ashanti was to be executed, there was the belief that its ghost had to know why it had died. Should a mother-to-be be decapitated, her child, if it was a real child and left within her, would never know the reason. To solve this dilemma an *enceinte* murderess was allowed to live until her child was born. Then both she and her tainted infant were killed.

The sex offenses that came to be treated as crimes in Ashanti were those that were looked upon as particularly repugnant. Of these there were five. Others remained "household" matters to be dealt with by the "bylaw" of the family, or within the framework of private law if it were an interfamilial affair.

Incest within either the *abusua* or *ntoro* was a capital crime. It would seem that under the old system the most the clan could do would have been to extrude the incestuous; other people could ostracize and ridicule them. The new death power of the central authority provided a more fearsome means of control that was readily put to use. So long as the lineage village was the extent of the community, it alone might suffer from the wrath of the lineage ancestors. On the other hand, when the whole tribe had become a cemented community, an act so distasteful to the ancestors as incest endangered the entire nation and threatened to destroy the universe.

Should the incestuous not be destroyed, hunters would have ceased to kill, children would have ceased to be born, the ancestral spirits would have been infuriated, gods would have been angered, clans would have ceased to exist, and all would have been *basa basa* (chaos) in the world. So thought the Ashanti. So thought the Old Testament Hebrews. So dire a condition the law strove to avoid.

Again, intent figured. When a couple unknowingly committed incest in ignorance of their relationship, they got off with fines and atonement assessments for sacrifices to the incensed supernaturals. This is also the modern penalty for incest with knowledge since the British mitigated the death sentence. In the 1920's the fine was £25, while the propitiation assessment consisted of a case of gin, a sheep to be sacrificed, and twelve yards of calico.

Many, if not most, primitive peoples hold that menstruation is inimical to the supernatural powers of men.[40] Menstruating women are deemed ritually unclean, even dangerous. Among the Ashanti, a man who had intercourse with a menstruating woman scoffed at the very foundation of Ashanti faith. The act was *oman akyiwadie;* the penalty, death.

Rape of a married woman in the bush was also a capital crime and not a matter for private prosecution.

Adultery with any of the wives of a chief, while an offense against

40 See R. H. Lowie, *Primitive Religion* (New York, 1924), chap. x.

the chief himself, came to be much more importantly an offense directly against the royal ancestors. Chiefs' wives were stool wives. When a chief died, or even when he was put out by impeachment, his wives stayed with the stool and became the consorts of his successor. The sexual interloper was tampering with women sacred unto the ancestors. Penalty: death in a truly hideous form, the *atopere,* dance of death, in which the condemned victim was with infinite pains dissected in small bits with such surgical skill that he was not killed during two or three days of exquisite torture.[41]

In discussing Trobriand law we raised the question as to whether certain offenses were legally private wrongs against the person of the chief or criminal offenses against the *publicum.* The drawing of an either/or distinction we hold to be artificial, although it will always make a profound difference in any law system whether the political leader is seen primarily as a person or as the head of state. It is the *patrimonium* versus the rights by tax question of our own medieval times. The essential difference is between *person* and *office.*

In Ashanti an offense against the chief as a person would merely mean a household suit with conciliation as its aim. Against the chief as the stool-holder, it would mean sin and death. "This fact of the social identification between the chief and the ancestors is still [1950] one of the difficulties of Ashanti law. It is very difficult to distinguish between offenses committed against the chief personally, and offenses against the stool or the ancestors. The Ashanti themselves appear to make no such distinction, for as long as a chief remains on the stool he is a sacred person in a special relationship with the ancestors."[42] A dangerous threat to personal liberty and the seeds of the tyranny that flowered in so many of the autocracies of early civilizations are implicit in the identification of the chief's individual self with that of the official-on-earth who embodied the whole society's relation to itself, its ancestors, its gods. A problem that has plagued generations of men emerged here as elsewhere with the rise of centralized government and the "divinity" of the ruler.

So it was that all assaults on the chief or his court retinue became capital crimes in Ashanti. So also treason. So also insults to the chief, as in the Trobriands.

[41] R. S. Rattray, *Religion and Art in Ashanti* (Oxford, 1927).
[42] Busia, p. 73.

For ordinary men, insults were private delicts. The same insults to a chief were reflections on the character of the royal ancestors. To say, "wo'ni" (your mother!), "wo'se" (your father!), "wo nana" (your grandparent!), carried a freight of implications that was enough.

According to Dr. Manet Fowler, among Negro boys in Louisiana twenty-five years ago the taunt, "Your mother!" was enough to start a good fight.[43] Louisiana is the one place in the United States to which we know the Ashanti were brought as slaves.

More explicit insults were: "The origin of your mother's genitals" —namely, the progenitors of your *abusua;* "The origin of your father's genitals"—namely, the progenitors of your *ntoro;* "May your ancestral spirits chew their own heads"; "May your ancestral spirits take their own bones [and eat them]."

There was no nose-thumbing or thumb-biting in Ashanti, but all of the above insults could be implied by holding the thumbs upward with the fists pressed close together. It was illegal, obviously, to do so.

Further, for any woman to call a man a fool was also a capital crime. Neither Rattray, nor Busia, nor any of the other Ashanti reporters (so far as I have discovered) indicate the rationale of this extreme piece of masculine egotism. There is the possibility that the Ashanti word translated as "fool" really means "unfit for being and for office." [44] The context of the insult could also imply incompetence on the part of a man's ancestors that they should beget such a one. Competence on the part of males does seem to be more important to the Ashanti than does the competence of the female. At any rate, more semantic and institutional detail are certainly necessary if this phase of the culture is to be understood.

Once on the stool, a chief had no personal property. Whatever he brought to the stool was "nationalized" and remained stool property forever. Hence any theft of a chief's property was a stool theft— theft from the ancestors: a capital crime. In the invention of this idea the Ashanti brought forth a really great intellectual achievement. How better could a society fuse the person in the office than to absorb his property wholly into the holdings of the office itself? Medieval European government lacked the idea. But *neither* line of government found it easy to control the revenue aspects of "justice."

43 Oral communication.
44 Suggested by K. N. Llewellyn. Personal communication.

Cursing the *Ashantihene,* which was done through the invocation of some spiritual power to cause the death of the king, was the crime most horrible of all. The Ashanti could not even speak of it by name; they had to resort to an inverted euphemism: "blessing the king." Here too, intent before the fact was treated as commission of the ultimate crime itself, for when a king died, his son ritually cleared the path to the royal mausoleum, and for a man to induce a small prince to clear the path while his father yet lived was a capital crime revealing a clear expression of intent to curse the king.

Revenge-suicide could be achieved by cursing the king and putting the blame on someone who drove you to the act. In a quarrel between two men one of them could reach the point when he felt the stand of the other went beyond all reason. Or, it could be that his own situation was untenable, and being unable to get out of it, he destroyed himself but also had the satisfaction of making a scapegoat out of his adversary by saying, "I call upon such and such a god to kill the King, and I do so on your head, and after I am killed may you pay 100 *pereguan* [45] to buy the Bongo's skin with which I shall be strangled." [46]

Curses were indeed taken seriously by the Ashanti, so much so that to push a man to the point where he cursed the king was almost as serious a crime as the curse itself. The penalty was not death, however, but a fine of £800 in gold dust—enough to force most men to enter into debt slavery. Like the threat of suicide among the Trobriand Islanders and the Cheyennes, it should have served to check extreme and outrageous demands in the enforcement of what might have been legal rights by reason of the social injury suffered by the person who was blamed for pushing the suicide to his extreme act.

As a further evidence of the heinousness of cursing the king, an incidental precaution taken in the royal courts when a man was condemned to death was for an executioner to thrust a stiletto through his cheeks and tongue so that he could not cry out a curse on the king before they got around to executing him.

Sorcery was classified as a special crime. It was murder, but a

[45] A packet of gold dust equal to £8 value.
[46] Rattray, *Ashanti Law and Constitution,* p. 312.

tainted murder utterly tabued by the ancestors. Condemned sorcerers were never decapitated; a witch's blood must not be shed. So they were strangled (like a curser of the king), clubbed to death, doused with oil and burned, drowned, or driven out to die of starvation. Witches were truly feared and hated. The social reprisal was an expression of sadism born of extreme anxiety.

As if these deadly crimes were not enough, every capital city had a list of local tabus the violation of which were *oman akyiwadie* and punished by death or buying back the head. The explicit origin of most of these tabus is unknown (at least as far as the reports go) and on the surface without reason. All of them, however, somewhere along the line, for some reason or another, became established as hateful to the ancestors. The functional theory of anthropology reminds us that they are not likely to be as capricious as they look on the surface, and they ought not to be condemned by the reader as wholly silly. On the other hand, the known tendency of culture to develop certain aspects beyond reason, and then to perpetuate them, reminds us that some tabus may indeed be quite without continuing reason so far as their specific content goes.

Here, in any event, is Rattray's list of local tabus for the district capital of Mampon.

1. A dog must not be allowed to run through the town.
2. A headrest must never be made of cloth.
3. A chicken must not be carried on top of any load.
4. Fish must never be cut up, if they are to be sold in the market.
5. Whistling is forbidden in the town because it is hateful to certain spirits.
6. A priest must never marry a priestess.
7. There shall be no farm work on Thursday. (This is actually a national and not a local tabu, for Thursday is sacred to the Earth throughout all Ashanti.)
8. An egg must not intentionally be broken upon the ground.
9. Nor a pot.
10. Nor may palm oil be spilt intentionally upon the ground. (The breaking of 8, 9 and 10 are local methods of invoking a curse on the chief of the district.)
11. Water must not be poured into palm oil.
12. A load must not be carried on the shoulders while in town.

13. A load carried on the head must not be raised up from the head while passing through the town. (This would have implied that the person considered the Mampon chief and elders as light and worthless—a nasty reflection on the judgment of their ancestors.)

14. No menstruating woman may speak to a priest or palace attendant.

If we shake down these particularistic rules of Rattray's and put some system in their arrangement, we get the following:

I. Acts which imply disrespect for the elders of the town are crimes because they reflect upon the judgment of the town ancestors.
    1. Criminal acts falling within this category are 2, 3, 12, and 13 (above).

II. Acts which are repugnant to the sensitivities of certain spirits are forbidden.
    1. Criminal acts falling within this category are 1 (?), 4 (?), and 5 (above).

III. No curse may be invoked on the chief of the district.
    1. In this locale the following acts, when performed, signify such invocation, and are forbidden as crimes.
        a. 8, 9, and 10 (above).

IV. Because of their special responsibilities priests and palace attendants may not be defiled.
    1. For a menstruating woman to speak to a priest is such defilement.

Finally, a brief note on special penalties: Impertinence was not serious enough as an offense to be considered a capital crime but neither was it to be countenanced. Conceited, disrespectful, swaggering, and overbearing men when brought before a chief for some minor misconduct would be cut back to size by slicing off the nose. If the man had not been too unbearable, the punishment would be lightened by notching his right ear—or cutting it off. Those who were charged with slander, if the slander had been against a chief or had been brought into a chief's court by means of an oath, when found guilty, had their lips cut off. And young boys found guilty of sexual insults, when the case had not been settled in household negotiations but had come into a chief's court on an oath, were castrated and kept as eunuchs among the palace attendants. Death or buying back the head were not the sole criminal penalties, after all.

The criminal offenses listed thus far had some antiquity among the Ashanti. They represent the culture in its more static aspects and they work to support conservatism. But Ashanti society was a society going through rapid expansion *and* consolidation. Ancestors as moral guardians are apt to have a stultifying effect. What went in their time is what they approve of today. The Ashanti called upon this dodge whenever it suited their purpose. But the Ashanti chiefs were too much bent upon expansion to let ancestorism hold them back. On the contrary, they used it to give sanction to new legislation by attaching a Great Oath to each new edict from the chief.

To speak the Great Oath is no more than to refer to the place and the day of the death (Koromante and Saturday) of Osai Tutu. The original event was one of sorrow and disaster, for it brought an end to the career of the greatest of the Ashanti. The ancestors grieved over it. Merely to mention the event wounded their memories and could even lead again to the death of the *Ashantihene* in battle. So, for a chief to attach the Great Oath to a new edict fixed the ancestors' attention on it and implied also that they approved the new act. Violations of laws with such "conditional curses" attached were hateful to the ancestors and it behooved the chiefs and elders to punish such defections as crimes. More exactly, it gave them a good excuse to deal roughly with obstructionists. The machinery worked nicely to smooth the path of social change.

By use of the same device the Ashanti arrived at the point where the criminal law could be made to supersede private law at every point. It reached the stage at which it flowered so luxuriantly as to all but choke out the gentle, conciliatory existence of the old household law.

It was enough for a disputant, no matter how trivial the original issue, to swear the forbidden oath of a chief or the King of Ashanti. The case was then immediately transferred to a royal court for criminal trial, with jurisdiction going to the court of the chief *whose oath had been used.* Unless it was a Kumasi case to begin with, the court of first instance was a trial court, and the Kumasi court the sentencing one, for only the King of Ashanti at Kumasi could "wield the knife." In any event, an appeal from the verdict of the trial court could always be obtained by swearing the King's oath against the local *Okyeame*. This device immediately raised the trouble case to the level of a crime against the king. On rehearing, if the verdict was reversed, the appellant paid a fee (*atitodie*) to the king. If not, he died. Since there is considerable evidence of venal urges on the part of Ashanti kings, appeal by oath would seem to be a good bet. The royal treasury profited by a reversal as it might not necessarily do on a sustaining of the lower court verdict.

Failure to settle a private dispute through household negotiations could lead to an ill-tempered bickering that produced some oath-naming. Then the private dispute became a crime. The normal path of such an untoward event runs as follows.[47]

Two men quarreled. They became angry with each other and began to say sharp things. One then slapped the other. (The assault was still nothing more than a somewhat aggravated household offense.)

He who got slapped then said, "Why did you strike me?"

To this he got the reply, "You abused me."

The slapper then said in effect, "By the great forbidden name (actually, he pronounced the tabued words of some oath), I did not."

He who got slapped then countered, "By the great forbidden name (the same one), you did."

All this had to take place in the hearing of a third person, or it went for naught. In such situations any citizen who happened to be around was under a royal duty to make an arrest. Not to do so was an offense, but we are not told to what penalty it was subject. He had to get a "log" and chain both men to it. The arrester then took both men along with their log to the chief's palace. When the chief was ready to hear the charge, they were brought before him. The *Okyeame,* or Speaker, opened the preliminary hearing by calling on the arrester to state the charge. A proper chief rarely talked in public. The arrester then merely reported that he had heard them both use the forbidden oath. Who used it first? He became

---

[47] No actual case records are presented in the literature, but Rattray does give us a model description of the ideology. *Ashanti Law and Constitution*, pp. 379 ff.

the First Defendant. The other became the Second Defendant.[48] A day was then set for the trial, and the hearing adjourned. Meanwhile, both prisoners were kept in chains and looked after by the arrester, who received a small fee, called *nsano,* paid by his prisoners.

On the day of the trial, the chief and elders assembled with other members of the royal entourage. The prisoners were led forward; then their custodian recited the cause of their arrest. Forthwith the *Okyeame* addressed the First Defendant, "State your case!"

This worthy then told his story. He asserted his claim as to the facts of the original dispute. He orated to the best of his ability without interruption by the court and until he had had his full say. Then he had to close with the set formula, "If the statement which I have spoken is not the truth, and if I have made up anything, then I stand to bear the penalty, for I have spoken the great forbidden name." He had thus placed his life in the hands of the court.

Then the Second Defendant was made to come forward. He, too, was ordered to state his case. This he did, in his own words, generally winding up by stating that the declaration of his adversary was a tissue of lies. Then he, too, recited again the formula of conditional self-curse.

What was the court to do now when confronted with diametrically opposed sworn allegations of fact?

First, the court record had to be corroborated. This was the job of the all-important *Okyeame.* Remember, the proceedings were those of a still-primitive people who had no manner nor means of writing but who had raised a formal judicial structure on which much hinged. The *Okyeame* therefore took his turn. Word for word and from memory alone he repeated the declaration of the First Defendant, ending with the challenge, "Were these the words from your mouth, or do I lie?" If an amendment was desired, the First Defendant offered it, but this was allegedly not usual. Then the statement was affirmed. The same process was next repeated with the statement of the Second Defendant.

The issue was now joined and one or the other of the litigants was presumed to be a liar. Although the facts of the original dis-

---

[48] Rattray calls them the "plaintiff" and the "defendant." In reality, there was no plaintiff in the ordinary sense of the word. Both men were on trial for perjury on the oath, and both were defendants. The state was the true plaintiff.

pute would remain critical, for guilt and innocence would be determined on these same facts, the offense under scrutiny by the court was one of perjury on a great oath. This was the deadly sin and the capital crime.

How to get at the fact? The elders cross-examined either or both litigants freely and informally. The chief usually restrained himself, as high magistrate he was to listen to the evidence, according to Rattray, but not probe it himself. Then "anyone else" could join the questioning. The trials were open to the public and the inference in Rattray's description is that "anyone" means "anyone." On this, however, it is reasonable to raise the presumption of doubt, since all groups of Ashanti are represented through spokesmen. It is hardly likely that young men would speak up when their lineage headmen would be there to talk for them. Women would most certainly not. But were there quasi-professional advocates who might be induced by the kin of a man to represent the interests of their relative at a trial? We would certainly think so, but we cannot tell. Nor do we know if these cross-examiners slipped in testimony of their own. That they make no positive assertions themselves is fairly implicit in Rattray's account. Nevertheless, as any good lawyer knows, loaded or leading questions can do the job as well. Rattray used the descriptive rather than the case method, so we have no actual account of cases in process, and there are no data that can give us insight into the nuances of Ashanti advocacy. We learn something about judges, but little about lawyers. And their ways are as, and sometimes more, important a part of the law process as are those of the judges.

Sooner or later in the cross-examination one of the prisoners would declare, "I have a witness," and he gave his name. The *Okyeame* asked the other if he agreed to having this witness called. If he did not, objection had to rest on "very special reasons." (Query: what were "very special reasons"?)

Now the elders asked the chief for a messenger to get the witness. He was sworn in with a conditional curse set by the *Okyeame*: "Swear by the god, ———, that you will not carry on any conversation at the place to where you are going."

The court messenger replied thus, "I swear by the god, ———, that he kill me, if I talk about what I have heard." Then he had also to speak the great forbidden word that he would not discuss the case where he was going, for he would then violate the name, and he would die.

When the messenger had gone, the *Okyeame* addressed the chief, saying, "Grandsire, we are going to set the main support."

The chief replied, "You may set it," because only a chief who talked too much would set it himself.

Now the *Okyeame* addressed the two prisoners. Summarizing the First Defendant's case in great detail, he warned them, "If that witness comes and says this, and this, and this (the First Defendant's allegations) then you (the First Defendant) will be right; but if he comes and says that he has not heard, in that case you are guilty."

Everything now turned on the testimony of one witness. Since it was obvious that the witness must not have been present at the testimony, one of the parties must have arranged ahead of time for someone to agree to serve as his witness and so to stay away from the court.

When the witness finally arrived (and he may have stayed away in another town so that the court had had to adjourn in the meantime), he was solemnly sworn in. The *Okyeame* called upon him to swear upon such and such gods to speak the truth. He did so. Then the *Okyeame* himself called on these same gods to kill the witness if he erred. Finally, he ordered the witness to speak the great forbidden name that he would not lie. Three times reinforced, the court sat back to hear the testimony.

The witness then related the facts of the original case as he knew them.

The elders then decided among themselves whose case the witness' assertion supported. On the basis of this judgment the *Okyeame* addressed the one against whom the judgment had gone. "You have heard what your witness has said," he intoned. "Had you not come here that we might take good ears to hear, then it would have been as if you had lifted some stick and clubbed the *Okyeame,* killing him, as if he were some brute beast; you are guilty."

All present cried, "E, e, e, e, e!"

Heralds came forward to sprinkle white clay on the back of the acquitted who then paid *aseda* to the chief as certification of his acquittal, and he was freed.

The guilty party was sentenced by the king or allowed to buy his head.

The role of the single witness in this account might well seem almost incredible. All we can do is to remind ourselves of the force of the religious premises underlying the Ashanti system. As long as the dogma of the active powers of gods and ancestors was universally held without tongue in the cheek, the system could work reasonably well. Rattray was convinced of its efficacy for the most part when he wrote, "The idea of a witness being friendly or hostile to one or other of the litigants seemed unthinkable. The sanctity and nature of the oaths taken and the deadly sanctions behind them seemed to the Ashanti mind to rule out most of the possibility of bias or lying." [49] So strong was this belief that kinship to a litigant did not rule out a person as a witness. The criminal law, ideologically at least, rose above kinship.

Witnesses were believed sometimes to give false testimony, nonetheless. Any witness who died shortly after a trial was suspect. In 1946, an *Akwamuhene* (village ambassador to the royal court) became ill forty days after testifying as witness in a homicide case. In the twenty-eighth day of his illness he confessed perjury. Subsequently he died.[50] If a witness died without confessing, an oracle would be consulted (by whom?), and if the *obosom,* or god, speaking through its priest, declared that the man lied under oath, his body was thrown into the bush, for burial was denied him. His personal property was confiscated and divided between the chief and the temples of the gods whose names had been used in perjury. If the condemned man was still alive, the original judgment was reversed. Had he bought his head, he got his money back. If he was already dead, it was just too bad. But whether the one who had gone free was executed or made to buy his head is not stated.

If the clan or lineage of the defunct witness wanted to go to the expense, it could buy his body from the chief for burial. As there was always a strong obligation on the kindred to see that their members were buried in the soil of the ancestral grove, they might do so by paying all the expenses of the trial and by assuming the debts of the man wrongly sentenced. It was not a light burden.

---

[49] Rattray, *Ashanti Law and Constitution*, p. 384.
[50] Busia, p. 24.

There was a possible out for the witness who fell ill, if he acted quickly enough. If he went to his god, and the priest told him his evidence was false, he might survive by refunding all the expenses as above noted and by sacrificing a sheep to the god.

What happened if the witness' account failed to corroborate the testimony of either party, or if his statement partly supported and partly refuted the testimony of both parties, we have no idea. Rattray's account, while it tells us much about the law as it is supposed to work, is silent on many of the salient points on which we would like to be informed.

With all this, the Ashanti trial procedure could not have been too strong in its techniques of objectively determining the facts in evidence. Much could have hinged on the behavior of the *Okyeame*. He supposedly gave verbatim records of the claims of the two parties. Persons who have had experience with the "tape recording" memory of illiterates from other cultures, especially of those who are specialists at the job, will not be surprised at this evidence of literal exactness. When exact memory is culturally important, as it is where there is no writing, it can be cultivated to a high degree. What is surprising is the absence of any comment by Rattray—who knew his law-stuff—on whether the *Okyeame* used or did not use tone and emphasis to *slant* the meaning of the words. Connotation has a lot of latitude in the sounding of the very same words.

There is also the possibility that a timid defendant might say "Yes" when the *Okyeame* challenged, "Are these the words from my mouth? Or do I lie?" Is a peasant before a great lord likely to say, "You lie!"? Maybe they do in Ashanti, but in the absence of contrary proof we would suspect it.

The problem of evidence in Ashanti disputes, as in so many advanced primitive law systems in which process was rather well developed, could also be met with recourse to ordeal in criminal cases other than oath perjuries. It was used primarily in witchcraft and adultery cases in which there were no witnesses. Ordeal was never imposed upon the defendant by the court but could always be requested by the accused. One form was to try to pass a needle through his tongue three times. If the needle failed, he was guilty. The other was ordeal by poison. On the request of the defendant, the man who had accused him was required to buy a large quantity of poisonous *odom* bark. This was steeped to form a brew, and after certain ritual preliminaries the man drank "potful after potful" of the vile stuff while his relatives anxiously exhorted him. The brew either nauseated him or began to take effect. Naturally, if he vomited, he would not die, and he was judged innocent. If, on the contrary, he showed signs of dying, the executioners rushed forward and chopped off his head. After all, a man must not be permitted to commit suicide.

In looking back over the Ashanti legal system it will be seen that for all its apparent complexity it was still basically simple. The monarchy had arisen not to suppress feud but primarily to gain power over enemies and to suppress intranational wars between the Ashanti tribes—which was the Ashanti equivalent of feud. Once the monarchy was established the people placed more and more of the dispute-settling process in the hands of the power-wielding third party —the royal state.

The total culture of the Ashanti, although still primitive, was elaborate enough so that it utilized more postulates than any of those previously analyzed in this book. They were as follows:

Postulate I. The gods and ancestral spirits control and direct the operation of all the forces of the universe.

Corollary 1. Man is subordinate to the wills of the gods and spirit beings; especially the spirits of ancestors.

Corollary 1'. The well-being of society depends upon the maintenance of good relations with the ancestors.

Corollary 1". The ancestors will severely punish any contravention of their will.

Corollary 2. The works of men are destined to be no more than the working out by human endeavor of forces of the universe that come within the ken of man.

Corollary 2'. The agents of government are under obligation to see that their regulations and all conduct among the Ashanti are in accord with "The Laws of Nature and the ancestors."

Postulate II. All men must be allowed to participate, directly or indirectly, in the formulation of laws.

Postulate III. All major contraventions of the will of the ancestors or the gods are sins.

Postulate IV. The ancestors will punish the group as a whole, if the group does not punish a sinner and atone for his misdeed.

Corollary 1. All sins are crimes.

Postulate V. The ancestors will "try" a man in the spirit world, if he takes advantage of a miscarriage of justice here.

Postulate VI. Past misfortunes are repugnant to the ancestral spirits.

Corollary 1. To mention such misfortunes (oath) causes the ancestors to take unfavorable notice of any situation to which an oath is attached.

Postulate VII. Men are endowed with conscious will, except when drunk or misdirected by an evil spirit in certain limited situations.

Corollary 1. A man is morally, legally, and individually responsible for his acts.

Postulate VIII. Blood is physical in nature and is inherited through the mother, thereby creating a physical bond of continuity in matrilineal descent.

Corollary 1. The primary loyalty of a person is to his maternal lineage.

Corollary 2. Social status, including chiefship, relations to property, residence, and burial, is primarily determined by membership in the maternal lineage and clan.

Postulate IX. Semen (the spirit) is inherited through the father.

Postulate X. Basic property belongs to the ancestors.

Corollary 1. Basic property is only administered in trust by its temporary possessors.

Postulate XI. A headman or chief is the carnal viceroy of the ancestors of the kinship group he governs, and a stool is symbolic of the collectivity of the ancestors.

Corollary 1. While in the official position of leadership, he is sacred.

Postulate XII. Men are bound to their chiefs by personal fealty as well as by kinship.

Postulate XIII. A man, except as he dies in battle or of natural causes, must know why he dies.

Corollary 1. Killing within the tribe must be done only by due process controlled by the king, for all other killing is hated by the tribe.

Postulate XIV. Cursing with a Forbidden Oath is killing.

Postulate XV. Incest destroys the universe.

Postulate XVI. Menstruation is spiritually unclean.

Postulate XVII. The sex rights of a husband in his wife are exclusive.

Through the application of these postulates as to the nature and quality of things the Ashanti worked out their functioning legal system and brought it to its great flowering.

PART III

Law and Society

10

Religion, Magic, and Law

Since the time of Sir Henry Maine it has been popular to hold that law has its origin in religion. Obviously enough, very little of the complex commercial and property law of contemporary industrial society can be tied to religious precepts, but in dealing with the history of law, it is another matter. In the latest edition of the *Encyclopaedia Britannica* Marrett perpetuates the old theme in closing his article on primitive law with this sentence, "In short, what early law prescribes and enforces is essentially a ritual—a system of observances, positive and negative, which in intention assimilates the human to the divine order."[1] As a generalization this is hardly correct. Primitive law is not usually ritualistic. The rituals of ordeal, conditional curse, and procedural formalism make up but a small part of the law of primitive peoples in general. Formalism and ritualism in law are by-products of legal specialism in the archaic and early modern legal systems. Such specialism does not exist among primitives.

The real problem is not, however, the question of the influence of ritualism on law. Rather: are religious precepts and beliefs the root of the norms of law? If they are not the root, what influence does supernaturalism—both religion and magic—exercise on the growth and the functioning of law? Because the facts force an answer to the first question that is largely negative, most of our inquiry will be a delving into the facts bearing on the second.

A word on Sir Henry Maine and the theory of the religious origin of law will not be amiss at the outset. Maine on religion has been misinterpreted by his overzealous followers and by a severe modern

[1] R. R. Marrett, "Law (Primitive)," in *Encyclopaedia Britannica,* 14th ed. (1949).

critic, A. S. Diamond, whose book, *Primitive Law,* is in large measure an attack on Maine in particular and the religious theory in general.[2] Diamond analyzes the several ancient codes (the Babylonian Code of Hammurabi, the Sumerian and Assyrian fragments, the Hittite, Hebrew (Pentateuchal), and Gortyn codes, the Twelve Tables and the Hindu Code of Manu) with great skill to demonstrate that except where amended with later priestly riders these first written formulations of archaic law are largely free of religious coloring. Thereby he believes he has cut the ground from under Maine—and this he makes the main theme of his book.

But Maine did not argue for a religious theory of law *in general,* and I thoroughly agree with Redfield's opinion that "he did not make the mistake of seeing religion as the source of law."[3] What Maine emphasized was the intertwining of law and religion in primitive societies. The very quotes cited by Diamond (and re-cited by William Seagle, who bases his discussion of the issue almost wholly on Diamond) to fasten the religious theory on Maine express no more than the idea of interdependence.[4] Maine's own words were, "Quite enough too remains of these collections [the codes], both in the East and in the West, to show that they mingled up religious civil, and merely moral ordinances, without any regard to differences in their essential character; and this is consistent with all we know of early thought from other sources, the severance of law from morality, and of religion from law, belonging very distinctly to the *later* stages of mental progress." And, "There is no system of recorded law, literally from China to Peru, which when it first emerges into notice, is not seen to be entangled with religious ritual and observance."[5]

Maine's cardinal error was in his idea as to the nature of primitive society. He thought it patriarchal, which it was not. And he thought the patriarch ruled as a despot unguided by any stable principles.[6] The commands of the patriarch came originally out of

[2] A. S. Diamond, *Primitive Law* (London, 1935).

[3] Robert Redfield, "Maine's Ancient Law in the Light of Primitive Societies," *The Western Political Quarterly,* 3:585 (1950).

[4] Seagle, "Law and Religion," Chap. X in *The Quest For Law.*

[5] H. Maine, *Ancient Law,* 3rd American ed. (New York, 1879), p. 15; *Dissertations on Early Law and Custom* (London, 1883), p. 5.

[6] Maine, *Ancient Law,* pp. 118 ff. "Law is the parent's word." "These early legal conceptions . . . still partake of the mystery and spontaneity which must have seemed to characterize a despotic father's commands."

nothing but his willful caprice. Maine's basic assumption was the direct opposite of the fundamental principle of regularity in norms that has emerged from the investigations of modern social science. So, when Maine theorized on the nature of law in societies that have gone beyond family atomism into kingship, he saw the early king giving "separate, isolated judgments," not "connected by any thread of principle." [7] The source of these judgments was said to be divine inspiration. The king had a trouble case; the gods gave him the answers. They simply came out of the blue. Such judgments in Homeric Greece were *themistes,* emanating as they did from *Themis,* the assessor of Zeus. Maine nowhere said the judgments were religious in content; they were by his assertion no more than god-inspired. They eventually provided the regularity of behavior by means of which custom was established. This is all there is to Maine's "religious theory of the origin of law." In his detailed analysis of the subsequent growth of the law in Rome and Greece he virtually ignored the idea, for he obviously found it of little use.

A much more useful key to the analysis of the relation of law to supernaturalism was offered by Maine in the closing sections of his great work. This is found in his characterization of the quality of primitive criminal law as compared to primitive private law.

"Torts then [as against crimes] are copiously enlarged upon in primitive jurisprudence: It must be added that Sins are known to it also . . . non-Christian bodies of archaic law entail penal consequences on certain classes of acts and on certain classes of omissions, as being violations of divine jurisprudence and commands . . . There were therefore in the Athenian and in the Roman states laws punishing *sins.* There were also laws punishing *torts.* The conception of offense against God produced the first class of ordinances; the conception of offense against one's neighbour produced the second . . ." [8] Certain sins were punished as crimes. Maine does, therefore, hold that much criminal law originated in religion. This does take place in primitive society, and I believe a review of the evidence will show that primitive criminal law coincides with certain notions of sin with remarkable frequency, albeit not exclusively. Private law, which predominates among primitives, rarely if ever undertakes to add its sanctions to tabu.

[7] *Ibid.,* p. 4.
[8] *Ibid.,* pp. 359–360.

A tabu is a social injunction that is sanctioned by supernatural action. It is not just anything forbidden. If it were, all laws would be tabus, as well as all violations of all norms. Better that usage confine the meaning of the term to its original Polynesian sense, which is that held here. A sin is the act of violating a tabu. Its punishment comes from the supernatural.

It is when the members of a society believe that the consequences of a sinful act may spread to the entire group, not confining its baleful effect to the sinner alone, that sins frequently become crimes, too. The sinner is punished by direct legal action through sanctions in the hands of men in addition to sanctions evoked by the supernatural. Then sin is crime as well. It may also be that men regard themselves as helpers of the supernaturals, their mundane agents. Then, as does the Ashanti chieftain, they lighten the burden of the supernatural and ingratiate themselves with it by punishing sinners instanter.

The supernatural also enters into the law-ways as the supporter of legal process not, it should be noted, as the source of substantive rules but as an instrument of judgment and execution when men's fallible means of determination of evidence are unequal to the task of establishing the facts. Recourse is had to conditional curse, divination and ordeal. The spirits know the truth. They are omniscient, or nearly so; and if properly appealed to, they will judge the case. They may also punish directly, or it may be that this job is left in the hands of human agencies. On the other hand, a man or a public official may judge a man to be a wrongdoer and so utilize magic to harm or kill him. This may or may not be a legal privilege-right, depending on the culture and the details of the situation. Misuse of supernatural powers—sorcery—frequently enters into the law as a tort against the victim and his kinsmen or as a criminal offense against the society.

Now to the facts.

Every single primitive society without exception postulates the existence of spirit beings and supernatural powers. Each of them attributes emotional intelligence to the spirit beings and holds to the belief that they respond with favor or disfavor to specific acts of men. They hold that in some or most of the important aspects of life man is subordinate to the wills of the spirit beings and that life must be made to harmonize with their dictates. Such presumptions are universal. Their influence is universally felt in the legal realm with the result that the elemental postulations of the supernatural also appear as jural postulates in all the type systems analysed in the earlier chapters. In Eskimo, Trobriand, Cheyenne, Kiowa, and Ashanti society their effect is direct and powerful. In Comanche, which is a highly secularistic society, they are weak.

Formal social control among the Eskimos has been shown to be much more religious than legal in nature. The many tabus are directly sanctioned by illness and bad luck. The shaman points them up and serves as the intermediary in relief of their ill effects. But— persistent refusal to follow the orders of the shaman in observance of the tabus leads to legal expulsion. Chronic sacrilege is a criminal offense, for the little Eskimo community must free itself of the dangerous effects of the supernaturally irresponsible acts of the chronically erring individual. In this, punishment is merely incidental. The aim is to free the band from the effects of guilt by association. Excessive sin is a crime; ordinary sin is only sin. Excessive sorcery is also a crime, as has been shown, not because too much sorcery is offensive to the spirits but because sorcery is a form of homicide and recidivist killing is not to be borne by the community.

Religious controls function in place of law for the most part in the Eskimo system, but law comes to the support of religion as a last resort when religious sanctions have failed to work and tabus are persistently ignored.

The issues of wife-stealing and man-to-man-killings that make up the bulk of Eskimo private law are wholly secular. The norms do not derive from religious injunction nor do they impinge on the supernatural field in any way.

Religion and the use of magic loom large in the lives of the Ifugao, it will be remembered from our previous description. Relations with the ancestors are of much concern to them. But tabu violations are entirely individual and family affairs to be expiated by extensive sacrifices and offerings to the spirits concerned. Because community consciousness is so poorly developed, there is no communal anxiety over a possible collective injury due to the sinful acts of mere individuals. No religious norms become crimes.

Nor is there much of supernaturalism in the extensive Ifugao private law, except indirectly. Rice fields have their magical potency, and failure to transfer the magical effect along with the soil when fields are bought and sold is a form of breach of contract. Sorcery is a tort punishable by the spearing of the sorcerer without too much likelihood of retaliation. It is only in the realm of evidence that supernaturalism assumes an important role among the Ifugao. And since this is a procedural rather than a substantive matter, it can hardly be said that Ifugao law has its roots in religion. Ordeal by red-hot bolo or removing pebbles from the pot of boiling water may be used to determine issues of fact in any sort of case except challenged parenthood. Then a kind of wager of battle with eggs or runo stalks is in order. Once the evidence is made clear by these devices it still remains the responsibility and privilege-right of the plaintiff to collect the damages or in some situations to kill the culprit, if the decision has gone against the defendant. The gods themselves take no further action. Barton's data indicate that not many of the numerous Ifugao lawsuits evoke an appeal to the supernatural. For all their religiosity and reliance on magic, Ifugao law is relatively free of religious influences.

Our three Plains tribes have shown us remarkable contrasts in the field of religion and law. Comanche tabus were absolutely a matter of individual medicine. They were in no respect a matter of tribal concern, and generated no law. Sorcery alone raised legal issues, but most sorcery cases were handled on the level of counter-magic. A few rare movements towards legal action by family members against sorcerers were instituted, but in only one recorded instance, and an intrafamily one at that, was it carried through to the actual application of physical force. Excessive sorcery, as with the Eskimos, became a crime but not as an offense against the supernatural; rather like dangerous and uncontrolled homicide.

Appeal to the Sun, Earth, and Moon deities was made when confronted by doubtful evidence in tort cases of alleged sorcery and adultery on the part of the wife. In the Comanche instance the deities judged and killed the guilty defendant. We see Comanche supernaturals supporting and aiding the law at a weak point, but no moral injunctions issue from the supernatural to form a base for substantive law.

The Cheyennes appeared before us as a sterling example of religious effect on law. Constitutionally their civil council derived its authority from religious fiat and was in part a sacerdotal body. Chiefs were sacred and hence their intervention in disputes was to be acceded to. Above all there was the notion of the polluting effect of homicide on the killer and the tribal fetishes and in consequence upon the well-being of the tribe. The killer was supernaturally punished with an ineradicable taint and legally punished with exile. The tribe "got shed" of him so as not to have to share the ill effects of his deed, and it collectively atoned for his act in the Medicine Arrow Renewal.

Here religious notions sharply influence the law, and the establishment of homicide as a crime follows directly from a religious injunction. Yet this is not to say, in the Cheyenne instance, that the legal prohibition of homicide originated in the religious ideal. Homicide, in one form or another, is subject to legal sanctions in every known society. In most of the law systems of lower primitives it is treated as a tort without an element of sin. It is prohibited on social grounds, not sacral. It is probable, in view of this fact, that the Cheyennes in their early history handled it in just this way. We know nothing of the history of the actual development of Cheyenne religious ideology, but it is probable that the secular norms checking homicide existed first and were later transformed into religious norms. In other words, it is highly improbable that the original Cheyenne law of homicide emerged from religion, although homicide as a crime undoubtedly did. What apparently happened was that when the Cheyennes acquired their tribal fetish and the idea of pollution was realized, it was seized upon as a genuinely effective way of stamping out feud for once and for all. Religion came in to complete the job that kin-based law among the simpler peoples can rarely handle by itself. It would be but another tribute to the social creativeness of the Cheyennes that they saw and seized the possibility which most other primitives missed.

The rest of Cheyenne law was essentially secular. The criminal law of the buffalo hunt was wholly so. Other legal activities of the military societies were likewise. Conditional curse on the buffalo skull to settle most points of evidence in coup-claiming disputes was there, but other forms of litigation were so relatively infrequent that cloudy evidence did not cause much trouble and the supernatural did not have to be called in for help.

In Trobriand law we discover a situation in which the relation of law to the supernatural is much more complex. The entire clan and subclan system with its attendant differences in rank, land rights, property inheritance, residence, economic exchange, and chiefly prerogatives is based on supernatural postulates: specifically, the mystic reincarnation of deceased ancestors through the maternal line and the supernatural emergence of clan ancestors from precisely located holes in the ground. There is in addition the overriding belief in the efficacy and necessity of magic for success in all operations.

The entire system of social organization and property rights is therefore tied to mystical concepts of a quasi-religious nature at the very least. Even so, the sanctioning of the maternal descent system as against the filial urge is almost entirely devoid of supernatural effect. The most important legal consequence of religious ideas might be said to be in the treatment of incest with its ancestral punishment as sin, and its social punishment as "crime"—if we accept "automatic" suicide on public exposure as representing public execution for the offense (and that is stretching it a bit). Be that as it may, this seems to be the only point at which gods or spirits serve as the source of a possible rule of law. On the other hand, magic and sorcery are potent instruments for applying legal force. The chief's drought magic has been noted as his top coercive weapon. His authority to command the services of professional sorcerers to destroy those who contravene his demand-rights gives him access to supernatural assistance on a somewhat lower level. Excessive sorcery by private individuals is in the Trobriands, too, a capital crime.

In Ashanti, we have the case *par excellence* of law controlled by religion. The situation there is so clear-cut that it needs only the briefest recapitulation. The Ashanti theory of the relation of law to the supernatural world is explicitly a Natural Law theory, and hence every legal prescription and action must nominally, at least, be squared with the ethics and requirements of religious belief. "The well-being of society depends upon the maintenance of good relations with the ancestors upon whom they depend for help and protection." All political heads of groups from the family and village headman up through paramount chief to king are viceroys of the ancestral spirits and gods in the administration of human affairs.

Their right judgments are *themistes*, inspired by the will of the spirit beings. Their wrong judgments are errors of the human will or defective intelligence and are set aside by the ancestors as invalid. Chiefs and kings are destooled for failure to follow social policy as the people understand it to have been set by the ancestors. Law and religion are inseparable. Tolerance of sin angers the ancestors against the entire group, and the group plays up to the ancestors by killing the sinner. Sin is crime and crime is sin. Some legal offenses may well stem from purely secular conflicts, as debt, but the mantle of religion can be thrown over them, if an oath is uttered. The gods also control all testimony through oath or ordeal, and the king is able to legitimatize his sovereignty as the descendant of the royal ancestral spirits, although these same spirits were not royal until their living Kumasi descendant, Osai Tutu, by military strength, political skill, and religious guile had made himself master of all the Ashanti tribes.

If we cast our eyes on some of the other primitive tribes, we see that the Andamanese and Caribs have not translated religious precepts into law, although religion and magic are basic to both their cultures. The lowly Australians, on the other hand, are led by their notions of spiritual anger and the mystic nature of the totemic group to impose the death sentence on incestors and presumptive interlopers who peer into ritual secrets that it is not their privilege-right to know.

The Pueblo Indian attitude toward law is much like that of the Ashanti. The universe is an ordered and delicately balanced system. Natural Law determines the functional interrelationship of all its parts. The main political offices are all priesthoods and even the post-Spanish, secular office of the governor and his staff is sanctified. The great burden of responsibility for all these men is to see that no individual deviates from the requirements of Natural Law. All legal regulation expresses presumptive religious doctrine. Law is heavily relied upon to support religion.

Similar patterns prevail throughout the *adat* of most of Indonesia, although with less specific religious dominance.

The facts, then, show that the simple idea that law originates in religion is overly naïve—the priority of the development of elaborate religious notions and practices in primitive society notwithstanding. However, the religious attitudes of a people naturally color and influence their legal development. After all, it is the basic tenet of functional realism that all aspects of culture and social forms interact upon each other. The religious complex, being universal and of primary importance in the primitive world, of necessity acts upon law and is in turn affected by it. Each has its distinctive sphere, however; religion is primarily concerned with human-to-superhuman relations while the main concern of law is with man-to-man relations. Religion does not embrace all life; nor does the law. Both set norms for human behavior and both supernatural and legal sanctions can be applied to the same norms—and are likely to be if the norms express behavior related to highly valued basic postulates as to the nature of things. The most significant fact that emerges from the evidence is that supernaturalism colors the law among primitive peoples most markedly when the society has a strong sense of oneness. In atomistic societies sin is less apt to take on the complexion of crime. Religion rarely enters as a progenitor of tort. Even so, much of primitive criminal law remains purely secular: cannibalism among the Shoshones, recidivist homicide and chronic lying among the Eskimos, violation of the hunt rules among the Plains Indians, for a few examples.

The law, for its part, consistently turns to religion when its techniques are not up to the problem of eliciting adequate evidence on which to settle a trouble case. Appeal to the supernatural to determine the facts through divination, conditional curse, oath, and ordeal appears to be universal. It even survives in our procedure in the swearing in of each witness with the conditional curse, "I swear to tell the truth, the whole truth and nothing but the truth. So help me God!" "Help" is a synonym for "smite." But our lawmakers and courts falter in their faith. They buttress the curse with laws and stiff penalties for perjury—Ashanti-like.

Sorcery and magic raise special problems. Each is a form of manipulation of supernatural powers, either spiritual or manaistic,[9] by control over the power through ritual formulas. When the formula is correctly followed, the magical effect is evoked without any element of choice on the part of the supernatural, providing some other magician does not upset the working of the formula by injecting

    9 Mana: supernatural power that does not appear in the form of a spirit being.

effective countermagic into it. The essential difference between magic and religion is that in the latter the spirit beings with which it deals can respond or not, according to their own volition.

Magic is another universal feature of culture. It can work with or against law and accepted morality and so impinges on the law. Sorcery is commonly lumped synonymously with magic in popular English usage. This is possibly a result of the medieval war of the priests against magicians and the triumph of the church as the sole custodian of man's relation to the supernatural. All magic was then condemned as bad, although unadmitted elements of magic still survive as residues in Christianity.

The moral duality of magic is still recognized, however, in "black magic" and "white," bad magic and good. The distinction rests on social values. The work of the official garden magician in the Trobriands is necessary to the growth of all crops. It is good magic. The work of the Trobriand sorcerer who kills people out of personal spite is bad magic. The work of the Trobriand sorcerer who kills at the behest of a chief, while not "good," is at any rate legitimate. It is used as a legal sanction.

The relation of law to magic is therefore one that is determined by the value and normative system of each particular society.

The most thoroughgoing and competent analysis of magical practices and their relation to social control that has yet been made is found in the works of E. E. Evans-Pritchard on the Azande of the South-central African Sudan.[10] The Azande are an advanced gardening people who divide into four main social classes: a nobility, commoners, foreigners, and slaves. They are spread widely over a vast territory, and like the Ashantis are organized into a number of tribes (Evans-Pritchard calls them "kingdoms") which in turn are subdivided into provinces administered by younger brothers, sons, and a few wealthy commoners appointed by the paramount chief. The governors in turn appoint local district deputies. The commoners, who are the true Azande, are descendants of the indigenous population. The nobility are conquerors from the outside.

[10] E. E. Evans-Pritchard, "Sorcery and Native Opinion," Africa, 4:22–55 (1931); *Witchcraft, Oracles and Magic Among the Azande* (Oxford, 1937), plus numerous other articles for which see p. 4, n. 1, of this cited work.

The commoners live in scattered homesteads, dispersed like American farms, rather than in compact villages. They differ from the Ashanti in this and in the fact that their several kingdoms have never been consolidated into a single political unit. And because the Azande state is still a raw conquest state in which the nobility remain a superprivileged endogamous caste, it reveals little of the constitutional system of responsibility that marks the Ashanti political system. The district and tribal courts impose the most brutal kinds of physical torture, of which incarceration in stocks for a number of days is one of the mildest. Most of these penalties are for offenses against the arrogant paramount chief, or king, who alone can authorize mutilation.[11]

The criminal law is revealed primarily as existing in support of the privileged position of the caste of conquerors and to be a true instrument of terror and exploitation in the hands of a ruling class that does no physical work whatsoever.

However, the central authority does also control the operation of private law much as our own state does. Numerous overt private trouble cases may be emended with damage payments arrived at through the procedure of private negotiation. But if the plaintiff does not succeed in getting a settlement that satisfies him and his kinsmen, he may not ordinarily move in to apply physical force on his own. He must present the case to a local royal deputy, a governor, or the chief himself for hearing or judgment. Refusal to accede to a court decision means physical torture or death plus much confiscation of property.

Now to return to the problem of magic, witchcraft, and sorcery. Azande private law is almost completely dominated by these forces. All untoward events in the life of a Zande are attributed to witchcraft. Witchcraft operates in everything. Minor misfortunes are shrugged off as due to witchcraft and without much feeling of rancor. No one should expect life to be a bed of roses. More serious events call for counteraction, for exposure of the responsible witch followed by corrective or punitive steps.

The power of witchcraft is an inherited one: from biological father to all his sons, from mother to all her daughters. Thus if one

---

[11] Under the British rule of the past forty years such sanctions have been suppressed and the position of the nobility much weakened.

man has it, all his male kinsmen have it. It is physically manifest as a form of organic growth that the Azande, like a number of other Africans, say can be found in the elbow or intestines of certain people. It is the witchcraft substance, and he who has it is *ipso facto* a witch. Being a witch, it follows from this, is a matter of constitution, not of volition. Witchcraft, since it kills people and spoils their activities in other ways, is antisocial—and illegal. No one wants to admit to being a witch, so detection cannot be by simple interrogation. Recourse is had to devices of divination for minor matters or for preliminary inquiry. Autopsy may be performed on a dead alleged witch to see if the witchcraft substance is in him. If it is, his family has to pay damages to the victim's kin or become victims of a legitimate vengeance magic. For preliminary inquiries every man has a rubbing board [12] or other divinatory devices. He also consults his board for all sorts of counsel on future events and whether the time is auspicious for this or that undertaking.

For serious witch hunting he uses *benge,* the poison oracle. A charge is spoken to the poison and a concoction of the deadly potion is forced into a chicken's throat, with the declaration that if the charge be true, let the fowl die, *and,* if the charge be false, spare the fowl. Two or more doses are administered to the chicken over a period of several minutes during which the charge is restated over and over. The questioning and dosing are not done by the man who is concerned but by some experienced operator whom he has engaged for the purpose.

When the poison has had its say, another chicken is subjected to the test, but this time the injunctions to the poison are reversed (if the charge be true, let the chicken live; if it be false, let it die). So it is that if the first chicken dies and the second lives, the allegation of witchcraft is confirmed; if the first lives and the second dies, the suspected witch is innocent and the accuser will have to dig up another name to try on the oracle. If the poison says one thing through the first chicken and another through the second, it is believed to be confused and no action can be taken on the result.[13] Purely secu-

---

[12] A little three-legged table on which he puts some plant juices and over which he rubs a wooden pestle. As the pestle sticks or moves easily he gets yes and no answers to his questions. See Evans-Pritchard, *Witchcraft, Oracles and Magic Among the Azande,* pp. 352–386.

[13] *Ibid.,* pp. 258–351.

lar grievances such as suspected adultery, theft, and arson are also put to the testimony of the poison oracle.

Witchcraft that has not caused death does not enter into the legal rubric. A man can do no more than to ask a witch to remove its effects, which he will ordinarily do. When a witch has caused a death and has been named, then the killing of the witch by vengeance magic (*bagbuduma*) is in order. But vengeance is held in check by the high chief, who first requires that the private poison oracle be confirmed by his own poison oracle. If his *benge* confirms that of the plaintiff, then permission is given to the kin of the witch's victim to loose vengeance magic against him. It will kill him, and its use as a sanction is a privilege-right. Vengeance magic so used is good magic (*wene ngua*). In earlier times, the kinsmen of a witch's victim frequently killed him outright, but only after the chief's permission had been formally obtained. Now, because the British rule no longer permits this, the use of vengeance magic has become more popular.

Adultery, theft, arson, and failure to pay debts are all perfectly mundane wrongs that should be brought to the chiefs' courts if the culprit is known or has been named by the poison oracle and will not settle.

There is another and, on the whole, easier and more certain way that is used by the Azande when the offender is not known. That is to have recourse to *pe zunga* magic in one of its several forms. As vengeance magic it "is the most destructive and at the same time the most honourable of all Zande medicines." In homicide cases in which the sorcerer is not known, "it is regarded as a judge which seeks out the person who is responsible for the death, and as an executioner which slays him." In the Zande's own words, "It decides cases." "It settles cases as judiciously as princes," for it acts only according to the merits of the case.[14] It is good magic, even though its effect is to kill, because it will work only when there is a just cause. Be the cause not just, the magic searches in vain for the alleged culprit and not finding him (because there is no culprit), returns to kill its maker, who is seeking not justice but spiteful personal injury to an innocent person. When punitive magic has been set to work, after a tort or a killing, and these are then compensated for with payment of a woman and a sufficient number of

14 *Ibid.*, pp. 388–389.

spears, the injured magic maker hurries to destroy his magic before it returns to kill him, because it absolutely will not harm the man who has already expiated his offense. *Pe zunga,* death-dealer though it be, is *wene,* good; it works only on behalf of the norms of right conduct.

Sorcery is the use of bad (*gbigbita*) magic. It has several forms, but all are alike in that they kill or sicken a selected victim without just cause. If a man has a just cause and knows his adversary, he should take it to court. If he has no cause, but acts only from hatred, envy, or spite, any good magic that he sends out will return to kill him. Only sorcery will work. And its work is unjustifiable homicide. The offense is a heinous crime; the penalty handed down in the princes' courts is death.

"Not only homicidal medicines are illegal but also medicines which corrupt legal procedure and which destroy a man's happiness and interfere with his family relations. Magic which influences the poison oracle in its verdicts is sorcery." [15]

Finally, there are some types of magic the moral and legal status of which is cloudy in the Azande mind.

Probably because of the fact that the royal caste which controls the political system is an alien group ruling through the sheer exercise of power, combined with the fact that the clans of the indigenous Azande are so widely dispersed territorially that they manifest little political effectiveness, Zande law expresses little religious influence derived from ancestral gods and spirits. It is clear enough by now that the kind of supernaturalism that permeates the law of the Azande is magical. Furthermore, the relationship of magic to law in Zande is the same as in almost every primitive culture, only it is more intensified. It is legitimately evoked to clear questions of evidence in adjective law. It is more intensified than usual because of the abnormal ubiquity of witchcraft (which is often nonvolitional, in contrast to sorcery). Sorcery in Zande as elsewhere is sheer aggression, covert murder. Repeated sorcery (and even a single aggravated case) is antisocial and illegal: a capital crime here as in the majority of primitive societies. Is it possible, also, that the Azande prefer to call on magic rather than the courts because the courts were not a product of their own making and are controlled by supercilious aristocrats of an alien, conquering caste?

[15] *Ibid.,* p. 395.

Before closing this discussion, note should be made of an interesting hypothesis recently advanced and tested by Dr. Beatrice Blythe Whiting.[16] In her fieldwork among the Harney Valley Paiute in Oregon she found that persons accused of being sorcerers are uncoöperative and antisocial persons who have records of being "mean." As she sees and reports it, sorcery is ascribed to people *ex post facto*—on the basis of a long record of general social dislike. Sorcerers are accused of causing the deaths of innocent people. They are evil, in contrast to other practitioners in magic who help people and are called "doctors." Sorcerers may be lynched or forced out of the band by common action.

Sorcery is sometimes used by these Shoshones as a subversive form of retaliation for a wrong done. It is easier than due legal process, which is uncertain and uninstitutionalized in the Shoshone situation. Fear of sorcery can thus serve to check violation of established norms of right conduct. But since excessive sorcery is a crime and persistent meanness. leads to being labeled a sorcerer, the fear of being tagged as an evil magician can work to hold potential deviants closer to the lines of conformity. Dr. Whiting advances the idea that reliance on sorcery and charges of sorcery to keep people in line is a function of the absence of any centralized legal authority in Shoshone society. She extends the hypothesis to postulate that the extent of sorcery is a function of the absence of centralized or supra-kin group authority in any society. Conversely, the presence of a central authority to handle serious trouble cases (homicide is her criterion) should mean an insignificant amount of sorcery in a culture.

She undertook to test the hypothesis with data from fifty tribes selected from the Yale Cross Cultural Survey. The fifty tribes were baldly classified thus:

(A) Sorcery important, homicide punished by victim's kin

(B) Sorcery important, homicide punished by central authority

(C) Sorcery unimportant, homicide punished by victim's kin

(D) Sorcery unimportant, homicide punished by central authority [17]

[16] B. B. Whiting, *Paiute Sorcery* (Viking Fund Publications in Anthropology, 15, 1950).

[17] Modified from Whiting, *Paiute Sorcery*, Table II, p. 87.

After classifying each tribe as best she could, she got the following numerical distribution:

(A)	30 (60%)	(B)	5 (10%)
(C)	3 (6 %)	(D)	12 (24%)

From this she obtained a tetrachoric correlation of .85 (reliable at .57) for the presence or absence of sorcery as a cause of illness with centralized (criminal) prosecution and punishment of homicide. Certainly this is a significantly high correlation which purportedly supports the hypothesis. The hypothesis makes sense and is probably basically sound. Sorcery when widespread in a society is very likely a form of fear projection—a manifestation of counteraggression when more open and aboveboard means adequate to solve head-on clashes of interests do not exist in a culture. Hence, it prevails in many societies that are limited in their politicolegal development, and it is less prevalent in the more highly organized ones. No student, however, should be misled by the sharp exactness of statistical correlations of the order worked out by Dr. Whiting. Statistical results, even when proper formulae are correctly manipulated, can be no more sound than the original units of count from which they are derived. The reduction of so varied a thing as sorcery into a two-class rubric (important and unimportant) is not realistic. There is so much subjectivity in the observer's judgment and so much sorcery must fall into an ambiguous middle position that a false objectivity is surely given to the unit totals used in the statistical formula. To decide whether superordinate justice and punishment prevail in a culture on the basis of the handling of homicide is too much of a tour de force. It ignores the variability of procedure among the actions that are found to occur when the original data are studied by means of the methods of functional realism. It relies overmuch on the more naïve procedures of the ideological approach.

Marvin Opler put his finger directly on the weakness of Whiting's methodology when he wrote, ". . . the inclusion of Trobriands in the grouping of *no* superordinate justice to go with such of their conceptions as *vada* sorcery is a warping of data to fit a two culture-type framework. Malinowski's account would seem to us to go deeper than that, as where he discusses chiefly prerogatives emanating from the richer districts of Kiriwina. Or, can the Cheyenne (along with Japan, Bali and Samoa!) have found their place under the rubric of 'superordinate justice' societies because of Hoebel's more definitive legal analysis as compared with Malinowski's preoccupation with magic? Such typologies, surely, do not do justice to the data. The danger of viewing correlations as more than correlations is one of which Dr. Whiting is aware, but to which the simplicity of her classification and the analysis of her cultures sometimes succumb. For analytic explanations no doubt, when we consider such cases as the Trobriands and BaThonga on their levels, or the Paiute on its own, we must still consider area, and history, and variations from a dual typology as conditions requiring analysis more penetrating at times than is here proposed in Dr. Whiting's pioneering effort." [18]

Legal institutions are not so simple that they can arbitrarily be put into one box or another of a limited two-box system. Statistics when used in the handling of complex cultural phenomena do not always prove as much as their numbers indicate. Nevertheless, the essence of Dr. Whiting's idea has the quality of being theoretically sound. Every society *does* have a social control system. Every society must have a means of holding its members close to the norms of behavior; to do this its norms must be clarified *and* sanctioned. If it does not do it with one set of means it must do it with another. Where overt mechanisms of law have not been worked out, covert methods of sorcery provide another and easily utilized device, for belief in the supernatural is universal and so is the existence of magic, which derives from this belief. Our studies have shown how difficult it is to create effective legal machinery. Most of the lower primitives are deficient in it. Sorcery is a treacherous alternative ready to hand. Yet law is a natural enemy of sorcery, for too much sorcery defeats its own purpose. So it is that as law triumphs sorcery withers and shrinks. But magic, the use of the supernatural for moral ends, long remains the handmaid of the law, mopping up where the broom of the law fails to sweep clean.

[18] M. K. Opler, Review of *Paiute Sorcery, Journal of American Folklore,* 64:243 (1951).

II

The Functions of Law

Law performs certain functions essential to the maintenance of all but the very most simple societies.

The first is to define relationships among the members of a society, to assert what activities are permitted and what are ruled out, so as to maintain at least minimal integration between the activities of individuals and groups within the society.

The second is derived from the necessity of taming naked force and directing force to the maintenance of order. It is the allocation of authority and the determination of who may exercise physical coercion as a socially recognized privilege-right, along with the selection of the most effective forms of physical sanction to achieve the social ends that the law serves.

The third is the disposition of trouble cases as they arise.

The fourth is to redefine relations between individuals and groups as the conditions of life change. It is to maintain adaptability.[1]

Purposive definition of personal relations is the primary law-job. Other aspects of culture likewise work to this end, and, indeed, the law derives its working principles (jural postulates) from postulates previously developed in the nonlegal spheres of action. However, the law's important contribution to the basic organization of society as a whole is that the law specifically and explicitly defines relations. It sets the expectancies of man to man and group to group so that each knows the focus and the limitations of its demand-rights on others, its duties to others, its privilege-rights and powers as against others, and its immunities and liabilities to the contemplated or at-

[1] Cf. K. N. Llewellyn, "The Normative, the Legal, and the Law-jobs: The Problem of Juristic Method," *Yale Law Journal*, 49:1355–1400 (1940). See also Llewellyn and Hoebel, chap. xi.

tempted acts of others. This is the "bare-bones job," as Karl Llewellyn likes to call it. It is the ordering of the fundamentals of living together.

No culture has a specific starting point in time; yet in the operation of the first function it is as though men were getting together and saying to each other, "Look here! Let's have a little organization here or we'll never get anywhere with this mess! Let's have a clear understanding of who's who, what we are to do, and how we are going to do it!" In its essence it is what the social-contract theorists recognized as the foundation of social order.

The second function of the law—the allocation of authority to exercise coercive physical force—is something almost peculiar to things legal.

Custom has regularity, and so does law. Custom defines relationships, and so does law. Custom is sanctioned, and so is law. But the sanctions of law may involve physical coercion. Law is distinguished from mere custom in that it endows certain selected individuals with the privilege-right of applying the sanction of physical coercion, if need be. The legal, let it be repeated, has teeth that can bite. But the biting, if it is to be legal and not mere gangsterism, can be done only by those persons to whom the law has allocated the privilege-right for the affair at hand.

We have seen that in primitive law authority is a shifting, temporary thing. Authority to enforce a norm resides (for private wrongs) with the wronged individual and his immediate kinsmen —but only for the duration of time necessary to follow through the procedural steps that lead to redress or punishment of the culprit. In primitive law the tendency is to allocate authority to the party who is directly injured. This is done in part out of convenience, for it is easier to let the wronged party assume the responsibility for legal action. It is also done because the primitive kinship group, having a more vital sense of entity, is naturally charged with a heavier emotional affect. In any event, when the community qua community acknowledges the exercise of force by a wronged person or his kinship group as correct and proper in a given situation, and so restrains the wrongdoer from striking back, then law prevails and order triumphs over violence.

We have also found in our studies of primitive societies that in a limited number of situations authority is directly exercised by the community on its own behalf. It takes the form of lynch law in some instances where clear procedures have not been set up in advance, as in the Comanche treatment of excessive sorcery and Shoshone treatment of cannibalism. Lynch law among primitives, however, is not a backsliding from, or detouring around, established formal law as it is with us. It is a first fitful step toward the emergence of criminal law in a situation in which the exercise of legal power has not yet been refined and allocated to specific persons. It is a blunt crude tool wielded by the gang hand of an outraged public.

Yet lynch law is rare among primitives. Even the simplest of them have crystallized standards as to what constitutes criminal behavior, and the exercise of public authority is delegated to official functionaries—the chieftain, the council of chiefs, and the council of elders.

Power may sometimes be personal, as is the power of the bully in the society of small boys, and as was to some extent the power of William the Conqueror. But personal tyranny is a rare thing among primitives. Brute force of the individual does not prevail. Chiefs must have followers. Followers always impose limitations on their leaders. Enduring power is always institutionalized power. It is *transpersonalized*. It resides in the office, in the social status, rather than in the man. The constitutional structures of the several tribes examined in this book have all clearly revealed how political and legal authority are in each instance delimited and circumscribed.

This point is emphasized only to dispel any residue of the hoary political philosophies that assumed without basis in fact that primitive societies existed under the rule of fang and claw.

However, the personal still obtrudes. An "office" although culturally defined is, after all, exercised by an individual. And who that individual is at any moment certainly makes a difference. There is leeway in the exercise or nonexercise of power just as there are limits. A man may be skilled in finding the evidence and the truth in the cases he must judge and in formulating the norms to fit the case in hand—or he may be all thumbs. He may be one who thirsts for power and who will wield all he can while grasping for more. Or he may shrink from it. Power defined through allocation of legal authority is by its nature transpersonalized, yet by the nature of men it can never be wholly depersonalized. A Franklin Roosevelt is not a Warren Harding.

Pertinent case evidence from the Bantu-speaking Tswana tribe of South Africa points this up nicely.

Tswana chiefs have evidently enjoyed law-making as well as law-enforcing authority for a long time. They lay down edicts that give the force of law to newly emerging norms, and they also rule that old laws have become obsolete, so denying support to claims based on once-valid legal principles. For example, in 1934, a young married man died childless; his younger brother, like Onan, refused to follow ancient levirate custom and act as "seed-raiser." His father then took up sexual relations with the widow, acting as a substitute for his derelict son. But then his own wife complained to the local headman, who rejected the complaint and upheld the behavior of her husband. She then appealed to the district chief. His councillors contended that the act was in accordance with their ancient usage and therefore a privilege-right. But, "the chief replied that the custom, if it did still exist, was obsolete and should be discouraged. He therefore ordered Bagwasi (the defendant) to stop cohabiting with the widow, and, when the order was ignored, punished him severely." [2] This chief could stretch the limits of power.

However, a Tswana chief cannot usually make an arbitrary ruling stick by mere say-so. "Many of the laws so imposed have been very difficult to enforce, or else have speedily lapsed owing to *widespread and continued* violation." [3] Authority cannot depart too far from use and wont. Thus, when in 1902 a member of the Kwena subtribe abducted the wife of another tribesman, the chief, Sebela I, upon trying the case, ordered payment of damages in the amount of ten cattle, and he added a new ruling that the abductor could keep the woman after paying damages. Immediately, his subordinate headmen saw the social consequences of such a policy. They objected that "it would be creating a bad precedent, which might lead

[2] Isaac Schapera, *Tribal Legislation Among the Tswana of the Bechuanaland Protectorate: A Study in the Mechanism of Cultural Change.* (The London School of Economics and Political Science, Monographs on Social Anthropology, No. 9, 1943), p. 6.

[3] *Ibid.*, p. 18 (italics mine). Compare Vinogradoff: "Laws repugnant to the notions of right of a community to its practical requirements are likely to be defeated by passive resistance and by the difficulty of constant supervision and repression." P. Vinogradoff, "Customary Law" in C. G. Crump and E. F. Jacob, eds., *The Legacy of the Middle Ages* (Oxford, 1926), p. 287.

wealthy men into breaking up others' homes, as it would be practically allowing a man to buy another's wife for ten head of cattle." Their pressure was such that Sebela reversed the rider to his judgment and ordered the defendant to have nothing more to do with the stolen woman lest he be deprived of all his property, which was in accordance with the old law.[4]

Thus it is as Julius Stone has written. "Transpersonalized power is economical of the use of force, by supporting it with group conviction; and conversely a group with strong convictions takes more readily to leaders identified with these convictions . . . Paradoxically, then, transpersonalization buttresses the power structure with group convictions, by adding to the subjects' submission tendencies, their tendencies to conform to the principle with which that power is identified; while, on the other hand, it checks power, since those in power, being identified with the rationalizing principle, tend to conform to that principle, lest by flouting it they undermine their own authority."[5] Such is the effect of the second function of law.

The third function of law calls for little additional comment, for the disposition of trouble cases has been our main methodological interest and has already been the subject of a large part of this book. Some trouble cases pose absolutely new problems for solution. In these cases the first and second functions may predominate. Yet this is not the situation in the instance of most legal clashes in which the problem is not the formulation of law to cover a new situation but rather the application of preëxisting law. These cases are disposed of in accordance with legal norms already set before the issue in question arises. The job is to clean the case up, to suppress or penalize the illegal behavior and to bring the relations of the disputants back into balance, so that life may resume its normal course. This type of law-work has frequently been compared to work of the medical practitioner. It is family doctor stuff, essential to keeping the social body on its feet. In more homely terms, Llewellyn has called it, "garage-repair work on the general order of the group when that general order misses fire, or grinds gears, or even threatens a total breakdown."[6] It is not ordinarily concerned with grand design, as is the first law-job. Nor is it concerned with redesign as

---

4 Schapera, p. 7.
5 Stone, *Province and Function of Law*, pp. 711–712.
6 Llewellyn, "The Normative, the Legal, and the Law-jobs," p. 1375.

is the fourth. It works to clean up all the little social messes (and the occasional big ones) that recurrently arise between the members of the society from day to day.

Most of the trouble cases do not, in a civilized society, of themselves loom large on the social scene, although in a small community even one can lead directly to a social explosion if not successfully cleaned up. Indeed, in a primitive society the individual case always holds the threat of a little civil war if procedure breaks down, for from its inception it sets kin group against kin group—and if it comes to fighting, the number of kinsmen who will be involved is almost always immediately enlarged. The fight may engulf a large part of the tribe in internecine throat-cutting. Relatively speaking, each run-of-the-mill trouble case in primitive law imposes a more pressing demand for settlement upon the legal system than is the case with us.

While system and integration are essential, flexibility and constant revision are no less so. Law is a dynamic process in which few solutions can be permanent. Hence, the fourth function of law: the redefinition of relations and the reorientation of expectancies.

Initiative with scope to work means new problems for the law. New inventions, new ideas, new behaviors keep creeping in. Especially do new behaviors creep in, nay, sweep in, when two unlike societies come newly into close contact. Then the law is called upon to decide what principles shall be applied to conflicts of claims rooted in disparate cultures. Do the new claims fit comfortably to the old postulates? Must the newly realized ways of behaving be wholly rejected and legally suppressed because they are out of harmony with the old values? Or can they be modified here and altered there to gain legal acceptance? Or can the more difficult operation of altering or even junking old postulates to accommodate a new way be faced? Or can fictions be framed that can lull the mind into acceptance of the disparate new without the wrench of acknowledged junking of the old? What *is* it that is wanted? The known and habitual, or the promise of the new and untested? Men may neglect to turn the law to the answer of such questions. But they do not for long. Trouble cases generated by the new keep marching in. And the fourth law-job presses for attention.

Recapitulation of just one Cheyenne case will throw the process into focus. The acquisition of horses greatly altered all Plains Indian cultures. One important Cheyenne basic postulate ran, "Except for land and tribal fetishes, all material goods are private property, but they should be generously shared with others." [7] When it came to horses, this led some men to expect that they could freely borrow horses without even the courtesy of asking. For horse owners this got to the point of becoming a serious nuisance, as in the cases of Pawnee and Wolf Lies Down.[8] Wolf Lies Down put his trouble case to the members of the Elk Soldier Society. They got his horse back for him with a handsome free-will offering of additional "damages" from the defendant to boot. The trouble case was neatly disposed of. But the Elk Soldiers did not stop there. There was some preventive channeling of future behavior to be done. Hence the "Now we shall make a new rule. There shall be no more borrowing of horses without asking. If any man takes another's goods without asking, we will go over and get them back for him. More than that, if the taker tries to keep them, we will give him a whipping." Here was the fourth function of law being performed. The lines for future conduct re horses were made clear.

Work under Function IV represents social planning brought into focus by the case of the instant and with an eye to the future.

The problem of reorienting conduct and redirecting it through the law when new issues emerge is always tied to the bare-bones demand of basic organization and the minimal maintenance of order and regularity. It may also shade over into work colored by a greater or lesser desire to achieve more than a minimum of smoothness in social relations. When this becomes an important aspect of law-work, a special aspect of law-ways activity may be recognized: the creation of techniques that efficiently and effectively solve the problems posed to all the other law-jobs so that the basic values of the society are realized through the law and not frustrated by it.

The doing of it has been called by Llewellyn "Juristic Method." It is the method not only of getting the law-jobs done but doing them with a sure touch for the net effect that results in smoothness in the doing and a harmonious wedding of what is aspired to by men and what is achieved through the law. It is the work not just of the craftsman but of the master craftsman—the kind of man the Polynesians call *Tui Thonga,* Great Adept.

[7] Postulate VII.   [8] Pp. 146–149 and 24 above.

Skill in juristic method may be the unique quality of a great judge or chief who judges for his people. In which case you may have a single man, or occasional men, cropping up to soften hard-shell legalism. Or it may become an institutional quality of a whole system in which a tradition of method is to keep one eye on the ultimate social goals of men and another on the working machinery to see that it is steering toward those goals. For juristic method, while it works on the immediate grievance to see that "justice" receives its due, also looks beyond to discern as far as possible the ultimate effect of the social policy that the *ratio decidendi* will produce. It weighs and balances the "rights" of the individual in *this particular case* against the need for order per se and the far-running needs of the group as a whole. It recognizes that regularity exists not only for the sake of regularity, which is no *Ding an sich,* but as a means to social and individual existence. But it also knows that absolute regularity is impossible in social physiology. It seeks as best it may to keep the working law flexible enough to allow leeway at the points where leeway will not cause the social fabric to part at the seams, and at the same time it seeks to maintain sufficient stiffness in the fiber of the law so that it will not lose its binding effect.

The Cheyenne Indians possessed effective juristic method as an institutional phase of their culture. A few men were shown up in our cases as not possessing the skill (like Bull Kills Him, who shot and killed the five horses in dispute on the ground that if he could not legally have all five, the other fellow would not either),[9] but in Cheyenne case after Cheyenne case it is shown at work in the action of any number of men. It was a general feature of Cheyenne law-ways, and on the matter of normality of juristic skill among the Cheyennes we wrote in 1940:

> The question recurs now on the matter of the generality or normality of juristic skill among the Cheyennes. One piece of the evidence is that neither Grinnell nor we had any word of persons famous for their wisdom in handling trouble-cases. If skill therein were not known, indeed familiar in the culture, this would mean nothing. But when skill is familiar in use, and recognized in its result, then absence of reputation for skill is a matter for remark . . . When an important skill exists and

[9] Llewellyn and Hoebel, p. 224.

is practiced with high frequency, but goes unremarked on by those among whom it is practiced, the simplest and most likely explanation is that the skill is too general to deserve explicit mention.[10]

Juristic method was at work on a low scale when the old men of an Australian tribe developed the ritual of expiatory combat and put it into effect as a means of lessening the harsh consequences of the legal rule of *talion*. It was blunderingly sought after by the Ashanti chief who put the culpability of the drunk and the madman to the test of the burning house. It is generally present in the successful work of the Ifugao *monkalun* with his cajoling, wheedling, and threatening suggestions of "reasonable" solutions of cases to both sides of hardheaded litigants.

It is absent in the poison ordeal of the Azande and the trial by red-hot bolo of the Ifugao.

Admittedly it would be hard, if not impossible, to scale a society on a measure of juristic method. Yet, grossly perceived, it can be seen to exist among primitives, often in large degree, and I venture to state in larger degree than in the archaic law of some of the Mediterranean civilizations, and in England after the Common Law had hardened and before Equity had been created to counteract its unreasonable effects.

If ever Sir Henry Maine fixed an erroneous notion on modern legal historians, it was the idea that primitive law, once formulated, is stiff and ritualistic (and by implication weak in juristic method).[11] The sample of case materials that has been set forth in this book has surely shown a large amount of flexible action in haggling (viewed dimly) and argument (viewed generously) over substance and penalty. In most primitive trouble cases the situation is surprisingly fluid, but flowing within channels that are built by the preëxisting law and moving to a reasonably predictable settlement. The channels, however, shift and bend like the course of a meandering river across the bed of a flat flood plain, though flowing ever in a given direction. Men are at work on the law.

The very fact that the bulk of the substance and procedure of primitive law emerges through case action involving claim and counterclaim, pleading and counterpleading, tends to keep legal be-

---

[10] *Ibid.*, p. 329.   [11] Maine, *Ancient Law*, esp. chaps. ii and iv.

havior relatively close to the prevailing social values. Which way a new issue will go will depend not alone upon the facts but also upon the skill of the litigants in framing the issue and arguing the relevance of their respective positions to the prevailing social ideas of right conduct and group well-being—or upon persuasiveness in argument that a new orientation of values is in order to meet changed conditions, even though the tough man and his kinsman, though "wrong," may sometimes make his position stick with naked force. Thus, the wise claimant argues his case not in terms of "this is good for me" but rather by maintaining "this is what we all want and should do." If he is a primitive advocate, it is more likely than not that he will also insist, if he can, that this is the way it has been from time immemorial. But the past certainly has no inflexible grip on primitive law.

Fiction [12] is one of the great devices of juristic method by means of which men fit new legal norms into old principles so as to reorient conduct without the need to junk long-standing postulates. Except for the universal practice of adoption, whereby outsiders are identified *as if* they are actually kinsmen, primitive men do not have to rely too heavily on the subterfuge of fiction to achieve legal change. Nevertheless, when the need is there many tribes have had recourse to its use.

An outstanding example may be found in adoptive marriage among the patrilineal groups of Indonesia. The important value for these people is to maintain the unbroken continuity of the paternal lineage. To do this, a family without sons adopts their daughter's husband as a "son" with the effect that her children remain within their clan and their inheritance will remain within their line.[13]

In Dahomey, in West Africa, where "bride price" means as elsewhere a payment by the husband's group for the forthcoming children who will belong to their group and not the bride's, a childless woman may buy a second wife for her husband and so escape being divorced. The children of her co-mate address her as "father"—a

---

[12] "Any assumption which conceals, or affects to conceal, the fact that a rule of law has undergone alteration, its letter remaining unchanged, its operation being modified." Maine, *Ancient Law*, p. 25.

[13] Ter Haar, *Adat Law in Indonesia*, pp. 175–176.

pure fiction that maintains the principle that he who pays for their mother is their father.[14]

Cheyenne Indian use of fiction had a nice touch. The induction of chiefs should traditionally take place in the great chiefs' lodge located in the very center of the tribal camp circle, but in 1890 the camp circle was a thing of the past. So Little Wolf said, "We'll just take this spot and say it is the center." During the drought of 1933, Black Wolf as head priest at a Peyote meeting brought forth commercial candied popcorn as one of the four sacred dishes to be served in the ritual breakfast at sunrise, saying, "We are supposed to have parched corn, but there is no corn in this country this summer. This is the same as corn."

Legislation by council and edict by king, or a fusion of the two, also find their places in the growth and reorientation of primitive law, and so serve as tools of juristic method. The not uncommon view expressed by Salmond that, "the function of the State in its earlier conception is to *enforce* the law, not to make it," is overstated.[15] Lowie is unfortunately guilty of the same overgeneralization in his assertion that, "All the exigencies of normal social intercourse are covered by customary law, and the business of such governmental machinery as exists is rather to exact obedience to traditional usage than to create new precedents."[16] This would be true for wholly static societies; but no society, not even the very primitive, is wholly static; new behaviors do call for new precedents and not all societies wait for acceptable precedents to be hammered out on the hard anvil of cases in process. Legislation always has a chance to contribute to juristic method.

Thus far in this chapter we have been concerned with the functions of law in their universal aspects. Do these lead to universal principles of content? Yes, but among the highly diversified cultures of the primitive world they are few and very generalized for the most part.

---

[14] M. J. Herskovits, "A Note on 'Woman Marriage' in Dahomey," *Africa*, 10: 335–341 (1937).

[15] Salmond, *Jurisprudence*, p. 49.

[16] Lowie, *Primitive Society*, pp. 358–359.

The one assumption of overwhelming importance underlying all primitive legal and social systems is the postulation of magico-religious forces as being superior to men, and also that spirit beings have emotional intelligence similar to man's. Its effect on the law systems was shown in the previous chapter to be variable. It is strongest in its consequences among those peoples whose religion emphasizes the role of ancestral spirits, and where the anger of spirits is believed to jeopardize the well-being of the entire society. The sins that arouse such anger are almost certainly taken up by the law as crimes. Almost universally, excessive abuse of personal control of supernatural powers (sorcery out of hand) is treated as a crime. On the other hand, appeal to the supernatural to solve problems of evidence through use of oracles, divination, conditional curse or oath is a very nearly universal legal device.

Homicide within the society is, under one set of conditions or another, legally prohibited everywhere. Likewise, it is universally recognized as a privilege-right under certain circumstances, either in self-defense against illegal, extreme assault (including sorcery) or as a sanction for certain illegal acts.

Virtually every society assumes the relative social inferiority of women (the Ifugao are one exception) and allows male relatives and husbands demand-rights and privilege-rights, powers and immunities, in relation to their female relatives and wives that do not find their equivalents on behalf of the women as against the males. Thus it appears to be universal on the primitive level (and general on the civilized level) that the husband may kill the adulterous wife caught *in flagrante delicto*. For the wife to enjoy such a privilege-right is most rare.

Law universally supports the principle of relative exclusiveness in marital rights. Adultery seems always to be punishable under the law, although just what constitutes adultery will be variable as marriage and kinship forms vary. The right to life and the right to wife are legal fundamentals. All legal systems, primitive and civilized, assume the importance of the kinship group, and all support it as a medium of inheritance of property rights.

All legal systems give cognizance to the existence of rights to private property in some goods; but among primitives land is legally treated as belonging directly or ultimately to the tribe or the kinship group; it is rarely sustained legally as an object of private property.

When the law-jobs get done, these norms inevitably become the common denominator of legal culture. But the functions of law, whatever the norms they may give rise to in any particular society, are what constitute the crucial universal elements of the law. Any one or half-hundred societies may select one rule of law and not another—the range is wide—but none can ignore the law-jobs. In the last analysis, that the law-jobs get done is more important than how they are done. Their minimal doing is an imperative of social existence. Their doing with juristic finesse is an achievement of high skill.

12

The Trend of the Law

There has been no straight line of development in the growth of law. The evolution of law as a phase of societal evolution has been no more an undeviating lineal development than has been the evolution of life forms in the organic world. Variation about a common core of organic structures and functions is characteristic of all forms of life. It is also characteristic of all forms of human culture and of the legal aspects of those cultures. Specific life forms and cultures have their own peculiarities resulting from variation and adaptation, and the natural history of each of them is unique. Therefore, it is an outmoded fallacy to suppose that the histories of all cultures shall move through identical steps or stages and that the resulting forms must be or have been close in similarity at specific points in their sequences of development.

Yet even as anthropology in keeping with all modern sciences is historical and evolutionary in one phase of its concern, so is the anthropology of law. Our primary concern, it is true, is functional: How does the law work as a whole? Why does it work as it does? How and why do its parts work as they do in relation to each other and to the cultural totality and the social entirety? But culture and society are not momentary things. They come out of the past, exist in the present, and continue into the future. They have historical continuity. What they are is the product of what they have been, worked upon by presently impinging conditions and forces. What they will be is the product of what they are, worked upon by the conditions and forces that shall engage them in the future. Neither the present nor the future can be understood without a knowledge of the past, although knowledge of the past alone does not hold the key to an understanding of the present or to an exact prescience of the shape of things to come.

Thus with the law; its present nature and functions are our chief concern, but its general history also has significance.

The trend of the law, like the trend of society and culture has been one of steadily increasing complexity. The study of this process is the aim of the evolutionary method, whose main interest, in the words of MacIver, "is not the modification of specific form into specific form but the emergence of a variety of more specific forms from the less specific." [1] Cultural evolution as conceived today may be taken to mean "the passage from simplicity to complexity, from homogeneity to heterogeneity, which, from empirical observation of living societies and their material remains may be deduced to have occurred and to be still occurring in the world of social life among men." [2] The society and legal life of the Ashanti are obviously further evolved than those of the Eskimo.

Viewed synchronistically, it is possible and wholly proper to treat the several law systems that are analyzed in this book as representing no more than a range of variation arranged on a scale of lesser to greater complexity with no inference as to growth sequence. Such a treatment may be called comparative—functional. When concern with growth sequence is added, the treatment becomes comparative—functional—evolutionary. The significance of the evolutionary aspect is, as demonstrated by modern science (both physical and social), secondary to the functional. Nevertheless, it is purblindness to let the primary interest wholly smother the secondary. It deserves its due.

The societies we have analyzed with respect to their legal aspects are all roughly contemporary to each other, and they were contemporary to nineteenth- and early twentieth-century European and American cultures. As societies we cannot comfortably say that one is appreciably older than the other—except perhaps that Eskimo culture has held its general form for a number of centuries longer than the others. This may also be true for Ifugao. As for the Plains cultures and the Ashanti, we know that they achieved their recent forms within the last several hundred years. They are not old. But

[1] MacIver, *Society*, p. 424.
[2] E. A. Hoebel, *Man in the Primitive World* (New York, 1949), p. 487.

they are nevertheless primitive. The point to be grasped is that among contemporary societies primitiveness does not necessarily mean antiquity, in spite of the fact that primary means first. What it does mean is that the cultural forms of primitive societies are more similar in their general characteristics to those that presumably prevailed in the early cultures of the infancy of mankind.

No scientifically restrained anthropologist of today will even hazard a statement as to what the specific details of any social institution may have been within the societies of early paleolithic men. When the Sunday Supplement writer calls for a statement on the love-life of Neanderthal Man, the most that can be reasonably suggested is that he undoubtedly had one. But whether he practiced monogamy or polygamy, levirate, sororate, cross-cousin, or husband's-sister's-son marriage—whether he had matrilineal or patrilineal clans, or none at all, there is no way of knowing for sure.

Yet a good deal is to be known—and *is* known—about those aspects of his social life that are closely linked to the enduring remnants of his material culture. We know specifically that his technology was limited to simple chipped stone and wooden tools. He did not even possess the bow and arrow. We know that he was limited to a direct hunting and collecting subsistence. He had no domesticated plants or animals; he was utterly lacking in the rudiments of a gardening, agricultural, or pastoral economy. His stock of capital goods was most meager. He built no permanent houses and raised no towns. These are all facts directly and unmistakably established by paleolithic archaeology.

These facts provide a starting point for formulation of certain inferences concerning the social life of Early Man, particularly with respect to population size of communities, to probable characteristics of political organization, and law-ways.

The methodology for such an undertaking is to scrutinize all contemporary or recently existing primitive societies that live by simple hunting and collecting devices to see whether there are any common social characteristics present or specifically absent from their cultures. If their presence or absence may be causally linked to the distinctive features of all simple hunting and gathering technologies, then we may reasonably infer the likelihood of the presence or absence of these very traits in early simple hunting and gathering societies. So also, when comparative anthropological studies establish a universal nuclear core of general traits as being present in all empirically observed cultures then it is scientifically reasonable to infer that these traits, which form the "common denominator of culture," were also probably present in early prehistoric cultures, even though they cannot be causally ascribed to any known archaeological evidence. The universal existence of an incest tabu would be an example in point.[3]

Although, as Murdock indicates, the universals may be specified in broad outline, they "rarely if ever . . . represent identities in specific cultural content."[4] The realized range of variation in culturally established norms is too great for that.

We cannot say with any reasonable certainty what the specific rules of law or any other forms of behavior were for any early society. But what we can do by comparative study and causal association with known material remnants of early cultures is to generalize the broad characteristics of social institutions that probably were present, and we can negatively assert their absence if such institutions and forms are not found in directly observed hunting and collecting cultures.

Thus can some of the main lines in the trend of legal forms from primal times to the present be sketched as they have unfolded through divergent evolution.

Prehistoric archaeology and comparative human biology have established unequivocally that man emerged from the subhuman, supersimian state a million and more years ago. The earliest human forms had only the slightest traces of culture, but through the subsequent ages man has been steadily increasing and diversifying his cultural inventory as he has moved up through the Dawn Stone, Old Stone, New Stone, Bronze, Iron, Steam, and Electrical Ages

[3] See G. P. Murdock, "The Common Denominator of Culture," in R. Linton, ed., *The Science of Man in the World Crisis* (New York, 1945), pp. 123–142.

[4] "For example, not only does every culture have a language, but all languages are resolvable into identical kinds of components, such as phonemes or conventional sound units, words or meaningful combinations of phonemes, grammar or standard rules for combining words into sentences. Similarly funeral rites always include expressions of grief, a means of disposing of the corpse, rituals designed to protect the participants from supernatural harm, and the like." Linton, *Science of Man,* p. 124. Yet no linguist could predict in advance what the language of an unknown people will be.

into the Atomic. In general subsistence economy he has moved from simple collecting and hunting into higher hunting on into hoe culture (gardening) or simple pastoralism, thence into agriculture (involving the use of the plow) or higher pastoralism, on into modern industrialism. A definite sequence is indicated here except that gardening and pastoralism have no priority with respect to each other. They are roughly contemporaneous alternatives dependent primarily on the type of physical environment a people inhabits. Grasslands and semideserts do not lend themselves to primitive gardening, which tends to be limited to forested areas, and so primitive grassland and semidesert dwellers usually take to herding as their advanced form of economy.

Economies may also be mixed. The Comanches were both hunters and herders. The Nuers of the East African Sudan raise millet and maize during the wet season when they live in villages; in the dry season they break up into small scattered camps as they seek pasturage for their cattle.

People who have achieved higher levels of economies rarely abandon completely the earlier forms of food-getting. Even our new atomic civilization utilizes extensive agriculture and herding, and some of its members occasionally take time off for hunting, fishing, or backyard gardening. The rubrics of subsistence classification are not exclusive, therefore; they merely indicate the predominating food-getting method.

The next point to get firmly in mind is that in its own particular history *a* society does not have to go through all the successive steps of the technological sequence. Borrowing may make great leaps possible. Eskimos are today serviced by airplanes and steamships. They moved from simple hunting savagery into a mechanical civilization within the span of a hundred years. But—in the evolution of culture, collecting and hunting came first; they endured throughout the Old Stone Age: a span of a full million years—95 per cent of all the time man has existed as man. The first domestication of plants and animals did not take place until Neolithic times—not more than 20,000 years ago. And the Machine Age got its start hardly more than three centuries back.

A society with a hunting culture *is* more primitive and less evolved than one with hoe-culture or simple pastoralism. These in turn *are* more primitive than one with agriculture or higher pastoralism; and these in turn *are* more primitive than one with industrialization.

Simple collecting and hunting societies are by no means all identical with each other; diversity and variation exist even on this low level. (Australian tribes show tremendous elaboration of kinship organization as against the Shoshone Indians or the Andaman Islanders, who are both on a very similar economic and social level of organization. Their religious forms are also markedly different in detail.)

As for law, simple societies need little of it. If the more primitive societies are more lawless than the more civilized, it is not in the sense that they are *ipso facto* more disorderly; quite the contrary. It is because they are more homogeneous; relations are more direct and intimate; interests are shared by all in a solid commonality; and there are fewer things to quarrel about. Because relations are more direct and intimate, the primary, informal mechanisms of social control are more generally effective. Precisely as a society acquires a more complex culture and moves into civilization, opposite conditions come into play. Homogeneity gives way to heterogeneity. Common interests shrink in relation to special interests. Face-to-face relations exist not between all the members of the society but only among a progressively smaller proportion of them. Genealological kinship links not all the members as it did heretofore but only a progressively smaller proportion of them. Access to material goods becomes more and more indirect, with greater possibilities for uneven allocation, and the struggle among the members of a given society for access to the available goods becomes intensified. Everything moves to increase the potentialities for conflict within the society. The need for explicit controls becomes increasingly greater. The paradox (albeit only a paradox for those who unwittingly *assume* that civilized people are more moral than uncivilized) is that the more civilized man becomes, the greater is man's need for law, and the more law he creates. Law is but a response to social needs.

The simple community of the lower primitive societies ordinarily consists of a few closely related families who comprise a kindred. Relationship is bilateral; i.e., kinship to the mother's relatives is felt to be equally as strong as to the father's. The community group, although it may be ethnologically a segment of a tribe, is autonomous and politically independent. There is no tribal state. Leadership resides in family or local group headmen who have little coercive authority and are hence lacking in both the means to exploit and the means to judge. They are not explicitly elected to office; rather, they lead by the tacit consent of their followers, and they lose their leadership when their people begin no longer to accept their suggestions—when they begin to accede to the ideas of some other man. As it is, their leadership is confined to action in routine matters. The patriarchal tyrant of the primitive horde is nothing but a figment of nineteenth-century speculation. The simplest primitive societies are democratic to the point of near-anarchy. But primitive anarchy does not mean disorder. Anarchy as synonymous with disorder occurs only temporarily in complex societies when in a social cataclysm the regulating restraints of government and law are suddenly and disastrously removed.

In the pristine state where all social relations are face to face, where the meager economic resources are open to all and shared by all, where interests are simple and common, basic order is maintained through the primary mechanisms of social control. There is little recognized need for any extensive suprafamilial authority. In the words of Murdock, "United by reciprocal relations and bound by a common culture, the members of the community form an 'in-group,' characterized by internal peace, law, order, and cooperative effort. Since they assist one another in the activities which gratify basic drives, and provide one another with certain derivative satisfactions obtainable only in social life, there develops among them a collective sentiment of group solidarity and loyalty, which has been variously termed syngenism, we-feeling, *esprit de corps,* and consciousness of kind." [5]

"Every member is ordinarily acquainted more or less intimately with every other member, and has learned through association to adapt his behavior to that of each of his fellows, so that the group is bound together by a complex network of interpersonal relationships." [6]

Whenever special questions of moment arise, we find that the

[5] G. P. Murdock, *Social Structure* (New York, 1949), p. 83.
[6] *Ibid.*, p. 82.

issue is discussed at length by all the adult males of the group until a consensus is arrived at. The legislative halls of civilization have their foundations in the "town meetings" of the primitive groups.

Although many writers, especially the earlier ones, have emphasized the kinship aspect of primitive society and its law, it is important to note that in the most primitive groups the isolated kindred is territorially discrete. "Every human society has some sort of territorial structure." [7] The members of the group are usually closely related *and* they live separately from other groups; they move about in their own recognized territory and their sense of cohesion rests equally on kinship and territorial bonds.

Every one of these small groups naturally has contacts with other local groups with whom they form a tribe. They generally intermarry, for the universal incest tabu forces local exogamy when all members of the community are closely related. They may also combine for ceremonial purposes or they may join for seasonal economic activities as in the Shoshone Indian pine-nut gatherings. For the most part, it is in conflicts of individual relations of members of different local groups within a tribe that such law as there is is engendered—always remembering, however, that almost all peoples conceive of some acts which are believed to endanger the group as a whole and are treated as offenses against the society per se.

If the orientation of the culture as a whole is noncompetitive, the data indicate that in the simple societies there is little development of legal forms and mechanisms. This is the situation that exists among the Negrito Andaman Islanders, who live in the southeastern part of the Indian Ocean. The Andamanese, who are strictly gatherers and hunters, live in small village communities and are absolutely monogamous. Kinship as such is slighted to an extent hardly approached by any other society; emphasis upon age-seniority and extensive lending and giving of goods and food serve as binding equivalents. The Andamanese were most fierce in their hostility to the rare outsiders who reached their shores. Many a shipwrecked crew was annihilated in the seventeenth and eighteenth centuries. But among themselves relations were tranquil for the most part.

---

[7] A. R. Radcliffe-Brown, Preface, in M. Fortes and E. E. Evans-Pritchard, eds., *African Political Systems* (Oxford, 1940), p. xiv.

Overgeneralizing the tendency, but still revealing its basic character, A. R. Radcliffe-Brown reports from his own field observations, "the only painful result of anti-social actions was loss of esteem by others. This in itself was a punishment that the Andamanese, with their great personal vanity, would feel keenly, and it was in most instances sufficient to prevent such actions. For the rest, good order depended largely on the influence of the more prominent men and women." [8] These more prominent men are the local headmen of whom there is at least one in each community, personable leaders who are naturally dynamic and who attract young men from other local groups as followers. Such headmen are spoken of as *er-ḵuro,* "big."

Now in spite of what Radcliffe-Brown says in the quotation just cited, he also reports that woundings, killings, theft, adultery, and malicious destruction do occur. Theft is particularly obnoxious to the Andamanese, since any object may be had for the asking and without pay, subject only to the expectancy of a reciprocal gift at a later date. The act of theft, although our reporter does not say so, apparently implies a form of deliberate and intended aggression against the victim, even as does malicious destruction.

Whatever the motivation of the thief, the response of his victim may be one of a variety of patterns ranging from do-nothingism through throwing a tantrum to an outright assault on the culprit. Dispute behavior was not studied in any detail by Radcliffe-Brown, whose interests have always centered on formal and generalized social structure rather than on the actions of people as such. Consequently, we know nothing about what causes one man to remain pacific while another indulges in a display of anger. No cases are offered or analyzed. We are given no idea of the relative frequency of theft or adultery; nor do we have any idea of how many aggrieved men do nothing, throw a tantrum, or spear the wrongdoer.

The tantrum follows a pattern that runs close to regulated combat. The wronged man lets loose a string of vituperation and smashes some property, his own and other peoples'. Or he throws a spear or shoots an arrow close to the offender without, however, actually trying to hit him. Nevertheless, people act so afraid of a man in his tantrums that the women and children flee to the jungle to get out

---

[8] A. R. Radcliffe-Brown. *The Andaman Islanders* (Cambridge, 1922), p. 52.

of his range, and if he is a formidable person, the men will sometimes take to the bush with them. However—and this is important
—intervention by an *er-ķuro* "would immediately bring such a scene
to an end." [9] In other words, the headman of the local group exercises a pacifying influence on behalf of the society to forestall the
possibility of a feud developing within his little community, for
killing an offender may lead to retaliatory killing by his immediate
kinsmen. It seems possible, too, that a Kiowa-like situation exists
here: the aggrieved party knows that he may relieve his feelings
in a public display of anger and a demonstration of intent to do
bodily harm to the wrongdoer without having to carry through his
threats, because a community "official" will come forth to calm him
down. He is able to set forth a warning to other men, however, that
he is not one to be trifled with too lightly.

In event of an actual killing, the reported course is for the killer
to flee to the jungle with such of his friends as want to hide out
with him. After a while he is supposed to be able to return without
great danger of retaliation; retention of feud or a lingering desire
for blood revenge are not Andaman traits.

Rudimentary law-ways are here then, but they are almost inchoate.
Theft and adultery do not elicit a demand for damages and hence
no procedural forms have been developed. The absence of a compensatory desire is, we suspect, a consequence of the fact that property
is so mobile among the Andamanese and possession of goods is not
valued. The blood revenge tendency is present, but it does not so-
lidify because the kinship sentiment is weak and the community
desire for internal tranquillity as informally expressed through the
intervention of the big man works to reëstablish a harmonious balance of relationships.

Brown found no instances of collective communal action on the
legal level and concludes that, "There does not appear to have been
in the Andamans any such thing as the punishment of crime." [10] Of
public delicts there were none.

As an additional example of a comparable low-level law system
the behavior of the Shoshone Indians of the Great Basin may be
noted. Specifically, the following account refers to the Seed Eater
(*Hзķandiķa*) band of Shoshones who occupy the desert just south

[9] *Ibid.*, pp. 40–49.   [10] *Ibid.*, p. 48.

of the Snake River and to the west of Pocatello, Idaho.[11] The Sho-shones are closely related to the Comanches linguistically and their culture represents the prototype from which the Comanche way of life originated.

Shoshone culture, as a result of impinging peripheral contacts, during the nineteenth century was somewhat less stable than that of the Andaman Islanders. But its basic organization was, in the large, generally similar. It differed most notably in lacking the age-grading that characterized the Andamanese. Legally it was similar in its lack of regularization of procedural reaction to aggressive acts within the band. It went beyond the Andamanese in planting the seeds of a criminal law in response to the ever-present threat of starvation. Alleged cannibals were destroyed and violators of the buffalo hunt rules were indirectly punished by means of whipping their horses. But remember, the Eskimos, when confronted by famine-induced cannibalism, made no move to punish it, although they handled chronic lying, excessive sorcery, and homicidal recidivism exactly as the Shoshones dealt with cannibalism. Similar situations may produce parallel cultural responses among different people, but they do not necessarily do so.

Another example of law on the simplest levels worthy of a brief description may be drawn from the Barama River Caribs as reported by Gillin.[12]

Although the Barama River Caribs do some gardening, they are essentially a hunting and gathering people. The tribe is distinct in language and in certain other cultural traits as well as in holding a discrete territory, but it "has no political functions and little social importance." The political unit is the local group formed of a set-tlement comprising fifteen to fifty persons and widely separated from other settlements. Each local group has its headman, chosen for "his strength." As is usual in all the simple societies, "In so far as the headman's personality carries weight his opinions are re-spected," but he "has no special power to enforce his orders."[13]

---

[11] E. A. Hoebel, "Notes on the Political-Juridical Behavior of the Northern Shoshone" (Appendix A, in *The Political Organization and Law-ways of the Co-manche Indians*), pp. 135–142.

[12] J. P. Gillin, "Crime and Punishment Among the Barama River Carib," *American Anthropologist*, 36:331–344 (1934).

[13] *Ibid.*, p. 333.

Most interpersonal trouble arises from intentional homicidal assault, adultery, theft, intentional poisoning, and sorcery.

The penalty for adultery ("regarded as a delightfully exciting game except when one's own wife becomes involved") is death to the man at the hands of the cuckold, assisted by his brothers—if the husband wants to invoke the penalty. The killing is a privilege-right and no retaliation is supposed to follow.[14]

An accidental killing, either by force of arms or poisoning, is legally excused on the basis of an interesting logic. As Gillin sees it, "The Carib philosophy on the matter of intent, stated in our terms, follows the reasoning that accidents are to be classed along with that whole group of natural incidents which are often injurious and inconvenient to human beings. The causes, however, are spiritual or supernatural, and the results are due to transgression, perhaps unconscious, of a tabu. If a man kills or poisons another by accident, he is merely acting as unconscious agent of the spiritual powers who constitute the effective agent and cannot be punished. Personal antagonism is eliminated in such a case, *the solidity of the group is unaffected, and retaliation has no function.*"[15]

Who still says primitive man is capable of acting only emotionally and without the guidance of reason?

The Caribs do not apparently like direct physical conflict. When they are befuddled at group drinking bouts, it is true that men frequently come to blows. And an adulterer caught *in flagrante delicto* will almost certainly be directly assaulted. But in more sober moments, rather than rely on open legal procedure, the aggrieved Carib prefers recourse to poisoning or sorcery, using either his own magic or that of a hired professional sorcerer. Such procedure is legitimate, for "public opinion supports the use of poison and sorcery as means of retaliating for an unprovoked offense," and "if a Carib who has committed an offense discovers his victim using either poison or sorcery against him as a retaliation, he devotes his efforts to self-protection [neutralizing magic] rather than to counter retaliation."[16]

Unlike the Andamanese, who reputedly take no group action on a legal level against the utterly antisocial person, the Caribs pro-

[14] *Ibid.*, p. 335.
[15] *Ibid.*, p. 337. (Italics mine).
[16] *Ibid.*, p. 335.

ceed as do the Eskimos against the not-to-be-borne-any-longer recalcitrant.

Occasionally a member of a group acquires a reputation among his
fellows as an undesirable character. He may repeatedly pilfer from others'
fields; he may trouble the women, be lazy, show himself ungenerous,
constantly pick quarrels, or make himself obnoxious in other ways. The
men of the settlement will talk to him, but if he does nothing to im-
prove his position in their eyes, he will be advised to leave on pain of
having life made very unpleasant for him.

If he persists in remaining he will find that he and his family are
social outcasts: they are not invited to drinking parties; he will be unable
to borrow anything; he will get no help in hunting, fishing, field cutting,
canoe building or other activities in which the men assist one another,
nor will his wife receive aid in her occupations; his household will be
excluded from the water-hole and bathing place. In short, he will lose
all advantages of group life. In aggravated cases, the other men may
beat him or even kill him . . . Ostracism within the group and violence
are, however, seldom necessary. Such a man with a vestige of common
sense leaves the settlement while he can comfortably do so. I know of one
man on the Barama who has been ejected from six settlements in this
way, so that he has become a permanent outcast.[17]

No single offense, it can be seen from this, constitutes a crime.
However, excessive malfeasance does. The spoken warning is followed by withdrawal of all social reciprocity, and here we have law
in Malinowski's sense. And if this fails to work, the culprit may be
beaten or killed (lynched) by the men of the community. Here we
have law in the full connotation of the word—the application, in
threat or in fact, of physical coercion by a party having the socially
recognized privilege-right of so acting. First the threat—and then, if
need be, the act.

One more interesting fact about the Caribs should be recorded.
The people, as we have already said, prefer to avoid outright physical violence. Consequently, when two men of distinct local groups
get into a serious quarrel, the members of the two groups break off
relations and place an injunction on social intercourse between all
members of the two groups.

This might be looked upon only as an expression of hostility, but it is quite clearly something more constructive than that. A person who defies the ban is scolded by his own headman and he may, if need be, be physically punished by his group leader. The object appears to be to prevent contact when tensions are high—contact that might lead to fighting and killing such as would involve the group in feud.[18]

When we take a look at the legal situation among the natives of Central Australia the basic outlines of the law-ways remain the same, but in specific detail there are notable differences as usual.

The amazing thing about the Australians is their luxuriant proliferation of the nuances of kinship. Here they are, by all counts on the most primitive level of recently living peoples, except in the field of kinship. And on this count they have showed a precocious ingenuity untouched by all the rest of known humanity. Don't ask, "Why?" and expect an answer. No anthropologist has even made a good guess. All we can do is to call attention to the fact that there is a human tendency in the elaboration of culture to seize upon some aspect and go all-out with it. "Cultural orthogenesis," it may be called, if we think of biological analogies; or "the tendency to skewed elaboration of culture," if we prefer statistical images. Sometimes we know enough about the culture history of a people to know why they have fixed on this or that phase of culture for elaboration, but the roots of the Australian situation are too deep in the unexposed soil of prehistory to make possible a reasonable guess. Nor is it to the point here to undertake any analysis of the maze of Australian kinship. What is significant for the purposes of our law studies is that the Australian consolidation of the kinship sentiments leads to a more definite formulation of legal patterns than is commonly characteristic of peoples on a similar economic and social level.[19] Suffice it to say that although the Australians live the greater part of the year in small, isolated, roving local groups or camps of which Harrasser identified more than five hundred, there are also totemic, moiety, and marriage class groupings that cut across local

---

[18] *Ibid.,* p. 340.

[19] For those who want a lead into this intricate and fascinating subject the following references are suggested: A. R. Radcliffe-Brown, "Social Organization of Australian Tribes," *Oceania,* I: (1939); this should be followed by W. E. Lawrence, "Alternating Generations in Australia," in G. P. Murdock, ed., *Studies in the Science of Society* (New Haven, 1937).

and even tribal lines.[20] Marriage regulations defining specifically whom a person may and may not marry are, as an expression of the elaborated kinship interest, strictly formulated and powerfully sanctioned. Most marriages are monogamous but all men in a husband's marriage class may usually have limited access to his wife without such activity constituting adultery. Sex relations between a woman and a man not of her husband's marriage class do constitute adultery and are severely punished. Regenerative rites are performed by initiated males in the utmost secrecy and the revelation of the secrets is also punished with extreme sanctions.

Headmen are met in some areas, but generally in Australia the council of old men prevails. Gerontocracy is the rule. Through the exercise of their power in support of the tribal norms the old men enter juridically into a number of dispute situations, and the line between private and criminal offenses becomes hazy indeed. Legal actions are frequent, for the Australians to even a greater degree than the Eskimos or the Comanches are prone to belligerent physical aggression. What, then, happens?

Personal quarrels stem mostly from charges of adultery, theft from trees marked as personal property, or from a man's hut in his absence, or from the appropriation of a wounded emu or kangaroo which was first struck by another hunter and which still bears his imbedded spear. It will make a difference as to whether both men are from the same or separate local groups.

In no event will compensatory damages to be paid in goods be asked or be given. The sanctions are wholly physical. In the event of theft from the hut, if the culprit confesses when confronted by his accuser, he should return the purloined object and beat his own head with stones before the hut of the offended party. If he fails to punish himself after confession, the victim of his theft may strike him with a boomerang or spear him in the leg. If the alleged thief refuses to confess, a fight is likely to take place, ending in the wounding or killing of one or the other. Then a true judicial process is invoked by the elders. They palaver over the facts to determine whether a theft had actually occurred. If they decide the charge was true, and if it had been the accused who was hurt or killed, then

---

[20] A. Harrasser, *Die Rechtsverletzung bei den australischen Eingeborenen* (Beilageheft zur vergleichende Rechtswissenschaft, Vol. 50, 1936), p. 11.

they rule the killing or wounding to be a privilege-right of the punisher and no further steps are taken. If the accuser was wounded and his accusation is judged just, the convicted thief is ordered to stand forth to be wounded in exactly the same part of the body, to the same extent and by the same type of weapon. If he had killed the accuser in the fight, he will be speared to death. Should he flee to escape the penalty, he becomes an outlaw to be killed on sight by any armed member of the local group.

The process is therefore stepped up through three stages: 1) the wrong is righted through confession to a charge initiated by the wronged party, plus return of the goods, plus self-punishment; 2) failing this, the wronged party undertakes self-redress through wounding or perhaps killing the defendant; 3) failing in this, with a resultant wounding or killing of the plaintiff, the council of elders enters with public action designed to see that justice is done through physical punishment of the thief equivalent to the physical injury suffered by the plaintiff, who gets no extra satisfaction for his injury but who does get the return of his stolen goods.

Self-redress is buttressed by public action in case of need.

Adultery seems to be handled in much the same way, except that rather than merely beat his head the contrite wrongdoer is expected to present his rump to be jabbed with a spear in the hands of the offended husband. An outright fight leads to consequences similar to those just described.[21]

This is the picture that prevails for interpersonal disputes *within* the local group in Central Australia. Public offenses are ideally handled much more summarily. Incest, which constitutes any crossing of the lines of sexual tabu defined by a person's own totem group, moiety, and marriage class, results in the spearing to death of both offenders after judgment by the elders. Revelation of the secret lore divulged by the old men to the younger as they go through the tribal secret initiation ceremonies results in a lethal spearing. For a woman or uninitiated man to come upon the elders *when engaged* in their *churinga* [22] ceremonies is fatal, even though

[21] C. Strehlow, *Die Aranda und Loritja-Stämme in Zentral-Australien,* ed. M. von Leonhardi (Veröffentlichungen des Völker-Museums Frankfurt-am-Main, 1907–20), 1915, pp. 9 ff.

[22] Painted slabs representing ancestral and personal spirits.

the meeting was entirely accidental. To know or to come into contact with the secrets of the universe when one has no right to these is a deadly crime; the old men exercise their power of control over knowledge and society with ruthless concern for their exclusive rights. But it is not merely domination over the uninitiated that the old men are striving to maintain. The grip of religion is so strong on their own minds, and they so greatly fear that any sacrilege will disturb the spirit forces in their relation to the band, that, theoretically at least, an initiate who disturbs the sacred ceremonies by late arrival can be condemned by the old men and killed by the younger.

Although the earlier reporters on Australia described these sanctions in ideological terms and indicated immediate and almost automatic application of the sanctions on the first breach, it is more reasonable to expect variations on the supposed norm and a good deal of backing and filling in response to personal factors and circumstances. There is in fact evidence enough to indicate that it frequently takes more than one transgression to cause a band to destroy one of its own members. Dawson observed that among the natives of West Victoria severe punishment (death) is applied, "should a person, through bad conduct, become a constant anxiety and trouble to the tribe." [23] The word "constant" is the important key. Once again, it is the case of the-not-to-be-borne-any-longer delinquent who builds up to the criminal who must be expurgated.[24]

Three specific cases recently reported in detail by Géza Róheim show the pattern clearly. The first, occurring between 1880 and 1890, is that of a man who was a member of the Ellery Creek band. He was "aggressively promiscuous," committing incestuous intercourse with women who were his classificatory mother, younger sister, sister's daughter and father's sister's daughter. Quite a string that, in a society in which a single transgression of incest is supposed to be punished with death! But he was *aknara* (strong and cheeky); he was capable of intimidating the women he consorted with and the men whose sense of propriety he outraged. "The thing went for a long time, because he was a strong man and very brave." Talk and mere disapproval did not faze him, for although "they [the old men] 'growled' in every camp . . . that did not stop him."

---

[23] J. Dawson, *Australian Aborigines* (London, 1881), p. 76.
[24] Harrasser, p. 34, cites a half-dozen similar notes for other parts of Australia.

Nor did individual husbands dare to lift a hand against him. It was not until the warriors of three communities (one his own) were convened under a leader who got them together that action was taken. They agreed on his death. But even with this mustering of force it was not done by them directly. The women were "ordered" to lure him into the bush, engage him in intercourse, seize him, and kill him. They did it with a vengeance. His own mother-in-law snared him in the sexual embrace. Then he was pounced on by the rest of the females who attacked him with their digging sticks. "First they pushed his eyes out and then they poked the heavy sticks right through his body, through the nostrils, through his head, etc., until they killed him." [25]

The second case is more cryptically presented. Bark was a promiscuous man who made a habit of traveling around without the company of his wife, as is regular. He committed incest with his mother-in-law, daughter, and classificatory mother—among others. At first, according to Róheim's report, he was ostracized. Finally, he was killed by "quite a lot of men." [26]

Then there was Lumps of Flesh ("i.e., he has committed incest and consequently has little lumps in his flesh"). He was promiscuous with "all degrees of relatives." Eventually the old men palavered and announced that they were going to decorate him for a totemic ceremony (the *illpangura*). He was innocently taken in, and when he sat down to be decorated, they held him fast while his throat was slit. To finish him off they cut him in pieces and hung the bits in the trees.[27]

Trouble between bands or members of different bands raises its own special problems for the Australians. Self-redress may possibly not be viewed as a privilege-right when an out-grouper comes to attack a member of the home body who has offended him. Remember that compensation through payment of damages does not exist among these people; the only recognized penalty is in physical punishment. An outright attack on an alleged wrongdoer from another camp almost certainly leads to armed resistance or a counterattack. Then a condition of intergroup war or intratribal feud exists, de-

---

[25] Géza Róheim, "The Primeval Horde in Central Australia," *Journal of Comparative Psychopathology*, 3:455 (1942).
[26] *Ibid.*, pp. 457–458.   [27] *Ibid.*, pp. 458–459.

pending on whether the local group or the tribe is looked upon as constituting the largest effective social unit. Among the Australians it is clearly a matter of feud, because although it is nominally within the discretion of each local group to decide what course of action will be taken, all local groups accede at some times to utilization of an institutionalized intergroup procedure for settling quarrels between their members. For ceremonial and social purposes the various independent hordes within the Australian tribes get together periodically for great ceremonies. This is important in their life-ways; unsettled quarrels between the groups make the enjoyment of such gatherings impossible, and so overriding common interests on a tribal scale have led to the development of adjudication and satisfaction-giving procedures in the form of regulated combat for which the Australian aborigines are so famous.

A classic example of the procedure is given by Howitt.[28]

When a serious offense occurred and the offender belonged to some one of the other local divisions, the custom was to send a messenger (Wirri-gir) to call on him to come forward and undergo punishment. In such a case, if he were a man of consequence, or if the affair caused much feeling among the people, all the totemites of each of the men assembled under their respective Headmen at the place agreed on.

Such a case occurred at the Mukjarawaint tribe, and was reported to me by a man of the Garchuka totem, whose brother and maternal grandfather had for some matter of personal offense killed a man of the black snake (Wulernunt) totem. They speared him at night, when he was sleeping in his camp, and escaped, but were seen and recognized by his wife. The relatives of the deceased sent a Wirri-gir to the offenders, telling them to look out for themselves and be prepared for revenge. A messenger was sent in reply saying that they should come with their friends, and that they would be prepared to stand out and have spears thrown at them. There was then a great meeting of the respective totems, the Garchuka being that of the offenders, and the Wulernunt that of the avengers.

Having met as arranged, at the time and place fixed, with their respective kindreds, the Garchuka Headman stood out between the opposed totemites and made a speech, calling upon his men not to take any unfair advantage in the encounter. Then he appointed a spot near

[28] A. W. Howitt, *Native Tribes of South-East Australia* (London, 1904), pp. 334–335.

at hand where the expiatory encounter should take place that afternoon, it being agreed that as soon as the offenders had been struck by a spear the combat should cease. Then the offenders stood out, armed with shields, and received the spears thrown at them by the dead man's kindred, until at length one of them was wounded. The Headman of the Garchukas then threw a lighted piece of bark, which he held, into the air, and the fight ceased. If it had been continued there would have been a general fight between the two totems.[29]

More details on the gradations and variations in the handling of intergroup delicts are given by Lloyd Warner for the Murngin tribe of Arnhem Land, just west of the Gulf of Carpenteria, in northern Australia.[30] Homicide among these people is frequent, Warner asserting that to his knowledge there had been seventy killings in a twenty-year period. Fifty of these are said to have been "clan retaliations," i.e., the killing of people of one totem group by those of another in reaction to a supposed offense. Fifteen of these were simple blood-revenge slayings. Ten were penalties for the abduction of women. Five were for alleged sorcery. And for these there were five counterkillings. Then there were five executions for looking upon totemic insignia by persons who had no privilege to do so. Quite a bloody record for a population of considerably less than 1,000—a record that indicates something of the destructive potentialities for a simple primitive people if the *lex talionis* were to go unchecked.

If a wife-abductor among the Murngin is to be killed, he alone is the selected victim, and he is waylaid in his sleep by a group of stealthy young men from the local group which he had raided. Although such attacks are usually done without the approval of the elders, the whole group of the killers is liable to retaliation through the "death adder," which is a night attack on the whole camp of the killers by all the warriors of the avenging group, who engage in a magical sham attack before they set out on the earnest enterprise.

It is to avoid the mutually disastrous effects of such bloodletting that the Murngin, like other Australians, may arrange a regulated duel, or expiatory combat. "The expiatory combats and regulated

---

[29] The tension-relieving aspects of ritualized conflict are readily observable in this kind of proceeding.

[30] W. L. Warner, "Murngin Warfare," *Oceania*, 1:457–477 (1930).

fights of the Australians are also all of them palpably means of ending a quarrel, or marking a point beyond which it must not go. They do not seek to punish a wrong, but to arrest vengeance . . . at a point which will save the breaking out of a devastating fight." [81] The purposes of the undertaking are to see that the injured group gets satisfaction by hurting the evildoer as he has hurt it *and* to reëstablish equilibrium between the groups by assuring a counterbalancing bloodletting which is not fatal.

In the Murngin way, the injured group is restrained by its elders until it has cooled down. Then it sends a messenger to the offenders with an invitation to formal "combat." If the invitation is accepted, the warriors of both parties arrive at the designated dueling ground on the given day. They come dancing and singing—for this is a ritual affair. Once there, they line up facing each other beyond the range of a hurled spear just to play it safe. The ceremony proper opens with the injured group approaching the offenders while doing its chief totemic dance. The dancing approach done, they turn and walk back to their places. Now the offenders dance and approach likewise, and then return to their places. The "fight" is now ready to begin.

The men who were accessories to the homicide, called "pushers," come forth to be thrown at. Headless spears are hurled by the warriors of the offended group, while the pushers dodge back and forth, shielded by two protectors who are close relatives of the throwers. Everyone throws at least one spear, while those who are not engaged in throwing spears hurl imprecations at the offending group who by usage cannot reply.

When there has been enough of this the actual killers come forth to be thrown at with headed spears. Yet they must not be hit, for such an accident will lead to a general fight in hot blood. So while all in the offended group are throwing spears to their hearts' content, their elders are exhorting them not to hit anyone. On the other side the old men are urging their young men not to lose their heads and become angry.

At last, when the offended party has spent its energy for spear-

[81] L. T. Hobhouse, C. G. Wheeler and M. Ginsberg, *The Material Culture and Social Institutions of the Simpler Peoples* (London, 1915).

throwing, the killers stand quietly while all the warriors of the offended group dance up to them. Now comes the crucial moment. If
a spear is jabbed through the thigh of one of the killers, it means
that all is over. If only a slight wound is given, it means that the
aggrieved group is not wholly satisfied and, after allowing a temporary truce, it will come for vengeance. No wound means immediate
vengeance and may lead to a general fight on the spot.

After all, there is no superior restraining power; it all depends on
the self-control of each group and the strength of the desire to raise
the interests of mutuality above the emotions of group antagonism.
The significant thing to recognize is that even on the very primitive
level a distinct effort is made to regularize and resolve disputes and
conflicts that endanger social well-being even when the local groups
involved are sovereign and there is no superior force to hold them
in check. In such instances as these they create the restraint (such
as it is) themselves.

Let us now move on to see what generalizations can be made
about law among the primitive peoples who have developed to the
level of the more highly organized hunters. The range of variation
in degree of political structuring and in forms of legal procedures
is obviously greater than among simple hunters and gatherers. The
size of the local groups is generally increased as a result of a richer
food supply. Population density is somewhat heavier but not intense.
The local groups, coming into more constant association with each
other, are frequently consolidated into a higher unit of organization
—the band (e.g., Comanches), and in some instances the bands may
be welded into a yet higher political structure—the tribal state
(e.g., the Cheyennes). Although the leader of the local group generally remains a mere headman, and so also the band leader, the
political heads of the tribes begin to take on the definite marks of
chieftainship. They possess attributes of authority that to some degree set them aside and above the usual run of men. A tendency to
hereditary succession to chieftainship tends to be felt, but it is not
yet ordinarily established as a fixed principle. It is merely that sons
or nephews of chiefs (if the society is matrilineal) are more likely
to become conditioned to family traditions of social responsibility

and ambition. Further, through generalization the young sprouts of chiefs are identified in the minds of the people with their fathers or uncles. An expectancy of leadership is attached to them.

Kinship may or may not be strongly emphasized: clans may be present, but by no means is it the regular pattern. Nevertheless, kinship continues to loom large in the law. Kinsmen stand together.

Homicide and adultery continue to be the chief sources of difficulty, and they remain almost exclusively private offenses. The higher hunters are generally warlike, as may well be expected of people who wrest their living from nature by force of arms. In interpersonal disputes there is a strong proclivity to resort to force. But there is an equally strong social interest in keeping internal resort to force within bounds. "There is always the enemy to fight." Aggression can be readily turned outside the tribe.

Another important factor that lends itself to the mitigation of physical exactions between members of the tribe is that through the higher development of material culture there is a richer inventory of economic goods. Goods can be equated with blood or physical and mental hurt. Composition is possible—private delicts become emendable.

Among the Australians, Andamanese, and for the most part among the Shoshones, as has been seen, this possibility does not exist. Indeed, Hobhouse, Wheeler, and Ginsberg found only six instances of composition predominating among fifty societies classified as Gatherers and Lower Hunters (12 per cent). But among the societies classified as Higher Hunters by these investigators 25 out of 75 (33 per cent) allowed composition of most wrongs.[32] Among these people, however, if the demanded (or acceptable) damages are not forthcoming, kinsmen of an aggrieved party back him in killing the offender or perhaps some other member of his group. Then there is once again the likelihood of retaliation and feud. But almost always there are the chiefs or other big men to be called upon to intervene to prevent this or to help to bring it to an end, if feud gets under way.

The weakness of the law on this particular level of social development is that the responsibility for adhering to established procedure still rests for the most part with the two contending parties. Each

[32] Hobhouse, Wheeler and Ginsberg, p. 80.

ordinarily determines for itself the justice of its cause without submission to a superior judicial authority except as a public consensus as to what is right and just may work to make itself felt in influencing the behavior of the litigants. Mediation there may be as among the Cheyennes; or Good Offices, or even arbitration. Still, the whole procedure may end in a resort to arms and internecine warfare. The well-being of the social body is precariously endangered.

The development of criminal law remains weak. The Cheyennes are exceptional in making all homicides a public offense. Special threats to the economic security of the tribe may come under a tribal criminal jurisdiction, as we have seen it develop in the Plains. Excessive sorcery universally does, while ordinary sorcery remains a private matter to be handled on the level of countersorcery with occasional recourse to procedure in private law.

The Law of Persons is still by far the bulkiest part of such law as exists, for property interests are not yet diversified enough to give rise to many clashing claims as to economic rights. Yet when such skewed elaboration as occurs among the Yuroks comes into play, law is built to deal with economic matters in considerable detail.

The law-ways of the Comanches, Cheyennes, and Kiowas as described and analyzed in Chapter VII exemplify the higher hunters sufficiently well so that further examples are hardly necessary. Still, as a reminder that wide variation is possible even though societies may be on the same general level of subsistence development, a brief consideration of the Indian tribes of the Northwest Coast of North America will be fruitful.

These people are primarily fishers and hunters of sea mammals, but they also trap and hunt the game of their rich forests. They are economically blessed by a prodigal environment, and through energetic application of their own skills they enjoy a high standard of living and a wide margin beyond the level of bare subsistence. Most of the tribes in the area exhibit a strong development of the kinship sentiment. They have moieties and clans (usually matrilineal) supported by elaborate mythologies objectively expressed in spectacular totemic art. Political and social rank are highly refined; chieftainship in each clan or village is inherited in "royal" lineages, and social rank must be achieved and maintained by competitive wealth manipulation, ostentatious display, conspicuous consumption, and the killing of people or the taking of slaves.

The functions of the chief are centered about economic, social and ceremonial activities—and warfare, if it can be dignified by this term. Only in a minor way are they concerned with political matters. Rather, the group tends to subordinate and coalesce itself in the personality of the chief, who thinks egotistically more than he does politically.

In each local group or tribe of the coast Tsimshian there is one house which ranks above all others. The head of this house is the chief of the tribe. In most tribes there are several chiefs' lineages in separate, though related, houses, but one is always recognized as the head chief, while the others are subordinate to him.

A chief is the social and ceremonial figurehead of the tribe, but has very little formalized political power. He has no control over the property or lives of his tribesmen, but exerts his authority mainly through the prestige of his position and his own personality. The cooperation of strong leaders in the tribe is necessary to any real extension of his power. Due to the fact that the reputation of the tribe among its neighbors depends largely on the chief and his potlatches, he is assured of his tribesmen's support and assistance.

A head chief holds the most powerful secular name, not only in his lineage, but also in his tribe, and possesses the right to the most dangerous and powerful sacred names and spirits. Leadership in the secret society activities was a chief's prerogative. It was he who conveyed supernatural power to a child for the first time and announced it ready for the secret society initiations. The organization of the winter festivities was in the hands of the chief and his councilors. They decided when the winter ceremonial season should start, who should give initiations and when they should be given. They could force initiations or prevent them as they saw fit. When the chief wanted to give a potlatch or a power demonstration no other tribesman might plan festivities that would interfere with his. Each head chief managed the winter season for his own tribe, assisted by the sub-chiefs. The head chiefs planned inter-tribal affairs among them. A chief decided when the winter ceremonials should end and it was he who removed the influence of the spirits from the dwellings and the people at large. Often the chief was called in to remove the tabus from initiates also, though that was not necessary. Only wealthy families could afford the services of a chief since he had to be paid much more liberally than anyone else.

While a chief can expect constant and liberal economic support from his tribesmen, he does not contribute to potlatches given by them. He is responsible for their economic welfare, must feed them when necessary and has to lay aside supplies for this purpose. He is also expected to be generous with his tribe and to give feasts to them from time to time. He constantly receives gifts from members of other tribes, either at potlatches or for services which he performs. Since his tribe furnishes him with wealth for his potlatches they expect to share in what he receives from others . . .

The main tie binding members of a tribe together is loyalty to their chief and participation in affairs that center around him. They elevate him to his position, support him, build his house, finance inter-tribal potlatches given by him and finally bury him. The members also protect him and avenge any wrong committed against the chief or a member of his family. If a member of another tribe should injure, insult or kill their chief, the tribe may demand payment through the successor and the leading men. In pre-white times if it was not made the offending tribe was raided. Should a tribesman kill a chief or chief's relative in another tribe, all of the murderer's tribesmen must contribute to pay the relatives of the slain man and his tribe.

Tribesmen are by no means passive followers of their chief. The lineage heads act as his advisers in all affairs of importance and withhold their support if they do not approve his plans. A number of generations ago the Gɪnax-angi · 'k tribe was so incensed because their chief allowed his son to take a copper shield that they had bought for the chief that they refused to furnish the wealth necessary to properly bury the chief and install his successor. More recently, Niəs-yaqana · 't's tribesmen voted to hold a housewarming in his new home instead of painting it for him. In spite of the chief's objection, the necessary funds were contributed and the party held. Quite as often the chief won, as when the same Niəs-yaqana · 't married a Nass woman over the protests of his advisers, and then willed his house to her. The system of checks and balances which were customary prevented a chief from becoming an autocratic ruler and also saved him from becoming a mere puppet in the hands of powerful lineage heads.[33]

A salient feature, along with elaborated rank order, of the Northwest Coast cultures, is egocentrism blown to the point of narcissism. The ego sense is strong but the ego is weak and vulnerable. It is

[33] Viola Garfield, *Tsimshian Clan and Society* (University of Washington Publications in Anthropology, Vol. 7, 1939), pp. 182–184.

easily injured and must be constantly reassured by means of external social gestures and symbolic acts on a grand scale: potlatch-giving or destruction of persons and property. Alternatively, legal settlements may also be sought, and even achieved. Individual offenses may be categorized as homicide, assault, negligence, etc., but in the native view they are basically all of a kind: defamation of character. The injured party is shamed, his (or his group's) reputation is tarnished by the insult; his social standing in the eyes of people is impaired. His overriding purpose is not to punish the wrongdoer but to reëstablish his prestige. Intent therefore plays no part in Northwest Coast law. The effect is the thing and the effect must be wiped out by some counterbalancing act.[34]

To understand this is important for understanding Northwest Coast behavior. Injury caused by nonhuman agencies produces the same wounded pride as do the acts of men. A potlatch must be given or property destroyed to recover esteem. Or, even more harshly, if a prince or high chief has died, his followers may go out to kill some other entirely innocent chief in the belief that it transfers the suffering to his lineage. So it was that when three relatives of a Kwakiutl chief were once accidentally drowned a killing expedition was sent out in order "to let someone else wail." [35]

In another typical instance, a Tsimshian village was shooting a cannon to honor their dead chief. In their usual enthusiasm for making a big show they overloaded the cannon. It exploded and killed a tribesman. They were much humiliated and "afraid of the slurring remarks of other tribes," so they decided to kill somebody in a neighboring lineage with whom they were on bad terms because of an inadequate settlement of a previous killing. They managed to wound the first man they met, and then the next day they cheerfully paid damages for the assault, after which the assaulted village joined with the others in the burial of the chief whose resounding mourning rites had touched off the event.[36]

Among the Tsimshians, when a killing occurs, either a feud or a legal action follows. Which it will be depends upon circumstances

[34] Cf. K. Oberg, "Crime and Punishment in Tlingit Society," *American Anthropologist*, 36:145–156 (1934).

[35] H. Codere, *Fighting with Property: A Study of Kwakiutl Potlatching and Warfare 1792–1930* (American Ethnological Society, Monograph 18, 1950), p. 102.

[36] Garfield, pp. 261–262.

and the tempers of the two involved lineages. Recourse to legal action occurs for exactly the same reason that the regulated combat is invoked in Australia; it is the only alternative to killing and more killing. The killing may be done, and a good deal of it is done, but it is too unnerving and upsetting to have it go too far.

The procedure of settlement is highly formalized and the whole undertaking hangs in delicate balance as can be seen in the following reliable account.

Men from the Gɪspaxlɔ·'ts and Gɪlusta'u tribes, who had their villages on opposite sides of the cove at Port Simpson, were gambling together when they got into an argument over the game. In the brawl that followed five Gɪspaxlɔ·'tx and three Gɪlutsa'u were killed. The Gɪspaxlɔ·'ts tribesmen then went up into the woods above the Gɪlutsa'u village and started firing on the dwelling of the chief, Niɔs-nawa. In his home as guests were a Haida chief and his two sons, who belonged to the Eagle clan. One of the sons was shot by Niɔs-mu·'tk, a Gɪspaxlɔ·'ts, also an Eagle clansman.

The lineage relatives of each murdered man asked indemnity from the murderer and his lineage. Since the procedure was the same in each case, a description of the request made by the Gɪspaxlɔ·'ts relatives of one of the murdered men will suffice. They selected the successor to the slain man to act as spokesman. Accompanied by his lineage relatives and spectators from the village, he went in front of the dwelling belonging to the murderer and his lineage and stood on the beach shouting many times, "Give me moose skins." His hair was tied in a knot over his forehead like a warrior's and he held an eagle tail feather in his hand. The G lutsa'u, knowing of the intended request, had gathered wealth and food for a feast. Soon the drum was heard in the house of the Gɪlutsa'u murderer and his relatives came down to the beach, scattering eagle down to signify their peaceful intentions. They laid a moose skin in front of the spokesman, placing him upon it and carried him into their house. Other Gɪlutsa'u gathered around him, shooting into the air, but he did not move. In the house he was placed in the seat of honor, his relatives around him.

The Gɪlutsa'u spokesman called for the compensation gifts, which were brought forward by the maternal uncle of the murderer and placed before the envoy. The latter arose, holding the eagle tail feather over his breast. He looked neither to right nor left, for to have done so would have indicated that he intended to kill for revenge. The tension was very great since the slightest move on his part could have precipitated general bloodshed. While the gifts were being brought in the relatives of the deceased sang one of their mourning songs. When the amount in front of the envoy satisfied him and his clan relatives he sat down. If they had not received sufficient gifts they would have walked out without a word and the negotiations would have had to be continued by the Gʌlutsa'u the next day When the amount was paid there was a general entertainment of songs and dramatizations, ending with a feast.[37]

In sum: the great legal problem for the tribes of the Northwest Coast is the restoration of balance between the local group aggregates that make up the larger society. Because the local groups themselves are small kinship bodies they are able to handle their internal personal problems on other than legal bases. Shaming suffices for this, "The big stick which is relied on in this control system [is] not physical punishment, but social attacks upon the extremely vulnerable egos of the members of the group." [38] But this same vulnerability leads to wanton killing and strains the weak legal machinery to the utmost.

The real elaboration of law begins with the expansion of the gardening-based tribes. With gardening an economic base is established that permits the maintenance of larger populations within a single community. More important, more communities can be maintained within a given geographical area. The pressures to maintain peaceful equilibrium between the numerous closely interacting communities become intensified. A further growth of law and a more effective law is demanded.

Land, a matter of little concern in the intratribal affairs of gatherers and hunters, becomes a matter of primary interest for families and individuals. Allocation of rights, duties, privileges, powers, and immunities with respect to real estate are now extremely important. Material culture proliferates; chattel goods become (though still in relatively limited degree) issues of interest. The law of things begins to rival the law of persons. Most important, however, is the fact that the societies now have the potentiality of becoming so large that face-to-face relationships between all of their members are no longer

[37] Garfield, pp. 259–260.
[38] W. C. Crane, *Kwakiutl, Haida and Tsimshian: A Study in Social Control* (Unpublished ms., University of Utah Library, 1951), p. 144.

possible. The family still exists, as it does in all societies, but even the extended family is no longer coterminous with the discrete society. It may still constitute the population of a single village, but the village becomes part of a larger whole.

The kinship principle has not atrophied; on the contrary it, too, expands along with the growing society. But to achieve this expansion its emphasis tends to shift from the bilateral kindred to fixation on a fictive device. The clan reaches its apogee. The fiction is that persons linked through one line of descent are more significantly related than are their kinsmen who are not linked through that line. The descent principle may be either matrilineal or patrilineal (among gardeners it is more commonly matrilineal) but the primary effect is the same either way. Half the genetic relatives of a person belong to his clan. The other half do not. Thus by an artificial discrimination, through an arbitrary process of paring down, the kinship group is enabled to retain a sharper identity in the face of expanding numbers. Thus it can continue to function as a body of mutual aid and protection, economically and legally; so can it continue to perform ceremonial and governmental activities. Yet it does this at the price of cutting off the individual in some degree from at least one of those who are his most intimate kinsmen: from either his mother or his father. One of them always belongs to a clan that is not his own. The Trobriand and Ashanti situations have revealed to us what manner of social and legal conflicts derive from this sacrifice in favor of the clan principle.

The clan is peculiarly suitable to gardening peoples because of its usefulness as an administrative unit in the allocation of land rights. In virtually every horticultural society it holds *de facto* control of the land. Even when the ultimate title is vested *de jure* in the tribal chief or the national king (viz., the Ashanti) the actual land-administering unit is the clan. The land is the stable base of all existence, and as long as the clan prevails no person or family goes landless, for no individual can alienate his holdings outside the clan, and the clan gives up its title only in utmost extremity. There is no agrarian problem for primitive societies.

Because it is such a potent institution, the clan looms large in the law of horticultural societies. And looming large, it intensifies the problems of maintenance of social order. Clan solidarity commits the clan to the challenge, "Strike my clan brother and you strike me." An offense against an individual is an offense against his entire clan. The reaction is collective, and a single disturbance can set hundreds of people into action. The upsetting consequences of an illegal act are apt to be magnified out of all proportion to the intrinsic significance of the act itself. Add this to the multiplied kinds of circumstances (debt, trespass, theft) that have proliferated on the new level of culture and the conflict disturbances that can internally disrupt the society are manifold.

We see a general situation, then, in which substantive law has become much more diversified through a new growth of the law of things (chattels and real property) and the active legal units *within* the society are much larger and more definitively exclusive.

Whether physical sanctions or damages in the form of property will be exacted by the injured person and his clansmen remains, among most of the less developed gardeners, mostly a matter of self-determination. Nevertheless, a trend toward composition is noticeable. Where Hobhouse, Wheeler, and Ginsberg found composition the regular form of sanction in twelve per cent of their sample of Gatherers and Lower Hunters, and in 33 per cent of their Higher Hunters, it becomes 45 per cent among the Horticulturalists.[39] In almost all instances, however, action for damages remains only a first step. Refusal or failure on the part of the defendant party to pay up leads to assault or killing. Then retaliation and feuding are the unhappy consequence.

As we have stated several times before, this is the fatal defect of most primitive law systems. Like the modern nation, each clan or kinship group determines for itself what the final action shall be, and no man, clan, or nation is competent to judge its own cause.

Several correctives come into play. Right standards of conduct make their influence felt in any society, and in a limited number of kin-dominated societies the clan will not raise a hand to prosecute an injury to one of its members when his conduct has been patently outrageous. Or they may make only a weak effort to collect light damages. In a few societies the extreme act of formal exclusion from the clan may be taken in order to free the clan from any necessity

[39] Hobhouse, Wheeler and Ginsberg, p. 80.

of paying damages on a wrongdoer's behalf and to free it from any need to get involved in a feud, if the culprit is killed by his victim's kinsmen. In a relatively few societies such as Samoa or Cheyenne the erring person or his kin group initiate atonement on their own. Direct action, for example, can be taken in consequence of private wrongs by the injured kin group in Samoa, but it frequently results in bloody feuds, which are eventually stopped by the intervention of the *fono,* the council consisting of all household heads. To head off direct action by the offended group the *matai,* or honored household head of the wrongdoer, humiliates himself by sitting all day before the house of the wronged man. Nothing is said, but at last if the injured man is willing to have the issue composed, he invites the *matai* in for *kava*-drinking and food. Subsequently, damages are paid in the form of five mats. Should he rebuff the *matai,* it means that an attack is contemplated and feud is in the offing. Homicide and adultery committed against ordinary men are serious torts, which, if the tortfeasor's household is of a mind to compound them, make it necessary for the entire kinship group to go and perform *ifonga,* as the act of self-humiliation is called.[40]

A number of offenses, incidentally, are clear-cut crimes against the society itself and they are directly tried by the *fono* in full sitting. The case is argued pro and con by accusers and the defendant, as well as by other persons of account who might feel they have something to say. It is done with all the high form of Polynesian etiquette. *Lèse majesté* against the person of the high chief (disrespect, adultery with his wives, assault on his person) is a first-order crime. No ambiguity as to whether such acts are merely personal offenses against the chief or crimes against the society exists here as it does in the Trobriand situation. For it is not the Samoan chief who institutes action and carries through the procedure. It is the council of household heads. Other public offenses are violation of ordinances (edicts) of the *fono,* insulting the village god (sacrilege), trying to stir up trouble between two household heads, excessive cruelty by a household head against his followers, incest, and refusal to settle a blood feud which threatens the security of the village. Lesser punishments imposed by the *fono* can take either the forms of fines

[40] Cf. Hogbin, *Law and Order in Polynesia,* p. 273.

(food to be eaten by the whole village) or enforced physical labor on public projects. For more serious individual crimes there is exile, or a variety of painful physical punishments to be endured immediately on the imposition of the penalty—or else death.[41]

When whole households act in defiance of the village good, the *fono* moves in a body against them in an official confiscation of their goods, followed by exile. A decision against a family once arrived at by the council, "the leading men of the settlement, rising from the place of meeting, proceeded towards the residence of the obnoxious family, attended by their followers, where they quickly seated themselves upon the ground in full view of the family they had decided to banish. The latter often heard of the sentence in sufficient time to enable them to remove their mats and other household property to a place of safety [Does this indicate that the offensive household was not invited or ordered to be present at the trial?]; but the livestock generally fell into the hands of the expelling party, who reserved them to feast upon after the work of the day."

. . . One of the judicial party rose to make a speech . . . for the benefit of the head of the doomed family, in which he informed him of the decision of the *fono,* and that they had come to enforce it. On the conclusion of this speech one of the judicial party rose up and commenced to ring the breadfruit-trees [which of course will kill them] . . . The commencement of this work of destruction was either the signal for resistance to be offered, or for the family to gather up their belongings and remove from the dwelling.

Whilst those proceedings were going on . . . the old men sat around the spot . . . chatting together apparently quite unconcerned, and waiting for the return of the young men who had been dispatched to plunder the taro patches . . . On the whole of the provisions being collected, they were cooked and eaten by the expelling party, who then returned to their homes.[42]

The supremacy of the council does not always go unchallenged, however. Powerful individual families still fight for family sovereignty—if they think they can get away with it. Or they threaten a

[41] Margaret Mead, *Social Organization of Manua* (Bernice P. Bishop Museum, Bulletin 76, 1930), p. 169.

[42] From J. B. Stair, *Old Samoa* (London, 1897), pp. 91 ff.; quoted in Hogbin, pp. 275-276.

fight on a scale that holds forebodings of serious consequences, and so force a compromise on the *fono*. One Samoan youth from a powerful household once stole a whole canoe-load of produce belonging to another village. His own *fono* condemned him, trussed him up like a pig, and took him over to the villagers from whom he had stolen. They were going to leave it up to them as to whether they would further punish the young man or have pity. His own household dissented from the action of their *fono* and let it be known that they would fight if the boy were hurt. To avoid the fight, the wronged village agreed to accept an indemnity, which was transmitted to them by some of the senior members of the thief's own *fono*.[43]

Stair also tells of a high-ranking chief with a large following who committed adultery with the wife of another chief. Because the wife of a chief was involved, it was a *fono* matter. The *fono* exiled the adulterer to a neighboring island, but his household and friends agitated for remission of the sentence. When it was not forthcoming, the chief and his henchmen returned in force. The *fono*, not wanting to face up to a general battle, formally approved his return. Then he, having won his point, decided caution and decency were the better part of valor and cleared out.

In Samoa, as in most other tribes on the middle levels of development, society is not yet so organized that preponderant power is surely and always in the hands of the official agents of the society as against its stubborn, subordinate elements. The society as a whole must compromise, no matter how much it goes against the grain. The situation is exactly that faced by the United Nations in its dealings with Communist China in Korea.

The salient feature of the struggle for law in the primitive societies that have evolved into settled populations of gardeners is the effort to establish the interests of the society as a whole as superior to the impulses and interests of the kinship groups within the society. Individuals as individuals, on the one hand, can rarely challenge the collective power of society with any enduring success. But it is otherwise with the kindred in the primitive world. The kinship group is frequently powerful enough, and it is commonly so self-conscious of its own solid identity and self-loyalty that it thinks

[43] G. Brown, *Melanesians and Polynesians* (London, 1910), pp. 289–290.

more of its own special interests than it does of the concern of the society at large. With such sentiments and such power it can confound the public law on occasion.

The struggle of the law through the ages of development on the primitive level has revolved about the problem of subordinating the kin-centered psychology to that of the community. The kin sentiment never dies, but ultimately public law triumphs.

It has been through the emergence of institutionalized chieftainship that this was in large part achieved, although in every case the chief is surrounded by a council not of his own choosing. The council both aids him in executive administration and serves as a check, either democratic or oligarchic, on personal dictatorship and individual whim.

Institutionalized chieftainship comes to mean a bestowal of power in the office of the chief that is a mighty lure for ambitious men. As a check on dangerously disruptive, self-seeking power struggles legitimacy becomes an important principle. The hereditary *tendency* to the bestowal of chieftainship almost inevitably becomes a hereditary principle when chieftainship is endowed with real power. Usually, as among the Trobrianders and Ashantis, a dominant clan or lineage is elevated to royal status and chiefs are chosen by fixed principles from within the designated line. As the Ashanti materials so clearly showed, these primitives are nevertheless aware of the dangers in a narrow and absolute rule of succession, which more often than not would put an heir to succession into the kingship who has no aptitude for the job. The king may then be a feeble weakling, or worse still, a dangerous egomaniac. In the one case, the state may fail to function effectively in times of crisis. In the other, tyranny may supplant social justice and men suffer under corruption. Hence the public checks on the choice of the successor to chieftainship from among a number of eligible heirs in the royal line. Hence the machinery for impeachment.

Functional flexibility may also be maintained by using the hereditary principle for one order of chieftain and a purely functional principle of selection for another. The Iroquois Indians exemplify this arrangement. The sachems, or peace chiefs, were chosen from among the possessors of certain names inherited within certain maternal lineages within the clans. On the other hand, the War

Chiefs could include any outstanding fighter who was elevated by the Council of Sachems on the basis of his record.[44]

The legal significance of the chief is, of course, that his personal law can with tribal backing become public law. The King's Peace becomes the law of the tribe. This is not the inevitable path to the consolidation of a tribe or nation under a centralized rule of law, but it is the line of development most easily followed, and it appears to be the one most commonly used in the later development of primitive societies, earlier civilizations, and in the transition from feudalism to nationalism in Europe. It has its modern counterpart in relapse to dictatorship when monarchy fails and the difficulty of operating a democratic machinery becomes too great for a people unskilled in political self-control or lacking in a highly developed sense of the common interest.

Ian Hogbin in his brief treatment of the rise of kingship in Ontong Java has an excellent account of one example of the process at work.

Some eight generations ago (*ca.* 1830?) one Ke hangamea organized a bunch of armed henchmen at whose head he set himself up as the first chief of all the tribe. He bullied and ruled by assassination of those who refused to obey his edicts. There was no legitimacy to his pretensions and his violence "led to a good deal of unrest." Eventually, like many another tyrant, he was himself assassinated. His example had revealed the possibilities in kingship, however, and so for three successive generations little civil wars took place between rival aspirants. Eventually, a man named 'Avi'o managed to attain the position and hold it against all comers. Apparently the people had by this time had enough of turmoil and to this day they have continued to support his descendants in the kingship. Kingship became legitimatized. And significantly, "succession has not followed any rules of primogeniture within the family but has been on the same lines as succession within the joint family." The most acceptable of the heirs becomes king.

Around 1870 two ambitious brothers hoped to overthrow the royal line, but the principle of legitimacy was by then too well established. The plotters murdered the royal heir as a rallying signal

---

[44] B. H. Quain, "The Iroquois" in Margaret Mead, ed., *Cooperation and Competition Among Primitive Peoples,* chap. viii.

for their revolt. But their *coup d'état* did not succeed. Only the men of their own joint family stood by them and some of these backed out when they saw how little support there was going to be. In the end, "there remained no more than two dozen supporters to fight the whole royal line with as many allies as it could muster." The eventual result was the death of the two ringleaders and most of their crew. The monarchy has never since been threatened.

Even so, in the area of law, the important kindreds continued to keep legal action in their own hands except for occasional intervention by the king on behalf of wronged persons whose kinsmen were too weak to be able to face up to the power of a stronger kinship group. The early kings also exhibited a sense of social justice by cutting off some of their own miscreant relatives so that they could be punished by their victims without fear of royal retaliation. The trend to royal intervention grew under later kings, until today "an offense against the individual has become a crime against the government."

"The natives do not in any sense resent the change," says Hogbin, "so it may be regarded as a justifiable one." In other words, the king's law has become the public law, for the people feel that the advantages under the administration of just kings outweigh the disadvantages of the old kin-regulated law. Yet the old feeling of personal interests remains strong; it is still difficult to get witnesses to offer evidence against an accused, for unless they have been personally injured, they say it is none of their business.[45]

It is not necessary to recapitulate the Ashanti story here. Suffice it to remind the reader that in the Ashanti development the full extension of criminal law was very nearly achieved on the primitive level and, indeed, in the enthusiasm of its freshness it very nearly outdid itself.

The reign of public law may also be achieved by other means than monarchy. Throughout Indonesia and among the Pueblo Indians in the American Southwest it has worked through the council. Both cultural systems represent high levels of achievement and organization on the basis of religiously oriented garden or agricultural economies with irrigation.[46]

The social systems of the two dozen pueblos of New Mexico and

[45] Hogbin, pp. 224–231.   [46] See Ter Haar, *Adat Law in Indonesia.*

Arizona are similar to each other in general configuration but highly variable in specific tone and detail of political institutions.

Of the nineteen New Mexican pueblos some sixteen represent established going concerns. But the same "old way" of government, "uncontaminated" by American influence, has produced in one pueblo (Sia) a strong semi-democracy, relatively unbothered by faction as distinct from personal power; in another (Santa Ana), a semi-democracy so factionalized that even individual power, leadership and vision are having a hard time reëstablishing any semblance of unity. In a third (Santo Domingo), we find an intrenched oligarchy forcing its will upon a relatively passive population, but largely for the common good as seen by the leaders. In a fourth (Taos), an intrenched oligarchy exploits the population with the high hand of substantial tyranny. In a fifth (Isleta), factions have split government to the verge of anarchy—yet somehow the pueblo has managed to hold together. In a sixth (Santa Clara), a similar factional situation led after twenty-five years to a "modernization" of government via compromise and a written constitution, which, now for fifteen years, has worked. In a seventh (Jemez), despite all "old style" form, the government has degenerated into helplessness against the unruly and into general unreckonability amid the pullings and haulings of persons and families, with justice either an accident or a mockery. Again, within a single pueblo the character of particular officers (in the annual succession in office) can be responsible for a cumulative solution of crises, building or rebuilding community structure and morale, or for a series of failures through weakness or blindness which precipitate new and greater crises. One pueblo (Laguna) has worked out a sort of federation of its seven sub-villages, with a machinery so elastic as to maintain the membership and loyalty, in addition, of two semi-self-governing "colonies," one in Arizona, one in California—and this although the old religious organization (which has been too lightly seen as the sole key to pueblo government) has in that pueblo been substantially disrupted.[47]

In like manner, there is no automatic connection between any legal measures or machinery and level of cultural development. There are only general associations and trends.

The details of Pueblo law are for future publication. The essential fact to be made at this point is that the administrative machinery of

[47] K. N. Llewellyn, Introduction for a forthcoming study of Pueblo Law and Social Control by K. N. Llewellyn and E. A. Hoebel.

the pueblos is a by-product of a most tightly-knit and elaborated religious–ceremonial organization of sacerdotal officers who form a village council for policy-making and judicial determination of all major infractions of pueblo norms, including interpersonal disputes between members of different families. The pueblo chief, or cacique, is almost exclusively concerned with ritual matters and religious contemplation. He exercises little direct legal power, athough the ultimate authority is theoretically his. The practical exercise of legal sanctions in all important matters is in the hands of the pueblo council. Minor affairs, if the breach is predominantly secular, are by tacit delegation left to the governor, who is a one-year appointee, or to the "war captain," if it is predominantly sacral. So overwhelming is the collective emphasis of pueblo social organization that little in the way of legally coercive privilege-rights is left to the individual or his kinship group in interfamilial trouble cases. The penal sanctions invoked on behalf of the total group were often harsh indeed: whipping, hanging by the thumbs, impounding in stocks, and death were once imposed consequences of the law. But this has not been the handiwork of chief or king but rather of the heads of the religious fraternities acting in common council through executive officers, the war captain and the governor.

The law of the tribes that have come under purview is obviously not the consequence of conquest, for the social structures that support these legal systems are not conquest states. Law is the inherent product of internal social forces, the creative consequence of a people's efforts to achieve and maintain a self-limiting order. This is not to deny the existence of conquest states with invidious law systems on the higher primitive levels, for east Africa abounds with them and in the Americas we have striking examples in the Inca and Aztec empires.[48] It does emphasize, however, the fact of the

[48] See K. Oberg, "The Kingdom of Ankole in Uganda," in M. Fortes and E. E. Evans-Pritchard, eds., *African Political Systems*, pp. 121–162; L. M. Nunez, *El durecho precolonial* (Encyclopedia Ilustrada Mexicana, No. 7, Mexico City, 1937); J. H. Rowe, "Inca Culture at the Time of the Conquest," in J. H. Steward, ed., *Handbook of South American Indians*, Vol. 2, *The Andean Civilization* (Bureau of American Ethnology, Bulletin 143, 1946), pp. 183–330. For a sound critical discussion of the conquest theory of the state, see R. H. Lowie, *The Origin of the State*, chap. ii.

primary development of law not as an instrument of exploitation but as a device shaped by the members of society in response to internal conditions in the search for ways and means to translate their basic social postulates into action, to preserve them and to resolve conflicts of interests.

The trend of the law as it has been thus far explored is one of increasing growth and complexity. It is also one in which the tendency is to shift the privilege-rights of prosecution and imposition of legal sanctions from the individual and his kinship group over to clearly defined public officials representing the society as such. The kinship group remains significantly important in all the higher primitive societies. Its interests and its members still continue to collide with those of other kinship groups within the same society, but in an increasing number of legal spheres it is no longer permitted to prosecute its own cause. The judicial function steadily wins out over the merely legal.

Sir Henry Maine, nearly ninety years ago, summed up the trend of the law in somewhat different terms. They took the form of a generalization that quickly achieved general acceptance. Most legal historians know it by heart. "We may say," wrote Sir Henry, "that the movement of the progressive societies has hitherto been a movement *from Status to Contract*." [49]

In fuller terms Maine explained the meaning of his generalization as follows. "The movement of the progressive societies has been uniform in one respect. Through all its course it has been distinguished by the gradual dissolution of family dependency and the growth of individual obligation in its place. The individual is steadily substituted for the Family, as the unit of which civil laws take account . . . Nor is it difficult to see what is the tie between man and man which replaces by degrees those forms of reciprocity in rights and duties which have their origin in the Family. It is Contract. Starting, as from one terminus of history, from a condition of society in which all the relations of Persons are summed up in the relations of Family, we seem to have steadily moved towards a phase of social order in which all these relations arise from the free agreement of individuals." [50]

Roscoe Pound, a generation ago, challenged the validity of Maine's

[49] Maine, *Ancient Law*, p. 165. [50] *Ibid.*, p. 163.

dictum as a universal generalization by showing that while it held for the historical development of Roman law from which it was almost exclusively drawn, it does not comfortably fit the phenomenon of the common law.[51] Morris Cohen, in noting the correlation between the expansion of commercial activity and the growth of the idea of contract (citing especially Hebraic and Hellenic law), like Pound reminds us that there is in reality a good deal more of status left in modern law than the contract enthusiasts who followed Maine allowed for.[52]

In surveying the truly primitive societies, those that lie beyond the newly emergent civilizations of the Mediterranean, no specific trend in the separation of the individual from his kinship group as a legal entity can really be discerned. Contracts, as specific agreements to assume limited duties (with reciprocal demand-rights) and to recognize limited privilege-rights (with reciprocal no-demand-rights) for specified periods of time, exist in Eskimo, Plains, Ifugao, Trobriand, and Ashanti law. Power in the Hohfeldian sense is an attribute of possibly all legal systems. Personal property in chattels may be alienated by "sale" or gift in exchange for implied counter-gift in any of these societies. And such gift exchange when supported by such "legal" responsibility as Malinkowski espoused is, broadly construed, contract. On the other hand, through the whole gamut of primitive societies basic property, real property, and family chattels of magic or prestige potency, cannot be alienated by contract of sale by action of any single individual. The individual who makes a contract for the pledging or sale of such goods is invariably no more than the agent or trustee for the family estate. He cannot act without family consent. Further, throughout the law of torts in all the primitive systems that have come under our purview the kinship group is never wholly separated from the individual in the matter of legal responsibility unless the kin, in self-defense or in support of the social norms, expel a notorious bad egg of their own volition.

The "Mainean shift" does not really become effective until after the beginning of the urban revolution in full neolithic times. It is

[51] "Moreover English legal history was not examined in making out the case, nor did the adherents of the political interpretation ever test it by an independent study of the common law." Roscoe Pound, *Interpretations of Legal History* (Cambridge, England, 1923), p. 55.

[52] M. R. Cohen, *Law and the Social Order* (New York, 1937), pp. 69–87.

then, not on the more primitive levels, that the individual begins to be loosened from his kinship group. For urbanization dissolves the strength of the kinship tie.[53] It concomitantly steps up the need for centralized legal control by throwing together multitudes of persons whose local, or tribal, backgrounds are different and whose customs and their underlying postulates are frequently in conflict at many points. City life proliferates law.

The really significant shift, however, in the development of primitive law is not a substantive shift from status to contract in the relations of individuals, even though this has been a noticeable characteristic of later European law; rather, the significant shift of emphasis has been in procedure. Privilege-rights and responsibility for the maintenance of the legal norms are transferred from the individual and his kinship group to the agents of the body politic as a social entity.

Legal historians have long envisaged primitive society as marked by retaliation and blood revenge: a veritable arena of violence ruled by "the law of the jungle." They have seen in their own mind's eye the very gradual substitution of composition for vengeance as a marked trend of the law. Over the vast span of the years, if we look at modern societies as against the primitive, it is true that a great change has taken place in this respect. Damages have generally replaced death as penalties in civil suits.

Yet there is an error in the conventional evolutionary idea. It lies in the notion that there ever was a time when torts were not emendable or a time when blood feud prevailed unchecked. The factual data make it very clear that the societies of man have from the outset wrestled with the problem of maintaining internal peace and harmony. The lowly Andamanese flees to the jungle when he has committed a homicide within his local group. His headman intervenes to pour oil on troubled waters when it appears that a dispute may lead to violence. The Eskimo meets killing with killing, but men who let the killing impulse run to feud and so kill more than once are removed by common communal action. The song duel exists as a substitute for violence to close issues of dispute without recourse to steps that may lead to feud. The lowly Australians have

[53] Cf. Robert Redfield, *The Primitive World and Its Transformations* (Ithaca, 1953).

no composition and they are plagued with feud, but regulated combat is used again and again in lieu of feud or to bring a standing feud to a close. The Ifugao have their procedural devices utilizing the good offices of a third party (as do the Yuroks) to see to it that trouble within the home district is adjusted without recourse to feud. The Cheyennes rely on a religious idea to make feud wholly impossible. The Kiowas follow suit, although with less sure effect. The Trobriand kinship group amends certain wrongs and killings even though retaliation is theoretically available. And finally, in Ashanti and Pueblo law feud is wholly impossible, for the right to take life is reserved absolutely to the central authority.

What emerges from the data is this: within loosely organized tribes in which the local group is autonomous, trouble involving members of different local groups frequently brews physical violence which often leads to feuding; feud marks an absence of law, for the killing is not mutually acknowledged as a privilege-right; yet it appears that every society has some set procedure for avoiding feud or bringing it to a halt; among the more organized tribes on the higher levels of economic and cultural growth feud is frequently prohibited by the action of a central authority representing the total social interest; this never happens on the lower levels of culture.

As the scope of commonality expands, as community of interest reaches out beyond the local group, beyond the clan and self-conscious kindred, men find the means to create and implement judicial and executive power in such a way that internecine strife within the bounds of the larger society is checked and ultimately suppressed.

It is argued by those who take the small view that because war between societies of men has always been, so war shall always be. War between societies is comparable to retaliation and feud within societies. The motivation and expression of both forms of behavior are much the same. But the urge to extend the realm of peace through law and the finding of the means to do it are clearly as old and as enduring as the urge to fight. The heartening fact is that for all the inadequacies of their judicial and administrative creations, for all the breakdowns of the machinery of social control that have occurred again and again in human history, the quest for law has never ceased on the part of men in society, and in the large the rule of law in the name of and on behalf of the social whole has grown and triumphed along with the expansion of the social horizon.

Today we find ourselves for the first time in a million years of social evolution at the point where technology has brought virtually every society into intermittent or enduring contact with nearly all the others. We have crossed the critical threshold into the realm where society on the world scale exists. The consciousness of World Society is just beginning to be born in the minds of men. World community is not yet a fully realized creation, for nations as segments of the world community are still, with reference to world society, on the functional level of the most primitive tribe. International law, so-called, is but primitive law on the world level. What has passed as international law consists of no more than normative rules for the conduct of affairs between nations and their citizens as they have been enunciated and agreed upon from time to time by means of treaties, pacts, and covenants. In addition, prevailing custom in international intercourse, recognized by tacit consensus or verbalized in arbitration and World Court awards, provides the other main source of its substance. Yet it has consisted of substantive rules without imperative legal sanctions.

Whatever the idealist may desire, force and the threat of force are the ultimate power in the determination of international behavior, as in the law within the nation or tribe. But until force and the threat of force in international relations are brought under social control by the world community, by and for the world society, they remain the instruments of social anarchy and not the sanctions of world law.

We are once again, in the long history of mankind, confronted with the stark bare-bones of the law-job. It is not this time a matter of society dribbling apart if the job fails to get done. It is the prospect of ghastly explosion.

Our studies have shown that the expanding societies of primitive men which have survived for our view mastered the problem, each on its own level, through expansion of the scope of the law, through creation of effective instruments of procedure, and the limitation and allocation of force in a way to make social authority prevail in the pinch. Had they not done so, they would not have survived for us to study.

No primitive society ever achieved this at a stroke. Nor should those who look for a better world in which there shall be a reign of peace through law expect that it can be done at a wave of the hand for world society.

The emergence of world law waits on the coalescence of a genuine sentiment of world community. The consciousness of the entity of the whole must outweigh the consciousness of limited national self-interest at points of critical conflicts of interest just as the sense of tribal oneness had to rise above local group and clan sentiment in simpler societies. Without the sense of community there can be no law. Without law there cannot for long be a community.

The lesson for today and the future is that a system of law for the world community must be created if the subcommunities, the nations and cities, are to survive.

A faltering step was taken in the old League of Nations. Humanity stumbled and fell. A new step has been taken in the formation of the United Nations, but it has not yet worked out the means, nor has it been allowed to take up the tools, to bring adequate force and the threat of force under the control of the world community, by and for the world society. An essential part of the process will be the formulation, step by step, of a realistic system of world law. The constitutional charter of organization is but the beginning; it sets the organic law and the structure of organization; the Bill of Human Rights expresses a body of fundamental, generalized postulates in one phase of personal law.

Governmental machinery is necessary to the total social control process in modern society. But government without law is limited to administration of services. These are essential and important without, however, making the whole piece. The creation in clear-cut terms of the corpus of world law cries for the doing. Even though present conditions do not look hopeful for the acceptance of world law, intelligent foresight demands that the eventuality must be anticipated. Much of the world law-to-be will be hammered out as specific issues catalyze action for the trouble case at hand. Like most socially accepted law it will be shaped of compromise of some interests. It will develop its shape in the arena of action. Underlying it all, however, if it is to be realized at all, there will have to be a minimum of general agreement as to the nature of the physical and ideational world and the relation of men in society to it. An important and valuable next step will be found in deep-cutting analysis of the major law systems of the contemporary world in order to lay bare their basic postulates—postulates that are too generally hidden; postulates felt, perhaps, by those who live by them, but so much taken for granted that they are but rarely expressed or exposed for examination. When this is done—and it will take the efforts of many keen intellects steeped in the law of at least a dozen lands *and* also aware of the social nexus of the law—then mankind will be able to see clearly for the first time where the common consensus of the great living social and law systems lies. Here will be found the common postulates and values upon which the world community can build. At the same time the truly basic points of conflict that will have to be worked upon for resolution will be revealed.

Law is inherently purposive. It deserves more purposive attention; for on its immediate growth hangs the fate of civilization. The science of comparative legal dynamics is called upon to add its catalytic effect to the crystallizing metamorphosis from primitive law to modern on the plane of world society.

If the fulfillment comes in our day, it will be our happy destiny to participate in the greatest event in legal history.

Bibliography

(Titles marked with an asterisk are cited)

Adam, Leonhard, "Criminal Law and Procedure in Nepal," *Far Eastern Quarterly,* 9:146–168 (1950).

—— "Methods and Forms of Investigating and Recording of Native Customary Law in the Netherlands East Indies Before the War" (mimeographed, African Institute, Leiden, 1948).

—— "The Social Organization and Customary Law of the Nepalese Tribes," *American Anthropologist,* 38:533–547 (1936).

*Aldridge, A. O., "The Meaning of Incest from Hutcheson to Gibbon," *Ethics,* 61:303–313 (1951).

*Austin, John, *Lectures on Jurisprudence,* rev. ed., ed. R. Campbell (1869).

*Baldwin, W. D., ed., *Bouvier's Law Dictionary* (Cleveland, 1934).

*Barton, R. F., *Ifugao Law* (University of California Publications in American Archaeology and Ethnology, Vol. 15, 1919), pp. 1–186.

*—— *Philippine Pagans: The Autobiographies of Three Ifugaos* (London, 1935).

*—— *The Half Way Sun: Life Among the Headhunters of the Philippines* (New York, 1930).

*—— *The Kalingas: Their Institutions and Custom Law* (Chicago, 1949).

*Benedict, R. F., *Patterns of Culture* (Boston and New York, 1934).

*—— *The Guardian Spirit Complex in North America* (American Anthropological Association, Memoir 29, 1923).

Bernard, Jessie, "Political Leadership among North American Indians," *American Journal of Sociology,* 34:296–315 (1928).

*Birket-Smith, K., *The Country of Eggedesminde and its Inhabitants* (Medelelser om Grønland, Vol. 66, 1924).

*—— *The Eskimos* (New York, 1936).

*Boas, Franz, ed., *General Anthropology* (New York, 1938).

*—— *The Central Eskimos* (Bureau of American Ethnology, Annual Report 6, 1888) pp. 399–669.

*——— The Eskimo of Baffinland and Hudson Bay (American Museum of Natural History, Bulletin 15, 1907).

*Bodenheimer, Edgar, Jurisprudence (New York, 1940).

*Boerenbeker, E. A., Het adatrecht de inlanders in de jurisprudentie, 1923–1933 (Bandung, 1935).

*Brown, G., Melanesians and Polynesians (London, 1910).

Bullock, C., Mashona Laws and Customs (Salisbury, 1913).

——— The Mashona: The Indigenous Natives of S. Rhodesia (Cape Town, 1938).

Burrows, E. G., "Breed and Border in Polynesia," American Anthropologist, 41:1–21 (1939).

*Busia, K. A., The Position of the Chief in the Modern Political System of Ashanti: A Study of the Influence of Contemporary Social Changes on Ashanti Political Institutions (Oxford, 1951).

Cairns, Huntington, "Law and Anthropology" in V. F. Calverton, ed., The Making of Man (New York, 1931), pp. 331–362.

*——— Law and the Social Sciences (New York, 1935).

Calhoun, G. M., The Growth of Criminal Law in Ancient Greece (Berkeley, 1927).

*Cardozo, B. N. The Growth of the Law (New Haven, 1924).

*——— The Nature of the Judicial Process (New Haven, 1921).

Cherry, R. R., Lectures in the Growth of Criminal Law in Ancient Communities (London and New York, 1890).

*Codere, Helen, Fighting With Property: A Study of Kwakiutl Potlatching and Warfare, 1792–1930 (American Ethnological Society, Monograph 18, 1950).

*Cohen, M. R., Law and the Social Order (New York, 1937).

*Cole, G. D. H., "Inheritance," Encyclopaedia of the Social Sciences, VIII (1932), 35–43.

Colton, H. S., A Brief Survey of Hopi Common Law (Museum Notes, Museum of Northern Arizona, Vol. 6, No. 7, 1934).

*Cook, W. W., "Hohfeld's Contributions to the Science of Law," Yale Law Journal, 28:721–738 (1919).

*——— "Ownership and Possession," Encyclopaedia of the Social Sciences, XI (1933), 521–525.

*Corbin, A. L., "Legal Analysis and Terminology," Yale Law Journal, 29:163 (1919).

Cory, H., and Hartnoll, M. M., Customary Law of the Haya Tribe, Tanganyika Territory (London, 1945).

Coxhead, J. C. C., The Native Tribes of N. E. Rhodesia, Their Laws and Customs (Rhodes-Livingstone Institute, 1914).

*Crane, W. K., *Kwakiutl, Haida and Tsimshian: A Study in Social Control* (unpublished M. A. thesis, University of Utah, 1951).

Danquah, J. B., *Gold Coast: Akan Laws and Customs and the Akim Akuakwa Constitution* (London, 1938).

*Dawson, J., *Australian Aborigines* (London, 1881).

de Jong, P. E. de J., *Minangkabau and Negri Sembilan: Socio-Political Structure in Indonesia* (Leiden, n.d.).

*Diamond, A. S., *Primitive Law* (London, 1935).

*Driberg, J. H., "Primitive Law in East Africa," *Africa*, 1:63–72 (1928).

Dundas, C., "Native Laws of Some Bantu Tribes of East Africa," *Journal of the Royal Anthropological Institute*, 51:217–278 (1921).

—— "The Organization and Laws of Some Bantu Tribes," *Journal of the Royal Anthropological Institute*, 45:234–306 (1915).

Durham, M. E., *Some Tribal Origins, Laws, and Customs of the Balkans* (London, 1928).

*Durkheim, Emile, *Les formes élémentaires de la vie réligieuse; le système totémique en Australie* (Paris, 1912).

*Ehrlich, Eugen, *Fundamental Principles of the Sociology of Law*, tr. E. Moll (Cambridge, 1936).

Elias, J. O., *Groundwork of Nigerian Law* (London, 1954).

Elkin, A. P., "Aboriginal Evidence and Justice in North Australia," *Oceania*, 17:173–210 (1947).

Elwin, Verrier, *Maria Murder and Suicide*, 2nd ed. (Bombay, 1950).

*Enthoven, K. L. J., *Het adatrecht de inlanders in de jurisprudentie, 1849–1912* (Leiden, 1912).

*Evans-Pritchard, E. E., "Sorcery and Native Opinion," *Africa*, 4:22–55 (1931).

*—— *Witchcraft, Oracles and Magic Among the Azande* (Oxford, 1937).

Firth, R. W., *Human Types* (London, 1938).

*Fortes, Meyer, ed. *Social Structure: Studies Presented to A. R. Radcliffe-Brown* (Oxford, 1949).

*—— "Time and Social Structure: An Ashanti Case Study," in Meyer Fortes, ed., *Social Structure*.

*—— and E. E. Evans-Pritchard, eds., *African Political Systems* (Oxford, 1940).

*Fortune, R. F., "Law and Force in Papuan Societies," *American Anthropologist*, 49:244–259 (1947).

*—— *Sorcerers of Dobu: The Social Anthropology of the Dobu Islanders of the Western Pacific* (New York, 1932).

*Frank, Jerome, "Lawlessness," *Encyclopaedia of the Social Sciences*, IX (1933), 277–279.

*Frazer, J. G., Preface, in B. Malinowski, *Argonauts of the Western Pacific* (London, 1922), pp. vii–xiv.

*Freuchen, Peter, *Arctic Adventure, My Life in the Frozen North* (New York, 1935).

Fyzee, A. A. A., *Outlines of Muhammedan Law*, 2nd rev. ed. (London, 1954).

*Garber, C. K., "Eskimo Infanticide," *Scientific Monthly*, 64:98–102 (February 1947).

*Garfield, Viola, *Tsimshian Clan and Society* (University of Washington Publications in Anthropology, Vol. 7, 1939), pp. 167–340.

*Gillin, J. P., "Crime and Punishment Among the Barama River Carib," *American Anthropologist*, 36:331–344 (1934).

*———— "Custom and the Range of Human Response," *Character and Personality*, 13:101–134 (1944).

Gluckman, Max, *The Judicial Process Among the Barotse of Northern Rhodesia* (Manchester, 1954).

*Goldschmidt, Walter, "Ethics and the Structure of Society: An Ethnological Contribution to the Sociology of Knowledge," *American Anthropologist*, 53:506–524 (1951).

Gomme, G. L., *Primitive Folk Moots or Open-Air Assemblies in England* (London, 1880).

Gongora, M., *El estado en el derecho indiano; epoca de fundación (1492–1570)* (Santiago de Chile, 1951).

Green, M. M., *Ibo Village Affairs: Chiefly with Reference to the Village of Umueke Agbaja* (London, 1947).

*Grinnell, G. B., *The Cheyenne Indians: Their History and Way of Life*, 2 vols. (New Haven, 1923).

Gutmann, Bruno, *Das Recht der Dschagga* (Munich, 1926).

*Haar, B. ter, *Adat Law in Indonesia*, tr. and ed. with an introduction by E. A. Hoebel and A. A. Schiller (New York, 1948).

Hailey, M. H., *An African Survey: A Study of Problems Arising in Africa South of the Sahara* (London, 1938).

Hall, R. de Z., "The Study of Native Court Records as a Method of Ethnological Inquiry," *Africa*, 11:412–427 (1938).

*Hallowell, A. I., "Psychological Leads for Ethnological Field Workers" (mimeographed; National Research Council, 1937); reprinted in D. G. Haring, ed., *Personal Character and Cultural Milieu*, rev. ed. (Syracuse, 1949), pp. 292–348.

Hamilton, R. W., "East African Native Laws and Customs," *Journal of Comparative Legislation*, 11:181–195 (1910).

Harley, G. W., *Masks as Agents of Social Control in Northeast Liberia* (Papers of the Peabody Museum of American Archaeology and Ethnology, Harvard University, 32, No. 2; 1950).

*Harrasser, A., *Die Rechtsverletzung bei den australischen Eingeborenen* (Beilageheft zur vergleichende Rechtswissenschaft, Vol. 50, 1936).

Harries, C. L., *Notes on Sepedi Laws and Customs* (Pretoria, 1909).

―――― *The Laws and Customs of the Bapedi and Cognate Tribes of the Transvaal,* rev. ed. (Johannesburg, 1929).

*Hartland, E. S., *Primitive Law* (London, 1924).

Hasluck, M., *The Unwritten Law of the Albanian Mountains* (Cambridge, Eng., 1954).

*Hawkes, E. W., *The Labrador Eskimo* (Memoir 91 of the Geological Survey of Canada, Anthropological Series No. 14, 1916).

*Herskovits, M. J., "A Note on 'Woman Marriage' in Dahomey," *Africa,* 10:335–341 (1937).

*―――― "The Ashanti Ntoro: a Re-examination," *Journal of the Royal Anthropological Institute,* 67:287–296 (1937).

*―――― "The Hypothetical Situation: a Technique of Field Research," *Southwestern Journal of Anthropology,* 6:1–20 (1950).

Hill, W. W., "Notes on Pima Land Law and Tenure," *American Anthropologist,* 38:586–589 (1936).

Hobhouse, L. T., *Morals in Evolution: A Study in Comparative Ethics,* 7th ed. (London, 1950).

*―――― G. C. Wheeler, and M. Ginsberg, *The Material Culture and Social Institutions of the Simpler Peoples* (London, 1915).

Hodgson, B. H., "Some Account of the Systems of Law and Police as Recognized in the State of Nepal," in *Miscellaneous Essays Relating to Indian Subjects* (London, 1880), XI, 211–250.

*Hoebel, E. A., "Fundamental Legal Concepts as applied in the Study of Primitive Law," *Yale Law Journal,* 51:951–966 (1942).

*―――― "Law and Anthropology," *Virginia Law Review,* 32:835–854 (1946).

*―――― "Law-ways of the Primitive Eskimos," *Journal of Criminology and Criminal Law,* 31:663–683 (1941).

*―――― *Man in the Primitive World: An Introduction to Anthropology* (New York, 1949).

*―――― "Primitive Law and Modern" (*Transactions of the New York Academy of Sciences,* Series 11, Vol. 5, 1942), pp. 30–41.

*―――― *The Political Organization and Law-ways of the Comanche Indians* (American Anthropological Association, Memoir 54: Contributions from the Santa Fe Laboratory of Anthropology, 4, 1940).

*——— A. A. Friedrich, P. W. Tappan, and J. Nathanson, *The Social Meaning of Legal Concepts: I, The Inheritance of Property and the Power of Testamentary Disposition* (New York, 1948).

*Hogbin, H. I., *Law and Order in Polynesia: A Study of Primitive Legal Institutions* (New York, 1934).

——— "Social Reactions to Crime, Law and Morals in the Schouten Islands, New Guinea," *Journal of the Royal Anthropological Institute,* 68:223–262 (1939).

*Hohfeld, W. N., *Fundamental Legal Conceptions as Applied in Judicial Reasoning and Other Essays,* ed. W. W. Cook (New Haven, 1923).

*Holland, T. E., *The Elements of Jurisprudence,* 8th ed. (New York, 1896).

Holleman, J. F., *Shona Customary Law: With Reference to Kinship, Marriage, the Family and the Estate* (London, 1952).

*Holm, G., *Ethnological Sketch of the Angmagssalik Eskimos* (Medelelser om Grønland, Vol. 39, 1914).

*Holmes, O. W., Jr., "Law in Science and Science in Law," *Harvard Law Review,* 12:443–463 (1899).

*——— *McDonald v. Maybee,* 243 U. S. Reports, pp. 90–91.

*——— *The Common Law* (Boston, 1881).

*——— "The Path of the Law," *Harvard Law Review,* 10:457–478 (1897).

*Hooton, E. A., *Man's Poor Relations* (Garden City, 1942).

*Howe, M. deW., *Holmes-Pollock Letters: The Correspondence of Mr. Justice Holmes and Sir Frederick Pollock 1874–1932,* 2 vols. (Cambridge, 1942).

Howell, P. P., *A Manual of Nuer Law* (London, 1954).

*Howitt, A. W., *Native Tribes of South-East Australia* (London, 1904).

Hozumi, Nobushigi, *Ancestor Worship and Japanese Law* (Tokyo, 1901).

Hudson, A. E., and E. Bacon, "Social Control and the Individual in Eastern Hazara Culture," in L. Spier, A. I. Hallowell, and S. Newman, eds., *Language, Culture and Personality, Essays in Honor of Edward Sapir* (Menasha, 1941), pp. 239–258.

*Hull, C. L., *Principles of Behavior* (New York, 1943).

*Human Relations Area Files, Inc., *Outline of Cultural Materials,* 3rd ed. (New Haven, 1950).

*Jablow, Joseph, *The Cheyennes in Plains Indian Trade Relations, 1795–1840* (American Ethnological Society, Monograph 19, 1951).

Jackson, H. M. G., "Some Reflections on the Relation of Law to Social Anthropology," *South African Journal of Science,* 24:549–552 (1927).

*Jeffreys, M. D. W., review of M. M. Green's *Ibo Village Affairs,* in *African Studies,* 9:99–104 (1950).

*Jenness, Diamond, *Life of the Copper Eskimo* (Report of the Canadian Arctic Expedition, 1913–18, Vol. 12, 1922).

*Jhering, Rudolf von, *Law as Means to an End,* trans. I. Husik (New York, 1924).

Jolly, J., *Hindu Law and Custom* (Calcutta, 1928).

Jolowicz, H. F., "The Assessment of Penalties in Primitive Law" (*Cambridge Legal Essays,* 1926), pp. 203–222.

Kaberry, Phyllis, "Law and Political Organization in the Abelam Tribe, New Guinea," *Oceania,* 12:79 ff., 208 ff., 331 ff. (1942).

Katz, Daniel and R. L. Schanck, *Social Psychology* (New York, 1938).

*Kluckhohn, Clyde, *Mirror for Man: The Relation of Anthropology to Modern Life* (New York, 1949).

*——— "Values and Value-Orientations in the Theory of Action: An Exploration in Definition and Classification," in Talcott Parsons and E. A. Shils, eds., *Toward a General Theory of Action* (Cambridge, 1951).

*Kocourek, A., "The Century of Analytical Jurisprudence Since John Austin," in A. Reppy, ed., *Law: A Century of Progress,* 3 vols. (New York, 1937), II, 195–230.

*——— and J. Wigmore, *The Evolution of Law: I, Sources of Ancient and Primitive Law; II, Primitive and Ancient Legal Institutions* (Boston, 1915).

*König, H., "Das Recht der Polar Völker," *Anthropos,* 22:689–746 (1927).

*——— "Der Rechtbruch und sein Ausgleich bei den Eskimo," *Anthropos,* 18 (1923), 19 (1924).

Kohler, Joseph, "Das Recht der Aranda und Loritja," *Zeitschrift für vergleichende Rechtswissenschaft,* 34:234–262 (1916).

*——— "Fragebogen zur Erforschung der Rechtsverhältnisse der sogenannten Naturvölker, namentlich in den deutschen Koloniolländer" *Zeitschrift für vergleichende Rechtswissenschaft,* 12:427–440 (1897).

*——— *The Philosophy of Law,* tr. A. Albrecht (New York, 1921).

*Kohler, Wolfgang, *The Mentality of Apes* (New York, 1925).

Koppers, William, "Stammesgliederung und Strafrecht der häuplingslösen Jamana auf Feuerland," *Proceedings of the 22nd International Congress of Americanists* (Rome, 1926).

*Kroeber, A. L., *Anthropology,* rev. ed. (New York, 1948).

*——— *Handbook of the Indians of California* (Bureau of American Ethnology, Bulletin 78, 1925).

*——— "The Superorganic," *American Anthropologist,* 19:163–213

(1917), reprinted in *The Nature of Culture* (Chicago, 1952), pp. 22–51.

*——— "Yurok Law," *Proceedings of the 22nd International Congress of Americanists* (Rome, 1926), pp. 511–516.

Kuper, Hilda, *An African Aristocracy: Rank Among the Swazi* (Oxford, 1947).

*Lawrence, W. E., "Alternating Generations in Australia," in G. P. Murdock, ed., *Studies in the Science of Society* (New Haven, 1937).

*Lee, Otis, "Social Values and the Philosophy of Law," *Virginia Law Review,* 32:802–817 (1946).

*Levi, E. H., *An Introduction to Legal Reasoning* (Chicago, 1948).

Lewin, Julius, *A Short Survey of Native Law in South Africa* (Johannesburg, 1941).

——— *An Outline of Native Law* (Johannesburg, 1944).

——— "Native Law and Its Background: The Limits of Tribal Law in Modern Bantu Life," *Race Relations,* 7:42–48 (1940).

——— *Studies in African Native Law* (Philadelphia, 1948).

——— "The Recording of Native Law and Custom," *Journal of the Royal African Society,* 37:483–493 (1938).

*Linton, Ralph, *The Cultural Background of Personality* (New York and London, 1945).

*———, ed., *The Science of Man in the World Crisis* (New York, 1945).

*——— *The Study of Man* (New York, 1936).

——— "Universal Ethical Principles: An Anthropological View," in R. N. Anshen, ed., *Moral Principles of Action: Man's Ethical Imperatives* (New York, 1952), chap. xxxii.

*Lips, J. E., "Government," in Franz Boas, ed., *General Anthropology* (Boston, 1938), chap. x.

*——— *Naskapi Law* (Transactions of the American Philosophical Society, Vol. 37, Pt. 4, 1947).

*Llewellyn, K. N., "Hohfeld, Wesley Newcombe," *Encyclopaedia of the Social Sciences,* VII (1932), 400–401.

*——— Introduction to "Pueblo Law and Social Control" (MS.).

*——— *The Bramble Bush: Lectures on Law and Its Study* (New York, 1930).

*——— "The Normative, the Legal, and the Law-jobs: The Problem of Juristic Method," *Yale Law Journal,* 49:1355–1400 (1940).

*——— "The Theory of Legal Science" *North Carolina Law Review* 20:7 (1941).

*——— and E. A. Hoebel, *The Cheyenne Way: Conflict and Case Law in Primitive Jurisprudence* (Norman, 1941).

Lowie, R. H., "Anthropology and Law," in H. F. Ogburn and A. Gold-enweiser, eds., *The Social Sciences* (New York, 1927).

*———— "Incorporeal Property in Primitive Society," *Yale Law Journal,* 37:551–563 (1928).

*———— *The Origin of the State* (New York, 1927).

*———— *Primitive Religion* (New York, 1924).

*———— *Primitive Society* (New York, 1920).

———— "Property Rights and Coercive Powers of Plains Indian Military Societies," *Journal of Political and Legal Sociology,* 1:59–71 (1943).

———— "Some Aspects of Political Organization Among the American Aborigines" (*Huxley Memorial Lecture for 1948, The Royal Anthropological Institute*).

*Lynd, R. S. and H. M., *Middletown* (New York, 1929).

*MacIver, R. M., "Government and Property," *Journal of Legal and Political Sociology,* 4:5–18 (1946).

*———— *Society: Its Structure and Changes* (New York, 1931).

MacLeod, W. C., "Aspects of the Earlier Development of Law and Punishment," *Journal of Criminal Law and Criminology,* 22:169–190 (1932).

*Maine, H. S., *Ancient Law: Its Connection with the Early History of Ideas, and Its Relation to Modern Ideas,* 3rd American ed. (New York, 1879).

*———— *Dissertations on Early Law and Custom* (London, 1883).

*Malinowski, Bronislaw, *Argonauts of the Western Pacific: An Account of Native Enterprise and Adventure in the Archipelagoes of Melanesian New Guinea* (London, 1922).

*———— *Coral Gardens and Their Magic: A Study of the Methods of Tilling the Soil and of Agricultural Rites in the Trobriand Islands,* 2 vols. (London and New York, 1935).

*———— *Crime and Custom in Savage Society* (New York, 1926).

*———— "Culture," *Encyclopaedia of the Social Sciences,* IV (1931), 621–645.

*———— "The Forces of Law and Order in a Primitive Community," *Proceedings of the Royal Institution of Great Britain,* XXIV (1925), 529–547.

*———— *Freedom and Civilization* (New York, 1944).

*———— "A New Instrument for the Study of Law—Especially Primitive," *Lawyers Guild Review,* 2:1–12 (1942); also *Yale Law Journal,* 51:1237–1254 (1942).

*———— "Primitive Law and Order" (*Nature,* Vol. 118, Supplement, 1926), pp. 9–16.

*———— *The Sexual Life of Savages in North-Western Melanesia: An*

  Ethnographic Account of Courtship, Marriage, and Family Life Among the Natives of the Trobriand Islands, British New Guinea (London, 1929).

  *———— "War and Weapons Among the Natives of the Trobriand Islands," *Man*, 21:10–12 (1920).

  *Marrett, R. H., "Law (Primitive)," in *Encyclopaedia Britannica*, 14th ed. (1949).

  ———— "The Nature of Sanction in Primitive Law," *Zeitschrift für vergleichende Rechtswissenschaft*, 50:63–69 (1936).

  *Marshall, Robert, *Arctic Village* (New York, 1933).

  *Marx, F. M., "Administrative Ethics and the Rule of Law" (MS.).

  *Masserman, J. H., *Principles of Dynamic Psychiatry, Including an Integrative Approach to Abnormal and Clinical Psychology* (Philadelphia, 1946).

  *Mead, Margaret, "Native Languages as Field Work Tools," *American Anthropologist*, 41: 189–205 (1939).

  *———— *Social Organization of Manua* (Bernice P. Bishop Museum, Bulletin 76, 1930).

  Meek, C. K., *Land Law and Custom in the Colonies*, 2nd ed. (London, 1949).

  ———— *Law and Authority in a Nigerian Tribe* (London, 1937).

  Meinhof, C., *Africanische-Rechtsgebrauche* (Berlin, 1914).

  *Meulen, J. E. van der, *Het Adatrecht de inlanders in de jurisprudentie, 1912–1923* (Leiden, 1924).

  *Mishkin, Bernard, *Rank and Warfare Among The Plains Indians* (American Ethnological Society, Monograph 3, 1940).

  Moor, L., *Malabar Law and Customs* (Madras, 1905).

  Moss, C. R., *Nabaloi Law and Ritual* (University of California Publications in American Archaeology and Ethnology, Vol. 15, 1920), pp. 207–343.

  *Murdock, G. P., "Bronislaw Malinowski," *American Anthropologist*, 45:445–451 (1943).

  *———— "Double Descent," *American Anthropologist*, 42:555–561 (1940).

  *———— "The Common Denominator of Culture," in Ralph Linton, ed., *The Science of Man in the World Crisis* (New York, 1945).

  *———— "The Science of Culture," *American Anthropologist*, 34:200–215 (1932).

  *———— *Social Structure* (New York, 1949).

  Nadel, S. F., "Land Tenure on the Eritrean Plateau," *Africa*, 16:1–22 (1946).

*Nelson, E. W., *The Eskimo About Bering Strait* (Bureau of American Ethnology, Annual Report 17, 1899).

Newell, W. B., *Crime and Justice Among the Iroquois Indians* (unpublished M. A. thesis, University of Pennsylvania, 1934).

Noon, J. A., *Law and Government of the Grand River Iroquois* (Viking Fund Publications in Anthropology, no. 12, 1949).

Northrop, F. S. C., "Criterion of Universal Ethical and Legal Norms," in R. N. Anshen, ed., *Moral Principles of Action: Man's Ethical Imperative* (New York, 1952), chap. vii.

—— "Philosophical Anthropology and World Law," *Transactions of The New York Academy of Sciences,* series II, no. 14 (1951), pp. 109–112.

—— "Jurisprudence in the Law School Curriculum," *Journal of Legal Education,* 1:482–494 (1949).

Nunez, L. M., *El durecho precolonial* (Encyclopedia Ilustrada Mexicana, no. 7, Mexico City, 1937).

*Oberg, K., "Crime and Punishment in Tlingit Society," *American Anthropologist,* 36:145–146 (1934).

*—— "The Kingdom of Ankole in Uganda," in M. Fortes and E. E. Evans-Pritchard, eds., *African Political Systems* (Oxford, 1940), pp. 121–163.

*Opler, Marvin, review of B. B. Whiting, *Paiute Sorcery, Journal of American Folklore,* 64: 241–243 (1951).

*—— "Themes as Dynamic Forces in Culture," *American Journal of Sociology,* 51:198–206 (1945).

*—— review of B. B. Whiting, *Paiute Sorcery, Journal of American Folklore,* 64: 241–243 (1951).

*Oppenheimer, Franz, *The State* (New York, 1922).

O'Sullivan, H., "Dinka Laws and Customs," *Journal of the Royal Anthropological Institute,* 40:171–191 (1910).

*Post, A. H., *Bausteine für eine allgemeine Rechtswissenschaft auf vergleichend-ethnologischer Basis,* 2 vols. (Oldenburg, 1880–81).

*—— *Einleitung in das Studien der ethnologischen Jurizprudenz* (Oldenburg, 1887).

*—— *Einleitung in eine Naturwissenschaft des Rechtes,* 2 vols. (Oldenburg, 1880–81).

*—— *Grundriss der ethnologischen Jurizprudenz,* 2 vols. (Oldenburg, 1894–95).

*Potter, P. B., "Mediation," *Encyclopaedia of the Social Sciences, X* (1933), 272–274.

*Pound, Roscoe, *Interpretations of Legal History* (Cambridge, 1923).

*———— "A Theory of Social Interests," *Publications of the American Sociological Society*, XV (1920), 1 ff.

*Provinse, J. R., "The Underlying Sanctions of Plains Indian Culture," in F. Eggan, ed., *Social Anthropology of North American Tribes* (Chicago, 1937).

*Quain, B. H., "The Iroquois," in Margaret Mead, ed., *Cooperation and Competition Among Primitive Peoples* (New York, 1937).

*Radcliffe-Brown, A. R., "Law, Primitive," *Encyclopaedia of the Social Sciences*, IX (1933), 202–206.

*———— "Patrilineal and Matrilineal Succession," *Iowa Law Review*, 20:286–303 (1935).

*————Preface, in Meyer Fortes and E. E. Evans-Pritchard, eds., *African Political Systems* (Oxford, 1940), pp. xi-xiii.

*———— "Sanction, Social," *Encyclopaedia of the Social Sciences*, XIII (1934), 531–534.

*———— "Social Organization of Australian Tribes," *Oceania*, 1:34–63, 206–246, 322–341, 426–456 (1930–31).

*———— *The Andaman Islands: A Study in Social Anthropology* (Cambridge, 1922).

*Radin, Max, "A Restatement of Hohfeld," *Harvard Law Review*, 51: 1141–1164 (1938).

Ramsay, T. G., *Tsonga Law in the Transvaal* (Pretoria, 1941).

*Rasmussen, Knud, *Across Arctic America* (New York, 1927).

*———— Grønlandsagen (Berlin, 1922).

*———— *Intellectual Culture of the Iglulik Eskimo* (Reports of the Fifth Thule Expedition, 1921–24, Vol. 7, 1929).

*———— *The People of the Polar North* (New York, 1908).

*Rattray, R. S., *Ashanti* (Oxford, 1923).

*———— *Ashanti Law and Constitution* (Oxford, 1929).

*———— *Religion and Art in Ashanti* (Oxford, 1927).

*Redfield, Robert, "La ley primitiva," *Revista Mexicana ed Sociologica*, 3:17–44 (1941).

*———— "Maine's Ancient Law in the Light of Primitive Societies," *Western Political Quarterly*, 3:574–589 (1950).

*———— *The Primitive World and Its Transformations* (Ithaca, 1953).

Riasanovski, V. A., *Customary Law of the Nomadic Tribes of Siberia* (Tsiensin, 1938).

*Richardson, Jane, *Law and Status Among the Kiowa Indians* (American Ethnological Society, Monograph 1, 1940).

Riesman, David, "Toward an Anthropological Science of Law and the Legal Profession," *American Journal of Sociology*, 57:121–135

(1951), reprinted in David Riesman, *Individualism Reconsidered and Other Essays* (Glencoe, 1954), chap. xxvii.

*Rivers, W. H. R., *Social Organization* (New York, 1924).

Robertson, J. A., "The Social Structure of, and Ideas of Law Among, Early Philippine Peoples; and a Recently Discovered Pre-Hispanic Ceremonial Code of the Philippine Islands," in H. M. Stephens, and H. E. Bolton, *The Pacific Ocean in History* (New York, 1917), pp. 160–191.

Rodnick, David, "Political Structure and Status Among the Assiniboine Indians," *American Anthropologist,* 39:408–416 (1937).

*Róheim, Géza, "The Primeval Horde in Central Australia," *Journal of Comparative Psychopathology,* 3:454–460 (1942).

Ross, E. A., *Social Control: A Survey of the Foundations of Order* (New York, 1901).

Rowe, J. H., "Inca Culture at the Time of the Conquest," in J. H. Steward, ed., *Handbook of South American Indians,* 6 vols. (Bureau of American Ethnology, Bulletin 143, 1946), pp. 183–330.

Royal Anthropological Institute of Great Britain and Ireland, *Notes and Queries on Anthropology* (London, 1951).

Saleeby, N. M., *Studies in Moro History, Law and Religion* (Manila, 1905).

*Salmond, J. W., *Jurisprudence,* 7th ed. (New York, 1924).

*Sapir, Edward, *Language: An Introduction to the Study of Speech* (New York, 1939).

*Sargent, S. S., and M. W. Smith, eds., *Culture and Personality* (New York, 1949).

Schapera, Isaac, *A Handbook of Tswana Law and Custom* (London, 1938).

*———— *Tribal Legislation Among the Tswana of the Bechuanaland Protectorate: A Study in the Mechanism of Cultural Change* (The London School of Economics and Political Science, Monographs on Social Anthropology, No. 9, 1943).

Schechter, F. I., "Law and Morals in Primitive Trade," in *Essays in Tribute to O.K. McMurray* (Berkeley, 1935).

Schiller, A. A., "Conflict of Laws in Indonesia," *The Far Eastern Quarterly* (November 1942), pp. 31–47.

———— "Pacific Affairs Bibliographies; No. 11: Native Customary Law in the Netherlands Indies," *Pacific Affairs,* 9 (1936).

*Schultz-Ewart, Erich, and L. Adam, *Das Eingeborenenrecht: Sitten und Gewohnheitsrechte der Eingeborenen der ehemaligen deutschen Kolonien in Africa und der Südsee,* 2 vols. (Stuttgart, 1929).

*Seagle, William, "Kohler, Joseph," *Encyclopaedia of the Social Sciences,* VIII (1932), pp. 587–588.

*———— "Primitive Law and Professor Malinowski," *American Anthropologist,* 39:275–290 (1937).

*———— *The Quest for Law* (New York, 1941).

Seebohm, Frederic, *Tribal Custom in Anglo-Saxon Law, being an essay supplemental to (1) 'The English Village Community' (2) 'The Tribal System in Wales'* (London, 1911).

Seymour, W. M., *Native Law and Custom, being a compendium of the recognized Native customs in force in the Native Territories of the Colony of the Cape of Good Hope, together with legislative amendments and reports of some of the more important decisions of the Native Appeal Court of Griqualand East, 1901–1909* (Cape Town, 1911).

Simons, H. J., "The Study of Native Law in South Africa," *Bantu Studies,* 12:237–242 (1938).

*Simpson, S. P., and Ruth Field, "Law and the Social Sciences," *Virginia Law Review,* 32:855–867 (1946).

*Spott, R., and A. L. Kroeber, *Yurok Narratives* (University of California Publications in American Archaeology and Ethnology, Vol. 35, 1943), pp. 143–256.

*Stair, J. B., *Old Samoa* (London, 1897).

Stafford, W. G., *Native Law as Practiced in Natal* (Witwatersrand, 1935).

*Steward, J. H., *Basin-Plateau Aboriginal Socio-political Groups* (Bureau of American Ethnology, Bulletin 120, 1938).

*Stone, Julius, *The Province and Function of Law: Law as Logic, Justice and Social Control: A Study in Jurisprudence* (Cambridge, 1950).

*Strehlow, C., *Die Aranda und Loritja-Stämme in Zentral-Australien,* ed. M. von Leonhardi (Veröffentlichungen des Völker-Museums, Frankfurt-am-Main, 1907–20).

*Sumner, W. G., *Folkways: A Study of the Sociological Importance of Usages, Manners, Customs, Mores, and Morals* (Boston, 1906).

*Thalbitzer, W., *The Ammassalik Eskimo* (Medelelser om Grønland, Vol. 39, 1914).

*Thomas, W. I., *Primitive Behavior: An Introduction to the Social Sciences* (New York, 1937).

*Thurnwald, Richard, *Die Menschliche Gesellschaft,* 7 vols. (Berlin, 1931–1953).

———— "Ermittlungen über Eingeborenenrechte der Südsee," *Zeitschrift für vergleichende Rechtswissenschaft,* 23:309–364 (1912).

—— "The Role of Political Organization in the Development of Man, with Suggested Applications in the New World," in S. Tax, ed., *The Civilizations of Ancient America* (Chicago, 1951), pp. 280–284.

Trimborn, H., "Das Recht der Chibcha in Columbien," *Ethnologica,* 4:1–55 (1930).

—— "Ein Mittelpunkt für die ethnologische Rechtsforschung," *Anthropos,* 46:995–996 (1951).

—— "Methode der Historischen Rechtsforschung," *Zeitschrift für vergleichende Rechtswissenschaft,* 43:416–464 (1930).

Tupper, L., "Customary and Other Law in the East Africa Protectorate," *Journal of Comparative Legislation,* 7:172–184 (1907).

*Tylor, E. B., "On a Method of Investigating the Development of Institutions; Applied to Laws of Marriage and Descent," *Journal of the Royal Anthropological Institute,* 18:245–272 (1888).

*Van Loon, H. W., *R. v. R., The Life and Times of Rembrandt van Rijn* (New York, 1930).

*Vinogradoff, Paul, and Hugh Goitein, "Jurisprudence, Comparative," in *Encyclopaedia Britannica,* 14th ed. (1949).

*—— "Customary Law," in C. G. Crump and E. F. Jacob, eds., *The Legacy of the Middle Ages* (Oxford, 1926), pp. 287–320.

*Wallace, Ernest, and E. A. Hoebel, *The Comanches: Lords of the South Plains* (Norman, 1952).

*Wardle, H. N., "Gifts, Primitive," *Encyclopaedia of the Social Sciences,* VI (1931), 657.

*Warner, W. L., "Murngin Warfare," *Oceania,* 1:457–477 (1930).

*Weakland, J. H., "Method in Cultural Anthropology," *Philosophy of Science,* 18:55–69 (1951).

*Weyer, E. M., *The Eskimos* (New Haven, 1924).

Whitfield, G. M. B., *South African Native Law* (Cape Town, 1929).

*Whiting, B. B., *Paiute Sorcery* (Viking Fund Publications in Anthropology, 15, 1950).

Williams, F. E., "Group Sentiment and Primitive Justice," *American Anthropologist,* 43:523–539 (1941).

Willinck, G. D., *Het Rechtsleven bij de Minangkabausche Maleiers* (Leiden, 1909).

Wilson, Godfrey, "Introduction to Nyakyusa Law," *Africa,* 10:16–36 (1937).

Wilson, Monica, *Good Company, A Study of Nyakyusa Age-Villages* (London, 1951).

*Wissler, Clark, Introduction, in R. S. and H. M. Lynd, *Middletown* (New York, 1929).

*Yerkes, R. M. and A. W., *The Great Apes* (New Haven, 1929).

INDEX

E. Adamson Hoebel

E. Adamson Hoebel is Professor and Head of the Department of Anthropology at the University of Minnesota. A leading authority on primitive law, he is the author of *The Cheyenne Way, Man in the Primitive World, Adat Law in Indonesia,* and *The Comanches.* His field research among the Indians of the United States is widely known.